Family Interaction

Family Interaction

A Multigenerational Developmental Perspective

FIFTH EDITION

Stephen A. Anderson
University of Connecticut

Ronald M. Sabatelli
University of Connecticut

Allyn & Bacon
Boston Columbus Indianapolis New York San Francisco Upper Saddle River
Amsterdam Cape Town Dubai London Madrid Milan Munich Paris Montreal Toronto
Delhi Mexico City São Paulo Sydney Hong Kong Seoul Singapore Taipei Tokyo

Publisher: Karen Hanson
Editorial Assistant: Alyssa Levy
Executive Marketing Manager: Kelly May
Marketing Assistant: Janeli Bitor
Production Manager: Fran Russello
Art Director: Jayne Conte
Cover Designer: Suzanne Duda
Editorial Production and Composition Service: Saraswathi Muralidhar/PreMediaGlobal
Printer: RRDonnelley & Sons, Inc.

Library of Congress Cataloging-in-Publication Data

Anderson, Stephen A. (Stephen Alan)
Family interaction : a multigenerational developmental perspective / Stephen A. Anderson, Ronald M. Sabatelli. — 5th ed.
p. cm.
Includes bibliographical references and index.
ISBN-13: 978-0-205-71083-6 (alk. paper)
ISBN-10: 0-205-71083-2 (alk. paper)
1. Families. 2. Interpersonal relations. I. Sabatelli, Ronald Michael. II. Title.
HQ728.A72 2011
306.85—dc22

2010017435

10 9 8 7 6 5 4 3 2 1—DOH—14 13 12 11 10

Allyn & Bacon is an imprint of

www.pearsonhighered.com

ISBN-10: 0-205-71083-2
ISBN-13: 978-0-205-71083-6

Contents

Preface

We are pleased and excited about this fifth edition of *Family Interaction: A Multigenerational Developmental Perspective.* When we started this project, we never anticipated that it would have such a long shelf life. We have added what we consider to be important new materials that highlight the ever-changing developments in the field of family studies. Most notably, the reader will find updated research findings throughout the text. Exciting new advances have been made in our understanding of the diversity that characterizes differing family structures and life-cycle stages. Recent research also has added considerably to our knowledge of parent–child relations; adolescent adjustment; couple communication; diversity of family structures and couple relationships, most notably same-sex couples; conflict resolution; and divorce. These and other new research developments have been incorporated in the text.

Beyond these exciting changes, the structure and primary focus of the text remain unchanged. This is still a basic text that is targeted for classes focusing on family interaction, family dynamics, and family functioning. Using a family systems and a multigenerational, developmental framework, this book highlights the challenges faced by contemporary families as they move through time. It offers a comprehensive overview of the major conceptual models that are used to understand the patterns and dynamics that operate in families. It provides readers with an overview of the basic first-order tasks that all families must execute regardless of their particular composition or living situation and, at the same time, offers readers an appreciation of the variety and uniqueness in how each family develops its patterns of interaction. That is, all families must develop a shared sense of identity, create a nurturing emotional environment, manage resources, and negotiate successful boundaries between individual members and with the outside world. Furthermore, all families must develop strategies for dealing with the second-order task of managing the ever-changing stresses they will encounter over the course of their development. Yet it is the uniqueness of each family—its structural organization and its particular cultural, ethnic, racial heritage, and gender orientation—that will influence the strategies that evolve to meet these challenges.

After providing a variety of conceptual lenses through which to assess and understand family functioning, we guide the reader through each successive stage of the family life cycle and later through a number of alternative developmental pathways brought about by the death of a family member, divorce, or remarriage. At each stage, current research findings and conceptual formulations are used to highlight the relationship between the family's interactional strategies and the functioning and well-being of individual family members and the family system as a whole.

We believe that this text offers a unique vantage point on the family. Its emphasis is on integration—particularly an integration of family systems and family developmental and intergenerational perspectives. We hope readers will come away with a respect for the complexities of family life as well as an appreciation for how our current conceptual models and knowledge about families can serve as useful guides to our assessment and understanding of families and their functioning.

Acknowledgments

We want to express our appreciation and gratitude to those individuals who contributed to the completion of this book. We are grateful to our families, who have supported us during the many hours that were devoted to this work. We are grateful to our colleagues and students who provided useful feedback and support. We are further indebted to Ted Knight, our project manager; Karen Hanson, our editor at Pearson; her assistant, Alyssa Levy; and to the production staff for their support and assistance in making this project proceed so smoothly.

PART I

Defining Families

Historically, family was defined as "married partners and children residing in a household." Over time there is no doubt that there has been a shift in the societal definition of families to include single parents, biracial couples, blended families, biologically unrelated individuals living cooperatively, and gay and lesbian couples, among others. The perspective taken with this book is that in spite of this diversity of family forms found in contemporary society, families share common tasks that they must execute. They must also develop unique interaction patterns and dynamics to manage these tasks. These common tasks and the patterns related to them are the primary focus of this text.

This book is guided by the assumptions that all families are unique and that this uniqueness is reflected in the patterns of interaction found within them. Aided by family researchers, theorists, and clinicians, the book focuses on a number of core concepts that help us to understand the unique interactional patterns found inside the family. To accomplish this objective, families are examined from a multigenerational developmental perspective. The book introduces relevant data on the changing character of contemporary families, presents research findings on how families cope with the stress of developmental transitions, and incorporates what is currently known about functional and dysfunctional families. Finally, the book touches upon some of the most common problems faced by families as they manage developmental transitions.

We begin this discourse by detailing the defining features of families when they are conceived of as a system. Despite the dramatic changes that families undergo over their life span, there are a number of predictable and identifiable tasks that all family systems must contend with regardless of the specific form that a family takes. That is, all family systems, regardless of who comprises the family, must (1) establish a clear identity for the family as a whole and for each individual member; (2) develop clearly defined boundaries between the family and the outside world and between individual members within the family; (3) manage the family household (allocate chores, handle finances, solve problems, etc.); and (4) manage the emotional demands of family life. In addition, families must adapt how they execute their tasks in response to the normative and non-normative stresses encountered over time.

It is the patterns of interaction that the family establishes for managing these basic tasks in the face of inevitable change that is the centerpiece of this book. In our view, family members establish routine, habitual patterns of interaction with one another over time that are then continually altered over the course of family development. These patterns give the family its distinctive identity, define the family's boundaries, determine how the household is managed, and prescribe the quality of the family's emotional environment. In sum, the exploration of the uniqueness of each of our families requires that we have at our disposal a conceptualization of the family that addresses the tasks that are common to all family systems and simultaneously embraces the diversity and distinctiveness of the patterns of interaction found within each family system. What makes each family unique are the distinct strategies it employs for executing a core of fundamental family system tasks. These unique strategies influence the trajectory of each family member's development—that is, the strategies determine how our lives unfold by influencing the patterns of nurturance and support we experience within our families, the values and attitudes that we come to embrace, and the developmental legacy that affects how we approach and sustain intimate relationships over our lifetime.

CHAPTER 1

The Family as a System

Chapter Overview

Focusing on family patterns of interaction requires a basic understanding of what is meant by the term "family." This chapter will define the concept of family, and provide an overview of the central assumptions and core concepts that are basic to an understanding of families when considered as a system. Within a family-systems framework, families are defined as complex structures consisting of an interdependent group of individuals who (1) have a shared sense of history; (2) share emotional ties to one another; and (3) devise strategies for meeting the needs of individual family members and the group as a whole. Implicit in the use of the system metaphor to define families is the premise that they are structurally complex. Families are comprised of multiple subsystems, have common purposes and tasks that must be fulfilled, and must devise strategies for the execution of these tasks. Within this systems perspective, the assessment of family functioning revolves around a theoretical consideration of the common tasks that a family must fulfill and the effectiveness of the strategies devised for executing these tasks.

The Family as a System

This book focuses on families and the interactional patterns and dynamics found within them. It further focuses on the developmental tasks that all families may encounter over their life course. This book's goal is simple: to provide an understanding of what a family is and how a family operates. Accomplishing this goal requires an ability to conceive of the family as a complex system and to conduct an in-depth analysis of the many forces that shape the patterns of interaction found within the family. Accomplishing this goal also requires an understanding of how the experiences of individuals within their families establish a legacy that influences their values and orientations, determines their strategies for dealing with people and events, and, ultimately, serves as the foundation for many of the choices those individuals make about their lives.

Writing a book about something with which everyone is familiar is a difficult challenge in that personal experiences, as well as exposure to family issues through books, television, and film, lead people to feel that they know all they need to know about the family. This can obscure one's objectivity and receptivity to new thinking. Consequently, at the outset of this book, readers are encouraged to be open to the diversity found within and among families. It is hoped that as a result of this openness readers will gain insight into their own family experiences—insight that will underscore the importance of the study of family dynamics and reinforce the view that the family touches on all aspects of our lives.

The Difficulty of Defining the Family

The task of defining the family is not a simple one, and the difficulty is derived from the mythology that surrounds the concept of family. When asked to define the family, most of us think of it as being comprised of a stable and harmonious group of people, monolithic in form, operating on the principles of harmony and love. We think of the family as comprised of a married couple and their biological children. This couple is happily married; the children all feel nurtured and supported by their parents; and each family member's experience of the family is the same—all share the perception of the family as a safe haven providing for each member's physical and emotional needs.

This idealized image of the intact, multigenerational family household distorts the diversity and instability that has always characterized American families (Hareven, 2000). The 1950s model of the white, middle-class, intact nuclear family, headed by a breadwinner father and supported by a homemaker mother, is only a narrow band on the broad spectrum of contemporary families (Teachman, Tedrow, & Crowder, 2000). In its place, the "postmodern family" has emerged (Stacey, 1996), characterized by a multitude of family structures—working mothers and two-earner households; divorced, single-parent, remarried and adoptive families; and domestic partners, both gay and straight.

For example, currently, married couples residing with their biological children account for only 24 percent of all households in the United States (U.S. Census Bureau, 2005a). Not surprisingly, single-parent households have become increasingly common, making up 26 percent of all American families with children under the age of eighteen, a dramatic 58 percent increase since 1970. There are now more than 12 million single-parent households, approximately 10 million of which are maintained by mothers (U.S. Census Bureau, 2005a). In an expanded look at the structure of the American family the U.S. Census Bureau reports that in 2007, of the nearly 74 million children under the age of eighteen living in the United States, 67.8 percent lived with married parents, 2.9 percent with two unmarried parents, 25.8 percent with one parent, and 3.5 percent with no parent present.

Consider as well the fact that a century ago, only 5 percent of married women participated in the labor market. In 1940, fewer than one married woman in seven worked outside the home. Since 1995, the dual-income family has become more common than the formerly more traditional one-income married household. Now over 60 percent of wives work outside the home (U.S. Census Bureau, 2006).

In addition, over the past thirty years, divorce replaced death as the most common end point of a marriage as the rates of divorce dramatically increased (Sabatelli & Ripoll, 2003). In the United States, the proportion of marriages begun each year that ended in divorce steadily increased from less than 10 percent in 1867 to over 55 percent in 1985 (Cherlin, 1992). Recent data suggest that since the mid-1980s the divorce rate in the United States has decreased slightly (Bramlett & Mosher, 2001). Even so, demographers expect that 25 percent of contemporary marriages will dissolve by their seventh year, and approximately half will end before their twentieth year as a result of divorce (Bramlett & Mosher, 2001; Pinsoff, 2002). Not surprisingly, these shifts in divorce rates have generated social and political discourse on the problems of divorce. With few exceptions (Ahrons, 2004), divorce has been defined as an undesirable end to marriage. Many studies have been devoted to the documentation of the deleterious short- and long-term effects of divorce on children and adults, and divorce has been viewed as a social disorder whose frequency approaches epidemic proportions and urgently needs to be reduced (Gallagher, 1996; Popenoe, 1996). The ending of marriages presumably threatens social order, disrupts kinship ties, creates economic instability, and potentially disrupts the lives of children. There is a lot at stake, in other words, when marriages fail to function as the pivotal and key subsystem within the family system.

In addition, the typical image of the family distorts the wide range of interpersonal dynamics found within the contemporary family. Certainly, most of us would be reluctant to label U.S. families as violent. "Violence" and "family" are not words that go together. Yet, research tells a different tale. The home is the single most violent location in U.S. society (U.S. Census Bureau, 2008). Statistics on intimate partner violence indicate that it is a widespread problem. For example, according to the U.S. Bureau of Justice Statistics (Catalano, 2006), more than 625,000 substantiated non-lethal violent acts were committed by current spouses, former spouses, boyfriends, or girlfriends in 2004 (the most recent year for which such figures are available). Other studies place the rates for intimate partner violence higher. Specifically, the National Violence Against Women Survey found that of the over 16,000 men and women surveyed, nearly 25% of the women and 7.6% of the men said that they have been raped or physically assaulted by a spouse, partner, or date at some point in their lifetimes. Within the previous 12 months, 1.5% of women and 0.9% of men reported incidences of violence. And if relatively minor acts of violence such as pushing, grabbing, shoving, and slapping were taken into consideration, the incidence of intimate violence would rise to more than 3 million for men and 5 million for women (Tjaden & Thoennes, 2000).

Furthermore, according to the U.S. Census Bureau (2008), there were about 900,000 substantiated cases of child abuse and/or neglect in 2005. Because the vast majority of child abuse incidents involve victims who cannot protect themselves and remain hidden from police and social service agencies, many researchers think that the actual figures are much higher. What is known for sure is that slightly over 1,500 children died of abuse or neglect in 2004, and 90% of the victims were killed by parents or other family members (Administration for Children and Families, 2006).

In summary, the typical view of the family includes several closely related but distinct myths about the family, myths bound up with nostalgic memory, selective perception, and cultural values concerning what is correct, typical, and true about the family. This typical view makes it difficult for us to consider the diversity in form found among families and the complexity of dynamics found within families. When defining the family, therefore, we must move beyond the mythological image of the family and address the basic or core features that comprise all families, while not losing sight of the diverse structures and dynamics within families.

The Characteristics of Family Systems

In recent years, in an effort to discuss the common features of families while embracing the complexity and diversity found within them, family social scientists have come to view the family as a system. When viewed as a system, the **family** can be defined as a complex structure comprised of an interdependent group of individuals who (1) have a shared sense of history; (2) experience some degree of emotional bonding; and (3) devise strategies for meeting the needs of individual family members and the group as a whole. Implicit in the use of the system metaphor to define the family is the premise that the family is structurally complex, is comprised of multiple subsystems, has common purposes and tasks that must be fulfilled, and devises strategies for the execution of these tasks.

When viewed as a system, the family is defined by two central dimensions: its **structure** and its tasks. Structure includes both the family's composition and its organization. Composition refers to the family's membership, or simply, the persons who make up the family. The family's structural organization refers to the unique set of rules governing the patterns of interaction found within the extended family system. Tasks refer primarily to the "business" of the family—its common and essential responsibilities. All families have tasks that they fulfill for society and family members alike.

Structural Properties of Families

Over the past thirty years, family systems perspectives have been widely accepted in the family sciences because they offer insight into the unique patterns and processes found within and between families (Whitchurch & Constantine, 1993). System thinking is grounded in the simple but elegant notion that what makes a system are the relationships among its parts and not the parts themselves. To simply illustrate this point, it should be evident that what makes an engineered system like a bridge unique is the relationships among the various components, or parts, of the bridge. That is, knowing the components that go into building a bridge can never provide sufficient insight into what makes a particular bridge a unique system. To understand the bridge as a system requires an understanding of how all of the component parts and subsystems—cement foundation, steel supports, and paved roadways—are connected to one another.

While of course the family is not an engineered system, the application of the systems metaphor to the family truly transforms our thinking about what contributes to the uniqueness of each family. When conceived of as a system, it becomes clear that the interrelationships among family members, more so than the individuals who comprise the family, are central to our understanding of the uniqueness of each family. Knowing that a single mother heads a family, for example, does not tell us anything about what goes on inside the family. To know what truly makes this single-mother-headed family unique (unique from all other single-parent-headed families and unique from all other types of families), we must understand how the members of this family interact with one another. That is, the unit of analysis is the relationships that occur among the members of the family. Consider the following illustration:

> *Judy is a thirty-eight-year-old mother of three children who has been divorced for nearly three years. Judy has a job as an executive assistant in a downtown insurance firm. Her three children range in age from seven to fourteen. Melissa, the oldest, is a ninth-grader. In order for Judy to manage her job, Melissa is responsible for much of the care of her sister, Molly, age nine, and her brother, Todd, age seven.*
>
> *At the start of each day, Judy wakes up and prepares for her workday. While Mom is showering and dressing, Melissa wakes her brother and sister, gets them dressed, prepares breakfast for the family, and makes lunch for the "kids" to take to school. Melissa, Molly, and Todd eat together while Judy has a cup of coffee and irons her clothes, puts on her makeup, gets dressed, etc. Molly and Todd talk with Melissa about the day ahead. They ask Melissa for help with the homework they did not finish the night before. Only after Judy, Molly, and Todd are settled does Melissa get herself ready for school.*

This illustration makes it clear that any effort to understand family dynamics must consider the rules of relating, or the unique patterns of interaction found within the family. In this particular family system, parental authority and responsibility have been delegated to Melissa by her mother. This arrangement is determined, in part, by the unique composition of the family and the demands placed upon it. Because Judy, a single parent, cannot manage the demands of the morning rush hour on her own, the younger children in this household interact with Melissa during breakfast as though she were their parent. They know whom to go to during this time with questions and concerns. Melissa, in turn, knows the boundaries of her roles and responsibilities, and Judy is free to get herself ready for work without worrying about whether her children are being cared for properly. This illustration makes it clear that any effort to understand the uniqueness of a family must consider its structural properties—both the people who make up the family AND the rules of relating that direct the unique patterns of interaction found within the family.

Wholeness

Family systems are characterized by the property of **wholeness**, that is, the family system is made up of a group of individuals who together form a complex and unitary whole (Buckley, 1967; Whitchurch & Constantine, 1993). The whole is distinctly different from the simple sum of the contributions of individual members, because each family system is characterized by structural rules of relating that determine how family members interact with one another. To understand the uniqueness of the family system, we must go beyond an analysis of the individuals who comprise the system. In the above example, we would not be able to understand the uniqueness of this particular family system simply by knowing that it is comprised of a single parent and her three children or by knowing the individual personalities of each family member. The uniqueness of this particular family can only be understood through an analysis of the rules that structure how family members interact with each other.

The property of wholeness suggests that there is a uniqueness to each family that can be understood only by understanding the interactional rules that structure the system. Knowing who is in the system is important because the composition of the family places demands upon the system and influences interactional patterns. At the same time, to analyze the uniqueness of each system we must consider what joins the individuals within the system together—in other words, the rules of relating within the system. When these rules become our focus, it becomes apparent that the system is greater than the sum of its parts.

Organizational Complexity

The term **organizational complexity** refers to the fact that family systems are comprised of various smaller units or subsystems that together compose the larger family system (Minuchin, 1974). Each individual family member can be thought of as a subsystem. Similarly, subsystems can be organized by gender, with the males in the family comprising one subsystem and the females comprising another, or each generation can be thought of as a subsystem within the whole. When considering subsystems in terms of generations, three primary subsystems are generally emphasized: marital, parental, and sibling. Each is distinguished by the family members who comprise them as well as by the primary tasks performed by each. The marital subsystem, for example, teaches children about the nature of intimate relationships and provides a model of transactions between men and women. The parental subsystem is involved with child rearing and serves such functions as nurturing, guidance, socialization, and control. Wives and husbands may comprise the parental subsystem; or others, such as grandparents or older children, may be involved. The sibling subsystem is typically the child's first peer group and offers opportunities for learning patterns of negotiation, cooperation, competition, and personal disclosure.

The tasks performed by each of these subsystems will be covered in greater detail in later chapters. For now, it is important to emphasize that the concept of organizational complexity addresses the organization of the family system as a whole and the relationship between the whole and its various subsystems. The operation and effectiveness of the whole system is influenced by the operation and effectiveness of each of the subsystems.

Interdependence

Implicit in the discussion of the structural dimension of a system is the idea that individuals and subsystems that comprise the whole system are mutually dependent and mutually influenced by one another (Von Bertalanffy, 1975; Whitchurch & Constantine, 1993). This mutual dependence and influence speaks to the **interdependence** among the system's members. In the context of the family system, even factors that appear to influence only one person have an impact on everyone. Similarly, a change in one part of the family system reverberates throughout the rest of the system.

Take, for example, the developmental changes that accompany adolescence. Adolescents need to establish their own identity as they prepare to make commitments to adult roles and responsibilities. While these developmental demands may appear to have consequences only for the adolescent, they affect the entire family system. The increased autonomy required by adolescents necessitates changes in the parental subsystem. Parents or other caretakers will have to adjust how they control their adolescents, just as the adolescents will have to change how much they depend on their parents and other caretakers. At the same time, the parents' or caretakers' changing relationship with their adolescent may have an effect on the marital relationship and other relationships within the family. Therefore, what appears as a change for one family member, in reality has a reverberating effect on the entire system.

The concepts of wholeness, organizational complexity, and interdependence encourage us to be aware of the many factors that potentially affect how a system operates. In this context, it is important to note that the family system is simply one subsystem within broader community and societal systems. The social, political, economic, educational, and ethical agendas of these broader social systems also have a reverberating impact on the family system and on the individuals within the family. In other words, both family system dynamics and functioning will be affected by the characteristics and functioning of these larger social systems.

Strategies and Rules

The patterns of interaction found within a given family system are structured in large part by the **strategies** that the family adopts for the execution of its tasks. In the above example of the single-parent family, it is clear that the family has evolved a set of strategies for dealing with the morning rush hour. The strategies involve having the older daughter, Melissa, take on parenting tasks to enable the mother, Judy, to get ready to go to work. This suggests that one way to make sense of the unique patterns of interaction observed within a family is to conceive of them as strategies that have been developed for managing its demands or tasks.

Consequently, all families are unique not only because they are comprised of a unique collection of individuals but because they evolve unique strategies and rules in an effort to execute their essential tasks.

The structure of the family is reflected in the unique strategies and rules that a family adopts for managing its demands or tasks. The strategies become the patterns of interaction observed within the family. As another example, consider the fact that all families have as one of their tasks the socialization of children. To accomplish this task, parents evolve socialization strategies and rules that determine how they purposively interact with their children. If the parents believe that boys should be masculine and girls feminine, they will interact differently with their sons and daughters. Daughters and sons will be encouraged to engage in different activities. The patterns of communication and interaction between the parents and their sons and daughters will be different as well. The strategies and rules employed by the parents create a unique interactional context that has a profound impact on the trajectory of each child's development.

Strategies are the specific methods and procedures used within a family to accomplish its tasks. These strategies are influenced by such factors as the historical era and the family's generational legacy, class, race, and ethnicity. Within each system, particular strategies become well established and routine over time. They recur with regularity and become the governing principles of family life.

These well-established strategies are called **rules.** Rules are recurring patterns of interaction that define the limits of acceptable and appropriate behavior in the family. By reflecting the values of the family system and defining the roles of individual family members, rules further contribute to the maintenance and stability of the family system.

Rules, in other words, can be thought of as the customs found within the family that govern the patterns of interaction found within it and, hence, define the family as unique. Each family, as an example, has a unique set of rules that are reflected in how meals are customarily managed. Who is responsible for different meal-time tasks, where individuals sit at the dinner table, what family members do during the consumption of the meal (e.g., talk, read, watch TV), and who is responsible for cleaning up after the meal (e.g., mom cleans up while dad watches the nightly news on TV) are a reflection of the unique rules that have come to be adopted within the family.

Rules may be **overt** or **covert.** Overt rules are explicit and openly stated. Covert rules are implicit, meaning that everyone knows the rules although no one has explicitly stated them. It appears as if most of the rules within a family system are covert or implicit. Referring to the meal-time example, in most families everyone has an assigned seat at the dinner table, even though the assignment of the seats has not been explicitly discussed. The existence of these seating rules becomes overt only when someone breaks the rule (i.e., think about what would happen in your family if you all of a sudden decided not to sit in your customary seat).

Families also develop **metarules,** or "rules about the rules" (Laing, 1971). There are always limits and exceptions to rules. There are circumstances in which they always apply and circumstances in which they can be violated. Some rules, in addition, are more important than others. All of this information about the rules—about the importance of different rules and about how and when the rules apply—is contained within the metarules. Metarules are the rules that apply to the family's rules.

Here are some examples of family rules: "You kids can always come to us and talk about anything and everything." "We always treat our children, all our children, equally." Each of these rules, however, could be qualified by a metarule. In the first instance, a metarule might specify what, in reality, can and cannot be discussed with the parents (e.g., sex and drugs). In the latter instance, the metarule might allow a particular child to be treated "more equally" than the others.

While it may appear as if the discussion of metarules introduces some unnecessary complexity to the analysis of family rules, an understanding of the ways in which metarules operate within systems contributes to an understanding of one of the more subtle, but nonetheless powerful, forces that direct the patterns of interaction observed within families. Metarules operate to modify and qualify family rules. These metarules, as do all family rules, delineate acceptable and appropriate behavior. They differ from overt and covert rules, however, in the sense that we are usually prohibited from having any insight into them (Laing, 1971). Although we can usually list the rules that apply to our family, it is much more difficult to arrive at an understanding of the metarules that apply to these rules.

In sum, each family is structurally complex. The family is comprised of individuals who are interdependently connected to one another. Together this interdependent constellation of individuals evolves a system of rules that shapes the patterns of interaction found within the family system. This system of rules is purposive (Kantor & Lehr, 1975) in the sense that the family has tasks that it must execute and therefore must evolve strategies for the execution of these tasks.

The Tasks That Families Must Execute

Implicit in the use of the system's metaphor to define the family is the view that the family is structurally complex. It is comprised of multiple subsystems, and the relationships among the members of the system and the subsystems are governed by a system of rules. This system of rules is reflected in how family members interact with one another, and is organized around the common purposes or tasks that all families must execute (Broderick, 1993). What makes a family unique, in other words, is the unique system of rules found within the family. These rules are organized around the tasks that all families must manage.

The tasks that the family must manage are a key defining feature of family life (Hess & Handel, 1985; Kantor & Lehr, 1975). Within this text we divide tasks into two broad categories—first-order and second-order tasks. **First-order tasks** can be thought of as the essential business of the family—the objectives that the family is charged with fulfilling regardless of its particular composition, socioeconomic status, and cultural, ethnic, or racial heritage. These first-order tasks are common to all families. Among family-systems theorists, there appears to be a consensus that all family systems must manage a constellation of identity tasks, regulate boundaries, regulate the emotional climate of the family, and devise strategies for the maintenance of the household. The strategies and rules that the family employs in its efforts to manage these tasks are in large part what determines the uniqueness of each family. And, it is these unique strategies that are evaluated whenever judgments of family functioning are made.

At the same time, all families must make adjustments in these strategies and rules in response to new information and the changes that occur within families over time. In this regard, systems theorists refer to adaptability as a property of all systems. **Adaptability,** as a system's concept, focuses attention on how the family customarily responds to stress or the demands for changes in its existing customs. Thus, families are not only charged with the responsibility for devising strategies for the execution of their basic tasks, but are charged with the responsibility of adapting the strategies and rules found within the family in response to new information and change. This sets adaptability off as a different kind of a task—a **second-order task**—in that it refers to the customs that exist within a family system for modifying existing strategies and rules (Bartle-Haring & Sabatelli, 1998). Effective families recalibrate or fine tune the ways in which they manage their first-order tasks in response to the changing developmental and contextual realities of the family system.

First-Order Tasks

Identity Tasks

All families must facilitate the development of a sense of identity for both individual family members and the family as a whole. In this regard, there are three interrelated identity tasks that family systems must execute: (1) constructing family themes; (2) socializing family members with respect to biological and social issues such as sexuality and gender; and (3) establishing a satisfactory congruence of images for the individuals within the family (Hess & Handel, 1985).

Family themes are those elements of the family experience that become organizing principles for family life (Bagarozzi & Anderson, 1989). They include both conscious and unconscious elements as well as intellectual (attitudes, beliefs, values) and emotional aspects. The family's themes become the threads that help organize the family's identity. These themes provide the individuals within the family with a framework of meaning influencing how family members interact with others and expect others to interact with them. Such themes also contribute to family members' personal identities by influencing how they orient themselves to others within and outside the family.

Family themes may also be related to ethnic and cultural heritage. For example, being Italian, Irish Catholic, or Jewish can become a family theme and influence the orientations and behaviors of family members. Other themes reflect the predominant values of a particular system. For example, the members of a family may share a view of themselves as competitors, survivors, winners, or losers, and these views may be accompanied by feelings of potency, elation, or despair. Each of these orientations or values translates into actions as individuals act in accordance with the themes.

In a related manner, family systems function to provide individuals with socialization experiences, which in turn further contribute to the development of each member's personal identity by providing additional information about the self. Through our ongoing interactions with significant others, we obtain information about how we are supposed to act as males or females. We also learn about our personal qualities, our physical and sexual attributes, our strengths and weaknesses, and the differences between right and wrong. These attributes likewise contribute to our framework of meaning in that they influence how we interact with others and how we expect others to interact with us.

Finally, each family strives to achieve a congruence of images (Hess & Handel, 1985) that reflects the shared views that family members have of one another. When the family holds an image of an individual that is consistent with the image the individual holds of himself or herself, this congruence facilitates social interaction. This congruence, furthermore, fosters one's personal identity by defining, in part, one's role and position within the family. Such critical identity images often endure for many years. Being the smart one, the athletic one, or the baby are family images that can have enduring influence upon how family members interact with one another over the years (Kantor, 1980).

It bears mentioning, in the context of discussing the identity tasks executed by the family system, that families can create family myths (Bagarozzi & Anderson, 1989; Ferreira, 1966). These myths can take the form of a family holding an image of itself that is incongruent with that held by outsiders. In this instance, the family themes may be inconsistent with the capabilities of the family and create tension between the family and other, outside systems. An example would be the situation in which a school system's effort to provide a child with remedial help conflicts with the family's theme of self-sufficiency. Such a myth can result in a family resisting the school system's intervention, with unfortunate consequences for the child.

In addition, a myth can take the form of an incongruence of family images; that is, the family may hold an image of a family member that is inconsistent with the abilities of the individual or the image the individual holds of himself or herself. For example, the family may hold an image of one member as being dumb when, in fact, the person is quite smart. Concomitantly, the family may hold to the belief that the women within the family need to be protected and are incapable of taking care of themselves. In each of these instances, the myth may serve to limit the behavior and potential of individuals and can create considerable family stress if individuals attempt to alter the image that others have of them.

Boundary Tasks

All families have as one of their tasks the establishment and maintenance of **boundaries** (Kantor & Lehr, 1975). A boundary marks the limits of a system, and boundaries delineate one system from other systems. Similarly, boundaries delineate one subsystem from other subsystems within a larger system. The concept of boundaries as applied to the family system is largely a metaphorical one (Steinglass, 1987), which suggests that information about family boundaries is not directly observable but rather is derived from the observer's subjective impressions of how the systems and subsystems relate to one another. In essence, the flow of information between and within systems provides insight into how systems and subsystems are delineated.

Two types of family boundaries exist: external boundaries and internal boundaries. External boundaries delineate the family from other systems. They determine family membership by delineating who is in, and out, of the family. External boundaries also regulate the flow of information between the family and other social systems. Internal boundaries regulate the flow of information between and within family subsystems. In addition, they influence the degree of autonomy and individuality permitted within the family.

Maintenance Tasks

All families strive to maintain the physical environment of the family in a way that promotes the health and well-being of the family and its members (Epstein, Ryan, Bishop, Miller, & Keitner, 2003). We readily recognize that families are responsible for providing basic necessities such as food, shelter, and education. To accomplish these tasks, families establish priorities and make decisions about the use of resources. Therefore, while maintenance tasks can be described in a direct and straightforward manner, the various decision-making strategies families develop to execute these tasks contribute substantially to the complexity of the family organization. Furthermore, the fact that the health and effectiveness of a family may be judged, to a large extent, according to how well these maintenance tasks are executed, attests to their importance.

Managing the Family's Emotional Climate

Family systems are responsible for managing the emotional climate of the family in a way that promotes the emotional and psychological well-being of its members (Epstein et al., 2003). Family systems function in this regard by providing for members' needs for closeness, involvement, acceptance, and nurturance. Management of its emotional climate requires the family to establish methods of dealing with conflict and distributing power within the family. Conflict is inevitable in all ongoing systems, and yet it has the potential to disrupt a system's functioning seriously. For these reasons, all systems must develop strategies for the management of conflict. In addition, patterns of authority, control, and power have the ability to promote or inhibit the experience of cohesion and cooperation within a system. The promotion of cohesion and cooperation is among those factors that contribute to the experience of intimacy and the emotional and psychological health of family members.

Second-Order Tasks

Adaptability and Managing System Stress

Quite clearly, events occur over time within families that require adaptations. All family systems must manage the need for change in their established structure. The concepts of **openness, stress,** and adaptability are linked within a system's perspective to the second-order task of managing the demands for change that occur within family systems over time.

The family system is conceived of as an open system in that it must adapt to changes from both within and outside the family. An open system is an information-processing system (Von Bertalanffy, 1975). Information is used by the system to determine whether the strategies employed by the system to execute its first-order task are operating effectively. In a sense, then, information-processing systems use information as a form of feedback. The feedback informs the system as to whether change or reorganization is required.

As an open system, the strategies employed by the family will need to be readjusted periodically in response to new information, such as family members' developmental changes. This information is often experienced within the system as stress. Stress is neither good nor bad in this instance. It simply tells the system whether established system interactional patterns require alteration (Von Bertalanffy, 1975; Whitchurch & Constantine, 1993). For example, over the life course of a family, individual and family circumstances change. These changes place stress upon established strategies and rules, and this stress can ultimately lead to a reorganization of strategies and rules such that a better fit is achieved within the family's present circumstances. Such reorganization is a form of system adaptability.

To understand the relationship between stress and adaptability, system theorists introduced the concepts of **morphostasis** and **morphogenesis** (Von Bertalanffy, 1975). Morphostasis refers to those processes operating within systems that resist changes in existing strategies. Morphogenesis, on the other hand, refers to those processes operating within systems that foster systemic growth and development. At all times, there exists within a system a dynamic tension between morphostasis (stability) and morphogenesis (change). Unless the need for reorganization within a system goes beyond some critical threshold, the system resists changing its existing strategies. This tendency to maintain constancy is referred to as morphostasis. When the need for reorganization exceeds some critical threshold, an adaptation or reorganization of system will occur, and this reorganization is referred to as morphogenesis. Both morphogenesis and morphostasis are essential for successful family functioning.

The changes that occur over time in the parent–child relationship help to illuminate the dynamic tension between stress and morphostatic and morphogenic processes. The toddler's growing need for more autonomy and personal control over the environment can place stress on the parents' current strategies for ensuring their daughter's physical safety and fostering her sense of competence and mastery. This stress results from two sources. First, parents may recognize that they need to change their strategies for managing their daughter's behavior. Second, their daughter's insistence that she be allowed greater autonomy will further increase their awareness that they need to change their parenting strategies. As this stress reaches a critical level, the parents will begin to alter the amount of autonomy and control they permit her to have. They may encourage her to dress herself and allow her to ride her bike down the street. This is an ongoing and dynamic process in the sense that the parents will not alter their existing parenting strategies (morphostasis) unless the demand for change goes beyond a critical threshold, thereby making change (morphogenesis) more rewarding than constancy.

The tension between the need to maintain constancy and the need to make changes exists in all family systems. Due to the open nature of the family system, the strategies it employs to execute its first-order tasks will periodically require readjustment. But these readjustments will not occur unless the need for their reorganization is sufficiently great. Stress and information are important concepts in this regard because it is the stress generated by the pressure to alter existing strategies that informs the system when a change is required.

Some systems, however, fail to make adaptations when they are required. These systems are often referred to as closed or rigid. Other systems make adaptations when none are required. They are often referred to as chaotic, random, or disorganized (Olson, Russell, & Sprenkle, 1989). In both instances, families, as open systems, are reacting to information and making adaptations. However, the adaptations made by these systems are not optimal, meaning that they may place the physical, emotional, and/or psychological health of family members at risk.

The Politics of the Family

Over the past couple of decades, our nation has become more concerned with the health and viability of the family, and the debate about the family has moved to the center of national politics. Much of this debate has focused on the problems of contemporary families and the prospects for the family's future. Views clearly differ about what form the family should take and about what factors contribute to the well-being of families. In the United States we debate the degree to which divorce and single parenthood undermine the quality of family life. We argue about the extent to which a mother's employment outside the home undermines the health and well-being of her children. Views clash whenever the question is raised as to whether gay and lesbian couples should be able to parent children or consider themselves a family.

At the heart of much of this debate are differences in opinion about the definition of (1) the family and (2) a functional family. From a systems perspective, a family exists whenever a group of individuals regularly interact with one another over time, experience some degree of emotional bonding, share a common history and legacy, and together devise strategies for the accomplishment of family goals and tasks. Typically, this type of structure results when individuals become related to one another, over time, by blood or marriage. It is clear, however, that blood and marriage ties are not the only ways in which family groups form. Rather, in the broadest possible sense, any group of individuals who share these properties and thus provide for the physical, social, and emotional needs of the individual members can be thought of as a family.

Central to this broad definition of the family is an emphasis on the first- and second-order tasks that the family must fulfill. What defines a family as unique is its structure, which is reflected in large part by the strategies the family employs to execute its first-order tasks. This is not meant to undermine the importance of the family's composition, because that composition influences the family's choice of strategies. The single-parent-headed family often evolves strategies different from those of the two-parent-headed household. The dual-worker system evolves strategies different from those of the traditional family system. The lesbian family system may evolve strategies different from those of the heterosexual family system. The composition of the family affects family dynamics by shaping the strategies employed in the system's effort to accomplish its tasks.

While the composition of the family shapes the strategies the family employs, it is not by itself an indicator of family functioning. Judgments about a family system's functioning must take into account the organizational structure of the family and, in particular, whether the family is able to execute its tasks effectively. Regardless of the particular composition of a family, family functioning is tied to family dynamics. When the structure and strategies of the family support the physical, social, emotional, and psychological well-being of family members, it is reasonable to conclude that the family is functional.

It should be clear as well that each society determines the appropriateness of essential family strategies; that is, prevailing cultural value orientations both direct how tasks should be executed and determine the appropriateness of each family's strategies. When the strategies a family employs are consistent with those endorsed within the society, the family is judged to be effective. When the strategies employed by a particular family deviate sufficiently from the cultural norms, the family is more likely to be judged ineffective. There is no way to divorce the issue of family functioning from the prevailing cultural value orientations of a given society. Within the United States, the cultural heterogeneity of the society contributes to a certain degree of debate as to the appropriate ways of executing family system tasks. The disciplining of children is a case in point. As a society we agree that children are expected to behave in socially appropriate ways, and parents are charged with the task of regulating the behavior of their children. We do not as a society agree, however, on whether physical force and punishment should be employed to control children. Some believe that hitting children should be against the law, whereas others believe that corporal punishment is essential to mold the character of our children.

The confusion that results from these two competing cultural value orientations makes it difficult to determine when a particular parent's discipline strategies have crossed the line from acceptable to dysfunctional. This illustration is used to point out how a determination of family functioning is culturally grounded. The strategies we approve of as a society become the standard by which effectiveness is judged. Therefore, the politics of the family are such that there is considerable disagreement about not only how a family should be comprised, but also how a family should operate. While a consensus has emerged over the years that the family is responsible for ensuring the physical, social, emotional, and psychological well-being of its members, there remains considerable debate as to what is, and what is not, an appropriate strategy.

Conclusions

A systems perspective focuses our attention upon the family's structural and functional features rather than on the family's particular composition. Specifically, it encourages us to be aware of the organizational complexity of the family and the reciprocal and interdependent relationships that exist between the family and broader social systems. Furthermore, a systems perspective encourages us to attend to the wide array of tasks that the family and each of its subsystems must execute in order for the family to function adequately. The family must devise strategies for executing these tasks. The family's choice of strategies is also at the heart of any judgment made regarding a family's effectiveness. The family's structural organization and its unique strategies only become apparent in examining the family's patterns of interaction. That is, only by observing the family's unique rules and patterns of interaction do we gain insight into how the family is structured and how it goes about fulfilling its basic tasks.

Finally, when the family is conceived of as an open system, we are encouraged to be aware of the dynamic and evolving nature of the family. Families, as open systems, develop in response to internal and external stresses that challenge the system to modify its way of executing its tasks. Each family system faces an ongoing challenge to accommodate the ordinary and extraordinary demands that are encountered over its life cycle.

Key Terms

Adaptability The capacity of the system to change its rules and strategies in response to situational or developmental stress.

Boundaries The concept used to delineate one system or subsystem from other systems or subsystems, or from the surrounding environment.

Covert rules Rules that are implicit rather than openly stated but are nonetheless understood by all family members.

Family An interdependent group of individuals who have a shared sense of history, experience some degree of emotional bonding, and devise strategies for meeting the needs of individual members and the group as a whole.

Family themes Those elements of the family experience that become organizing principles for family life, including both conscious and unconscious elements as well as intellectual (attitudes, beliefs, values) and emotional aspects.

First-order tasks The tasks that are common to all families regardless of their particular composition, socioeconomic status, and cultural, ethnic, or racial heritage. Examples of first-order tasks include the formation of family themes, the regulation of boundaries, and the management of the household.

Interdependence The idea that individuals and subsystems that compose the whole system are mutually dependent and mutually influenced by one another.

Metarules Rules about rules.

Morphogenesis Those processes operating within systems that foster systemic growth and development.

Morphostasis Those processes operating within systems that resist changes in existing strategies.

Openness The ease with which members and information cross the boundary from one system or subsystem to another.

Organizational complexity The organizational structure whereby family systems are comprised of various smaller units or subsystems that together comprise the larger family system.

Overt rules Explicit and openly stated rules.

Rules Recurring patterns of interaction that define the limits of acceptable and appropriate behavior in the family.

Second-order tasks The responsibility that all families have for adapting their strategies and rules in response to stress, information, and change.

Strategies The specific policies and procedures the family adopts to accomplish its tasks. Also the unique patterns of interaction that each family establishes to execute its basic tasks.

Stress Information transmitted to the system about whether established interactional patterns require alteration.

Structure Both the family's composition and its organization. Composition refers to the family's membership, that is, the persons who make up the family. Organization is the collection of interdependent relationships and subsystems that operate by established rules of interaction.

Wholeness The idea that systems must be understood in their entirety, which is distinctly different from the simple sum of the contributions of the individual parts.

CHAPTER 2

Family Strategies

Chapter Overview

This chapter focuses in depth on the concept of family strategies. Key to any effort to understand family patterns of interaction is an understanding of the relationship between family tasks and family strategies. Each family system shares a common core of tasks. Themes and identities must be developed. Internal and external boundaries must be established. The physical environment must be managed. The emotional environment must be regulated. And the family system periodically must be reorganized in response to ongoing stresses and strains. Each of these tasks requires the development of strategies and rules, and the specific strategies employed within a family system result from the dynamic interplay among a variety of historical, social, cultural/ethnic, and intergenerational family forces. It is important to understand that the strategies and rules employed to regulate each of these specific family tasks interdependently influence one another. This interdependent cluster of strategies and rules serves as the foundation for assessing the patterns of interaction and functioning observed within the family system.

Family Strategies

A systems view of the family requires an understanding of the interdependence that exists among (1) the family's particular composition; (2) the tasks the family must negotiate; and (3) the strategies the family employs in meeting these tasks. Although families exist in many forms, we assume that all families, over the course of their life span, must execute similar tasks. To state that all families must execute similar tasks is not to say that all families are alike, however. All families are unique, and this uniqueness is reflected in the strategies and rules the family adopts when carrying out these tasks. These strategies and rules form the unique patterns and dynamics of interaction found within each family.

The Development of Strategies

Several factors affect a family's choice of strategies. Family systems are embedded within broader social, economic, religious, educational, and political systems, and each of these broader systems can influence the predominant strategies selected by families. In addition, the historical context must be considered. The predominant strategies for the execution of family tasks may vary in different historical eras. This variability occurs when educational, political, or religious philosophies change over time.

The legacy of the family is another factor influencing the strategies established within a particular system. Research has shown that families tend to repeat patterns of interaction from one generation to another (Bartle & Anderson, 1991; Fine & Norris, 1989). This is not meant to suggest that individuals simply adopt the patterns of interaction they experienced in their own families of origin when they establish their own family. Rather, it makes sense to view one's family of origin experiences as an important source of influence. The family of origin serves as a model or blueprint. Whether or not we follow this blueprint when we establish priorities and strategies for our own family has a lot to do with how we experienced our family of origin while growing up. If we had good experiences, in our family of origin, we are likely to want to repeat what we learned. If we had bad experiences, we may not be so inclined to want to repeat them in our own family. We may instead become committed to establishing new and different strategies. However, as we will see in later chapters, ineffective family strategies may be repeated despite our best intentions. The broader point, however, is that, good or bad, family of origin experiences influence the strategies families establish and pass from one generation to another.

It should be apparent that, at all times, the strategies employed within the family result from the dynamic interplay among various cultural, historical, social, and family forces. Societal forces constrain and limit family behavior by establishing norms and mores that delineate the limits of appropriate and acceptable family behavior. In spite of these broader social constraints, each family's patterns of interaction remain unique. This uniqueness results, in part, from the influence of the family of origin, and also from the fact that we remain active agents in shaping and changing the strategies of our own families.

The following sections examine how families develop strategies for executing each of the tasks outlined in Chapter 1. This discussion begins with the family's identity tasks as these determine how the family defines itself to its own members as well as to outsiders.

Identity Strategies

Family themes and images provide family members with a framework of meaning. This framework supplies the information that becomes part of the family's shared identity as well as each member's personal identity: information about who we are and how we should act with others (both outside and inside the family). Family themes and images also provide members with a set of expectations about how others will act toward them and how they should behave toward others. The family's framework of meaning significantly influences patterns of interaction by prescribing the expectations that all members are to follow.

The choice of family themes is not random but purposeful, that is, there are reasons specific themes are emphasized in a particular family. Some themes have been passed down from earlier generations as part of the family's legacy (Boszormenyi-Nagy & Krasner, 1986; Byng-Hall, 1982; Kramer, 1985). These themes may be linked to long-standing traditions or core family values. For instance, the Kennedy family has established deep commitments to social and political causes that have spanned at least three generations. This theme has clearly influenced the family's view of itself and the career paths of many Kennedy family members.

Other themes may have ethnic origins. Italians know, for example, that they are supposed to have a zest for celebrating, loving, and fighting (Giordano, McGoldrick, & Klages, 2005). Scandinavians, in contrast, know that maintaining emotional control is essential (Erickson, 2005). Still other themes may derive from religious beliefs. Family themes of humility or respect for authority may derive from an orientation that recognizes in some manifestation the existence of a higher power. Finally, themes may represent unresolved emotional issues in one or both parents' families of origin. Themes of rejection, retaliation, engulfment, abandonment, aggression, sacrifice, helplessness, or deprivation in the present family may be a result of unresolved issues in past generations (Bagarozzi & Anderson, 1989).

Families tend to enact those behaviors that are congruent with their primary themes. Depending on the theme, the accompanying behavioral patterns may be positive or negative. That is, they may either foster or interfere with the growth and development of the family and its members. For instance, a theme of mastery and competence may enable family members to remain optimistic when unforeseen events such as a father's job loss or a mother's major illness occur. On the other hand, a theme of family deprivation may lead parents to neglect their children just as they themselves were neglected by their own parents. In either case, the family's themes serve an identity function by regulating how members believe they are supposed to behave in response to a variety of situations.

The selection of particular themes also may represent the family's strategy for attempting to control how others perceive the family. For example, themes such as "intellectual superiority," "courage in the face of challenge," and "serving the needy" all help to determine how members view themselves, how members are supposed to act toward others, and how the family is to be viewed by outsiders. In some families, the priority may be to have others in the community view the family in a positive light. Other family systems may be indifferent to how others view them, while still others may actively encourage others to adopt a negative view of them.

It is important here to point out that we gain insight into the themes existing within the family by paying attention to how resources are deployed within the family. Time, energy, and money can be thought of as the primary resources managed within a family (Kantor & Lehr, 1975). The central themes within the family are reflected in how these resources are used. It is a pretty good bet that if the family invests a lot of time, energy, and money in the education of the children within the family, then education is a central theme within the family. Similarly, if all the children within the family have to play a musical instrument and time and money are used in the pursuit of music lessons, then the family has "being musical and artistic" as one of its themes.

Furthermore, themes can create an emotional climate that permeates all aspects of family life. The theme of "service to the needy" contributes to the belief that family members should help the needy and perhaps should feel guilty when they do not. Similarly, the theme of "being perfect" can result in family members feeling shame and guilt if they wind up judging themselves as deficient in some ways. For example, the negative emotions that a child feels as a result of having difficulty with math in school will be amplified by the theme of perfection.

In sum, the specific themes present within the family direct the flow of resources, determine the behavior of family members, and create an emotional climate all at the same time. All families, regardless of their composition and makeup, develop themes. The particular themes adopted by a family contribute to the evolving identities, skills, and emotional well-being of individual family members.

Personal images evolve within the family system in a manner consistent with themes. People see themselves as having distinct attributes such as "I am smart," "I am attractive," "I am lazy," or "I am overweight." The attributes that we ascribe to ourselves are, to a large extent, socially created; that is, they are by-products of our social interactions (Hess & Handel, 1985). These attributes are influenced, in other words, by our perception of how others see us and by how we compare ourselves to others. While it is necessary to acknowledge that others outside the family (e.g., peers, teachers, coaches) will contribute to the development of personal identity, the family remains a major force in its development.

The attributes emphasized by the family reflect the identity strategies the family establishes for its members. Within some families, the strategies include encouraging individual family members to feel good about themselves, and to feel capable and confident in dealing with the challenges of life. When these are important values, the family acts to encourage the development of these personal identities. When interacting with their children, such parents will encourage them to view themselves as possessing positive rather than negative traits. Parents will highlight the strengths of the child and provide the child with opportunities to master skills and succeed.

While such goals are common in many families, they certainly do not characterize all families. We need, in this regard, to develop some way of understanding how negative identities become established in some family members. Here the legacy of the family becomes critical. For example, parents may not be capable of acting generatively toward their children due to their own negative family history and poor self-concept. They may find themselves unable to acknowledge the positive traits and abilities of their children and able to see only negative ones. In other situations, persons who feel bad about themselves develop strategies for making themselves feel better at someone else's expense. We have probably all had some experience with individuals who attempt to make themselves feel good by making others feel bad about themselves. When one can walk away from these individuals without caring what they think, such strategies have a minimal effect on one's personal identity. However, it may be quite different when the critical person is a close family member. When a mother makes herself feel better by telling her daughter that her breasts are too small or her nose is too big, the effect can be dramatic and enduring.

Interestingly, identity strategies typically differ for each family member. Gender is of particular interest when the discussion turns to differences in the personal identities of family members (Goldner, 1988; Walter, Carter, Papp, & Silverstein, 1988). The beliefs families have with respect to males and females influence how children are socialized. Interactions with children can be decidedly different depending on the sex of the child. Boys may be taught the importance of acting in a masterful way and taking on challenges. They may be taught that they are valued because of what they can accomplish. Girls, in contrast, may be taught the value of social skills and the importance of nurturing others. Girls, in addition, may be taught that they are valued based on physical attributes. This type of gender indoctrination defines and limits the behavior and personal identities of male and female children. Given that few families consciously think about their gender belief systems, and that most families are invested in influencing family members' gender socialization, these differing gender orientations often have a pronounced effect on the personal identities and behaviors of family members.

Finally, families vary in terms of the extent to which the family uses strategies to attempt to control the identities of its members. While all families exercise some control over the identities of their members, some families attempt to exert more control than others. The critical question is whether a given family's strategies for fostering its members' identities are flexible and accommodating or rigid and predetermined. That is, do family members have the freedom to develop their own identities, based on their own unique strengths and potentials, or are they constrained by expectations that require them to develop a particular identity that may not fit with their innate skills and abilities?

When the family's strategies include greater control over the identities of its members, the rules that develop will be qualitatively different from those in families who allow greater latitude to individual members. Parents may argue, for example, about which side of the family a child resembles. When a child does well in school, the parents may beam and say, "Just like your father!" In these instances, the family is controlling, to some extent, a child's identity. The child's identity is kept "in the family," so to speak. This form of control is quite benign so long as the child is given the freedom to grow and change over time, and so long as the freedom to explore his or her own identity exists both within and outside the family.

In some families, however, parents live vicariously through their children (Stierlin, 1981). These parents are highly invested in controlling how children are viewed by others, and their own sense of worth and accomplishment is derived from the actions of their children. This severely constrains the children's ability to explore their own identities because they are pressured to fulfill the dreams and expectations of their parents. For many children, this burden can be a disabling force throughout their lives.

The goals of socializing children and assisting children in the development of their family and personal identities add distinct complexity to an understanding of the patterns of interaction that occur between parents and children. The ways in which interactions develop are related to the type of orientation desired (positive versus negative) and the degree of control that the family exercises over these orientations. In this regard, while all parents succeed in influencing the personal identities of family members, not all facilitate this process in ways that are beneficial to the child. Fostering a negative identity disadvantages the child. Controlling the child's identity can be equally disruptive as the process robs the child of the right to exercise personal control over who he or she is and how he or she would like to be seen by others.

Boundary Strategies

External Boundaries

Some boundaries delineate the family's relationship to other external systems. In other words, families establish strategies and rules for interacting with outsiders and manipulating their physical environment to maintain their integrity, cohesiveness, and separateness in relation to the external environment (Kantor & Lehr, 1975; Whitchurch & Constantine, 1993). In general, the ways in which these external boundaries are regulated vary according to their degree of permeability. **Permeability** refers to the degree to which the family's boundaries are open or closed.

Family systems with relatively open external boundaries are those in which the home is literally open to others. Family membership may be loosely defined, and people can come and go freely from the home. In addition, information about the family can flow easily to outside systems. In relatively closed systems, the home is literally closed to others. Children, for example, cannot have friends visit their homes. There is a heavy emphasis on privacy, and rules are established prohibiting the discussion of family matters with outsiders ("What we say within the home stays within the home"). The physical environment around the home is structured in a way that communicates this interest in privacy. For example, trees may be planted in strategic places to block the view of others to the home.

The type of external boundaries established by the family is one of the factors that contributes to each family's uniqueness. While most families fall somewhere in the middle of the "open/closed" continuum, typically maintaining some balance between being entirely open and entirely closed, each system has unique boundary strategies and rules. The importance of these boundary strategies and rules is twofold.

First, these strategies and rules influence our interactions with others. We generally structure our interactions with others to conform with the family's boundary rules. That is, the family system's boundary rules define the parameters of appropriate and inappropriate behaviors with outsiders. While there may be some conscious planning and discussion of these strategies, for the most part family members are not conscious of the decisions that they have made about how their external boundaries will be structured.

Second, the family's boundary rules influence the level of members' comfort with and trust of those outside the family system. In general, the more open a family's boundaries, the more comfortable members feel with others. Similarly, the more closed a family's boundaries, the less comfortable members are likely to feel outside the family's orbit. Individuals also tend to be more comfortable with persons who come from families with boundary strategies and rules similar to their own. This is because similarity fosters the ease of interaction. When the rules and strategies differ, each individual's assumptions about how the boundaries should be structured are violated by the other's behavior. These violations result in discomfort with the interaction and distrust of the other.

In sum, external boundaries structure the ways the family and its members relate to outsiders. These boundaries influence the sources of information that individual family members are exposed to. In subtle but distinct ways, these boundaries influence how each family member's life unfolds. For example, a child needing remedial help with math may wind up not getting this help if the closed nature of the family boundaries results in the child's parents tending to mistrust teachers and school administrators.

Internal Boundaries

Internal boundaries mainly concern how internal distances between individuals and subsystems are regulated within the family (Hess & Handel, 1985; Kantor & Lehr, 1975). How these boundaries are regulated is reflected primarily in the degree to which each member's individuality and autonomy are tolerated within the family system. This tolerance for individuality and autonomy has been understood as existing along a continuum. Those systems with a low tolerance for individuality are conceived of as having **enmeshed** internal boundaries. Those systems with a high tolerance for individuality are conceived of as having **disengaged** internal boundaries (Minuchin, 1974; Olson & Gorall, 2003).

When boundaries are conceived of as enmeshed, the strategy of the system is to limit the expression of individuality and autonomy. This is accomplished by structuring interactions to encourage individuals to be dependent on others in the family. Little privacy is permitted, and the "business" of the individual is the business of the family. Therefore, when one member of the family has a problem, all members share in the problem. The rules established within the family require that each individual discuss his or her problems, thoughts, concerns, and so on, with the family. The family is free, in addition, to intrude on the personal life of family members.

When boundaries are structured in a disengaged way, the strategy of the system is to promote the expression of autonomy. At the extreme end of the disengaged continuum, individuals are left to fend for themselves. Rules within the family are established that encourage individuals to keep to themselves and not expect assistance or advice from others in the family. In other words, autonomy is valued and expected. Family members would not think to intrude in the business of other family members.

The strategies employed by families as they establish and regulate these internal system boundaries are clearly related to the effectiveness of the family. Olson and colleagues (1983, 1989, 2003) suggested that optimal family functioning is more likely to occur when families achieve a balance between enmeshment and disengagement. In more functional families, the boundary rules allow for both the expression of individuality and the experience of a secure connection to the family. Olson and colleagues further noted that boundary strategies and rules need to be adjusted in accordance with the changing developmental needs and capabilities of individual members. We would expect parents to be more enmeshed with an infant than an older child who is more capable of acting in an independent and self-reliant way.

It is clear that considerable tension can exist within families around the structuring of these internal boundaries. This tension occurs when the goals for the system and the goals for individuals are not consistent. For example, the family may have strategies for maintaining a strong external boundary and sense of security by limiting members' autonomy and encouraging them to depend only on one another. However, as children develop they may desire more autonomy than the parents are willing to tolerate. This conflict around the regulation of autonomy can result in tension and stress that may eventually lead to a restructuring of the family's internal (and perhaps external) boundaries.

Boundary strategies are influenced to a significant extent by cultural and ethnic orientations. Certain ethnic groups (e.g., Italians) tend to structure boundaries in a more enmeshed way than other ethnic groups (Giordano et al., 2005). This means that cultural and ethnic orientations normalize the patterns of distance regulation observed within the family. Enmeshment is then embraced because it is what is expected. However, a potential source of stress may emerge when outsiders have a different view of how boundaries should be structured. An example of this is a marriage between persons from different ethnic backgrounds.

Finally, it must be emphasized that the discussion of boundaries centers around how distances are regulated between both individuals and subsystems of the family. Two points are important in this regard. First, it is possible that the patterns of distance regulation will be similar for all family members. It is just as feasible, however, that some subsystems will develop patterns that differ from other subsystems within the family. For example, siblings may be enmeshed with one another in a household where the parents remain disengaged from the children. The central point here is that we should avoid talking about enmeshed and disengaged families and instead talk about the boundary strategies that characterize particular relationships and subsystems within the family.

The second point is that boundary strategies may or may not result in the experience of intimacy. We may be tempted to assume that enmeshed boundaries represent a high degree of intimacy and concern among family members and that disengaged boundary patterns occur because individuals do not care for one another. While this may be true in some instances, we should avoid these generalizations. Family members who are overinvolved with one another may not like one another very much. Similarly, individuals may act with a great deal of autonomy within their families and yet still experience considerable family support.

Maintenance Strategies

All families have maintenance tasks involved with providing food, shelter, clothing, and education to their members. While this may seem relatively straightforward, we seldom think of the patterns of decision-making connected to these basic maintenance tasks.

Themes run through all aspects of family life. It should come as no surprise, thus, that family themes are closely connected to how maintenance tasks are executed. That is, all families, based on their themes, establish priorities in terms of how they want the family to be maintained. To live in accordance with these priorities, decisions must be made about the use of the family's resources. **Maintenance resources** consist of time, energy, and money that the family must use to accomplish its maintenance tasks. Since each of these resources is finite, the system's values and priorities establish how the family's resources are to be used.

Making decisions about the use of family resources is a complex and dynamic process. In essence, decision-making strategies delineate who has control over the resources and provide insight into the power hierarchy within the system. They also determine who is involved in the decision-making process and how each one is to be involved. How resources are to be used is also of interest.

The maintenance strategies that evolve in a system, therefore, reflect the priorities of the system and involve decisions about the use of resources. For instance, living in an exclusive neighborhood may be a system priority. To accomplish this objective, decisions about the use of system resources, particularly money, must be made. In some instances, this particular priority will not affect other maintenance strategies because the family has an abundance of money. In other instances, however, the money used to accomplish this objective will leave the family with little money for the accomplishment of other maintenance tasks. The family may have to skimp on food, be unable to buy furniture, or have insufficient money to finance the education of the children. In other words, because maintenance tasks involve the strategic manipulation of family resources, how one maintenance task is accomplished has an interdependent effect on how other tasks are accomplished.

The maintenance strategies adopted by a family are also reflected in the various plans and procedures adopted by the family for maintaining the household in terms of cleaning, cooking, managing finances, and so on. The specifics of each strategy are determined to some extent by the structure of the family and the resources available to it. Children in single-parent-headed households, for example, may be assigned considerably more responsibility for maintenance tasks than children in two-parent-headed households. This may occur because limited parental resources require the use of children as resources for household management.

Each maintenance strategy and rule is characterized by a level of complexity and organization. Some strategies are quite flexible and perhaps even inconsistent. Others are highly rigid and defined. Within underorganized systems, consistent maintenance strategies are not established. There may be no well-defined strategy for paying bills and handling finances. Meals are seldom planned, for example, and, when they are, the necessary ingredients are not present within the house. This requires a trip to the market, which uses some of the time, energy, and money available to the system. Because the meal takes longer to prepare than was originally planned, the organization of the children's schedules is disrupted. Thus, in a cyclical fashion, the failure to establish consistent maintenance strategies contributes to the level of chaos present within the system.

Within overorganized systems, the maintenance strategies are extremely organized and rigid. There are strategies for when different maintenance chores must be done and who is responsible for doing them. The laundry is done on Saturdays, for example, and housecleaning on Sundays. All school lunches for the upcoming week are made on Sunday evenings and placed in the freezer. While these systems are efficient in executing the maintenance tasks, the rigidity present within them can undermine both spontaneity and creativity.

A family system, no matter how organized or disorganized, is adequate so long as the maintenance tasks are accomplished. This is not to suggest that we do not evaluate the effectiveness of a family's strategies and plans. Clearly an evaluation of the maintenance strategies employed within a family is a major part of any evaluation of the effectiveness and functioning of the family (Epstein et al., 2003; Fisher, Ransom, Terry, & Burge, 1992). If the house is not maintained, if children are not fed and clothed, if clothes and children are dirty, for example, we judge the family to be ineffective. It is true, as well, that when making these assessments, it is important to consider the level of chaos or rigidity characterizing the maintenance strategies being employed. In this regard, optimal strategies allow for a relatively high degree of organization and stability as well as enough flexibility to foster spontaneity and creativity (Anderson & Gavazzi, 1990; Beavers & Hampson, 2003; Olson & Gorall, 2003).

The priorities, resources, and strategies adopted by a system result in the formation of rules that define how family members are supposed to act. These rules reinforce the priorities of the family and are intended to help the family effectively use its resources. When money is limited and providing food for family members is a priority, for example, rules around eating may evolve ("You can't leave the table until your plate is clean!"). These rules will be enforced in different ways. Some families lecture their children about the importance of eating but eventually allow them to leave the table without eating everything. (Kids learn the rules and know if they just "stick it out" they will not have to eat the lima beans!) Other families may make their children sit at the table for hours until all the food is eaten. Other families might literally force-feed the children. Others might give the kids a beating if they do not eat their food.

Rules may remain quite stable over time or may change from one generation to the next. These changes often occur because the resources of the next generation of the family have changed. Referring back to the example of rules around eating, if adult children have more money than their parents, they may, when they have children of their own, still have the priority of providing food for family members, but their greater affluence may result in rules about eating that are more flexible. It is interesting to note how this alteration of rules can become a source of conflict between the generations.

In summary, an understanding of family system maintenance tasks is relatively straightforward. All families must execute these tasks. Considerable variation exists, however, in how they are executed. Maintenance strategies vary as families establish different priorities for how they want to maintain themselves. These different priorities are reflected in the various ways families strategically use their resources and in the rules they establish about the use of resources. Each strategy and subsequent rule results in the patterns and dynamics of the family taking on a unique form and organization. It should also be clear that the maintenance strategies and rules employed by the family carry considerable weight in terms of how we evaluate the family's functioning.

Strategies for Managing the Family's Emotional Climate

Management of the emotional climate of the family involves the evolution of strategies for nurturing and supporting individual family members, building family cohesion, and managing conflict and tension. The successful development of positive strategies for managing emotional expression has been found to promote the health and well-being of family members, while the absence of such strategies has consistently been associated with a host of health complaints and symptoms (Fisher, Nakell, Terry, & Ransom, 1992; Jacob, 1987).

While it would be naive and simplistic to assert that all families seek to create a secure emotional environment, it is reasonable to assume that this is a priority of most families. When the strategies of the family fail to include interactions for promoting the emotional and psychological well-being of its members, we immediately question the effectiveness of these systems.

That most families desire to promote the emotional and psychological well-being of family members does not mean that all families accomplish this task in similar ways. The strategies adopted for nurturing and supporting family members are quite diverse. Just think of all the different strategies that can exist for supporting family members. Are family members free to talk about their feelings and share their problems? Are family members willing to listen to others? When they listen, do they provide support, advice, or both? In addition, consider all the different ways that families express affection and intimacy. In some families, love may be expressed verbally, and in other families by doing things for others ("You know we love you because we take care of you. Why should we have to say it?"). In some families, affection is physically expressed with hugs and kisses. In other families, physical displays of affection are clearly "against the rules."

In other words, the family's nurturance and support strategies become the family's nurturance and support rules. Whether they are implicit or explicit, we all know what these rules are in our own families. Somehow we know what is, and what is not, acceptable behavior. Of interest in this regard is that, so long as we abide by the rules, interaction proceeds smoothly. What is also interesting is that there are no right or wrong ways to express nurturing and support. What matters is how the strategies and resultant rules are experienced by members of the family. The critical issue to consider when evaluating the effectiveness of a family's strategies for nurturing and supporting its members is the fit between the behaviors employed and how these behaviors are experienced by family members.

When family members share expectations and assumptions about acceptable ways of expressing support, not only do interactions flow smoothly, but the behaviors are effective at communicating support. Dissimilar expectations and assumptions are likely to result in tension and conflict. Teasing is an example of a strategy that could be employed to promote closeness. So long as everyone understands the meaning of this behavior ("We only tease people we care about!"), teasing will be experienced as an expression of nurturing and support. But a very different outcome is likely when we interact with others who do not share this framework. Unless we share similar frameworks, we cannot be sure that teasing someone will be experienced as an expression of closeness and support.

Building family cohesion requires strategies that distribute power in ways that allow members to feel positive about their involvement in the family. Power is a complex issue within families. On the one hand, as noted, maintenance of the family requires the creation of power hierarchies and decision-making strategies. On the other hand, power hierarchies and decision-making strategies can operate against the creation of cohesion and the experience of intimacy in close personal relations. Issues of power and decision-making will be examined in greater detail in later chapters. However, the key point at this juncture is that the choice of strategies for managing family resources can have either an "everybody wins" or a "win–lose" outcome. Those strategies that enable all family members to feel confirmed, accepted, involved, and acknowledged will promote family cohesion. Those strategies that benefit some members at the expense of others who feel unconfirmed, slighted, or ignored will not promote the development of family cohesion.

One critical issue in this regard is the legitimacy of the power and decision-making strategies employed by the family. We react to power situations differently depending on whether we perceive the people making decisions as having a legitimate right to do so. When people are perceived as having the legitimate right to make decisions and control resources, they are viewed as exercising authority rather than control. Authority is the legitimate use of power, whereas control and domination are the nonlegitimate uses of power (Scanzoni, 1979b). In the family system, power and decision-making strategies reflecting the legitimate authority of family members to control resources do not operate against the experience of family cohesion. When power and decision-making strategies are perceived as efforts to control resources and dominate others in nonlegitimate ways, the injustice of being unfairly treated is likely to contribute to an erosion of family cohesion. Successful management of the family's emotional climate must include decision-making and control strategies and rules that foster cooperation and cohesion.

Managing the emotional climate of the family also requires the evolution of strategies for dealing with and managing conflict. In all family systems, conflict is inevitable and has the potential to disrupt the functioning of the system. Conflict-management strategies are complex in that some can protect the system from major disruptions and yet be ineffective at promoting the emotional and psychological health of family members. Ideally, conflict-management strategies successfully manage conflict and promote the well-being of family members.

Families use various strategies for the management of conflict. Some families simply deny that any conflict exists. While denial may minimize the disruptive effects of conflict for the system, it may not allow vital information to enter the family that may be essential to the emotional and psychological health of family members. An example of this would be family members' denial of a parent's alcoholism or substance abuse. Although this may in some instances minimize overt conflicts in the family, it may inadvertently contribute to that parent's occupational, social, or physical health problems and, in turn, bring highly disruptive problems into the family.

Other conflict-management strategies might involve the denial of conflict until it reaches a point at which an "explosion of conflict and anger" occurs. At one moment, interactions are subdued and controlled, and, at the next, family members are yelling and screaming at one another. In some instances, these eruptions can become out of control and threaten the physical safety of family members.

Other family systems manage conflict by detouring the conflict between two persons onto a third person or some other object. A number of terms have been used to describe this process, including scapegoating (Vogel & Bell, 1968), triangulation (Bowen, 1978), coalition (Minuchin, 1974), and projection (Framo, 1970). These concepts will be discussed in much greater detail in subsequent chapters. In general, detouring strategies involve misdirecting conflicting feelings toward one person onto another person, often one perceived as less threatening, such as a child. The feelings may be in the form of anger, worry, overprotectiveness, support seeking, or some other manifestation of unresolved tension and anxiety. Conflicts may also be detoured onto some other object or activity rather than another person. For instance, some individuals detour conflicts onto their work, their favorite hobby, or even excessive television watching.

In each instance, conflict-detouring strategies are employed instead of dealing directly with the source of the conflict. For example, instead of dealing with the conflict he experiences with his wife, a father criticizes one of his children about how irresponsible he or she is. Alternatively, the father may confide in one of his children about how unreasonable the mother is. In the first instance, the stress created by the conflict is managed by using a child as a replacement. In the second instance, the child is used as a support to confirm the father's negative view of his wife. Both of these strategies, however, place the child in a potentially unhealthy situation. The child may develop a negative self-image as an irresponsible person or risk the loss of a supportive relationship with the mother to maintain a positive relationship with the father. In the latter instance, the child's loyalty conflicts may become even more pronounced should the mother choose to seek out the same child for her support.

Alternatively, the mother may seek out a different child to become her support. If this occurs, the members of each group are at odds with the members of the opposing group. The formation of subsystems around detoured conflicts, therefore, creates patterns of interaction that reverberate throughout the entire family system. If consistently applied, these strategies of managing conflict clearly have the potential to become dysfunctional patterns of family interaction (Beavers & Hampson, 2003; Bowen, 1978; Minuchin, 1974).

In contrast, more successful strategies for managing conflict are those that promote open acceptance of conflicts and responsible efforts to negotiate compromise solutions between family members. Minor irritations are addressed as they occur rather than being saved up until they can no longer be tolerated. In this way, potentially explosive outcomes are avoided. Finally, conflicts that originate within a particular relationship are addressed within that relationship without the need to rely on a third party for detouring the accompanying tension and anxiety.

The broader point here is that there are a variety of strategies for managing conflict. These different strategies are more or less successful at bringing about conflict resolution and at promoting the emotional and psychological health of family members.

In summary, the emotional climate of the family affects our emotional and psychological well-being. The management of this emotional climate is one of the primary tasks of the family system. Our emotional and psychological health are dependent on whether family members (1) feel nurtured, supported, and valued by the members of the system; (2) work cooperatively to accomplish common goals; and (3) are willing to take the risks necessary for the management of the inevitable conflicts that occur.

Strategies for Managing Stress: Adaptability as a Second-Order Task

Coping within Families

As an organizationally complex, dynamic, and open system, the family is ever-evolving. Family system perspectives assume that the changing circumstances of family life mean that the family is always under some degree of stress. As a result, the family will, periodically, need to alter how it executes its first-order tasks. Managing stress and making adaptations are important second-order tasks that are related to the ability of the family to function effectively over time.

Stress within Family Systems

When we use the term **stress**, most individuals think of a negative emotional state characterized by the experience of excessive pressure, anxiety, and tension. Although this is one way of conceptualizing stress, this is not the way the concept of stress is used within system's perspectives. Stress, from a family systems perspective, is the degree of pressure exerted on the family to alter the strategies it employs to accomplish its basic tasks. Stress, in this regard, can be conceived of as a specific type of information or feedback about the functioning of the system and whether morphogenetic changes are necessary to enhance that functioning. These morphogenetic changes are accompanied by transformations in the family's interactional patterns and rules of relating. The growth and development of an adolescent, for example, "stresses the family system" because patterns of relating must be adjusted to accommodate to the changing developmental needs and abilities of the adolescent. That strategies and rules need altering is not necessarily a negative experience for the system. The pressure to transform these rules and strategies is needed for the system to continue to function effectively.

Stress is experienced in response to events that require changes or adaptations on the part of the family. There are two types of stressor events encountered by families: **normative stressor events** and **non-normative stressor events**. Normative events refer to those expected and ordinary developmental transitions affecting the family. Their key distinguishing features are that they are expected, occur regularly over the course of time, and carry with them ordinary difficulties. Examples of normative events include marriages, births, and the deaths of elderly family members.

Non-normative stressor events are unexpected events. These events create unanticipated hardships for the family, and require adaptations or alterations in the strategies used by the system to execute some or all of its basic tasks. A house fire, for example, cannot be anticipated. This non-normative event will require the family to alter substantially many of the strategies it uses to fulfill its tasks. The damage done to the home will disrupt the usual flow of day-to-day living. Basic maintenance strategies will need altering. Furthermore, the emotional turmoil and anxiety in the aftermath of the fire will result in family members needing more emotional and social support than usual. The fire will require some readjustment in how the emotional climate of the family is maintained.

The conceptualization of stress from within family systems perspectives has been further elaborated by Carter and McGoldrick (2005a) in their discussion of horizontal and vertical stressors. Horizontal stressors are the demands placed upon the system as it moves through time, dealing with changes and transitions that occur over the life cycle. These include both unexpected, non-normative events and expected, normative events. The degree or level of stress experienced within a family is influenced as well by vertical stressors, or by the patterns of relating and functioning that are transmitted from generation to generation within the family system. These vertical stressors include the attitudes, expectations, taboos, secrets, and unresolved emotional issues each generation of a family is exposed to while growing up. This suggests that the multigenerational patterns of interaction that exist within a particular family potentially contribute to the overall level of stress experienced by a family as it moves through time. Each family system is characterized by a unique historical and evolving legacy that interacts with the ongoing ordinary and extraordinary demands to influence the level of stress experienced within a family system.

As suggested in Figure 2.1, a family's overall level of stress is determined by both horizontal and vertical stressors. Given enough stress on the horizontal axis, any family can appear disorganized and dysfunctional. For instance, a family dealing simultaneously with the parents' divorce, the oldest child's marriage, a grandparent's death, and the youngest child's chronic illness would be likely to evidence a high level of stress, confusion, and disorganization. It would be difficult for such a family to meet its basic tasks successfully in the face of such a high demand on its available resources.

By the same token, a family with minimal horizontal stress and an intense level of vertical stress can appear just as disrupted. For instance, a daughter announces her plan to marry and leave home. In some families such an event may be a cause for celebration ("We're not losing a daughter but gaining a son."). However, imagine that the daughter's parents are emotionally cut off from one another after years of intense marital conflicts. Further imagine that the father

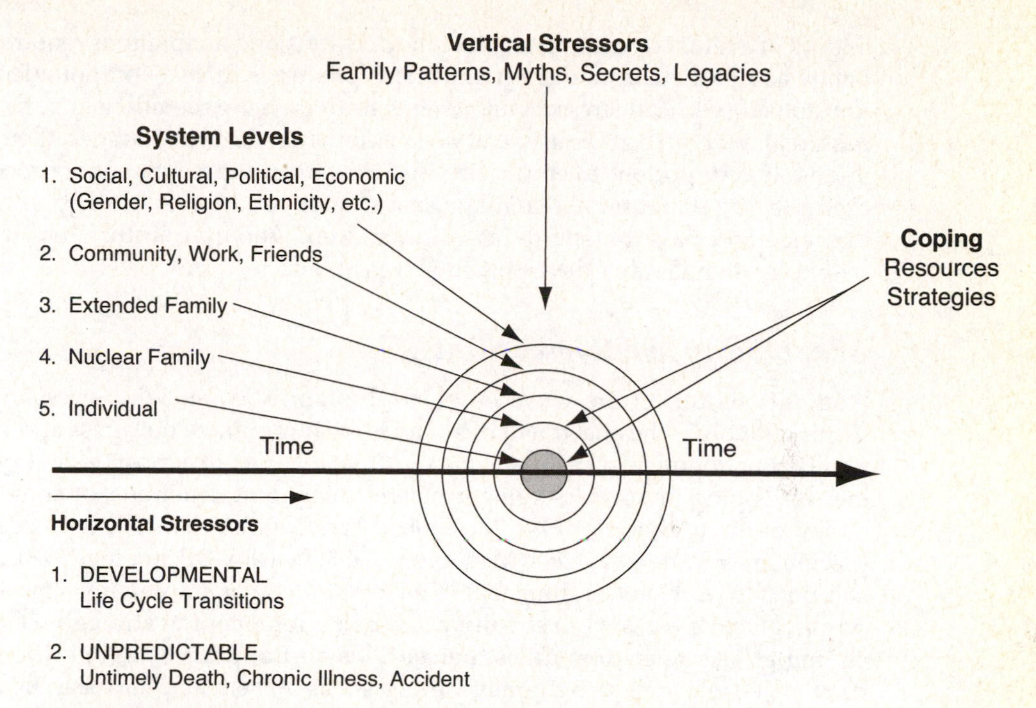

FIGURE 2.1 Horizontal and Vertical Stressors

Source: Adapted from Betty Carter and Monica McGoldrick (Eds.), *The Changing Family Life Cycle: A Framework for Family Therapy*, 2e. Published by Allyn and Bacon, Boston, M A. Copyright © 1989 by Pearson Education.

immersed himself in his work while the mother turned to her daughter for emotional support. Both parents learned this pattern of cutting off from one another emotionally in their own highly conflicted families of origin. They developed this strategy to tune out their own parents' frequent arguments and the verbal abuse they both personally received.

In this family, the daughter's departure may precipitate intense stress and anxiety. The mother may feel betrayed by her daughter and reject the daughter's partner. The daughter, in turn, may feel guilty about leaving while, at the same time, be extremely angry at the mother for her attitude toward her fiancé. The father is also likely to be quite apprehensive about the added emotional demands his wife may place on him when the daughter leaves. Therefore, the stress of past generations becomes an important factor in determining this family's response to the current developmental transition.

It should be clear that families must contend at any point in time with a **pile-up of stressor events** (McCubbin & Patterson, 1983; Mederer & Hill, 1983). Families seldom deal with one event at a time. Instead, stressor events overlap. Normative events overlap (you graduate from college, take a job, and marry within a year), and this overlap is complicated by the potential presence of a non-normative event (during this period your brother dies in a car crash). The consequence of this pile-up of events is a magnification of the demands and adaptations required of the family at a particular moment in time. This pile-up is further compounded by the unresolved (vertical) stressors and strains from earlier generations that have been passed along both consciously and unconsciously as legacies, images, themes, and myths. It is important to emphasize that this is a multigenerational process. For example, the daughter above may use a similar tuning-out strategy in her own marriage and pass it along to her own children, who may, in turn, use it to deal with their own family's developmental transitions.

Adaptability and Coping Strategies

Adaptations reflect the ways in which the family copes with stressor events. **Coping** involves the enactment of strategies that minimize the stress and keep the family functioning in an efficient and effective manner. In a most basic way, strategies for coping involve resolving problems, managing emotions, or some combination of the two (Klein, 1983; McCubbin, Joy, Cauble, Comeau, & Needle, 1980; McCubbin & Patterson, 1983; Menaghan, 1983; Pearlin & Schooler, 1978). Seeking solutions to problems and managing the emotions that accompany stressful periods involve the use of both **cognitive** and **behavioral coping strategies**. Cognitive coping efforts refer to families' perceptions and appraisals of specific stressor events. The way in which a family views a stressor event and the meaning and significance attached to it frame the event. This frame in turn influences the ways in which the family attempts to respond to the stressor behaviorally.

A significant aspect of successfully coping with stress events, therefore, is the ability to define adaptively the crisis situation. Cognitive coping efforts by the family include clarifying the hardships it must contend with such that they become more manageable, deemphasizing the emotional components of the crisis, and trying to maintain the functional properties of the family system such that it can continue to support members' social and emotional development (McCubbin & Patterson, 1983).

Think, for example, of all the times you have seen a reporter interview the victims of a non-normative crisis. These situations clearly promote insight into how the victims are cognitively coping with the hardship. One individual will say, "Well, I'm sorry we lost the house in the fire, but at least no one was hurt." This type of framing accentuates the positive rather than the negative aspects of the event, thereby helping to manage the emotional components of the crisis. This individual might go on to say, "This is why homeowner's insurance exists. We'll get in touch with our insurance company and begin the process of rebuilding." Here again, this appraisal of the situation frames the event in a way that allows the hardships to become more manageable.

Other individuals react quite differently to the stressor event. In some interviews, people simply keep saying over and over again, "Why me?" Others might focus on their lost possessions and say, "Everything is gone. We won't be able to replace some of what we lost. It's devastating!" These ways of framing the event may result in the emotional aftermath of the crisis interfering with attempts to manage the crisis event and the other demands of family life.

Behavioral coping strategies refer to what the family actually does to manage stress (McCubbin et al., 1980). As do cognitive responses to stress events, behavioral strategies vary considerably from family to family. It is useful to think of specific behavioral strategies as reflecting the general coping orientations of the family. Families vary, for example, in terms of the degree to which they actively pursue solutions to problems. Some families remain complacent, doing little to address sources of stress and strain, while others are active. Furthermore, families vary in the degree to which they seek help and support from outsiders or experts.

These general orientations influence the specific manner in which coping strategies are implemented. For example, if a family shuns support and assistance, family members will not ask for directions when they find themselves hopelessly lost while traveling. Although not asking for directions is a rather benign example of a behavioral coping strategy, try to imagine how this family might respond to the loss of a job, a house fire, the unexpected illness of a family member, or the demands imposed by the birth of a baby.

Coping Resources and Coping Efficacy

The specific cognitive and behavioral problem-solving strategies used to respond to stressor events depend on the **coping resources** possessed by the family. Coping resources refer to the properties of a family and the attributes and skills possessed by individual family members that serve to minimize the vulnerability of a family to stress (McCubbin et al., 1980). Family systems can be thought of as having different resources that influence their choices of coping strategies. Examples of coping resources include the unique skills, knowledge, temperaments, and personalities of individual family members. They also include the various sources of social support available to families when they are confronted with stressful situations. The transition to parenthood, for example, can be thought of as a stress event that requires adaptations on the part of the family system. The coping strategies employed by a particular family in response to this event will be influenced by the knowledge and information the new parents have available to them. The family's response to this event also will be influenced by the various social supports available to them.

The interrelationships among stress, coping resources, coping efforts, and family adaptability are depicted in Figure 2.2. This model provides a graphic illustration of how each element of the family stress and coping process is connected. It also offers a way of understanding how the abilities of the family to manage stressor events is tied to the ongoing stress levels found within the family and the functioning of the family over time.

The main point here is that all families are under stress, although the level of stress will vary over time. The degree of stress within the family is related to the demands placed upon it to alter or adjust its manner of functioning. These demands stem from the horizontal and vertical stressors experienced by the system at any point in time. At certain times there are few pressures to alter existing strategies, and at other times the demands are excessive. When these pressures are sufficiently great, the system will need to make adaptations in an effort to reduce

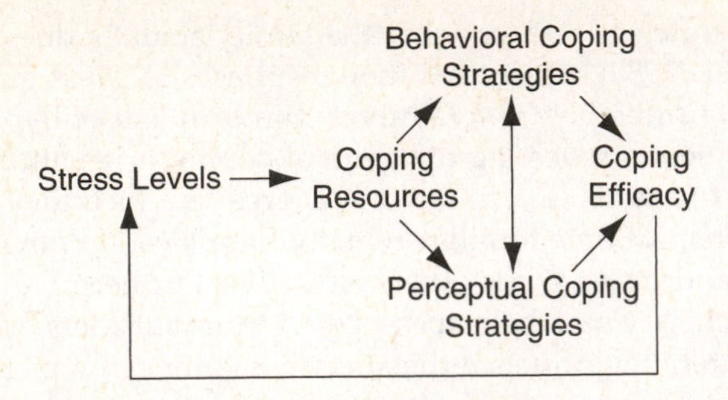

FIGURE 2.2 The Family System's Responses to Stress Events

stress. These adaptations, if successfully executed, will result in new strategies being employed to accomplish the tasks of the family.

How a system responds to stress is determined by the coping resources present within the family system. Based on the degree and type of resources within the system, the family evolves unique coping strategies. There is obviously a great deal of variation in the ways families can respond to stressor events, and not all coping strategies are equally effective at reducing stress. **Coping efficacy** refers to the adequacy of the efforts undertaken by the family to reduce stress. The most efficacious coping efforts are those that produce adaptations that reduce stress while supporting the growth and well-being of all family members. Other, less effective coping efforts may reduce systemwide stress but do so in a way that is detrimental to particular family members. Conceiving a substitute child to replace another child lost prematurely to a chronic illness may relieve the feelings of loss felt by parents and other family members but may eventually constrain the identity of the newborn who is raised to be just like the lost child. Still other coping efforts may result in systemwide adaptations that fail to reduce stress or actually increase the stress experienced by the family and its members. Denying the situation's seriousness and refusing to have the family's water tested despite reports that a local toxic waste dump has been leaking, may fail to reduce stress and, over time, increase family stress and the danger to family members' well-being.

In sum, the effectiveness of a family's coping strategies is reflected in the ability of the family to cultivate the resources and skills that will enable them to meet the challenges of life. By doing so, these families are able to continue to effectively execute their basic tasks. This ability to cultivate the strengths that will allow the family to respond effectively to both normative and non-normative stressors and to jump back from the demands placed on the family has been termed "family resiliency." Insights from numerous studies (McCubbin, McCubbin, Thompson, Han, & Allen, 1997) suggest that resilient families, the ones that cope most effectively with stress events, share several characteristics:

- Commitment is a balance of dedication and accountability. It includes actions that demonstrate loyalty, determination to work things out together, and sacrifice for the benefit of all.
- Cohesion indicates the degree of family togetherness with emphases on respect for each person's uniqueness and emotional closeness and practical dependence on each other.

- Communication involves respectful listening and speaking skills, including openness, clarity, accuracy, honesty, and mutuality.
- Spirituality includes the capacity for going beyond self-interest, living with a positive purpose, and reverencing life. In families it may mean having shared purpose and values.
- Connectedness is the capacity for contributing to and receiving from the extended family, the community, or the nation.
- Resource management involves the effective use of time, money, and energy when handling stress events.

Within the families lacking resilience, family members feel alienated and isolated from one another, anxious, and perhaps depressed. Family members' roles and responsibilities become confused. The family breaks into factions. Coalitions and triangles disrupt the ability of the family to manage conflict and support its members. The family environment is experienced as chaotic and disorganized. Family members no longer are assured of receiving needed physical, social, emotional, and psychological benefits and the survival of the family may be in question.

Clearly, the inability to keep pace with the stressful demands of family life further contributes to the pile-up of demands and the levels of crisis experienced within the family. This state of crisis is brought about because there is a residue of demands left unmanaged by the family system (McCubbin & Patterson, 1983). That is, in a recursive way unresolved demands feed back into the horizontal and vertical stresses experienced within the family, thereby amplifying the levels of stress experienced within the family and interfering with the ability of the system to adapt to ongoing system demands.

Conclusions

Family patterns of interaction are profoundly influenced by the strategies adopted within the family system for the execution of its basic tasks. These patterns are determined by the structure found within family systems, which is in essence a system of rules that determine how each of these different tasks is to be executed. The unique identities of each family member evolve within this context, and individuals develop strategies and styles for interacting with family members as well as outsiders.

In a most basic way, the effectiveness or functioning of the family is tied to the manner in which these basic tasks are executed. In the best of all circumstances, family themes and identities, boundary processes, emotional processes, and the management of the family's maintenance needs promote the physical, intellectual, social, and emotional welfare of family members.

In addition, through the examination of family stress and coping processes we gain insight into important factors that influence patterns of family interaction and functioning. Family interactions are profoundly affected by the family's need to adapt to the changing demands of family life. Stressor events place demands on the family to alter its interactional strategies.

While all families must periodically alter their strategies, these changes must be coordinated in a way that allows the family to continue to execute its tasks effectively. In this regard, coping strategies can be thought of as the vehicle through which the family maintains a balance between morphostatic and morphogenic processes. Under stress, the family experiences pressure to change. This pressure to change will ordinarily be resisted (morphostasis) until the stress goes beyond a critical threshold, at which point changes will occur (morphogenesis). In this way, changes occur only when they are necessary for the family to continue to function effectively.

The coping process breaks down when the system fails to maintain an effective balance between morphostatic and morphogenic processes. When this balance is violated, either changes occur when they are not required, or changes do not occur when they are required. In the first instance, new strategies are adopted when old ones are still efficient and effective. In the second instance, old strategies are maintained when new ones are clearly required. In either of these instances, alterations in the coping process may result in a deterioration of the family's ability to manage some or all of its tasks.

Key Terms

Behavioral coping strategies What the family actually does to manage stress.

Cognitive coping strategies The perceptions and appraisals that people and families make with regard to specific stressor events.

Coping The cognitive and behavioral problem-solving strategies that are used to respond to a stressor event.

Coping efficacy The adequacy of the efforts undertaken by the family to reduce stress.

Coping resources Those properties, attributes, or skills individuals, families, or societies have at their disposal when adapting to novel and demanding situations. Coping resources serve to minimize vulnerability to stress.

Disengaged The concept used to describe systems' boundaries characterized by a high tolerance for individuality.

Enmeshed The concept used to describe systems' boundaries characterized by a low tolerance for individuality.

Maintenance resources The amount of time, energy, and money that the family has available to accomplish its maintenance tasks.

Non-normative stressor events Unexpected events that create unanticipated hardships and require adaptations or alterations in the strategies used by the system to execute some or all of its basic tasks.

Normative stressor events The expected and ordinary developmental transitions affecting the family. Their key distinguishing features are that they are expected, occur regularly over time, and carry with them ordinary difficulties.

Permeability The degree to which the family's boundaries are relatively open or closed.

Pile-up of stressor events The total number of events, both normative and non-normative, that a family must contend with at any point.

Stress The degree of pressure exerted on the family to alter the strategies it employs to accomplish its basic tasks.

PART II

Models of Family Functioning

From a systems perspective, family functioning is tied to family process. An effective family is one in which established patterns of interaction enable the family to execute its tasks in ways that foster the physical, social, and psychological health and well-being of family members. An ineffective family is characterized by patterns of interaction that interfere with the family's ability to manage its basic tasks. The strategies adopted by ineffective families increase the likelihood of individual family members being physically, socially, and/or psychologically at risk.

Over the years, many models of family functioning that emphasize the importance of family processes have been developed. Within the next three chapters, a number of these process models of family functioning are presented. These and other models provide a basic orientation for understanding the key issues that influence how families develop and change over time. However, it is important to emphasize at the outset that each model of family functioning is simply a point of view, reflecting the values and beliefs of the theorists who developed it. Theorists' values and beliefs are, in turn, influenced by the prevailing cultural value orientations, as was noted in Chapter 1.

From our perspective, each model of family functioning to be discussed can be thought of as emphasizing certain basic family tasks while deemphasizing others. As discussed in Chapter 3, the structural model's value is in its ability to describe the core structural and organizational characteristics of the family. It emphasizes the family's boundary tasks by attending to the composition of family subsystems and the regulation of boundaries. It further concerns itself with the task of managing the family's emotional environment by addressing how power and authority are distributed throughout the system and how conflicts become patterned in family relationships.

The intergenerational models discussed in Chapter 4 emphasize the importance of the family's identity tasks in understanding family functioning. The importance of intergenerational models is further derived from their focus on how experiences within one's family of origin come to influence the patterns of interaction found within subsequent generations; this is a major theme throughout this text.

Finally, the contextual models presented in Chapter 5 stress the need to consider each family's unique heritage, values, and customs. Factors such as a family's race, culture, ethnicity, religion, and socioeconomic status influence how the family's identity is shaped, boundaries between family members and with the outside world are established, resources are managed, the emotional environment is regulated, and stress is handled. While it seems clear that no one model can give us all the necessary information that we may need in determining how successfully a given family is operating, knowing something about all of these different models broadens our ability to assess and evaluate multiple aspects of family functioning.

CHAPTER 3

Structural Models

Chapter Overview

An effectively functioning family is characterized by patterns of interaction that enable the family to execute tasks to foster the physical, social, and psychological health and well-being of family members. This chapter examines family processes that influence individual and family functioning. In particular, it focuses on the structural model—a specific process model of family functioning that is based on three major assumptions about the nature of behavior. First, all individuals operate within a social context that, among other things, defines the parameters of their individual behaviors. Second, social context can be thought of as being organized into a structure, or an invisible set of rules regulating how, when, and with whom family members relate. Third, some structures are better than others. Those systems built on solid structures are more adaptable to the changing demands of family life, whereas those systems built on faulty structures are less adaptable to the ordinary and extraordinary demands of family life. The family's organizational structure encompasses (1) the manner in which family subsystems are organized; (2) the hierarchical relationships between family subsystems; and (3) the clarity of the boundaries within and between subsystems. The structural model considers family members' developmental level, the family's resources, and the family's composition.

Structural Models of Family Functioning

The Importance of Context

Models of family functioning operate similarly to the lens on a camera, offering a different perspective on what contributes to effective family functioning. While various process models focus on somewhat different tasks, strategies, and rules as the keys to understanding individual and family functioning, all share several basic premises. They are all influenced by family systems theory and, thus, focus on the rule-governed patterns of interaction present within the family. The primary focus of process models is on the relationships between family members and, most specifically, the reciprocal patterns of interaction that recur with regularity between family members. These systems-oriented models take the position that forces within the family system operate to elicit particular thoughts, feelings, and behaviors from family members. The system, therefore, provides the context that must be considered if the goal is to understand the social and psychological functioning of individuals.

The importance and power of the family **context** become evident when we consider how our feelings and behaviors often differ from one social context or system to another. In our families, we think, feel, and act in ways that are consistent with our position and role in the family. For example, we may find that our actions are consistent with the prescribed role that we were expected to play throughout our developing years. Perhaps we were expected to be the "family clown" who lifts the family's spirits, or the "big sister" to whom others go when they need comfort and support. Because we and other family members share these role identities, they become a force in determining how we act within the context of the family.

When the context changes, however, as when we interact with others at school or work, we often find ourselves behaving in very different ways. These differences emerge, in part, because these systems are different. That is, our position and role in these systems and the rules that govern behavior differ. Therefore, while we may believe that we have to be serious when interacting with family members, we may feel free to act in a more carefree manner with friends. While we may be distant and removed when in the company of family members, we might be quite comfortable being the center of attention in a peer group. The point is that our inner thoughts, feelings, and actions can be quite different depending on the social context, and these different contexts have the potential to elicit responses from us that are more or less adaptive.

Care must be taken when addressing the importance of the context as an elicitor of behavior to avoid giving the impression that (1) behavior is determined by forces outside the control of individuals; and (2) individuals are not responsible for their behavior. Process models highlight the need to consider the context of the family system when attempting to understand why people behave the way they do. The family context—the priorities, strategies, and rules established by the family—shapes and constrains behavior. Individuals, however, must be held responsible, ultimately, for choosing to act in accordance with the pressures embedded within this context.

For example, the cultural heritage of Italian Americans emphasizes the importance of food and eating at family gatherings. If an Italian were to eat to excess at a social gathering, however, it would not be appropriate to hold the cultural context responsible for this behavior. In a different context, growing up in a dysfunctional family and being physically abused as a child may help to explain why an individual physically abuses his or her own children, but the context does not relieve this individual from personal responsibility. Individuals ultimately are responsible for how they respond to the social pressures embedded within their social systems.

Another caution at the outset is that we must be careful in the use of the labels "functional" and "dysfunctional" to describe families. "Functional" simply means workable. "Dysfunctional" means unworkable and is often associated with symptoms of distress (Walsh, 2003). Although many of the models discussed in this chapter refer to different types of families as functional or dysfunctional, they are referring more specifically to the particular strategies and rules families adopt to achieve their goals. Thus, it is preferable to identify a particular strategy or pattern of interaction as dysfunctional rather than the entire family. The important question is to ask whether a certain strategy or pattern is functional to what end, for whom, and in what context (Walsh, 2003). A strategy that is functional in one context may be dysfunctional in another. For example, it may be functional for a child to maintain eye contact when communicating with other family members in a white, Anglo-Saxon family but dysfunctional to do so in a Hispanic family where such a behavior is considered disrespectful. Or, it may be functional for a married couple to minimize conflicts in their relationship by using a child as a scapegoat and focusing instead on the child's misbehavior. However, such a pattern is not likely to be functional for the child.

Process models of family functioning all emphasize the importance of the family system as a principal mediator of individual development and adjustment. These models highlight the ways in which the regular, patterned, and predictable patterns of interaction that occur within the family elicit predictable responses from family members. To understand how an individual functions, we must look into the ways in which the family system elicits adaptive or maladaptive thoughts, feelings, and behaviors from its members.

The Structural Model

The structural model was developed by Salvador Minuchin and his colleagues (Minuchin, 1974; Minuchin, Montalvo, Guerney, Rosman, & Schumer, 1967) from their research on normal families and their clinical work with multiproblem families. This model is based on three major assumptions about the nature of behavior. First, all individuals operate within a social context that, among other things, defines the parameters of their individual behaviors. As noted, this means that systems establish rules, goals, and priorities that shape and constrain behavior. The second assumption is that this social context has a definable structure. **Structure**, according to Minuchin (1974), refers to the invisible set of functional demands that organizes the way family members interact with one another over time. The term "structure" here is used to label the strategies families develop for regulating how, when, and with whom family members relate. The third assumption is that some structures are better than others. Those systems built on solid structures are more adaptable to the changing demands of family life. Those systems built on faulty structures are less adaptable in response to the ordinary and extraordinary demands of family life.

The structural model, therefore, adopts the view that the family system, like mechanical and biological systems, has a structural foundation that contributes to the system's effectiveness. Some bridges are built on a better foundation than others. With a better foundation, the bridge is better able to stand up to the various pressures and stresses it encounters; that is, it is better able to withstand changes in weather, temperature, and weight. Similarly, the family is built on a structural foundation that is either enabling or disabling. The structural foundation of the family is not necessarily related to whether the family has problems, as all families have problems. The structural foundation of the family addresses, rather, whether the family is effective at managing its problems. The relationship between structure and how families manage their problems is the key to understanding the structural model's view of pathology (Steinglass, 1987).

Minuchin (1974) suggests that three dimensions are relevant for understanding the family systems structure: (1) the family's organizational characteristics; (2) the degree to which patterns of family transactions are appropriate for the family system's developmental level and its available resources; and (3) the family's response to stress.

The Organizational Characteristics of the Family

Family organization is determined by examining three interdependent characteristics: (1) the manner in which family subsystems are organized; (2) the hierarchical relationships between family subsystems; and (3) the clarity of the boundaries within and between these subsystems.

The family differentiates and carries out its functions through **subsystems** formed by generation, sex, interest, or function (Walsh, 2003). The primary subsystems comprising the family—the parental, marital, and sibling subsystems—all have tasks they must execute. The parental or executive subsystem must perform the tasks necessary to nurture, guide, socialize, and control children. To do this, parents or other caretakers must be able to support and accommodate one another to provide the necessary balance between nurturance and firmness. Parents also must be able to negotiate and accommodate to changes in their children as they grow and mature.

The tasks of other subsystems are interdependent with, yet different from, those of the parental subsystem. For instance, the tasks of the marital subsystem include establishing a confirming and respectful method of communication, negotiating a balance between intimacy and individuality, and establishing a mutually satisfying sexual relationship. The more successful the couple is in executing these tasks, the better their chances of effectively working together as parents. The tasks of the sibling subsystem include offering subsystem members mutual support and providing opportunities to practice and develop social skills.

Subsystems, according to the structural model, must be hierarchically organized in order for the family to function effectively. **Hierarchy** refers to the idea that well-organized systems have clear distinctions between the levels of the system. In a corporation, there are clear lines of authority among the president, vice-presidents for various operations, supervisors, and workers. In a good chicken coop there is a clear pecking order with only one rooster assuming authority over the other chickens (Minuchin, 1986). So, too, in families there must be clear lines of authority between the generations, with parents in charge of children. This is not to say that children are not listened to, acknowledged, affirmed, or conferred with. However, the critical point is that a family is not a democracy, and children are not the parents' equals or peers. Parents, by virtue of their age, experience, and parental responsibilities, must be in charge of decisions that affect the family and its members.

It is from this base of parental authority that children learn to deal with authority and interact in situations in which authority is unequal (Becvar & Becvar, 2000). This power and authority hierarchy is flawed when power and control rests with the children, or when parents rely on their children for nurture, support, and care. Such a process is referred to as **parentification**. Parentification can undermine the ability of the family to address the needs of the children responsibly and, therefore, increases the likelihood that the family will become dysfunctional.

Boundaries are another integral component of the family system's structural organization. They define who is in the system and its subsystems and regulate how family members are to interact with one another. They help to establish and reinforce the hierarchical relationships among members and subsystems by prescribing the flow of information within the system.

The effectiveness of the family's structural foundation is tied to the clarity of the boundaries that exist within the system. A well-structured family is one in which subsystem boundaries are clear. Within these families, everyone knows his or her position or role in relationship to one another. Clear parent–child boundaries, for example, allow information to flow freely from children to parents as well as from parents to children. Clear boundaries also help to establish a tolerance for individuality that allows both children and parents to feel respected and valued. Clear boundaries between the marital and parental subsystems allow parents to attend to their own adult needs for intimacy while still fulfilling their parental responsibilities to meet the needs of their children.

In addition, clear sibling subsystem boundaries allow children to be children and experiment with peer relationships (Becvar & Becvar, 2000). This means that parents at times are willing to let siblings negotiate, compete, work out differences, and support one another without parental interference. It also means that some information shared between siblings stays within the sibling subsystem. For instance, sisters may seek advice about boyfriends from one another rather than from Mom or Dad.

Unclear Boundaries, Coalitions, and Family Functioning

Boundaries that are not clear are either too rigid, resulting in **disengagement** between family members, or too diffused, resulting in **enmeshment** or overinvolvement between family members. When the boundaries between subsystems in the family are not clear, hierarchies are likely to become confused, and problems in the family's functioning are likely to occur. A primary indicator of such problems is the presence of rigid and recurring coalitions. A **coalition** refers to one member of the family siding with a second member against a third. This three-person pattern is closely linked with the concept of power, because the result of the coalition is to shift power away from the more removed member and toward the twosome. A coalition contrasts with an **alliance**, in which two family members share an interest with one another that is not shared by the third. Alliances allow family members to share interests and companionship in a way that does not interfere with the functioning of the family.

Within the structural model, the presence of a **cross-generational coalition** is viewed as particularly disruptive to the functioning of the family. A cross-generational coalition occurs, for instance, when a parent persuades a child to side with him or her against the other parent, or when wives or husbands side with their own parent against their spouse. When such coalitions happen occasionally, it is a minor matter. However, when these patterns become firmly established and recur continuously, their presence interferes with the ability of the subsystems to execute their tasks, and participants are likely to experience subjective distress (Haley, 1987).

The presence of cross-generational coalitions in the family system implies that generational and subsystem boundaries have been breached and are no longer clear. Take, for example, the situation of young Johnny. Mother tells Johnny to go pick up his toys. Johnny refuses and goes to complain to Dad about Mom's unfair treatment of him. Dad insists that Johnny obey his mother. So far, this interaction appears to be one in which the parents are operating in harmony within the parameters of their parental subsystem and are establishing clear limits for Johnny's behavior.

However, let us say that Dad's style of reinforcing Mom is to yell at Johnny in a way that Mom feels is unacceptable. Mom now turns to Dad and scolds him for being too harsh with the boy and making him cry. Mom then withdraws from Dad to comfort Johnny for the treatment by his "mean" and "insensitive" Dad. In this instance, Mom has entered a coalition with her son against her husband and, in the process, has undermined the integrity of the parental subsystem. Johnny, by virtue of his support from Mom, has been elevated to a position of greater power in the system. He may learn, for instance, that whenever he wants to undermine his father's discipline, all he has to do is to cry and complain to his mother about his "mean" Dad. If this pattern becomes well established in the family, conflicts will become common, family cohesion will be disrupted, the effectiveness of parents to work effectively with one another will be damaged, and subjective distress will be experienced by all participants. Dad may feel undermined as an effective parent, Mom may feel unable to rely on her husband for support, and Johnny may be deprived of a positive relationship with his father.

When boundaries between subsystems are well defined, subsystem functions can be carried out without interference, and family functioning is enhanced. The presence of a cross-generational coalition means that at least one parent-child relationship has become enmeshed and that the child has become the primary support for the parent. When this happens, generational boundaries have been breached, and the functioning of both the marital and parental subsystems is undermined. Such coalitions also interfere with the child's ability to act autonomously and are an important factor in the development of symptoms and dysfunctional behavior (Fish, Belsky, & Youngblade, 1991; Fullinwider-Bush & Jacobvitz, 1993).

The Developmental Level, Resources, and Composition of the Family

The structural model highlights the relationship between family structure and the circumstances surrounding family life. All families are viewed as needing to establish boundaries and hierarchies if effective family functioning is to be achieved. However, the specific boundaries and hierarchies that are established must consider family members' developmental level, the family's resources, and the family's composition.

Clearly, the age and developmental capabilities of family members must be considered when establishing boundaries and regulating power and authority within the family. We expect older children to be allowed greater autonomy than younger children within a family system. Furthermore, we expect that parents will assume a position of power and authority when relating to younger children and that they will soften this position as the children move into their adult years. An effective family is one that establishes boundaries and hierarchies that are sensitive to the developmental capabilities and needs of family members.

Similarly, families vary in terms of their resources, that is, the time, energy, and money that they have at their disposal. These variations can also affect how subsystems are organized and how hierarchies and boundaries are established. For example, the chronic illness of a parent may prompt changes in the functioning of the parental subsystem, forcing the healthy parent to assume more responsibility. As a consequence, caring for the ill spouse may severely limit the amount of time and energy this parent has to devote to the children. Children may have to learn to do more for themselves, thereby shifting some of the support and nurturing functions away from the parental subsystem into the sibling subsystem.

The family's unique composition also affects its structural organization. The structural features of a family with two children may be quite different from those of a family with nine children. Siblings in the larger family system may organize themselves into several smaller sibling subsystems according to age or gender differences. So, too, the structural features of a single-parent-headed household are likely to differ from those of a traditional nuclear family.

The composition of a single-parent-headed household and the resources available to this system, for example, might require the formation of subsystems that cut across generational lines and appear to establish inappropriate hierarchies. In some single-parent-headed households, a grandparent may assume many of the parental responsibilities in order for the parent to work. In other single-parent households, an oldest child may be left in charge of other children. When viewed from a nuclear family perspective, these structural features might be viewed as interfering with the ability of the family to execute its tasks successfully. These arrangements, however, make sense given the available resources and the current demands facing the family.

These alternative structural arrangements will not interfere with the ability of the family to function effectively so long as the boundaries and lines of authority and responsibility are clearly drawn (Walsh, 2003). In other words, having a grandmother assume parental responsibilities will not be a problem so long as the boundaries and hierarchies clearly establish that the mother, and not the grandmother, is ultimately responsible for the children. Similarly, putting a child in charge of other children will not pose problems for the system so long as the parent retains a position of authority within the system.

Such a pattern will become a problem, however, if the parent assumes no responsibility for the children and delegates all authority to the parental child. Too much responsibility can become overwhelming for the parental child and interfere with his or her own growth and development. Parental children often develop an identity centered on meeting the needs of others while sacrificing their own needs. Furthermore, a heavy emotional investment within the home may interfere with the child's own developmental need to socialize with peers and engage in other age-appropriate activities.

The effectiveness of a family's organizational structure is determined by the interplay of the family's subsystems, hierarchies, and boundaries. The clearer the boundaries, the more definable the family's subsystems and their hierarchical arrangement will be. So long as the family's organizational structure places the ultimate responsibility for children in the hands of the parents, the family will function effectively and the development of individual members will be enhanced. In dysfunctional family structures, recurring cross-generational coalitions place children in positions of power and authority over adults. As a result, the boundaries defining subsystems are vague, and the hierarchy is confused. Such structures are likely to interfere with the growth and development of family members (Haley, 1987; Minuchin, 1974).

Families need different organizational structures (subsystems, hierarchies, and boundaries) depending on their composition, resources, and circumstances. In this regard, the structural model encourages us to be sensitive to the various forces that influence how family structures become established. The structural model further encourages us to evaluate the family on the basis of whether its structure enables it to execute its tasks effectively.

Stress and Adaptation

Family life places demands on the family system that require modifications in family patterns and dynamics. As discussed in previous chapters, these demands for systemic changes are experienced as stress. When stress goes beyond a critical threshold, changes in patterns and rules generally occur. All family systems must manage stress and periodically make changes in response to stress. The changes that families make in response to stress can be either adaptive or maladaptive.

The structural model is quite concerned with the concept of **adaptation**. Here, adaptation refers to how the family reorganizes its structure in response to internal demands and external social or environmental events. Functional systems are those that are flexible and able to change their subsystems, hierarchies, and boundaries when necessary. Dysfunctional systems are those that are rigid and unable to make such changes when they are required (Minuchin, 1974).

Internally, changes may be required as a result of either an individual family member's maturation or unforeseen developments. For instance, as children age, personal and subsystem boundaries will require readjustment to allow them more autonomy and independence. Or, as noted, the chronic and prolonged illness of a parent may require adaptations within the marital, parental, and sibling subsystems. In each of these instances, so long as the adaptations maintain the integrity of the essential subsystems, the family is likely to continue executing its varied tasks effectively. However, if the family fails to modify and adapt its structures, the likelihood of dysfunctional behavior significantly increases.

In the most basic sense, then, the structural model highlights the interdependence that exists among the family's structural features, the family's vulnerability in stressful periods, and the family's flexibility in altering its strategies and rules in response to stress. Families that have clearly defined subsystems, hierarchies, and boundaries; have adequate resources (and thus less vulnerability); and can flexibly adapt their structure when necessary will execute their basic tasks more effectively. Families that have rigid and poorly defined structures and greater vulnerability to stress are less likely to execute such tasks effectively. The outcome for these families is likely to be greater stress and a progressive deterioration of family functioning.

For example, family systems that rely on a parentified child for support and nurturance are likely to be excessively stressed when the time comes for this child to leave home. The family may prefer to adapt to this situation by maintaining the present structure and discouraging the parentified child from leaving. However, as developmental pressure builds for the parentified child to leave, pressure on the system to change also will increase. Mom may, at this point, have a "nervous breakdown," which again places pressure on the child to stay at home to help. If Mom's breakdown does not thwart the child's determination to leave, Dad may suddenly start drinking to excess. The family's inadequate structure is evident in its weak parental and marital subsystems and in its rigidity in the face of required change. Such a structure is likely to adapt to stress in a manner that interferes with the social and psychological adjustment of family members. In this instance, the mother's, father's, and child's social and psychological adjustment are all jeopardized.

Mapping the Family Structure

The structural perspective provides us with a way of mapping the structured patterns of interaction that occur within the family. Each family's map is defined by its boundaries, the hierarchical relationships among family members, and by the alignment of subsystems within the system. In an effective family, the expectation is that the boundaries will be clear, the hierarchical relationships between parents and children will be generationally and developmentally appropriate, and the subsystem alignments will result in the primary coalition within the family being among spouses rather than between children and parents.

To capture the structural form and organization of the family, the boundaries, hierarchies, and alliances can be mapped. As a way of illustrating how to construct these maps, consider the following example depicted in Figure 3.1. Some of the keys to interpreting the map are presented in Figure 3.2.

M F (executive subsystem)

\- - - - - - -

Son Daughter (sibling subsystem)

FIGURE 3.1 Clear Boundary between Parents and Child

\- - - - - - - clear boundary

. . . . diffuse boundary

rigid boundary

affiliation

over-involvement

conflict

coalition

detouring

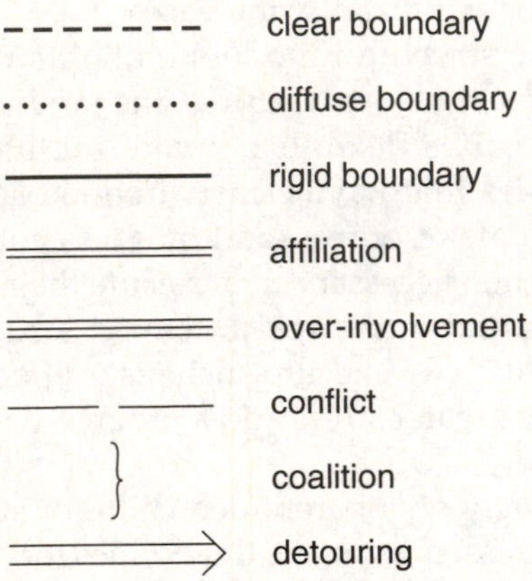

FIGURE 3.2 Keys to Interpreting Structural Maps

The information conveyed by this structural map suggests that the mother and father within the system are aligned with one another, are hierarchically higher than their children, and the boundary between parents and children is clear. A structure such as this suggests that the parents are comfortable with their marital relationships and act together as the executive subsystem within the family. This means that authority lies in the hands of the parents, neither child is in a coalition with either parent, and neither child occupies a position of higher authority within the system relative to one another.

Consider the following additional examples drawn from Minuchin (1974). A father (F) and mother (M), stressed at work, come home and criticize each other but then detour their conflict by attacking a child. Such a pattern reduces the danger to the spouse subsystem, but stresses the child. Graphically, this system is mapped in Figure 3.3.

Given the same situation, however, within a different family system, the husband may criticize the wife, who then seeks a coalition with the child against the father. The boundary around the spouse subsystem thereby becomes diffuse and an inappropriately rigid cross-generational subsystem of mother and son excludes the father. Graphically, this system is presented in Figure 3.4.

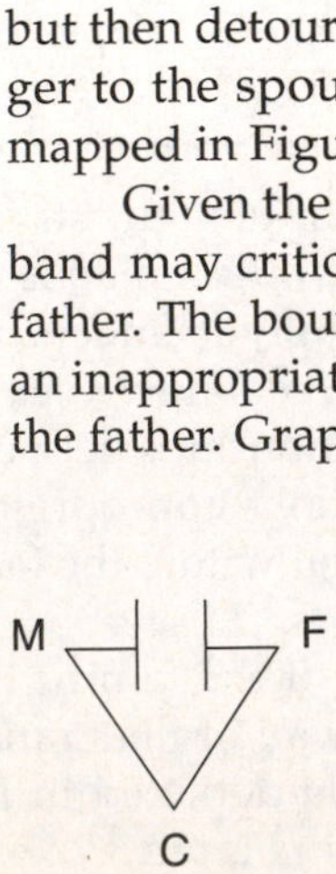

M F

C

FIGURE 3.3 Conflicts Detoured onto a Child

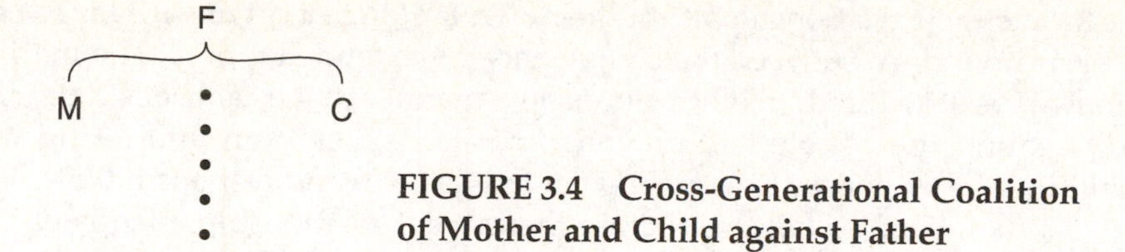

FIGURE 3.4 Cross-Generational Coalition of Mother and Child against Father

A map, in other words, is a tool to graphically represent the form and organization of a particular family system. The map takes into account the members of the system, their positions in relationship to one another, the boundaries that define these relationships, as well as the distribution of authority within the system. By mapping the family, it is possible to draw inferences about the functioning of the family system and to derive insight into how the patterns of interaction within the family might need to be adjusted.

For example, in Figure 3.3, the danger to the marital subsystem is reduced by the fact that both partners find unity in their attacks on the child. Such a pattern is detrimental to the child and requires the introduction of different and more constructive conflict-management processes. The marital subsystem in Figure 3.4 also needs to more constructively deal with conflict. In addition, the coalition between mother and child reduces the ability of the parents to act as a parent within the system. Structurally, mother is too aligned with the child to exercise parental authority. Father is excluded from many of his parental functions. The system needs to be restructured to enable the parents to coordinate their parental responsibilities and allow the mother to exert authority and the father to experience a mutually rewarding and intimate relationship with his child.

Structural Patterns and Dysfunctional Behavior

How well the many tasks of the family are managed depends on the establishment of boundaries, alignments, and hierarchies that maintain the integrity of the family's subsystems during stressful periods. When the foundation of the family is built on a solid structure, its subsystems can effectively execute their tasks. When the structural context of the family is flawed, however, it is increasingly likely to elicit disordered thoughts, feelings, and behaviors from family members. In other words, each person's experience of the family system is derived, in part, from how the entire system is structured.

To illustrate this point, let us examine the relationship between the functioning of the marital subsystem and the abilities of other family subsystems to execute their tasks. Research has consistently linked a strong marital bond and the absence of destructive conflict to effective family functioning (Anderson & Cramer-Benjamin, 1999; Cummings & Davies, 1994; Demo & Cox, 2000; Fincham, 1994). When the marital subsystem functions well, spouses negotiate issues related to balancing intimacy and individuality. They establish satisfactory methods of communication that are affirming and respectful of each other's unique abilities and differences. They establish a satisfactory sexual relationship and successfully negotiate their relationships with their own families of origin such as to establish a clear boundary between the couple and the extended family. The marital relationship is structured, in other words, in a manner that establishes a clear boundary around the couple and prevents marital issues from interfering with the abilities of the spouses to assume other family roles and responsibilities.

When couples fail to structure the marital relationship adequately, the absence of clear marital boundaries may allow marital conflicts and tensions to permeate other subsystems and disrupt their functioning. Commonly, when the marital subsystem breaks down, the ability of spouses to assume parenting roles and responsibilities becomes impaired. Children may be neglected as tension within the marital relationship interferes with the ability of parents to take on the expected responsibilities of parenthood.

Spouses in troubled marital relationships may look to their children for support, thus forming cross-generational coalitions. These coalitions subsequently block the child from having a supportive and nurturing relationship with the excluded parent. Formation of these coalitions is also likely to interfere with the ability of brothers and sisters to establish appropriate sibling relationships if the siblings find themselves in opposite camps.

In other instances in which the marital subsystem fails to function adequately, a child may begin to misbehave or become symptomatic as one family strategy for containing marital strife. In this situation, the child learns to act out or become troubled whenever the stress within the marital relationship becomes too great and threatens the stability of that relationship. The distraction posed by the child's dysfunctional behavior allows spouses to put aside their differences and perhaps even experience some intimacy with one another while they attend to their "needy and troubled" child. The "problem" child can be thought of as a scapegoat or an "emotional distance-regulator" for the unresolved conflicts present in the marital relationship (Byng-Hall, 1980; Vogel & Bell, 1968). The child's role in this situation is to help the parents get along.

In still other instances, a child may come to be viewed as being responsible for the difficulties within the marriage. When this occurs, the child may be emotionally abused and rejected as parents convey the message that they wish the child did not exist, would die, or go away. Children in such a situation may also be physically abused as parents alleviate the tensions they experience within the marriage by pushing, kicking, and beating them. This pattern of holding the child responsible for tensions within the marriage and other problems within the family is one factor consistently associated with children running away from home (Stierlin, 1981).

Conclusions

The structural model, with its emphasis on structure, subsystems, hierarchies, and boundaries, offers a means of assessing family functioning by examining the degree to which the structured patterns of interaction foster an environment that supports the physical, social, emotional, and psychological needs and well-being of all family members. Effective family functioning is enhanced when the family's hierarchies, boundaries, and generational alignments remain clear. The recurring presence of cross-generational coalitions suggests that the systems boundaries are not clear and that problems in functioning may occur. Clear and flexible boundaries further imply that the structure of the family and its subsystems are capable of changing in response to developmental or external stresses, thereby ensuring the growth and stability of the system.

Key Terms

Adaptation How the family reorganizes its structure in response to internal demands and external social or environmental events.

Alliance A pattern of interaction formed when two family members share an interest with one another that is not shared by others.

Boundaries Within the structural model, definitions of who is in the system and its subsystems. Boundaries regulate how family members are to interact with one another.

Coalition An interactional pattern characterized by one family member siding with a second member against a third.

Context The set of circumstances or facts that surround a particular event, situation, individual, or family.

Cross-generational coalition An inappropriate alliance between one parent and a child against the other parent that undermines the executive functions and authority of the parental subsystem.

Disengagement The lack of involvement among family members that results from rigid boundaries.

Enmeshment The overinvolvement among family members that results from diffuse boundaries.

Hierarchy The clear distinctions between the levels of a well-organized system.

Parentification An imbalance in the family's power and authority hierarchy that develops when power and control rest with the children, or when parents rely on their children for nurturance, support, and care.

Structure According to Minuchin (1974), the invisible set of functional demands that organizes the way family members interact with one another over time.

Subsystem A group formed within a larger system that shares common functions or other features such as gender, generation, or interest.

CHAPTER 4

Intergenerational Models

Chapter Overview

In this chapter, Bowen's intergenerational model of family functioning is reviewed. Bowen's model of family functioning focuses on how experiences in the family of origin establish a legacy that affects (1) the development of individual family members and (2) the patterns of adjustment found in subsequent generations of the family. The concept of differentiation is most basic to Bowen's model and is used to refer both to properties of the family system and to attributes of the individuals within the system. The level of differentiation found within a particular family system refers to the patterns and dynamics of interaction found within the family that directly and indirectly affect the development of the self. Differentiation processes are reflected in how identity tasks are managed, how boundaries are regulated, and how the emotional climate of the family system is managed. When applied to the individual, differentiation refers to the abilities of family members to express their individuality and act autonomously while remaining emotionally connected to others. The premise underlying Bowen's theory is that individuals from poorly differentiated families will manage their unresolved issues with their family of origin in ways that are destructive to the self and subsequent generations of the family. According to Bowen, poorly differentiated individuals organize their relationships with others outside their families by using one of three distinctly destructive strategies: the creation of conflict, the establishment of rigid and complementary patterns of interaction that encourage dysfunctional behavior, or the projection of these unresolved emotional attachments or conflicts on to one or more of their children.

Intergenerational Models of Family Functioning

A common question when examining the strategies and rules adopted by a family system is how these patterns and dynamics become established in the first place. The structural model provides insight into how current patterns of family interaction can contribute to effective family functioning. The structural model does not, however, address how functional or dysfunctional interactions or strategies become established. In this chapter, intergenerational models of family functioning are discussed. These models offer valuable insight into how forces that operate within the family over time can contribute to the development of effective or ineffective patterns of interaction.

Intergenerational models focus on how experiences in the family of origin establish a legacy that affects the development of individual family members and the patterns of adjustment found in subsequent generations of the family. These views take the perspective that symptoms and problems result primarily from unconscious attempts by individuals to reenact, externalize, or master intrapsychic conflicts originating in their families of origin (Framo, 1970). It is assumed that childhood experiences in the family of origin affect identity development and the establishment of future adult relationships. Effective or ineffective strategies are passed from generation to generation and help to determine the system's ability to manage its basic tasks. One of the best known intergenerational models of family functioning is offered by Bowen (1978). His theory includes a number of interlocking concepts that he developed early in his career when conducting research on families with a schizophrenic member. His theory has undergone further elaboration as a result of his later research with average families, his own treatment of families in family therapy, his later work in training psychiatric interns in family therapy, and his career-long efforts to understand the interactional forces operating within his own family of origin. His theory provides a framework for understanding how family interactions become established, affect the personal development and adjustment of family members, and are carried into future generations of family life.

Core Concepts in the Bowen Model

The concept of **differentiation** is most basic to Bowen's intergenerational theory. Bowen uses this term to refer both to properties of the family system and to attributes of the individuals within the system. When applied to the family system, differentiation refers to the patterns and dynamics of interaction that directly and indirectly affect the development of the self. Bowen contends that some families facilitate individual development and adjustment while other families provide a context that inhibits adjustment and fosters dysfunction. When applied to the individual, differentiation refers to the abilities of individual family members to express their own individuality and act autonomously while remaining emotionally connected to others. This ability to act in a self-differentiated manner enables individuals to make mature commitments to adult roles, responsibilities, and relationships.

Differentiation as a Family System Property

In Bowen's scheme, all families are characterized by a level of differentiation falling along a continuum from well differentiated at one extreme to poorly differentiated at the other extreme. The level of differentiation is a reflection of the degree to which difference is tolerated within the family system (Farley, 1979). Within well-differentiated systems, there exists a high tolerance for difference. Within poorly differentiated families, there exists a low tolerance for difference.

According to the intergenerational perspective, these tolerances become reflected in three interlocking processes: (1) how the family regulates its internal boundaries; (2) how the emotional climate is managed; and, most importantly, (3) how identity tasks are executed.

Differentiation and Boundary Processes

The basic tolerance for difference that exists within the family system is reflected, in part, in how internal boundaries are structured. All families evolve boundary strategies that balance how separateness and togetherness are regulated. Families with a high tolerance for individuality allow family members to act in appropriately independent and autonomous ways. They respect the rights of others. The desire for privacy is honored, and individuals are viewed as having the right to think, feel, and act independently of other family members.

Poorly differentiated systems are characterized by a low tolerance for individuality. According to Bowen (1966), they are "emotionally stuck together." Bowen originally used the term **undifferentiated family ego mass** to refer to these families, but later abandoned this term and instead emphasized the notion of **fusion** as it operates in the poorly differentiated family system. In poorly differentiated families, the forces of fusion are strong enough to negate family members' individuality, viewing it as disloyal and threatening to the family's stability. Such families operate with a sense of emotional oneness. The fears, anxieties, stresses, or even joys of one family member are felt intensely and personally by all family members. The degree of closeness can be so great in some poorly differentiated families that all members may come to believe that they know each other's thoughts, feelings, fantasies, or dreams (Goldenberg & Goldenberg, 2000).

Differentiation and the Management of the Emotional Climate

The tolerance for difference that exists within the family system is reflected, as well, in how the family manages its emotional climate. Within the well-differentiated family system, family members respect one another. They tend to act with sensitivity and empathy toward the problems and concerns of others. In well-differentiated families, the strategies employed for managing the emotional climate contribute to the experience of intimacy, integration, and cohesion. The absence of such empathy, sensitivity, and concern is one feature that distinguishes the poorly differentiated from the well-differentiated family.

Well-differentiated and poorly differentiated families also differ in the amount of conflict and interpersonal tensions they experience and in how their conflicts and tensions are managed. The more poorly differentiated the family, the greater the conflict and tension experienced and the greater the tendency to rely on a strategy called **triangulation** (Bowen, 1966). This process is similar to the concept of coalition described in Chapter 3. Triangulation describes a three-person interaction in which the tension and conflict experienced between two persons is displaced onto a third party.

Bowen pointed out that any relationship can become unstable at times due to conflict and tensions. Even in the best of families, parents occasionally get angry with their children, spouses disagree and fight, and children compete and fight with their siblings. According to Bowen, whenever these tensions exceed the level of tolerance for that particular relationship, a third person is brought into the relationship to relieve the excess pressure. The partner most uncomfortable with the relationship at this point is the one most likely to seek outside support. This might take the form of making complaints about the partner, telling a story about the partner, gossiping about the partner, or portraying the partner as unreliable, intolerable, or annoying. The partner who seeks such outside support is generally comforted by the third party and thus relieved of tension.

The uncomfortable partner and the third party form a positive bond that contrasts with the negative one experienced between the original pair. It should be noted here that the third party need not always be another person, although it may be. It might also be work, a hobby (e.g., excessive reading, television watching, bird watching), or alcohol or some other form of substance abuse. Any object that redirects the tension in a relationship away from the pair to another source can serve this triangulation function.

According to Bowen, although all relationships to some degree or another rely on this process to relieve excess tension, triangulation is more likely to occur in poorly differentiated systems. Triangulation interferes with family members acting in responsive, respectful, and nurturing ways toward one another.

In addition, a great deal of conflict goes unresolved, and this becomes a factor that contributes to the system being under stress. When Dad plays golf and Mom complains to her children rather than dealing directly with Dad, the conflict that exists between them remains unresolved. The emotional climate of the family remains highly charged, which works against the goal of family members feeling at peace with one another.

Therefore, Bowen's view is that the triangle, or three-person arrangement, is the basic structure of all family relationships. Within less effective families, however, the tendency is for triangulation processes to occur more frequently and to pattern rigidly how the family deals with stress, anxiety, and conflict. The strategies used to manage the family's emotional climate not only fail to alleviate stress but, in fact, increase the level of stress by leaving a residue of unresolved conflict and anxiety. The result is a loss in the family's overall ability to support its members.

Differentiation and the Management of Identity Tasks

According to intergenerational models, the family's tolerance for individuality is reflected in the degree to which the family attempts to control the identities of its family members. Within well-differentiated family systems, an optimal tolerance for individuality allows family members to be recognized as having unique individual characteristics and to act in appropriately autonomous ways. This helps to create a family environment in which individuals feel supported and encouraged to be themselves.

Within poorly differentiated families, family rules make it clear that individuality and autonomy will not be tolerated. When family members attempt to express their individuality, they are often viewed as being disloyal to the family. Family members are easily made anxious in such situations as they become rebellious or dependent on the approval of others.

It is clear that intergenerational models are concerned with how patterns and dynamics of family interaction provide a context for personal development and adjustment. According to Bowen, the differentiation levels within the family system affect individual family members by influencing their abilities to act in self-differentiated ways. As Bowen (1978) argues **differentiation of self** refers to the extent to which one has successfully resolved emotional attachments to one's family of origin. This is reflected in the individual's level of psychological maturity. Bowen conceives of self-differentiation as existing on a continuum or scale ranging from zero to one hundred. The metaphor of a scale allows individuals to be plotted along a conceptual continuum for assessment purposes.

Well-differentiated families tend to produce children who operate at the high end of the self-differentiated continuum. In well-differentiated families, the tolerance for individuality and acceptance of each individual's right to control his or her identity facilitates self-differentiation and allows individuals to operate with a clear sense of self. Here **self** refers to a superordinate personal structure, the purpose of which is to organize an individual's experiences (cognitive and emotional, conscious and unconscious) into a coherent and meaningful whole (Bagarozzi & Anderson, 1989). The self includes personal knowledge as well as knowledge about the self in relationship to significant others (Anderson & Sabatelli, 1990). Individuals with a clear sense of self are capable of separating their emotional from their intellectual functioning. Objectivity and clear reasoning characterize their feelings. They may make decisions based on a careful assessment of the important facts rather than on how they feel at the time. Persons at the high end of the differentiation scale perceive their lives to be under their own control rather than at the mercy of uncontrolled emotional forces (Bowen, 1978; Kerr & Bowen, 1988).

The higher the differentiation of self, the less likely individuals are to experience fusion with others in personal relationships; that is, they are able to act as individuals while still being emotionally connected to others. In essence, well-differentiated individuals manage the pressure to fuse with others in a fluid and flexible manner. Such individuals can temporarily lose their sense of self in a relationship (as in falling in love or engaging in a sexual encounter) but are also able to disengage from this heightened state of connection and maintain a clear sense of themselves as individuals. This fluid manner of merging with others (e.g., empathizing with the other's feelings, sharing the other's thinking, or placing the needs of the other above one's own) and then disengaging from them to refocus on the self to attend to one's own needs is a characteristic of those with a higher level of psychological maturity.

Individuals at the low end of the self-differentiation continuum operate with no clear sense of self. Individuals with an unclear sense of self in turn have difficulty separating their emotional from their intellectual functioning. Feelings dominate over objectivity and clear reasoning. They may make decisions based on how they feel at the time, rather than on a careful assessment of the important facts. Because the search for love and approval from others is a dominant force, little energy remains for pursuing goal-directed tasks. Such persons may be so preoccupied with the need for approval and acceptance that they cannot fully engage themselves in jobs, school, favorite activities, or other meaningful experiences. Persons at the low end of the differentiation scale are more vulnerable to stress and to the development of physical or psychological symptoms in times of stress, and require more time to recover from stress and the accompanying symptoms (Bowen, 1978).

Persons with a lower level of differentiation experience extremes of fusion in their interpersonal relationships. They are either unable to disengage successfully from the emotional oneness with another person once it is established or unwilling to lose whatever sense of self they possess to merge with another person, even temporarily. The analogy of a magnet is useful here. If the forces of two magnets are especially strong, they will be pulled together and difficult to separate. Alternatively, we could decide to keep the two magnets far enough apart to ensure that their magnetic forces cannot act upon one another. In either instance, the ability to move fluidly closer together temporarily and then to disengage is lost. If the magnetic forces are not as strong, it is easier to move the magnets together and separate them later.

The point is that, when the family system attempts to control the identity of its members, the members' ability to act in a self-differentiated manner is severely limited. When self-differentiation is limited, individuals tend to structure their relationships within the family in one of two extreme ways. In the first instance, poorly differentiated individuals give up attempting to control their own identities by fusing with the family, that is, by allowing the family to control their sense of self. Being in this situation is likely to arouse a great deal of anxiety and tension. Individuals are prone to feel guilty if they displease others and to feel extremely loyal and obligated to those to whom they are connected. The importance of these emotional reactions is that they further interfere with the individual's ability to act in a self-differentiated manner.

Conversely, when self-differentiation is limited, individuals may be unwilling to risk closeness with others. In some families this strategy can become so extreme that it results in **emotional cutoffs**. Individuals thus affected emotionally detach themselves from the family of origin in an attempt to exercise some control over their sense of self. In some cutoff situations, members may maintain such extremes of distance that they have no physical contact with one another for years. Alternatively, participants may remain in physical proximity to one another and yet stay emotionally and psychologically divorced. In other words, cutting off from the family of origin represents one strategy for gaining control over, and protecting, one's sense of self. Unfortunately, control over the self is gained at the expense of closeness with others.

In Bowen's conceptual scheme, even persons operating at the lowest levels of the self-differentiation continuum, such as those who are considered to be schizophrenic or actively psychotic, have some basic sense of self. So, too, persons who are believed to be highly differentiated in Bowen's scheme tend to have some degree of unresolved emotional attachment to the family and, therefore, must continually strive to rework these family relationships in order to grow and mature. Bowen further points out that levels of self-differentiation are not fixed. In particular, the notion of stress is important here because the level of personal stress can cause individuals to seem to be more or less differentiated than they might otherwise appear. During periods of heightened stress, individuals and families will operate at a lower level of differentiation, and during periods of relative calm, they will function at the higher end of their own potentials.

Managing Unresolved Issues with the Family of Origin

Intergenerational perspectives assert that unresolved issues within the family of origin interfere not only with children's current adjustment but also with their ability to enter adult roles and relationships successfully later in life. Individuals who have unresolved issues with their family of origin are viewed as carrying a heightened degree of anxiety about themselves into their relationships with others. This anxiety about the self becomes an unstable foundation for ongoing interpersonal relationships. The greater the problems with self-differentiation, in other words, the more likely one's relationships with friends, lovers, and children will be structured in ineffective or destructive ways. Although this model remains underresearched, available studies have supported this basic assumption (Anderson & Sabatelli, 1992; Charles, 2001; Sabatelli & Anderson, 1991).

According to Bowen, poorly self-differentiated individuals organize their relationships with others outside the family by using three distinctly destructive strategies. The first involves the creation of **conflict** as a strategy for maintaining distance from others and protecting one's sense of self. Conflict and disagreement can help to maintain an illusion of difference. Therefore, conflict allows individuals to reaffirm that they are indeed different and distinct as individuals.

Along these lines, relationships involving poorly differentiated individuals tend to be dominated by a high degree of emotional reactivity. Anxiety about the self and inability to merge in a mature and intimate way with another create an emotional environment that is highly charged. Whenever the behavior of another is viewed as a threat to the sense of self, the poorly differentiated individual is likely to react to this perceived threat in a highly emotional way. Strong and powerful emotional reactions—extreme anger, shouting, and name-calling, for example—are likely to occur in such situations. Although we all react when the behavior of a partner threatens our basic sense of self, poorly differentiated individuals are more easily threatened and more prone to react in extreme ways.

Therefore, when faced with the challenge of maintaining a personal identity within an intimate relationship, poorly differentiated individuals, because of their anxiety about the self, are unable to express their individuality in a way that allows them to remain connected to others. Instead, they may create conflict and find faults with the partner to protect their sense of self. Clearly, however, this sense of difference is maintained at the expense of intimacy.

A second strategy employed by poorly differentiated individuals for managing unresolved differentiation issues within the family of origin is the establishment of rigid and complementary patterns of interaction that can, ultimately, encourage dysfunctional behavior. In this instance, poorly differentiated individuals may compensate for their anxiety about the self by cultivating relationships that reduce or minimize this anxiety. One way of doing this is to interact only with submissive and underfunctioning individuals. In this situation, overcontrolling or overfunctioning behavior enhances the individual's sense of competence and reduces anxiety about the self. Using this strategy for managing unresolved differentiation, however, restricts one's relationships to people who are unable to exercise any authority in relationships. In other words, the success of this strategy relies on being able to locate someone who is willing to underfunction in relationship to this overfunctioning behavior.

Alternatively, the strategy employed for managing poor self-differentiation can take the form of finding a parental figure who provides care, nurturing, and support that was missing in the family of origin. These individuals, therefore, assume a child-like position in relationships with others. This strategy requires finding someone who is willing to function in the capacity of the parent. Such relationships can take on an **overfunctioning/underfunctioning** complementarity in that the ability to assume the dependent position of a child requires the construction of a relationship with another who is willing to take control of the relationship.

A further consequence of this pattern of interaction is the development of dysfunctional behaviors in the underfunctioning member of the dyad. When experiencing stress or anxiety, an underfunctioning individual will often become less able to function. This dysfunction becomes one way of eliciting support from the partner. Conversely, when overfunctioning members of a dyad are under stress, they may actively encourage their partners to become dysfunctional. Being superior to the other or being able to rescue the other becomes one way of maintaining the illusion of a strong identity and adequate sense of self. Often, underfunctioning members comply because the failure to do so would threaten the security they derive from the relationship.

It is not possible, therefore, to attribute sole responsibility for this rigid pattern of overfunctioning and underfunctioning to one member of the relationship. Although on the surface the overfunctioning partner may appear to benefit more from the arrangement, both partners contribute to and benefit from this outcome. Each partner, by transferring some responsibility for the self to the other, minimizes the ongoing anxiety about the self. The rigidity of the pattern, however, keeps both partners from experiencing a full sense of self, one that includes the capacity to be vulnerable and taken care of by the other combined with the capacity to be competent and to care for the other. On the contrary, each partner is rigidly locked into a role. According to Bowen (1978), "one denies their immaturity and functions with a facade of adequacy. The other accentuates their immaturity and functions with a facade of inadequacy. Neither can function in the midground between overadequacy and inadequacy" (p. 19).

It should be clear, then, that one strategy for dealing with unresolved conflicts and tensions around issues of self-differentiation is to reenact these conflicts in current relationships. The creation of an overfunctioning and underfunctioning complementary relationship is one way of dealing with the anxiety about the self that is generated from these unresolved issues. The result, however, is a high degree of dependence on the relationship, which inhibits spontaneity, creativity, and, perhaps most importantly, intimacy. There is, in other words, a fragility to the bonds that exist in these relationships, as any semblance of intimacy is based on patterns of interaction that discount the worth and ability of one partner (Papero, 1991).

The third strategy for handling fusion in family relationships is through the **family projection process**. In this instance, parents project (displace) part of their own unresolved emotional attachments or conflicts onto one or more of their children. Typically, the parent is more responsive and reactive to one child than to the others, but in highly stressful and anxious situations more than one child may be affected. The parent's own level of anxiety is lessened by focusing on the child. That is, as the parent's anxiety increases, he or she responds as if the anxiety were a problem for the child rather than for himself or herself.

The parent's feelings can become intense and range from overly positive to highly negative. If highly positive, the child may be overvalued, overprotected, and treated as immature. If highly negative, the child may be treated in harsh, punitive, and restrictive ways. In either case, the child becomes attuned to the parental anxiety and responds in ways that appear to justify the parent's concerns (Papero, 1991). For instance, if the parent is overly concerned about the child getting hurt, the child may become accident prone. Similarly, if the parent repeatedly scolds the child for never listening, the child may respond by misbehaving. The child who is the object of the projection becomes the one most emotionally attached to the parents and develops a lower level of self-differentiation than his or her siblings. Therefore, this child becomes more vulnerable to stress, more anxious, more concerned with receiving love and approval, and less successful at completing goal-directed tasks than other children in the family.

The process occurring between parent and child is generally seen as a product of the anxiety and fusion present in the relationship between the mother and the father. The unresolved issues between them are submerged and redirected, typically through the triangulation process, as concern for the child. It is important to note that neither the child nor the parents are viewed as at fault for this pattern. Parents themselves have been similarly involved with their own parents, and likewise their parents with their parents, over numerous generations. The parents may have some or little awareness of the familiarity of these patterns, but in any case be unable to change them. Therefore, the strategies in one generation represent the cumulative effects of the succeeding generations (Bowen, 1978; Papero, 1991; Roberto, 1992).

The Multigenerational Transmission Process

How is it that an individual develops either a high or low level of differentiation of self? According to the intergenerational perspectives, this is largely determined by the emotional forces that operate in one's family of origin. Essentially, Bowen

(1978) believes that spouses marry individuals who are at the same level of differentiation as themselves. Therefore, a person from a poorly differentiated family would likely marry someone from a poorly differentiated family, and a person from a highly differentiated family would likely marry someone from a highly differentiated family. Each marriage partner would then bring into the marriage similar levels of unresolved emotional attachments to his or her own family of origin and issues with fusion and differentiation of self. The greater the severity of these unresolved issues, the greater the likelihood that similar difficulties will develop in the marital relationship and the nuclear family. In other words, personal issues that remain unresolved from one's own family of origin are likely to be reenacted in one's future relationships.

Transmission of unresolved emotional attachments over the generations has been referred to as the **multigenerational transmission process**. Over the generations, some offspring gain higher levels of differentiation than their parents, and some develop lower levels. These outcomes are determined by the child's position in the family projection process. The closer (i.e., the more attached) the child is to the parents and the more involved the child is in alleviating anxiety in a parent or in the marital relationship, the lower the child's level of self-differentiation. The less involved a particular child is in these emotional patterns, the greater his or her potential level of differentiation. With less of their attention focused on the family's tensions and anxieties, such children are able to engage more freely in age-appropriate tasks, such as participating in peer relationships, achieving academically, or developing other unique physical or mental abilities.

When children marry, they select a spouse at the same level of differentiation as themselves. The lower the differentiation of the couple, the greater the tension and anxiety to be managed through conflict, the creation of overfunctioning/underfunctioning patterns of interaction, or family projection. For example, both overfunctioning and underfunctioning partners may have learned their respective roles in their own families of origin. The overfunctioning partner may have been trained to become a parental child or to make decisions for others in the family, whereas the underfunctioning partner may have been trained to go along with the decisions of others (Papero, 1991). The reenactment of these learned behaviors in adult relationships becomes both a source of unresolved conflict in the marriage and a means to maintain emotional equilibrium in the system (Kerr & Bowen, 1988).

Therefore, the patterns in the family of origin are replicated with more or less intensity depending on the position of each spouse in the family of origin. In each succeeding generation, some offspring will develop lower levels of differentiation, while others will develop higher levels. Over time, families will have some offspring who operate at progressively lower levels of functioning and others who will function at progressively higher levels. The multigenerational transmission of unresolved emotional attachments will continue until they are dealt with successfully.

This notion of transmitting unresolved attachments over succeeding generations has much in common with the notion of **legacy** introduced earlier in the discussion of the family's identity tasks (Boszormenyi-Nagy & Spark, 1973). Family members acquire a set of expectations and responsibilities toward each other based on the patterns and dynamics that have operated in the extended family system over time, and on the particular position they held in their own family of origin. The legacy includes a sense of loyalty and indebtedness to the family as well as a **family ledger**. This ledger is a multigenerational "accounting system" of who, psychologically speaking, owes what to whom (Boszormenyi-Nagy & Krasner, 1986; Boszormenyi-Nagy & Ulrich, 1981). These debts, while not entirely consciously acknowledged, will have either a primarily positive or negative balance. When members believe that they have been treated responsibly, equitably, and fairly, their sense of loyalty to the family will dictate that they return similar experiences to others in the family, either their parents and siblings or their spouses and offspring. When members believe that they have been treated irresponsibly, inequitably, and unfairly, their sense of deprivation will leave their "accounts" unsettled. Such unsettled grievances carry legacies of mistrust, deprivation, and entitlement that may have to be paid by succeeding generations.

Therefore, the legacy of individuals more attached to their own families of origin and more involved in their family's projection process is one of poor identity development and a sense of having been treated unfairly and unjustly by others. In turn, themes of deprivation, entitlement, mistrust, inequity, and exploitation are likely to be carried into future generations. In contrast, more differentiated individuals are likely to carry into their own families themes of justice, fairness, trust, generosity, and affection.

The Genogram: Insight into Intergenerational Processes

One way to gain insight into intergenerational patterns of differentiation and adjustment is through the examination of a family's genogram, a diagram depicting the biological and interpersonal relationships of the generations within the system. It provides information about the individuals within the extended family system and about the relationships between its members. The genogram is also useful for probing the significant events that occur within a family that affect subsequent patterns of interaction.

The genogram uses a set of standard symbols for diagramming the family system (cf. McGoldrick, Gerson, & Petry, 2008). Figure 4.1 provides a key to the construction of a genogram. The basic information contained within the genogram includes the name, chronological age, and generational position of each family member. In addition, significant nodal events are depicted in the genogram (e.g., dates of marriages, divorces, and deaths of family members).

In constructing the genogram, a historical depiction of the multiple generations comprising the family is created along with a chronology of the major events that the family has experienced. This historical information becomes even more useful when the emotional ties and patterns of interactions among family members are explored. In essence, the purpose of the genogram is to gather insight into the existing patterns of family system differentiation and how they affect the adjustment of individual family members.

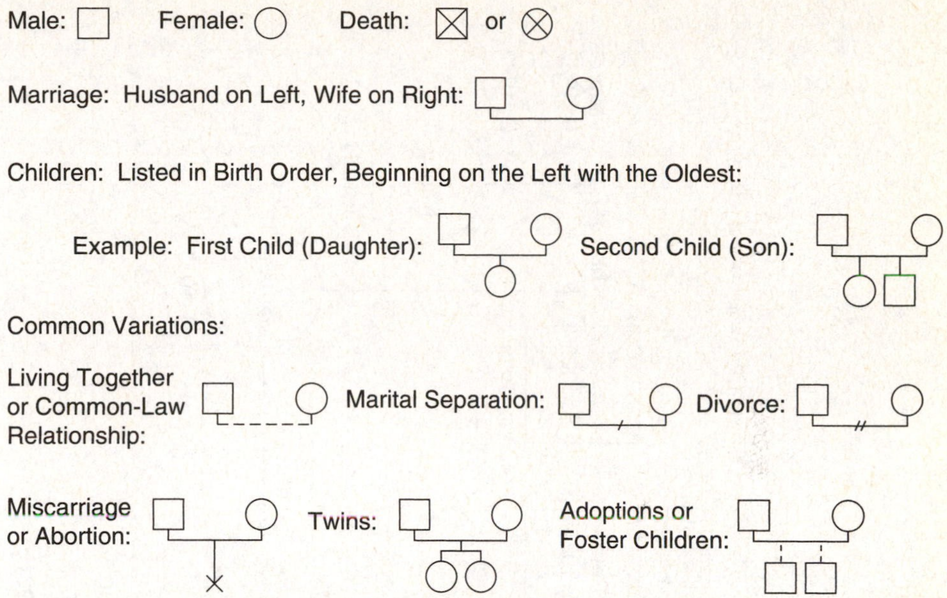

Male: Female: Death: or

Marriage: Husband on Left, Wife on Right:

Children: Listed in Birth Order, Beginning on the Left with the Oldest:

Example: First Child (Daughter): Second Child (Son):

Common Variations:

Living Together or Common-Law Relationship: Marital Separation: Divorce:

Miscarriage or Abortion: Twins: Adoptions or Foster Children:

FIGURE 4.1 Key to the Use of the Genogram

A Genogram Illustration: The Johnson Family

To illustrate how the information contained in the genogram helps to provide insight into family processes and family adjustment, the case of the Johnson family is presented. The genogram for three generations of the family is presented in Figure 4.2. The Johnson family came to family therapy as a result of a list of problems that Margaret wants fixed. Specifically, she is unhappy with her husband, Tom; concerned about her son Ben's (age fifteen) obesity; and having increasing difficulty controlling her younger son, John (age twelve), who has become profane and abusive toward her when she disciplines him. In exploring the details of the family's history as depicted on the genogram, many of the important issues leading to the difficulties become apparent.

Tom, born in 1949, never knew his biological father as his father. His mother, Lilian, divorced shortly after his birth and remarried Pete in 1951, when Tom was two. Pete is described by Tom as being an alcoholic who was abusive to his wife and children. Pete and Lilian had three children in four years, which means that Tom has one biological older brother and three younger half-siblings. In 1962, when Tom was thirteen, Lilian deserted her family. Tom's adolescence was a troubled one, which he attributes to his obesity. Tom was raised by Pete through his adolescence, got a job as a machinist at age eighteen, and left home a year later. Although there were many children in the household when he was growing up, Tom reports that he has little contact with any of his brothers and sisters now, and that he has not seen Pete or Lilian in years. His primary recollections of childhood are of sadness at having been abandoned by his biological father and mother.

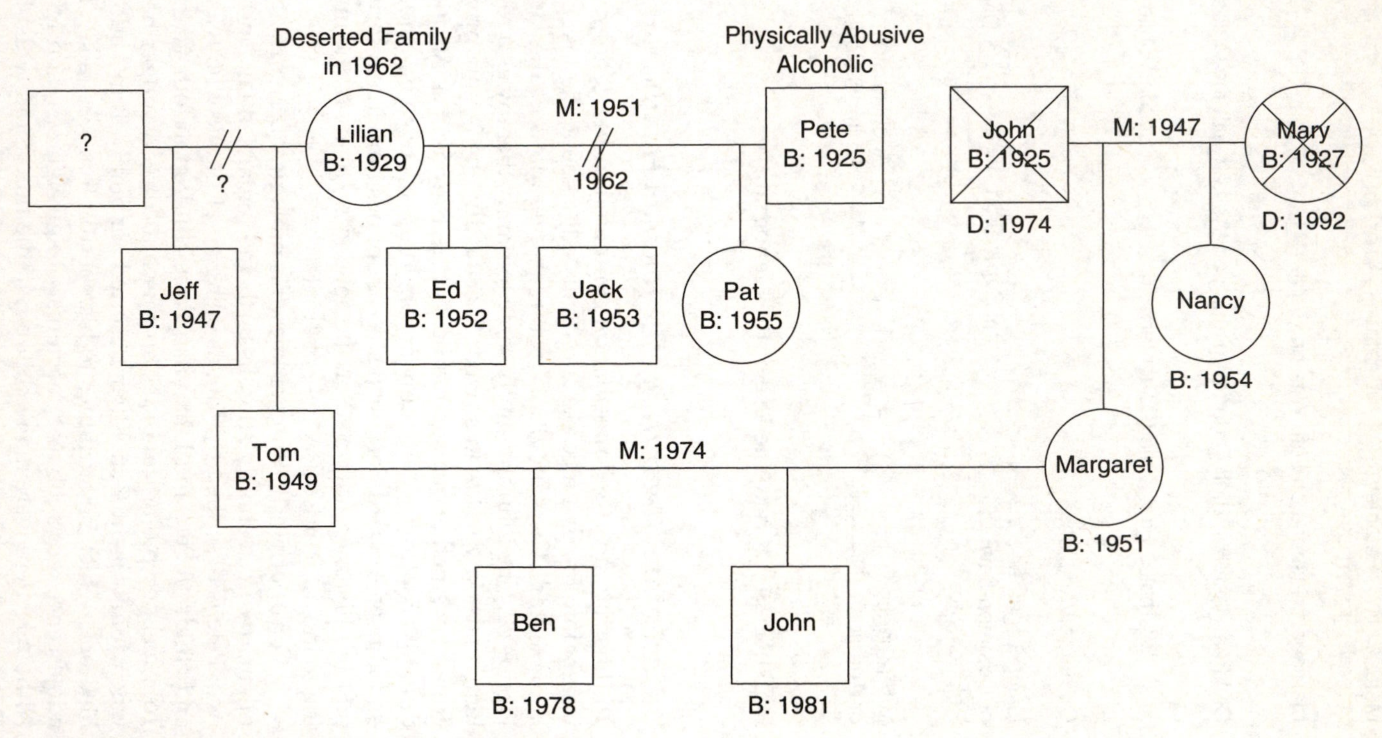

FIGURE 4.2 The Johnson Family's Genogram

Margaret, born in 1951, is the older daughter of John and Mary, both of whom are deceased. Margaret's father died in 1974 when she was twenty-three and her mother died in 1992. Margaret has one younger sister, Nancy. Margaret's mother and sister were always close to one another, and she often felt excluded from their conversations. Margaret reports that her mother and father had a troubled marriage—she characterizes them as the "classic example" of a couple who stayed married for "the sake of the children." She was close with her father and felt that her mother treated him badly. She was distressed by his death. After his death, Margaret's relationship with her mother and sister became even more strained. Margaret's sister, Nancy, "always took her mother's side" in the conflicts between her parents. It is interesting to note that Tom and Margaret married in the same year that Margaret's father died.

Tom and Margaret met when he was twenty-four and she was twenty-two. They dated while her father was ill. Tom reports being very lonely and inhibited due to his obesity and feeling grateful for Margaret's kindness toward him. Margaret, on the other hand, was grateful for the support that Tom offered her during her father's illness. They married shortly after her father died. Not surprisingly, since Margaret and her mother did not get along, Tom did not get along with Margaret's mother at all.

The marital relationship of Tom and Margaret was characterized initially by a "mutual neediness." Each relied heavily on the other for support. Over the years, however, Margaret has become increasingly bothered by Tom's inadequacy and child-like dependency. She complains about his inability to lose weight and his inadequacies as a father. The tension in their relationship threatens Tom a great deal. His recollections of being abandoned by his mother and cut off from his family make him feel particularly vulnerable when Margaret threatens to leave him. Unfortunately for Tom, when he is stressed by these feelings, he eats more, thereby further disappointing Margaret.

In exploring what happens in the family when conflicts between Tom and Margaret occur, it becomes clear that much of the tension between them is triangled onto Ben, whose overeating has become a major preoccupation of the family. Ben's weight, in other words, buffers the marital stress and tension that threatens to break the family apart. It is important to point out that neither parent acts supportively toward Ben and his weight problems. Rather, they get impatient with him for failing to diet and attack his character. Ben, as a result, is often depressed, has low self-esteem, and feels that he "won't amount to anything." Not surprisingly, he fails at all reasonable efforts to diet.

The relationship between John and his mother is conflicted and is part of a triangle involving Tom, Margaret, and John. Tom enjoys a close relationship with John, and feels that Margaret is too harsh and rejecting toward John. Margaret gets angry at Tom's unwillingness to support her efforts to control John. John rebels against Margaret's authority, yelling and screaming at her. In some ways, it appears that Tom enjoys the discomfort that John creates for Margaret.

This example illustrates how the genogram and the intergenerational model can be used to shed insight into how intergenerational patterns of interaction become established. Within Tom's family of origin, there is a strong theme of abandonment. This emotional legacy results in Tom being dependent on Margaret for her emotional support. Quite naturally, he feels extremely threatened by Margaret's threat to divorce him. This anxiety interferes with Tom's ability to function in a number of domains. He loses control of his eating when under stress, a factor that only serves to increase Margaret's disdain for him. Under stress he gets extremely rejecting toward Ben. This can be understood as Tom projecting his own anxieties about his inadequacies onto Ben. He also attempts to deal with these anxieties by forming a close bond with his son John. This coalition, however, only results in more tension permeating the system as Margaret becomes furious with both Tom and John.

Margaret's attraction to Tom can be understood as stemming, in part, from his ability to help her deal with the loss of her father and her lack of closeness with her mother. Over the years, however, as she has adjusted to her father's loss and achieved some distance from her mother (perhaps assisted by her mother's death), she has become less reliant on Tom for this support. As this reliance on Tom lessens, she becomes more critical of his "inadequacies." In other words, as the purpose of the marriage shifts from helping Margaret deal with her intergenerational legacy, her perception of the man she married shifts as well.

Although family dynamics cannot by themselves be held responsible for Ben's obesity, they certainly can be viewed as having a role in supporting his weight problem. Ben has been assigned an identity within the system—he is the one with a problem. The difficulty in correcting the trouble, however, lies in the fact that the family system has come to rely on its presence to mitigate against the stress and conflict between Tom and Margaret. It is interesting to note how Tom's anxiety about his own weight and the difficulties that he had with weight during his own youth have not led him to have a great deal of empathy for Ben. He acts, instead, in a harsh, punitive way toward his son. Both parents seem to blame Ben for his weight problem. In the process, Ben feels unloved and unrespected, which results in him eating more (a pattern that parallels Tom's own behavior under stress).

John and Margaret's difficulties stem, in part, from Tom's satisfaction when John stands up to Margaret. The more Tom feels the threat of being abandoned by Margaret, the more he tries to protect himself from this threat by aligning himself with John. This cross-generational coalition, however, undermines Margaret's authority and creates tension in her relationship with John. Margaret is correct in being angry at Tom for not supporting her, but Tom's anger at her and his emotional neediness keep him from responding to her requests for support. John, as a consequence, is set free by these dynamics. He is free to stand up to Margaret, the only controlling force in his life.

Conclusions

One of the main contributions of the intergenerational perspective is the insight it provides into how strategies and rules evolve within families. The patterns and dynamics of interaction observed within a family system are shaped and molded by the experiences of all family members within their respective families of origin. In effective families, the overriding tolerance for individuality that exists within the system allows family members to express their individuality and remain comfortably connected to the family. In other words, there is a context of effective strategies for managing boundaries, providing nurturance, and promoting personal identities that results in children developing a healthy sense of self and the capacity to act in responsible and supportive ways in intimate relationships.

Conversely, poorly differentiated families, like the Johnson family, structure boundaries, manage the emotional climate of the family, and assign identities in ways that impede the development of individual family members. These poorly differentiated individuals take from the family context a great deal of self-anxiety and an overriding lack of tolerance for the individuality of others that is transmitted from generation to generation. The Johnson family illustrates how the emotions and dynamics of the family of origin affect mate selection, marital dynamics, and patterns of adjustment in succeeding generations.

Key Terms

Conflict In intergenerational models, a strategy for maintaining distance from others and protecting one's sense of self. Conflict and disagreement can help to maintain an illusion of difference.

Differentiation When applied to the individual, differentiation refers to the ability of family members to express their own individuality and act autonomously while remaining emotionally connected to others. At the family level, differentiation refers to the degree to which difference is tolerated within the family system.

Differentiation of self The extent to which one has successfully resolved emotional attachments to one's family of origin. This becomes reflected in the individual's level of psychological maturity.

Emotional cutoff An attempt to emotionally, psychologically, or physically detach oneself from the family of origin in an effort to avoid fusion and maintain control over one's sense of self.

Family ledger A multigenerational "accounting system" of who, psychologically speaking, owes what to whom.

Family projection process The process by which parents project (displace) part of their own unresolved emotional attachments or conflicts onto one or more of their children.

Fusion The tendency to submerge one's sense of self in relationships with others, thereby losing the distinctions among emotional and intellectual functioning, self, and other.

Legacy The set of expectations and responsibilities family members develop toward one another based on the patterns and dynamics that have operated in their extended family system over time, and on the particular position they held in their own family of origin. The legacy includes a sense of loyalty and indebtedness to the family.

Multigenerational transmission process The process by which the family's level of differentiation and the parents' unresolved emotional attachments are reenacted in future relationships and passed along to succeeding generations.

Overfunctioning/underfunctioning A reciprocal pattern of interaction in which one participant assumes a competent, caretaking position in relation to the other, who assumes a dependent, child-like position.

Self A superordinate personal structure whose purpose is to organize an individual's experiences (cognitive and emotional, conscious and unconscious) into a coherent and meaningful whole.

Triangulation A three-person interaction in which the tension and conflict experienced between two persons is displaced onto a third party.

Undifferentiated family ego mass A poorly differentiated system characterized by a low tolerance for individuality in which members appear to be "emotionally stuck together."

CHAPTER 5

Contextual Models
Family Diversity

Chapter Overview

This chapter focuses on how theorists and researchers have approached issues of culture. More specifically, it addresses issues of ethnicity, race, economic status, and other factors that affect the strategies families develop to manage the tasks they must perform. A metaperspective on issues of diversity within families is presented. This perspective highlights the point that cultural sensitivity can be enhanced only when the predominant beliefs, customs, and practices of particular ethnic groups are appreciated. This information must be balanced, however, by an awareness of a resultant tendency to overgeneralize about ethnic groups. That is, an understanding of ethnicity must include both an understanding of the central tendencies of each group and an appreciation for the variations found within and between cultural groups.

While cultural tendencies may result in certain family themes and strategies being more common than others within each ethnic group, the chapter points out the many factors besides ethnicity that contribute to the diversity found within families. To this end, factors such as the reasons for immigration; the length of time since immigration; whether the family lives in an ethnic neighborhood; the upward mobility of family members; political and religious ties; the extent of family intermarriage with, or connection to, other ethnic groups; and the family members' attitudes toward their ethnic group are discussed as contributing to the diversity found within families. In addition, the chapter highlights the effect of socioeconomic factors and acculturation processes on the variations within ethnic families. It ends with a review of the more salient and enduring themes highlighted within the social science research associated with selected ethnic groups.

American society is culturally heterogeneous, a composite of many racial, ethnic, and cultural heritages. Because the family system is embedded within broader social systems, racial, ethnic, cultural and subcultural values and orientations influence the strategies and organizational structure of a family. It is important to examine these factors more closely as they relate to the dynamics within the family.

Race, Ethnicity, and Culture

Race is the term used most typically to refer to categories of individuals who share common inborn biological traits, such as skin color; color and texture of hair; and shape of eyes, nose, or head. It is often assumed that people within the same racial categories also share behavioral, psychological, and personality traits that are linked to their physical similarities. Because race is often thought of as an inherited and permanent biological characteristic, it can easily be used to divide people into mutually exclusive groups (Newman, 2007).

The concept of race is, however, not so straightforward. People who consider themselves "white," for example, may have darker skin than those who consider themselves "black." Furthermore, there is tremendous variability within racial groups. Currently the largest minority racial group in the United States is Latino or Hispanic—comprising nearly 15% of the total population (U.S. Census Bureau, 2008). Yet, within this and other racially designated groups there is much variation. Latinos include Mexicans, Puerto Ricans, Cubans, and others from Central or South America or the Caribbean. Asian Americans include Japanese, Chinese, Vietnamese, Laotians, Cambodians, Koreans, Filipinos, Native Hawaiians, Samoans, and other Pacific Islanders. While these groups share many commonalities, they also display many differences in their customs and practices.

So what ultimately ties people together in a particular racial group is not a set of shared physical characteristics but the shared experience of being identified by others as members of that group (Piper, 1992). During the process of growing up and creating an identity, people learn three important things. They learn the boundaries that distinguish group members from nonmembers, the perceived position of particular groups within society, and whether membership in a group is something to take pride in or be ashamed of (Cornell & Hartmann, 1998). In other words, race is a social construction.

Sociologists typically use the term **ethnicity** to refer to a group that shares a common identity based upon nonbiological traits such as shared ancestry, culture, history, language, and beliefs. Ethnic groups or subgroups reside within a larger culture and yet maintain their own autonomous identity and structure. Ethnicity has also been defined as a sense of commonality or community derived from shared networks of family experiences. The term implies that the commonalities found within ethnic groups make them distinct from other groups. One's ethnic identity is fostered through the processes of socialization and enculturation (Newman, 2007). However, ethnicity is more than membership in a particular group. It involves conscious and unconscious processes that fulfill a deep psychological need for personal identity and a sense of historical continuity. It is a fundamental determinant of values, perceptions, needs, modes of expression, and behavior that is derived in large part from unique family experiences (McGoldrick, 2003).

The concepts of ethnicity and culture are closely linked. **Culture** can be defined as "highly variable systems of meanings," which are "learned and shared by people or an identifiable segment of a population." Culture represents "designs and ways of life" that are normally "transmitted from one generation to another" (Rohner, 1984). The main point is that ethnicity and culture mutually influence one another and are reflected in the language, customs, and beliefs that provide members of a group with a common identity. That is, both ethnicity and culture are terms used to understand the meaning that people give to events. Ethnicity and culture define groups of people who share particular habits, customs, rituals, concepts, and interpretations of the world because of reasons of geography, historical period, religion, and other contingencies that play a role in establishing a degree of homogeneity to their perspectives (Pare, 1996). Family members' cultural and ethnic origins can play an important role in determining how various family tasks will be managed, such as how identities will be shaped, how family boundaries will be structured, how the family's resources will be spent, how the physical environment will be maintained, and how the emotional climate will be managed.

When trying to understand family patterns of interaction, it is important to think of race not as a biological category but as a social construction that is given meaning and significance in specified historical, political, and social contexts. Historically, "racial differences" based upon physical characteristics have served to legitimize prejudice and discrimination on the basis of these supposed differences (Omni & Winant, 1994). Race becomes an important factor within the family because the family must respond to the broader society's construction of their race. These social constructions, inevitably, will influence family themes, the construction of external boundaries, and other customs designed for the execution of basic family tasks.

In an effort to talk meaningfully about differences among people without legitimizing stereotypes, prejudice, and discrimination, contemporary social scientists shy away from the use of terms such as "race" and instead embrace terms like "ethnicity" and "culture." In the United States and Europe, ethnicity is commonly associated with membership in a nondominant group. That is, groups that are not of predominant European ancestry are perceived as constituting a different culture because of their language, style of dress, political views, food, music, or religious practices.

Embracing ethnicity and culture in place of race has shifted the discourse about human differences and family differences from one based upon biology to one that is shaped by social and historical experiences. Family patterns and processes are thought to be shaped by the social constructions of the races and by ethnic and cultural traditions. These ethnic and cultural traditions are an important part of the family's legacy. Hence, in order to understand the patterns of interaction found in contemporary American families, we must have an appreciation for their diverse ethnic and cultural heritages.

Two perspectives have emerged in the field of family studies that help us to better understand the ethnic and cultural diversity of families. The first of these perspectives is termed the **multidimensional perspective**. In this instance the term **cultural diversity** is used as a broad and encompassing term that takes into account many subcultural influences and the multiplicity of contexts with which families must contend. It takes into account not only ethnic, racial, and religious differences but also variations in socioeconomic status, family structures, sexual orientations, gender roles, and life stages (Allen, Fine, & Demo, 2000). Also important to consider are setting (rural, urban, or suburban), language, nationality, employment, education, occupation, political ideology, migration, and stage of acculturation (Falicov, 1995).

This multidimensional perspective can be contrasted with another position that has emerged within the field, namely the **culture-specific perspective** (Gates et al., 2000; Jencius & Duba, 2002). The emphasis here is on examining the specific cultural attitudes, beliefs, feelings, and behaviors that characterize members of a particular ethnic or racial group. The focus is on general characteristics that differentiate one ethnic or racial group from another. For instance, members of Irish families tend to marry late, and in African American families, the extended family is an important source of practical and emotional support (Falicov, 1995; Pinderhughes, 2002).

Both of these perspectives—the multidimensional and the culture specific—have particular strengths as well as limitations. The multidimensional perspective calls attention to the importance of understanding the uniqueness of each family system and the need to assess each family's "ecological fit" within its own broader context. However, this definition of cultural diversity makes generalization from the individual family to other similar families much more difficult (Falicov, 1995). Every family is viewed as unique. The culture-specific perspective provides valuable information about differences between ethnic groups and helps us develop sensitivity to these cultural differences. Unfortunately, it assumes homogeneity among all members of an ethnic group and ignores the significant variations that exist even among families of a particular ethnic group.

In this chapter, we will examine these two differing perspectives. We will discuss how theorists and researchers have approached the general issues of culture as well as the more specific issues of ethnicity, race, economic status, and other factors that define membership in our pluralistic society. We will focus our attention on how issues of culture affect the strategies families develop to effectively manage the myriad of tasks to which they must attend. Later in this chapter, we will illustrate how ethnicity influences family patterns of interaction by reviewing what family social scientists have found to be the more salient and enduring themes associated with a selected number of ethnic groups. Before proceeding with these summaries, however, we present a metaperspective that takes into account the strengths of both the multidimensional and culture-specific perspectives.

A Metaperspective on Cultural Diversity

Systems perspectives encourage us to understand each family as a unique system with its own predominant strategies for managing family tasks. For instance, all families construct identities and central themes. For some families, these identities and themes may have been strongly influenced by racial constructions and ethnic and subcultural identifications. However, others may have been less influenced by such factors. Since culture is about the meaning a family derives from its racial, ethnic, religious, historical, geographical, and subgroup identifications, we cannot know to what extent the family is influenced by these factors without communicating with family members or observing their interactions. For instance, if we note that a family observes all religious holidays and is active in religious activities, we may conclude that religion has a strong influence upon the family. Or if family members tell us that their most deeply held convictions are the same as the ones their grandparents learned in the "old country," we might begin to appreciate the significance of their ethnic origins.

The essential issue here is that we must have the necessary firsthand information to form reliable conclusions about the extent to which a family is influenced by culture and ethnicity. The absence of such information means that any conclusions will be based on assumptions, conjecture, and stereotypes.

If we cannot know the extent to which culture and ethnicity shape the form and organization of a particular family without actually observing or communicating with that family, then of what value are ethnic-focused profiles of different ethnic or subcultural groups? How do these profiles help or hinder us in assessing family functioning?

They help us by sensitizing us to the possibility that difference might be equated with dysfunction. Recall, for example, the discussion in Chapter 3 about the structural model of family functioning, which proposed that families balanced between enmeshment and disengagement were more functional than those that fell in the extreme regions of enmeshment or disengagement. Yet, families with Hispanic or Southeast Asian ethnic origins or from Mormon or Amish religious backgrounds often operate more in the connected and enmeshed regions without dysfunction (McGoldrick, 2003; Olson & Gorall, 2003).

The main point is that although there may be identifiable differences among groups, knowing these differences is not the same as judging these differences. To determine that a difference is bad or dysfunctional requires evidence that the difference results in the development of family strategies that work against the family accomplishing its tasks. To conclude that a difference is bad or dysfunctional simply because it deviates from the dominant culture is at best judgmental and naive, and at worst potentially discriminatory and dangerous.

By the same token, ethnic- or culturally focused group profiles become problematic when they obscure the tremendous diversity that operates within cultural and ethnic groups. That is, focusing too much attention on differences among groups can obscure the differences within groups. Consider the following generalizations drawn from existing research.

Among Irish Catholics, there is a heavy emphasis on church authority and a tendency to assume that anything that goes wrong is the result of a person's sins. This type of orientation means that Irish Catholics are often unlikely to seek help from others for problems (McGoldrick, 2005a).

These conclusions are essentially generalizations based on central tendencies among Irish Catholics. That is, the generalizations simply represent modal, or the most frequently occurring, patterns that have been observed. The fact that these patterns occur more frequently than others is important. However, this does not mean that all Irish Catholic families share these characteristics. Attention to the modal patterns obscures the diversity within these families and results in a simplistic view of the patterns of interaction characteristic of different ethnic groups.

It is also important to refrain from making cross-group comparisons on the basis of available group profiles. We are tempted to use group profile data to infer that all members of one particular group are qualitatively different from members of another group. Take, for example, the following conclusion: "While all cultures value the family, Italians appear to give it higher priority than most other groups do. For Italians, family life is their primary orientation" (p. 349). There is a strong emphasis on family bonds and a tendency for parents to be overinvolved with their children (Giordano et al., 2005). Again, these statements could be construed as implying that this strong family emphasis is true for all Italian families but not true for families of other ethnic origins. Although an emphasis on family is important in many Italian families, and although additional themes emerge in research on families from other ethnic groups, we should not conclude that other groups do not value the importance of family.

Several important considerations have been raised in this section. One is that cultural sensitivity can be enhanced when we appreciate the predominant beliefs, customs, and practices of particular ethnic groups. However, this information must be balanced with an awareness of a resultant tendency to overgeneralize about ethnic groups. An understanding of ethnicity must include both an understanding of the central tendencies characteristic of each group and an appreciation of the variations found within and between groups. Pluralism is not only a characteristic of the culture as a whole but also of each ethnic group and each family within that group.

Another consideration is the distinction between knowledge of cultural diversity and tolerance for differences. Knowledge of cultural diversity is often promoted as a strategy for achieving a tolerance for differences, and it may in fact be necessary to achieve such a tolerance. However, it alone is not sufficient, because generalization of the central tendencies of a particular ethnic group to all members of that group can actually undermine a tolerance for difference. This happens when too much attention is paid to differences *between* groups and insufficient attention is paid to variations *within* groups.

In sum, it is essential that we consider how ethnicity serves as an important filter influencing family themes and images, boundary processes, resource priorities, and predominant orientations to the management of emotional issues. At the same time, while there is a need to acknowledge a certain level of cultural similarity within ethnic groups, we also need to acknowledge the variability that exists within these groups. Furthermore, we need to refrain from assuming that ethnicity has a uniform and, hence, predictable impact on each family's patterns of interaction.

The Broader Racial and Ethnic Context

The diversity found within and between ethnic and racially diverse families results from a constellation of factors. While there may be cultural tendencies that result in certain family themes and strategies being more common than others within each ethnic group, it is important to recognize that each family is unique, a product of not only its ethnic heritage but also its intergenerational themes and legacies, its level of education and socioeconomic status, its present living conditions, its level of assimilation into the majority culture, and many other factors that define the family's current social context. McGoldrick (2003) has noted, for instance, that many factors influence the extent to which traditional ethnic patterns will surface in any particular family within that ethnic group. Among these factors are the reasons for immigration, the length of time since immigration, whether the family lives in an ethnic neighborhood, the upward mobility of family members, family political and religious ties, the extent of family intermarriage with or other connection to other ethnic groups, and family members' attitudes toward the ethnic group and its values.

Thus, it is fair to conclude, for example, that there is no such thing as the black, Hispanic, Italian, Irish, Jewish, or Asian family. For example, Taylor (2000) points out that there is no such thing as *the* black family, as black people in this country do not comprise a monolithic group. There are, for example, differences between black families from the North and those from the South. There are also important urban versus rural differences. In addition, black African American families may be distinct from those black families with cultural ties to the West Indies. Similarly, the Puerto Rican culture is clearly a product of many diverse influences, including Spanish, African, and Caribbean Indian.

In the following section, we shall highlight several of the more prominent factors that further contribute to the diversity found within family systems. These issues are discussed with the goal of promoting sensitivity to the many factors that contribute to the uniqueness of each family system.

Class, Socioeconomic Status, and Family Diversity

Any perspective on the diversity found within and between family systems must consider how **socioeconomic status (SES)** and social class affect family strategies. Clearly, families from different socioeconomic strata may establish different family strategies partly in response to the different economic circumstances in which they live. It is also the case that individuals from different socioeconomic strata may approach family life in distinctly different ways due to variations in attitudes, beliefs, and values. In embarking on this discussion, however, we must remain mindful of how the metaperspective on cultural diversity discussed previously also applies to issues of social stratification. That is, we neither want to overgeneralize the tendencies within families of various socioeconomic strata or exaggerate the differences between socioeconomic groups. While the terms SES and social class are often used interchangeably, there are some basic definitional differences. In general, **social class** implies discrete categories of people who are similar in their levels of education, income, occupational status, housing, and lineage (Hoff, Laursen, & Tardif, 2002).

This definition has the advantage of considering class as a cohesive whole that organizes families' experiences at different class levels. This encourages us to think of middle-class families as being discretely different from working- or upper-class families. However, it should be clear that the multiple variables that constitute class (i.e., education, income, occupation, and so on) are not perfectly correlated. Thus, one problem with defining classes as distinct categories is that assignment to a class for any one family may depend on what variable or combination of variables is used in the definition of class. There is also the problem of overgeneralizing the similarities within classes and exaggerating the differences between classes.

Like social class, SES is a composite variable defined primarily by the education, income level, and occupational status of the family. In contrast to social class, however, SES is more typically used in the research literature to connote a more continuous variable, meaning that all families fall somewhere on an SES continuum from relatively low to relatively high. This SES continuum has the advantage of highlighting the tendencies that might be found within families of different socioeconomic strata while also highlighting the fact that the differences noted may be only ones of relative degrees.

Perhaps one of the areas in which SES is noted to affect family patterns of interaction most prominently is parenting strategies. The parenting research clearly demonstrates that parents' values, beliefs, and attitudes toward children vary by their level of SES (Hoff et al., 2002). For example, higher SES parents have greater expectations for their children's academic performance and talk to their children more often about school than do lower SES parents (Bradley & Corwyn, 2002). In addition, SES has been found to covary with the behaviors that parents value in their children. Lower SES mothers, for example, tend to rate proper demeanor, which includes obedient, respectful, and quiet behavior, as being more important than do higher SES mothers (Harwood, 1992). This preference of lower SES mothers for "proper demeanor" may be a specific example of a more general preference among lower SES parents for conformity to societal prescriptions, while, in contrast, higher SES parents want their children to be self-directed and to value creativity (Hoff et al., 2002).

Thus the education, income, and occupation of parents have a potential impact on the structure and experience of family life. While cultural diversity adds to the complexity found within family systems, culturally diverse family systems are further diversified in terms of SES. We cannot speak, for example, of Italian family systems or Irish family systems as monolithic entities. In part, this results from the unique ways in which SES affects the goals, values, beliefs, and context of these ethnic families. Concomitantly, we cannot speak as if there are family patterns and processes characteristic of working-class or middle-class families independent of their ethnic and cultural heritage.

Poverty, Racism, and Family Life

In discussing SES, it is important to be aware of how poverty in particular influences the structure and experience of family life. While there are ongoing debates within the social sciences about how to define social class and where to draw the lines between classes, it is reasonable to suggest that a realistic image of American life includes a substantial number of families living in or near **poverty**. For example, in 2008, about 7.6 million U.S. families (approximately 10% of all families) were considered poor—meaning their income level fell below the official poverty line as set by the federal government (U.S. Census Bureau, 2008). The **poverty line or level** is defined as the least amount of income needed for a family to purchase a minimally adequate amount of basic goods such as food, clothing, and shelter throughout the year (Rank, 2001). The poverty level is adjusted each year to account for inflation. Poverty levels vary by household size. It is important to note that this official poverty line was set in 2002 by the federal government as an income of $18,244 or less for a family comprised of two adults and two children. This means that a substantially larger percentage of families, although not officially poor, are clearly economically disadvantaged and grapple with economic hardships in their efforts to manage the ordinary and extraordinary demands of family life.

Regardless of where the official poverty line is drawn, poverty leads to high rates of infant mortality, poor nutrition, inadequate housing, mental illness, and family disruption (Lerner, Rothbaum, Boulos, & Castellino, 2002). Research clearly shows that poverty is perhaps the most pervasive stressor in adults' lives, especially when it is combined with unemployment (Wilson, 1996). The effects of poverty are also especially severe for children (Rank, 2001). Economic disadvantage presents chronic stressors and insecurity as well as daily stressors or irritants (McLoyd, 1990). These stem from the inability to plan ahead, a sense of loss of control over one's life, feelings of relative deprivation in terms of material possessions, poor housing, lack of food, cold in the winter and heat in the summer, untreated illnesses, dangerous neighborhoods, and lack of access to proper educational experiences for one's children (Rank, 2001; Wilson, 1996). These stressors associated with poverty take their toll on marital relationships as well as child-rearing practices. Marital stress, dissatisfaction, domestic violence, and divorce are all more likely among those in poverty (White & Rogers, 2000). Adults become more easily irritable and tempers flare. Recriminations are exchanged, and mutual supports fail when they are most needed. Men often withdraw from family life as a result of feeling that they cannot contribute because they have failed in their role as provider. Child-rearing practices become harsher, less sensitive, and more inconsistent (Conger, Conger, Elder, Lorenz, Simons, & Whitbeck, 1992; Elder, 1979).

In addition, poverty is clearly confounded by race, with the multigenerational existence of poverty affecting many African Americans and other minority groups, particularly those in working and inner-city families (Boyd-Franklin, 2003). These families must manage the demands of family life while confronting the duel difficulties of racism and life in an economically deprived context. They are faced with such threats as drug and alcohol abuse, gangs, crime, homelessness, increasingly dangerous public housing, violence, early death, teenage pregnancy, high unemployment and school dropout rates, poor educational systems, and ongoing issues with the police and justice systems (Boyd-Franklin, 2003). They see few options for their children and may feel trapped, which leads to what Pinderhughes (1982) has termed the "victim system":

> *A victim system is a circular feedback process which... threatens self-esteem and reinforces problematic responses in communities, families and individuals. The feedback works as follows: Barriers to opportunity and education limit the chance for achievement, employment and attainment of skills. This limitation*

can, in turn, lead to poverty or stress in relationships, which interferes with adequate performance of family roles. (p. 109)

Many of the poor, and in particular the poor found within racial minorities, who must confront issues of both racism and poverty, feel trapped, disempowered, and increasingly full of rage. Men in these communities who are unemployed are less attractive as prospective mates, and, thus, may remain unmarried. This in turn contributes to the high rates of female-headed single families (Pinderhughes, 2002). Unemployed men may also be reluctant to marry because of concerns about being able to fulfill the role of provider. For men of color, success in the role of provider is highly important (McLoyd, Cauce, Tacheuchi, & Wilson, 2000).

Their poor economic conditions mean that these families live within a context in which they fear for themselves and for their children. Adolescence begins early within poor, inner-city communities, where, at a very young age, children are faced with choices related to sexuality, household responsibility, drugs, and alcohol use. Random violence, particularly drug-related violence, has become a major concern for such families. Parents struggle with feelings of being powerless to prevent the streets from taking over their children (Boyd-Franklin, 2003; Osofsky, 1997).

The broader point here is that the social context of family life can profoundly influence the trajectory of individual and family development. While it would be erroneous to conclude that all poor families are beset with problems and function in marginal or erratic ways, it would be equally wrong to ignore the profound ways in which poverty affects the quality of family life. Furthermore, we cannot dismiss the complex interplay of factors such as race, racism, class, and poverty that influence the structure and experience of family life. In the final analysis, while we cannot predict exactly how many of these factors will affect family life, it is clear that education, economics, employment histories and opportunities, and racism weave their way into the fabric of family life and influence both the strategies used to execute the family's tasks and their effectiveness.

Acculturation and Family Diversity

The process by which families combine their ethnic/minority identities with the dominant cultural values, attitudes, and practices reflects their own process of acculturation. Traditionally, **acculturation** has been conceptualized as a process of adaptation that involves learning about a new culture and deciding which aspects of the culture of origin are to be retained or sacrificed. It refers to the changes in attitudes, values, and behaviors made by members of one culture as a result of their contact with another culture (Handelsman, Gottlieb, & Knapp, 2005). The process of acculturation is dynamic and occurs over time in the context of family life and broader social experiences (Zuniga, 1992). Although the process is ongoing, discontinuities may be expected due to family relocation, economic and social constraints, formation or disruption of important relationships, or traumatic experiences.

Acculturation occurs with respect to many sociocultural family characteristics, including language, occupational status, attitudes, food preferences, recreational activities, customs, rituals, and attitudes toward child-rearing (Falicov, 2003). The degree of family acculturation may be characterized along a continuum. At one end of the continuum are those ethnic families that maintain a strong identification with the traditions and practices of their cultural heritage. At the other end are those ethnic families that abandon their cultural traditions and quickly adopt the mainstream values and attitudes of their host culture. Within the mid-range of this continuum are ethnic families thought of as bicultural, emphasizing both traditional and mainstream values (Falicov, 2003).

Acculturation, thus, helps to explain the diversity found within ethnic and racial families as these families change at different rates over time in response to their contact with the dominant culture of the United States. The rate at which the acculturation process occurs is influenced by many factors, including migration experience, generational status, degree of **assimilation** into the dominant culture, likelihood of returning to the homeland, ongoing contact with the culture of origin, and length of time within the host culture. Uncertainty regarding whether the family will remain in the United States, for example, would favor maintaining traditional ethnic values.

Three adjustment patterns to the process of immigration that underscore the individual variability that can be expected during the process of acculturation have been identified (Fitzpatrick, 1988): (1) escaping from the immigrant group and becoming as much like the dominant group in as short a time as possible; (2) withdrawing into the old culture and resisting the new way of life; and (3) trying to build a "cultural bridge" between the culture of origin and the new culture. It is this last group of immigrants—who seek to establish themselves in the new society but continue to identify themselves with their culture of origin—who are actually striving toward biculturalism.

Thus, the concept of acculturation is especially useful because it underscores the heterogeneity within ethnic and minority groups while emphasizing individual differences among members of the same group. Many variations exist within ethnic groups, particularly among the most recent immigrant groups, due to the degree to which acculturation has occurred. Thus, it is difficult to generalize about ethnic and racial families because it is impossible to determine a priori the degree to which the acculturation process has affected the structure and experience of each family life.

Ethnicity, Race, and Family Strategies

The general themes and orientations found within various ethnically and racially diverse families are presented here to illustrate how a family's structure and strategies may be influenced by its cultural heritage. The examples demonstrate how cultural themes are woven into the fabric of family life in ways that affect patterns of interaction and functioning. Again, we are reminded of the metaperspective presented earlier. That is, we must remain aware of the many ways in which these group profiles can be helpful in understanding the differences in the patterns and dynamics observed within families and at the same time be misleading, particularly if insufficient attention is given to variations within groups and if cross-group comparisons are made.

Jewish families, for example, place a very strong emphasis on preserving their heritage and connection to previous generations. This also includes a very strong family orientation in which marriage and children play a central role (Hines, Preto, McGoldrick, Almeida, & Weltman, 2005). Children and grandchildren are often perceived as the very essence of life's meaning (Rosen & Weltman, 2005). Parents in Jewish families tend to have democratic relationships with their children. In fact children may be asked to play a meaningful role in resolving family problems. There is a less clear-cut boundary between parents and children than in other ethnic groups (Rosen & Weltman, 2005). Because children are expected to be such a source of pride and pleasure for parents, they may at times feel challenged to balance obligations to family with their own independent strivings (Hines et al., 2005). There is also a strong concern for children's emotional, social, and intellectual development and a strong value placed on intellectual achievement and financial success. Jewish families value education, learning, and open debate. Conflict is directly and openly expressed. Cynicism and criticism are often expressed in Jewish families to get family members to react and respond. What may appear to others as anger or hostility is often perceived within the family as a way of showing caring. The fact that Jews live so often in situations of oppression and anti-Semitism helps to account for Jewish families' strong emphasis on tradition and community (Hines et al., 2005; Rosen & Weltman, 2005).

Within Irish families it is important to maintain a positive image. Expressing feelings or admitting a problem, especially to other family members, often produces feelings of embarrassment and shame (Hines et al., 2005; McGoldrick, 2003). As a result, conflict within these families is dealt with indirectly. Ambiguous communication and keeping secrets are also common strategies for dealing with conflicts within the family (Hines et al., 2005). Humor and sarcasm are other important ways of dealing with stressful and difficult situations (McGoldrick, 2005a). Within the Irish family, the mother has characteristically played the central nurturing role with the father remaining peripheral. The Irish sense of duty is a strong value, and parents generally want to do the right thing for their children. There is a tendency to focus more on their children's conformity to rules than on other aspects of the children's emotional needs such as self-expression, assertiveness, and creativity. Consequently, children are raised to be respectful and well behaved. Discipline is traditionally strict and may be enforced with threats of damnation ("you'll go to Hell for your sins"). Physical expressions of affection are rare (Hines et al., 2005; McGoldrick, 2005a).

While all cultures value the family, Italians revere it as the highest source of influence in their lives (Giordano et al., 2005). For Italians, family life is their primary orientation. There is a strong emphasis on family bonds and a tendency for parents to be overly involved with their children. The family system is patriarchal in structure, with authority tending to reside with the males within the household. The Italian mother, on the other hand, is at the heart of the Italian home. She is responsible for the affective realm of the family, and it is expected that her life should center around domestic activities. Her personal needs are expected to take second place to those of her husband and children. While parents expect loyalty from their children, in general, and while children experience a strong sense of obligation to the family, sons and daughters are socialized somewhat differently. For example, sons are given considerably greater latitude in controlling their lives than are daughters. Daughters, in contrast, are often restricted socially and are taught to devalue personal achievement in deference to the needs and wishes of the family. Italians have learned to take maximum advantage of the present. That is, they have a tremendous ability for intense enjoyment and involvement in eating, celebrating, fighting, and loving (Giordano et al., 2005; McGoldrick, 2003).

The historical experience of slavery, the difference in skin color, and the ongoing impact of racism and discrimination all have a continuing and pervasive impact on how African American family life is structured (Hines & Boyd-Franklin, 2005; Pinderhughes, 2002). Racism, for example, influences how boundaries with outsiders and social support are structured. For black families, the mistrust of broader social systems is among those factors that result in the development of strong kinship networks. Kinship ties, however, are not exclusively structured by blood ties, as relatives with a variety of blood lines are often absorbed into a coherent network of mutual emotional and economic support (Hines & Boyd-Franklin, 2005).

African American families consider children to be very important. Because of the degrading messages children receive from society, an important part of parenting is instilling a sense of racial pride and positive identity in children. This involves educating children to the realities of racism and discrimination. Parents also must struggle to overcome a sense of futility and disempowerment that characterizes many poor African American families. Values of loyalty and responsibility to others, especially those within the extended family network, are also emphasized (Boyd-Franklin, 2003; Hines & Boyd-Franklin, 2005).

For many black extended families, reciprocity—the process of helping each other and exchanging and sharing support as well as goods and services—is a central part of their lives and has important survival value (Boyd-Franklin, 2003). Because of the economic realities faced by many black families, parenting roles are rather flexibly structured. In addition, "informal adoption," an informal social service network that has been an integral part of the black community since the days of slavery, occurs whereby adult relatives or friends of the family take in children and care for them when their parents are unable to do so (Boyd-Franklin, 2003).

Latino families in the United States, which make up 15 percent of the population, include many groups with unique histories and cultures. Mexican Americans are the largest subgroup (58.5%), but Puerto Ricans, Cubans, Central Americans, and South Americans are also heavily represented (U.S. Census Bureau, 2008). In comparison with other racial groups, Latinos have larger families and lower divorce rates (Zuniga, 1992). In traditional Latino cultures, children symbolize fertility and security for the future (Garcia-Preto, 2005). This means that children are important within families to the point that the parent–child relationship may be considered even more important than the marital relationship, and parents may be expected to sacrifice for their children (Zuniga, 1992). Because of this emphasis, it is not uncommon for parents to maintain an intense connectedness with their children from infancy through adulthood.

Familism, a strong identification with the family, is central in most Latino cultures. Family includes not only nuclear and extended family, but the larger network of friends and neighbors with whom an enduring bond is established. Family loyalty, respect for parents, and a sense of duty toward other family members are emphasized. While this strong family orientation can be a source of social support, it can also interfere with individual advancement. That is, group cooperation, obedience, and the ability to get along with others may be considered more important than success in the outside world (Hines & Boyd-Franklin, 2005; Garcia-Preto, 2005).

Male dominance and female submissiveness describe traditional gender-typed roles in Latino families. However, this traditional pattern appears to be slowly modifying in response to acculturation, current social conditions, and the economic context. Thus, in response to social changes and acculturation, there appears to be a range of gender role patterns observed within Latino families, including shared decision-making and egalitarianism.

Only 3.6 percent of the American population is Asian, but that number is expected to double during the next 50 years (U.S. Census Bureau, 2008). Immigration patterns have resulted in a very diverse group of Asian Americans, including Chinese, Filipino, Japanese, Koreans, and Southeast Asians. The earliest immigrants were primarily farmers and laborers, while more recent groups have tended to be highly educated professionals (Chan, 1992).

The central values in many Asian cultures are rooted in Confucian principles that emphasize family, harmony, and education. Virtues such as patience, perseverance, self-sacrifice, and humility are held in high regard. Self-interest is subordinated to the good of the group, and connectedness is emphasized while individualism is minimized. Parents, thus, for example, will readily sacrifice their personal needs and wants in the interest of their children and the family (Chan, 1992).

In traditional Asian families, roles are strongly influenced by the age, gender, and birth order of family members. Women have primary responsibility for childrearing, while men are financial providers and disciplinarians. While there tend to be strong emotional ties among family members in Asian families, a mother's strongest bond may be with her children rather than with her husband. A father's primary attachment may be with his own mother rather than with his wife. Oldest sons are often expected to guide the development of younger siblings (Chan, 1992; Lee, 1996).

In most Asian American subcultures, education is highly valued, and children are taught to respect learning and knowledge (Chan, 1992; Lee, 1996). There is a cultural tendency to attribute academic success to effort rather than innate ability (Stevenson & Lee, 1990). Guided by this belief, parents feel responsible for their children's academic performance, and children in turn feel that they honor their parents by performing well in school (Chan, 1992). This emphasis on education supports biculturalism for Asian American families living in the United States (Garcia Coll & Pachter, 2002). In other words, within many Asian American families there is a respect for their cultural traditions as well as a high emphasis on assimilating into the mainstream of American culture through education and employment that lead to upward mobility.

Conclusions

It is critically important to pay attention to the ways in which culture, race, ethnicity, class, SES, and acculturation affect the strategies that families employ in their efforts to execute the tasks of family life. All families evolve themes, and these themes may reflect the ethnic and cultural heritage of the family. Such ethnic traditions and cultural themes provide the family with a framework of meaning and orientation that may affect the priorities of goals of the family, the values and attitudes of the family members, and the strategic manner in which issues such as power, decision-making, intimacy, and child-rearing are managed.

The metaperspective on diversity presented within this chapter is meant to remind us that we cannot assume that culture, race, and ethnicity have a predictable impact on the structure and experience of family life. Many, many factors, such as SES, poverty, racism, and acculturation, modify or perhaps intensify how cultural factors are integrated into the fabric of family life. We thus need to be aware of how culture influences the family. But we also need to recognize that family systems are decidedly complex and unique. A truly tolerant perspective on families requires that we be aware of the heterogeneity found within families and the factors that accordingly contribute to the uniqueness found within them.

Key Terms

Acculturation A process of learning about a new culture and deciding what aspects are to be retained or sacrificed from the culture of origin.

Assimilation The process by which a minority group gradually adopts the customs and attitudes of the dominant culture.

Cultural diversity A broad and encompassing term that takes into account the many subcultural influences and variety of contexts that shape people's lives and account for differences among people in a given culture. This includes variations due to ethnicity, race, religion, socioeconomic status, family structure, sexual orientation, gender, and life stage.

Culture A group of persons who share particular habits, customs, rituals, concepts, and interpretations of the world because of geography, historical period, religion, and other factors that play a role in establishing a degree of homogeneity of their views.

Culture-specific perspective A view that regards cultural diversity as being derived from a consideration of factors related specifically to race and ethnicity. Here the emphasis is upon examining the specific attitudes, beliefs, feelings, and behaviors that characterize members of a particular ethnic or cultural group.

Ethnicity The characteristics of a unique subgroup possessing an autonomous identity and structure that reside within a larger culture.

Multidimensional perspective A view that regards cultural diversity as being derived from a consideration of a multiplicity of factors rather than solely from the effects of race and ethnicity.

Poverty The condition of the life of families or individuals whose income falls below a certain level established by the federal government for a given year. In 2002, this figure was $18,244 for a family of four.

Poverty line or level The least amount of income needed for a family to purchase a minimally adequate amount of basic goods such as food, clothing, and shelter throughout the year.

Race The physical characteristics of particular groups of people.

Social class Discrete categories of people who are similar in their levels of education, income, occupational status, housing, and lineage.

Socioeconomic status (SES) A continuous research variable based upon the subject's education, income, and occupation.

PART III

Family Developmental Stages

This part of the text addresses the relationship between family interactions and the developmental changes that occur within families over time. The multigenerational/developmental perspective highlighted here focuses on the stages in the family life cycle, the tasks the family must execute during each stage, and the impact that transitional periods have on the patterns of interaction and functioning found within the family.

As a family system moves through time, patterns of interaction are shaped and influenced by developmental stress. As was noted in Chapters 1 and 2, all family systems encounter developmental stress, which originates from two basic sources: (1) the changing needs and abilities of individual family members as they mature; and (2) the changes in the family system as a whole as it undergoes modifications and revisions over time.

From a family systems perspective, the changing needs and abilities of individuals over their life courses are thought to affect the family's patterns of interaction. As individuals grow and mature, their physical, social, emotional, psychological, and cognitive needs and abilities change. Each family member's development affects how the family will execute its basic tasks. The family's physical maintenance, boundaries, emotional environment, and identity tasks will vary according to the needs and abilities of its members. For example, the physical, social, and emotional needs of an infant are far different from those of a school-age child. The family must be capable of altering its interactional strategies in response to these changes if the family is to continue to meet its primary goal of facilitating the growth and development of its individual members.

Each family system can also be thought of as having its own developmental course. Over time, the family will undergo changes in its composition as members are added or lost. These transitions can produce periods of instability, disorganization, stress, and potential change. Critical family transitions, generally marked by the arrival (through marriage, birth, or adoption) or departure (through school entrance, launching, or death) of members into or out of the family system, demand adaptations and modifications in the family system. During such times of structural reorganization, tasks must be realigned, roles redefined, and strategies revised. For example, the birth of the first child moves the family from a two-person to a three-person system, adding the new role of parent to the family's previously existing roles. This reorganization leads to changes both in the family's structural composition and in how the family will execute its basic tasks. Maintenance tasks must now include attending to the basic physical needs of the infant. Resources previously directed toward other priorities must now be focused upon the child. The family must realign its internal boundaries to account for a parental as well as marital subsystem. External boundaries must shift to accommodate interactions with child-care professionals (such as pediatricians and day-care provider) and other families with children.

As more attention is focused on the needs of the newborn, the emotional climate of the family may become disrupted. Conflicts may arise over how much time and energy are directed toward parental versus marital responsibilities. The family's identity must shift from that of a married couple to that of a family with a child. Attention must be given to the establishment of the child's own identity through the selection of a name or gender-appropriate clothing (blue for boys, pink for girls?). Each of these task realignments will require modifications in the family's former behavioral strategies. New decisions, plans, and procedures must be implemented in order to meet each of these changing demands.

Consequently, the following chapters highlight the issues confronted by family systems as they deal with specific developmental transitions. Before proceeding, however, we need to call attention to two important points. First, for the sake of simplicity more than for any other reason, family developmental perspectives focus primarily on normative patterns of development (those experienced by a majority of families in American culture). This somewhat narrow focus is not meant to obscure the fact that all families must contend with developmental issues. That is, all families must make adaptations that are shaped and constrained by the family's unique composition, structure, and circumstances. For example, the married couple that chooses not to have children does not have to contend with stressors such as bearing children, forming a parental subsystem, sending children off to school, or launching children into adulthood. Yet both partners must still deal with their own and each other's aging, and the impact this change will have on their marital relationship. They must also deal with the aging of their own parents and the demands and adaptations associated with these developmental changes.

Similarly, a blended family—a family comprised of remarried adults, stepchildren, and stepsiblings—faces issues that are substantially different from those dealt with by a traditional nuclear family. Yet blended families, like traditional nuclear families, must also adapt to the changing developmental needs and abilities of their individual members. The fact that some systems may be less common means only that they may encounter greater uncertainty and a smaller repertoire of established strategies for adapting to the demands they face.

Second, it is always important to remain aware of the multigenerational implications of our discussion of family developmental transitions. A truly systemic perspective on family development must be mindful of the multiple generations that comprise the family system. Each generation is interdependently connected to others, and each generation experiences developmental transitions and change.

As such, change in one generation has reverberating impact on the stresses and strains felt in the other generations of the family. A multigenerational developmental perspective encourages sensitivity to this fact.

Take, for example, an elder generation of a family that is dealing with the premature removal of a spouse from the work force due to a debilitating illness. The couple's family resources may become strained due to increasing health-care needs and reduced income. Such changes may prompt concern from adult children, who respond by making more frequent trips home to help care for the ill parent, contributing to medical costs, or providing emotional support to both the well and the ill parent. This shift in focus to the elder generation may come at a time when the adult children's own families are undergoing developmental changes. Perhaps the oldest child is preparing to leave home and marry, or the youngest child is having a difficult transition to middle school. The needs of these children may remain unmet as resources shift to the elder generation and new strategies are enacted to address their needs. Clearly, the stress within the nuclear family is amplified whenever developmental changes occur in other generations of the family.

If we are to take seriously the notion of life cycle, then we must view the multigenerational family system as moving continually through time as each generation moves through a series of successive stages. There is no clear beginning or end. This cyclical nature of the family life cycle creates a dilemma, however, when it is desirable to discuss the developmental issues associated with each stage of the cycle. How is it possible to discuss discrete stages if the family system experiences many or all stages at the same time? Within this text, this dilemma was resolved by discussing the stages experienced by only the nuclear family rather than the extended family. We punctuate the life cycle of the family, somewhat arbitrarily, by selecting as a starting point the period during late adolescence or early adulthood when the individual exits his or her family of origin. The separation of young adults from the family of origin can be considered the beginning stage of the family life cycle, because this event becomes the foundation for the establishment of the next generation of the family when these young adults marry. The early marriage years in the life cycle are then followed by the parenting years, which include the transition to parenthood, the parenting of young children, and the parenting of adolescents. The parenting years terminate with the launching of children. The postparental family stages involve the family with those issues that adult family members encounter as they move through middle adulthood and old age.

The key to understanding how developments during these stages affect families is to keep in mind that all families have tasks that they must execute. The execution of these tasks must be tailored to the family's particular stage in its life cycle. Transitional periods in the cycle are stressful because it is during these times that strategies and rules for the execution of tasks must be altered. In this way, the changing abilities and needs of individuals and families over time are among the key factors influencing family interactional patterns and dynamics. Furthermore, family transitions and family patterns of interaction are both integrally related to family functioning. When transitions are successfully mastered, family functioning is enhanced and family members carry fewer vertical stressors with them into subsequent life-cycle stages and transitions.

CHAPTER 6

The Transition from Adolescence to Adulthood

Chapter Overview

The concept of individuation is introduced in this chapter to describe the tasks associated with moving from adolescence to young adulthood. Although individuation is generally viewed as a lifelong developmental process, it is during adolescence and young adulthood that the need to establish the self as separate and distinct from significant others takes on added importance. It is during this developmental period that individuals attempt to redefine their relationships with parents and other caretakers in terms of greater equality and self-sufficiency. However, their strivings for greater autonomy occur in a context of ongoing emotional connection to parents and other significant adults who remain their primary sources of encouragement and support.

Successful individuation and the transition from adolescence to young adulthood are influenced by the family's level of differentiation. When a family's patterns of interaction support the young adult's bids for autonomy and self-sufficiency and their needs for connectedness and support, individuation is enhanced. When the family's patterns of interaction are skewed in one direction toward either too much connectedness or too much separateness, the individuation process is inhibited.

The successful resolution of separation–individuation during later adolescence and early adulthood is defined by the establishment of (1) a clear sense of personal identity; and (2) the capacity for intimacy with others. Failure to negotiate separation–individuation successfully during this developmental period has been associated with a host of interpersonal and psychological problems, including abuse of drugs and alcohol, eating disorders, suicide, running away from home, and involvement in cults, to name only some.

The Transition from Adolescence to Adulthood

Examination of the family life cycle begins by considering how individuals negotiate the transition from adolescence to young adulthood. The developmental pressures experienced by young adults center on their need to evolve a mature identity and make commitments to adult roles and responsibilities. To accomplish these tasks, individuals must achieve an "adequate separation" from the family of origin (Carter & McGoldrick, 2005b). This adequate separation enables young adults to exercise control over their lives and take personal responsibility for the consequences of their decisions and behaviors (Williamson, 1981).

The developmental demands arising during this transition period raise a number of important questions that will be explored in this chapter. For instance, how do young adults successfully leave home to begin caring for themselves, supporting themselves financially, and establishing their own residences? How do young adults successfully negotiate the change in their relationship with their parents from one of parent–child dependency to adult-to-adult mutuality? How do young adults establish a clear sense of self or personal identity? Finally, how do young adults develop the necessary interpersonal skills and confidence to be successful in developing satisfying intimate relationships with friends, dating partners, and prospective marital mates?

The answers to these questions are complex and involve many factors. This chapter will examine the relationship between family system dynamics and the individual's development during late adolescence and early adulthood. The goal is to consider how the family either aids or interferes with the young person's emergence from adolescence to young adulthood. It is important, however, to bear in mind that the family of origin, while having an important impact on development, is only one of many factors influencing how individuals mature from adolescence into adulthood. Other factors, such as cultural norms and subcultural values, particularly as they affect gender-role socialization, also influence how males and females develop during this period. The temperament of each individual; his or her physical, intellectual, and cognitive abilities; the quality of peer relationships; the availability of role models and mentors; and the kinds of supports available in the community all play a part in determining how each individual's development will proceed.

The Individuation Process

The model presented here emphasizes the relationship between individual development and family system dynamics. A central concept within this model is that of **individuation**, a developmental process through which a person comes to see the self as separate and distinct within the relational (familial, social, cultural) context (Karpel, 1976). The degree to which individuation has occurred is the degree to which the person no longer experiences himself or herself as fusing with others in personal relationships. Defining characteristics of fusion include the dissolving of ego boundaries between the self and the other, the inability to establish an "I" within a "we," and a high degree of identification with and dependence on others (Anderson & Sabatelli, 1990; Karpel, 1976).

Individuation can be thought of as a process through which an individual builds a background of knowledge about the self in relationship to others. The individuation concept has much in common with Bowen's (1978) notion of self-differentiation. Both concepts emphasize the individual's ability to develop and maintain a coherent sense of self that is separate and distinct from others

(Anderson & Sabatelli, 1990; Karpel, 1976). As was noted in Chapter 4, individuals always operate within a social, interpersonal context. Within this context, there is a universal demand to negotiate a balance between one's own self-interests and the interests of significant others. Both the individuation and self-differentiation concepts emphasize the extent to which a person can interact intimately with others without becoming fused, dependent, or overidentified with them. Well-individuated persons can remain in emotional contact with significant others and also dare to be different, express a personal point of view, show a unique ability, or seek fulfillment of a personal need.

However, the individuation concept differs from Bowen's (1978) notion of self-differentiation in one important way. Individuation is thought of as a universal, lifelong developmental process (Cohler & Geyer, 1982; Grotevant & Cooper, 1986; Guisinger & Blatt, 1994). When conceived of as an ongoing developmental process, individuation accounts for the progressive changes that occur over time in each individual's abilities to express his or her individuality. For children, individuation is most closely associated with the parent–child relationship, but as individuals mature, individuation must be thought of as operating in any relationship with a significant other. This might include relationships between husbands and wives, between friends, between employers and employees, and between teachers and students (Allison & Sabatelli, 1988). In each adult relationship, it is essential to balance needs for affiliation, closeness, or intimacy with those for distance, separateness, and individuality.

To progress developmentally, each individual must successfully balance, in an age-appropriate manner, autonomy (self as individual) and interdependence (self as related to other). This age-appropriate balance of separateness and connectedness enables children to exercise greater control over their lives, which, in turn, enables relationships with parents and other family members to be gradually reconstituted on a more mutual and adult level. The symbiotic, fused attachment that characterizes the parent–child relationship during early infancy (Mahler, Pine, & Bergman, 1975) evolves toward a dependent, symmetrical parent–child relationship during childhood followed by a progressively more independent and mutual relationship during adolescence and early adulthood (Anderson & Sabatelli, 1990). At each of these successive periods, the child's different needs for autonomy must be balanced with the corresponding need for emotional support and affiliation. This is best accomplished in a parent–child relationship characterized by an authoritatively firm but gentle pattern of discipline that allows the child age-appropriate freedom and autonomy (Baumrind, 1991b).

Indicators of Mature Individuation in Early Adulthood

The individuation process is characterized by progressive shifts in the individual's ability to take personal responsibility throughout adolescence and into adulthood. The ability is reflected in each individual's **functional, financial,** and **psychological autonomy** from the family of origin (Arnett, 2000, 2006; Steinberg, 2005; Herman, Dornbusch, Herron, & Herting, 1997).

During adolescence, individuals strive to renegotiate their relationships with their parents and other members of the family to achieve greater autonomy and self-sufficiency. However, residues of dependency often remain. Adolescents will, for example, exercise more control over how they dress and where and with whom they spend their time. In contrast, they may remain dependent on their parents for emotional support, advice about relationships, or occupational choices (Sabatelli & Anderson, 1991; Steinberg, 2005). Often adolescents continue to rely on the family for financial assistance with clothing purchases or educational expenses.

During young adulthood, these lingering dependencies must be altered if individuals are to succeed at managing the demands of adult roles and responsibilities. Young adults must become more functionally autonomous, that is, capable of managing and directing their own personal affairs without help from family members. Functional autonomy is furthered by the achievement of a sufficient degree of financial autonomy and self-sufficiency (Gavazzi, Sabatelli, & Reese, 1999).

Adolescents also need to renegotiate their psychological autonomy with their families. This means that they must take control of their own lives while remaining intimately connected to others. When psychological bonds are not adjusted in age-appropriate ways, an individual feels excessively controlled by the family or becomes highly emotional and reactive. This, in turn, interferes with the person's ability to make clear and rational choices about the future. Exercising control over our lives, in other words, means that we feel free to act without worrying about what our family will say or think about the choices we have made.

Reworking our psychological connection to the family of origin affects the emotions, cognitions, and behaviors that accompany our efforts to act in a personally responsible manner. One important indicator of individuation is the degree to which young adults are emotionally dependent on or emotionally reactive to the family. **Emotional dependence** can be defined as the excessive need for approval, closeness, and emotional support (Gavazzi et al., 1997). **Emotional reactivity** refers here to the degree of conflictual feelings, including excessive guilt, anxiety, mistrust, resentment, and anger, toward one's parents (Bowen, 1978). Whether emotional dependence or reactivity interferes with our abilities to exercise appropriate control over our lives depends on the cognitions and behaviors that accompany the emotions that we experience. For instance, needing the approval of one's parents or feeling excessively loyal or obligated to one's parents may be accompanied by thoughts such as "I must make my parents proud of me," or "my parents' wishes are more important than my own." These thoughts, in turn, can influence our choice of behaviors. Ultimately, it is how we respond behaviorally to our feelings and thoughts that determine our success at reworking our psychological ties to our families and becoming appropriately individuated.

Because individuation is a lifelong process, it is important that parents and other adults continually encourage children to act in accordance with their own unique potentials and competencies. However, at earlier stages of development, when emotional dependencies are strong, children are more likely to conform to their parents' rather than to their own wishes. The relationship between parents and children throughout adolescence and early adulthood may continue to evoke demands for conformity to the parents' wishes. However, these demands and the accompanying feelings of guilt, loyalty, obligation, or anger generally become less intense during early adulthood. Adolescents and young adults are generally more capable of acting in accordance with their own personal opinions, needs, and desires than are younger children.

The well-individuated adult, under conditions of conflict or demands for conformity, chooses to respond to feelings of guilt, loyalty, obligation, or anger by behaving in ways that promote intimacy while allowing for personal authority or fulfillment (Williamson, 1981, 1982). For example, in response to a parent's disapproving remark about a new hairstyle, an adult child may decide not to lash out in anger even though this may be the initial emotional reaction. Instead, he or she may point out to the parent the hurt this comment has caused, or acknowledge the anger and hurt internally while simply pointing out that styles have changed and that he or she is quite pleased with it. Either of these options maintains the personal relationship and allows for further interaction.

Less individuated individuals respond behaviorally in ways that interfere with their ability to make mature decisions and that threaten or damage family relationships. Such behaviors include reacting to feelings and cognitions by attacking the family or acting defensively. For example, an adult child could counter the criticism of his or her hairstyle by telling the mother that her hair looks even worse. Such a response, however, may result in both the child and the parent getting more upset or defensive. The result may be development of a pattern of attack–counterattack or emotional distance that will jeopardize the personal relationship.

Another less individuated response is one of rebellion or defiance of parental wishes. In this case, individuals respond to conflicts by behaviorally retreating, or cutting off, from the family system (Bowen, 1978). The family's demand for unending loyalty or its hostile rejection of the member may leave the separated individual no other recourse but to seek functional or financial autonomy at the expense of connectedness and intimacy. The irony here, of course, is that, while the individual may appear to be in control of his or her life, it is the emotions and the response to these emotions that are really dictating the life course.

Finally, less individuated responses can include conforming to parents' wishes at the expense of personal autonomy and individuality. In this instance, the individual's need for autonomy is sacrificed in response to the family system's demand for fusion, loyalty, and connectedness. This can lead to a **pseudo-individuation**, in which expressions of individuality appear to be successful but instead leave the person dependent on the family. Such individuals have difficulty making commitments to others outside of the family or assuming age-appropriate responsibilities. They also may tend to avoid conflicts, view themselves in need of others' continued assistance, call on family members for approval and support, and, in doing so, appear to remain functionally and financially dependent on the family (Anderson & Sabatelli, 1990).

Of course, for most young adults, the individuation process inevitably proceeds. Most will eventually develop the ability to exercise control over their lives and remain intimately connected to their families. That is, most young adults develop a sufficient level of functional, financial, and psychological independence to proceed through subsequent stages of personal development. They leave home, establish their own separate households, enter into new and meaningful personal relationships, and assume various other adult responsibilities. However, to the extent that individuation efforts are impeded, these and other developmental tasks will be more difficult to master. To understand how individuation efforts become disrupted, we must examine the dynamics operating within the young adult's family of origin, particularly the family's level of differentiation.

The Individuation Process and Family Differentiation

If individual development is viewed as occurring in the context of family development, the family must be thought of as a significant codeterminant of the individuation process. Family differentiation can be thought of as the essential counterpart to the individuation process. While individuation is conceived as an individual developmental process, differentiation is considered an interactional property of the family system. As was noted in Chapter 4, **differentiation** refers to the manner in which the family's boundaries, emotional climate, and identity tasks are managed. In well-differentiated families, an optimal tolerance for individuality allows family members to be recognized as having unique individual characteristics and to act in appropriately autonomous ways. This helps to create a family emotional environment in which members feel supported and encouraged to be themselves.

Poorly differentiated families display either a low **tolerance for individuality** or a low **tolerance for intimacy** (Farley, 1979). When tolerance for individuality is absent, this is manifested in distance-regulation patterns that are enmeshing and interfere with the abilities of individuals to express their needs for autonomy and individuality. The boundaries between members and subsystems are blurred, and members are fused with one another. As a result, the ability to act autonomously and express individuality is inhibited.

The absence of tolerance for intimacy is manifested in patterns and dynamics that communicate little respect, regard, and concern for individual family members. In these systems, family members' bids for autonomy are permitted, but their needs for support, responsiveness, and mutual-relatedness go unmet (Minuchin, 1974; Stierlin, 1981). Such patterns of interaction inhibit individuation in that they foster emotional reactivity rather than emotional relatedness. The choices and commitments individuals make can become heavily influenced by anger and resentment felt toward the family of origin. Individuals from emotionally deprived systems may also become preoccupied with seeking and winning the approval and regard that they lacked in the family of origin. Such needs may interfere with the ability to make mature and rational commitments to adult roles and responsibilities.

As noted, the family's strategies for regulating individuality and intimacy are, in part, determined by its intergenerational legacy. A parent's own unresolved individuation often engenders unconscious attempts to reenact unresolved conflicts in the family of procreation. The interactional patterns of separateness and connectedness and the tolerance for intimacy established by parents define the context within which children must master their own age-appropriate level of individuation. Parents whose own individuation has been curtailed are more likely to establish interactional patterns that include intense emotional cutoffs, triangles, coalitions, conflicts, or family projection processes (Allison & Sabatelli, 1988, 1990). The presence of such patterns has consistently been found to be associated with adolescent adjustment difficulties (Bomar & Sabatelli, 1996; Bray, Adams, Getz, & Stovall, 2001; Steinberg, 2005). Some of these difficulties will be examined in more detail in a later section of this chapter.

In contrast, when the parents' own individuation has been more or less successful, they are more likely to establish patterns and dynamics within the family that enhance rather than inhibit individuation (Stierlin, 1981). The genuine respect and concern that parents feel for their children enable them to act in a generative way. Children are encouraged to explore their own interests, and parents take pride in the accomplishments of their children. When the time comes, during adolescence and early adulthood, parents are able to support their children's autonomous behaviors and expressions of individuality.

During adolescence and early adulthood, the family must respond to the increased pull toward individuation as the young adult's essential movement is away from the family toward the wider social environment. The family's responsiveness to these separation efforts will ensure an ease of transition away from the family and promote a comfortable interdependence among generations. Families with a low tolerance for individuality are more likely to initiate responses associating individuation with disloyalty, thereby inhibiting successful separation. Families with a low tolerance for intimacy may push young adults into premature separation before they are psychologically ready, thereby engendering feelings of rejection or alienation.

The Individuation Process and Subsequent Development and Adjustment

The individuation process influences each individual's present and future development. During early adulthood, two principal indicators of the relative success of this developmental process are the extent to which the individual has established (1) a coherent personal identity; and (2) the capacity for intimate relationships.

Identity Development

A fundamental assumption of most theories of life-span development is that the resolution of adult developmental tasks requires the formation of a mature **identity** during late adolescence and early adulthood. For instance, Erikson's (1963, 1968) theory of psychosocial development asserts that the establishment of a secure identity provides the foundation for the commitments one makes to a personal ideology, occupation, and lifestyle (Erikson, 1968).

Identity development during early and later adolescence is influenced by a number of factors. The emergence of a mature ego contributes to personal identity by providing a framework of meaning that the individual subjectively applies to experience (Marcia, 1980). The consolidation of maturing cognitive abilities is also associated with identity formation. Adolescents acquire the ability to view themselves, their parents, and the larger society more critically. Adolescents also become capable of taking multiple perspectives, which contributes to self-understanding by allowing them to consider new roles and view themselves as they are seen by significant others (Steinberg, 2005).

Finally, identity is further enhanced by the adolescent's movement into the peer group. Peer relationships provide individuals with opportunities to experiment with new roles and responsibilities and engage in same- and opposite-sex relationships. These opportunities to explore different identities provide individuals with information that is vital to the consolidation of the mature identity that is carried into adulthood (Steinberg, 2005).

Individuation, Family Dynamics, and Identity Formation

Within the traditional developmental perspectives it is assumed that adolescents must develop a sufficient level of autonomy, or a "good-enough" level of individuation, from parents for these identity-enhancing changes to occur. Autonomy is viewed as requiring the rejection of parental identifications and authority, which in turn fosters the adolescent's movement into the peer group and the wider society. This movement facilitates the adolescent's search for such factors as new personal values, self-knowledge, and career choices (Erikson, 1968; Josselson, 1980; Marcia, 1966, 1976). Identity is thus linked to a break with or separation from the parental family (Arnett, 2000; Steinberg, 2005).

Traditional life-span perspectives, therefore, view individuation as (1) a synonym for autonomy; and (2) a prerequisite for identity development. When these assumptions are examined from a perspective that integrates individual and family development, however, two distinct issues arise. One is the exclusive focus on autonomy as the principal indicator of individuation. Clearly, a more balanced view is achieved when autonomy is considered as one polarity in the ongoing dialectical process of individuation. In this view, identity is defined as the distinctions the self makes against the backdrop of relationships with significant others. Identity is accomplished, therefore, not by breaking the psychological and emotional ties with one's parents and family, but by renegotiating these relationships. Dependent parent–child relationships evolve toward adult-to-adult mutuality and interdependence. Emphasis is placed as much on ongoing relatedness as it is on separation and disengagement.

The second issue is that traditional developmental perspectives do not account for the family context within which these changes occur. The family system, over the course of its development and especially during the period of adolescence, must establish interactional strategies that foster the individuality of its members. From this vantage point, the family of origin is not a constant from which separation occurs but a fluid, changing context within which the level of tolerance for individuality can vary from rigid and restrictive to open and responsive (Allison & Sabatelli, 1988).

Both parents and adolescents undergo changes that must be accommodated by other family members. Parents must relinquish physical and psychological control over their children while transforming their own roles and identities (Stierlin, 1981). Adolescents and young adults must renegotiate the level of connectedness with the family and master the progressive changes in their evolving identities. These changes require that the asymmetrical patterns of authority present in parent–child relationships during early and middle childhood gradually become reorganized on a more mutual and symmetrical basis (Bomar & Sabatelli, 1996; Grotevant & Cooper, 1986). It is the relative success of the renegotiation of these parent–child positions vis-à-vis one another that is hypothesized to be related to the young adult's personal adjustment.

The Capacity for Intimacy

Successful emergence from childhood into early adulthood reflects not only the development of a personal identity but the capacity for intimacy in one's relationships. Traditional life-span developmental theories such as Erikson's (1968) have generally depicted the capacity for intimacy as developing in young adulthood following the establishment of a clear sense of identity during adolescence. In Erikson's (1968) framework, **intimacy** is defined as the "capacity to commit oneself to concrete affiliations and partnerships and to develop the ethical strength to abide by such commitments even though they may call for significant sacrifices and compromises" (p. 263). Further, "it is only after a reasonable sense of identity has been established that real intimacy with the other sex (or for that matter with any other person) is possible" (Erikson, 1968, p. 95). The implication is that mastering the task of establishing intimacy occurs after the establishment of a sense of identity, primarily in one's peer relationships.

Here again, the role of the family is deemphasized as the major thrust of development is assumed to be directed outside the family toward the wider social system and one's extrafamilial peer relationships. Although it is undoubtedly true that young adults' primary developmental movement is toward the external social environment, this does not necessarily have to occur at the expense of ongoing relatedness to the family of origin. Furthermore, such a view minimizes the role of the family in providing the basic modeling and interpersonal skills necessary for establishing close relationships with others.

Much as the family's tolerance for individuality either facilitates or hinders the young adult's development of a sense of identity, so, too, does the family's tolerance for intimacy either foster or inhibit the individual's capacity to establish intimate relationships. When the family's tolerance for intimacy is low, family members' bids for autonomy may be permitted, but their needs for support, responsiveness, and mutual relatedness are likely to go unmet (Minuchin, 1974; Stierlin, 1994).

In Chapter 4, it was noted that individuals leave their families of origin with a set of expectations and responsibilities toward others based on their particular family experiences. When the family's emotional environment leaves individuals feeling abandoned, rejected, isolated, or deprived, this legacy is then carried over into their future close relationships. As young adults, such individuals may experience considerable ambivalence about making intimate commitments, fearing further rejection or abandonment. Alternatively, they may enter relationships with strong dependency needs and seek to have past injustices righted in the present relationship. Should current partners fail in meeting these unresolved needs, which is often the case, the outcome may again be conflict, disappointment, frustration, and ambivalence about committing to other intimate relationships.

In contrast, young adults who have experienced a familial environment in which the tolerance for intimacy is high are more likely to carry a positive family legacy into future relationships. Those who have experienced a legacy of affiliation, nurturance, equity, affection, and support are in a much better position to enter into new relationships with the trust and openness necessary to make new commitments possible.

To summarize briefly, the successful resolution of separation–individuation during later adolescence and young adulthood is defined by the establishment of a clear identity and the capacity for intimacy with others. These tasks can be viewed as reciprocal rather than linear processes. The clearer one's sense of self, the more one is able to risk involvement in an intimate relationship with another. Truly intimate connections to others enable us, in turn, to evolve a clearer and more mature sense of self.

The capacity to view the self as separate and to remain in emotional contact with the other is a dynamic tension that operates in all relationships. In the family of origin, the capacity to establish effective strategies for managing this dynamic tension between separateness and connectedness fosters the young adult's individuation efforts. In true systemic fashion, the young adult's level of individuation, in turn, influences the capacity of future generations of the family system to balance their tolerance for individuality with their tolerance for intimacy.

Individuation Difficulties and the Problems of Youth

A number of psychological and relationship problems are related to a breakdown in the individuation process during adolescence and young adulthood. In this section, several of these more common and contemporary problems are examined. It should be noted that we will not review all of the potential problems that young adults face. Instead, we will highlight the research that has established a relationship between selected problem behaviors and the family's strategies for managing its members' separation–individuation efforts.

In general, problem behaviors in youth are tied to the dilemma created when the young person's need to evolve a mature identity is blocked by the presence of individuation-inhibiting patterns and dynamics within the family system. When confronted with this developmental bind, youth are likely to become highly anxious. They may attempt to solve their dilemma by behaving in dysfunctional or self-destructive ways. Therefore, one way of framing dysfunctional behavior is to view it as an attempt by the individual to find a solution to a dilemma that arises when his or her developmental needs are blocked by the family's interactional strategies.

When the family's strategies inhibit individuation, or overly control the young adult's identity, the young adult will generally seek to solve this developmental bind in one of three ways. Some will simply fuse with the family, allowing the family to control their identities. In this instance, the young adult sacrifices individuality and the freedom to move developmentally beyond the family's domain of influence. Others rebel, separating from the family and reactively choosing an identity that clearly distinguishes the self from the family. In yet other instances, the anxiety engendered by this developmental bind may lead the youth to attempt solutions that are compromises between leaving and staying at home. In these situations, the attempted solutions become part of the problem (Watzlawick, Weakland, & Fisch, 1974). These young adults may behave in ways that enable them to appear as if they are controlling their individuality, but, paradoxically, they also remain dependent on the family. These behaviors, therefore, interfere with the youth's ability to manage life independently. In other words, such solutions can have a serious impact not only on the young person's present functioning but also on the mastery of subsequent life-cycle transitions and tasks.

The Abuse of Drugs and Alcohol

Both substance dependence (also referred to as addiction) and substance abuse have come to be referred to as "psychoactive substance use disorders." Dependence on a psychoactive substance such as cocaine, marijuana, amphetamines, heroin, or alcohol can be defined as (1) the persistent use of the substance; and (2) the experiencing of a cluster of cognitive, behavioral, and physiological symptoms that indicate that the person has impaired control of the substance use and continues to use the substance despite adverse consequences. Dependence on the substance may include such physiological indicators as tolerance and withdrawal symptoms. Tolerance refers to the need for increased amounts of the substance to achieve the desired effect or to a diminished effect with regular use of the same amount. Withdrawal symptoms (e.g., morning shakes, malaise relieved by substance intake) occur when the substance use is stopped or decreased. Substance abuse, in contrast to dependence, refers to a less intense pattern of behaviors and symptoms that involves continued use despite knowledge that the substance use is causing social, occupational, psychological, or physical problems. A problem with substance abuse might also be indicated when the individual continues to use the substance in physically hazardous situations such as when driving a car or using dangerous equipment (American Psychiatric Association, 2000).

The prevalence of illicit drug and alcohol usage among adolescents has varied considerably over time. The percentage of youth who used these substances at some point in their lives reached a peak in 1979, then declined through the 1980s before hitting a low in 1991 and 1992. A new period of increased usage followed during which the proportions of youth reporting use of any illicit drug increased from 18 percent to 29 percent among eighth graders, from 31 percent to 45 percent among tenth graders, and from 44 percent to 54 percent among twelfth graders

(Johnson, O'Mally, & Bachman, 2001). Over the past four years, these rates have tended to decline slightly and then stabilize with small variations of usage among different drugs (Mason, 2004).

The most recent data from the National Survey on Drug Use and Health (Substance Abuse and Mental Health Services Administration, 2003) indicate, for instance, that the percentage of teens who reported ever using marijuana declined from 21.9 percent in 2001 to 20.6 percent in 2002. However, the lifetime usage of other illicit drugs increased between 2001 and 2002 from 2.3 percent to 2.7 percent (cocaine) and 9.6 percent to 11.2 percent (nonmedically used prescription drugs).

The survey also noted the importance of age when considering adolescent substance use patterns. The percentage of youth who reported illicit drug (heroin, cocaine, cannabis, hallucinogens, stimulants) or alcohol dependence or abuse in the past year increased with age. Among twelve- to thirteen-year-olds the rate was about 2 percent, but it rose for fourteen- to fifteen-year-olds (8 percent) and sixteen- to seventeen-year-olds (17 percent) before peaking with eighteen- to twenty-year-olds (22 percent). About 29 percent of all adolescents between the ages of twelve and twenty reported using alcohol in the past month. Of these, 19 percent were binge drinkers (five or more drinks at least once in the last thirty days) and 6 percent were heavy drinkers (five or more drinks on at least five of the last thirty days). The highest rates of binge drinking (50 percent) and heavy drinking (20 percent) were among twenty-one-year-olds. Those enrolled in college were more likely (19 percent) to be heavy drinkers than those not enrolled in college (13 percent). Next to alcohol, marijuana continues to be the most frequently abused substance, followed by prescription drugs (pain relievers, tranquilizers, stimulants, sedatives), cocaine, hallucinogens (LSD, PCP, peyote, mescaline, ecstasy), and inhalants (amyl nitrate, cleaning fluids, gasoline, paint, glue) (SAMHSA, 2003).

Alcohol and drug abuse among adolescents and young adults is generally recognized as a multidimensional problem, including such factors as negative peer influences, poor school performance, having been a victim of crime or violence, and neighborhood disorganization (poverty, crime, drug trafficking) (Hawkins, Catalano, & Miller, 1992; Kilpatrick, Aciero, Saunders, Resnick, Best, & Schnurr, 2000; Mason, 2004). However, the family, and in particular, a breakdown in the family's separation–individuation process, has been identified as a critical factor (Bray, Adams, Getz, & Baer, 2000; Bray, Adams, Getz, & Stovall, 2001; Levine, 1985; Spotts & Shontz, 1985; Vakalahi, 2002; van Schoor & Beach, 1993). Families with substance abusing adolescents have been found to have high levels of conflict (Bray, Adams, Getz, & Baer, 2001; Hawkins, Herrenkohl, Farrington, Brewer, Catalano, & Harachi, 1998). These families also have been identified as having fears related to separation, perhaps due to previously unresolved deaths or other losses (Kaminer, 1991; Levine, 1985). The marital relationship when intact is often conflicted, and the adolescent's substance abusing behavior can serve to keep the focus off the couple's unresolved conflicts (Bray, Adams, Getz, & Baer, 2001; Bray et al., 2000; Todd & Selekman, 1989). One or both parents are likely to have a history of alcohol or drug abuse as well (Hawkins et al., 1992; Kilpatrick et al., 2000). Parent–child interactions have been described as lacking closeness (Bray, Adams, Getz, & Baer, 2001; Hawkins et al., 1998). Permissiveness, poor discipline, and a lack of parental involvement and monitoring are common (Bogenschneider, Wu, Raffaelli, & Tsay, 1998; Hawkins et al., 1992; Mason, 2004; Vakalahi, 2002). A lack of perceived family and parental support are serious risk factors that predict adolescent substance abuse (Hawkins et al., 1992; Kilpatrick et al., 2000; Wills, Resko, Ainette, & Mendozza, 2004).

The patterns and dynamics present within these families, in other words, tend to be characterized by excessive conflict, tension in the marriage, cross-generational coalitions, and the use of triangulation to manage conflicts. The substance abusing youth in these families are often caught up in the bind of needing to individuate from a system that does not offer optimal conditions for this to occur. As noted earlier, successful individuation occurs when the young person can gradually assume greater independence and personal responsibility while remaining connected to a context of close and supportive relationships with parents and other family members (Youniss & Smoller, 1985). In this context, the young adult's substance abuse has been viewed as a form of both pseudo-individuation and protection for the family (Stanton, 1977; van Schoor & Beach, 1993). Abusing drugs appears to be a form of rebellion against the family and its values, that is, it is an expression of individuality. At the same time, however, these behaviors keep the young adult dependent and, therefore, unable to separate.

Consequently, the use of chemical substances may help the addict to maintain some emotional distance from the family while remaining enmeshed in the system. Under the influence of the substance, the young adult can become assertive toward the family; stand up for the self; and express autonomy, freedom, and individuality. However, these expressions are easily discounted by the family as being caused by the drug, not by the young adult (Stanton & Todd, 1982).

In sum, the abuse of drugs and alcohol among youth can be thought of as a compromise, but dysfunctional, solution to their needs to separate sufficiently from individuation-inhibiting families. The use of substances allows youth to maintain some control over their individuality and identity. The repeated failure to maintain an independent lifestyle or succeed in the outside world that goes hand in hand with the abuse of substances, however, keeps the young adult closely involved with the family. The use of substances, in this regard, allows the young adult to postpone the process of individuating from the family, and protects the family from changing or having to face the prospect of another separation and loss.

Eating Disorders

The main types of eating disorders are anorexia nervosa, bulimia, and binge eating disorder. The peak period of onset is during adolescence and early adulthood (Becker, Grinspoon, Klibanski, & Herzog, 1999; Lewinsohn, Striegel-Moore, & Seeley, 2000). Females make up the vast majority of cases.

Anorexia nervosa means a nervous loss of appetite. In this sense, the name of the syndrome is somewhat inaccurate, for those who are afflicted by anorexia nervosa do not necessarily suffer from a lack of appetite, but they deliberately and willfully limit their food intake in spite of desires to eat (Dwyer, 1985). The process of eating becomes an obsession. The person becomes preoccupied with food, and unusual eating habits may develop. Avoiding food or meals, eating only small portions of food, or carefully measuring and portioning food are common (Becker et al., 1999). Individuals who were previously thought by their parents to be good, compliant, successful, and gratifying children often become angry, stubborn, negativistic, and distrustful. They often claim not to need help and care, and become insistent on their right to eat as they wish and be as thin as they want to be (Dwyer, 1985). Common symptoms of anorexia nervosa include (1) resistance to maintaining body weight at or above minimally normal weight for age and height; (2) intense fear of gaining weight or becoming fat, despite being underweight; (3) disturbances in the ways one's body weight is perceived (individuals see themselves as overweight even though they are very thin); (4) strong influence of body weight and shape on one's self-evaluation; (5) denial of the seriousness of the weight loss; and (6) infrequent or absent menstrual periods (American Psychiatric Association Work Group on Eating Disorders, 2000).

The occurrence of anorexia nervosa appears to have increased, especially in the past twenty-five years, when rates have more than doubled. Recent lifetime estimates of its prevalence range between .5 percent and 3.7 percent of all females. Only 5 percent to 15 percent of those who suffer from anorexia or bulimia are male (National Institute of Mental Health [NIMH], 2007). **Bulimia** is a pattern of behavior characterized by the recurrent episodes of binge eating followed by purging behavior (e.g., abuse of laxatives, self-induced vomiting, enemas). Those suffering from bulimia often experience a lack of control over eating during the episode. They generally recognize their binge eating as abnormal, and often experience depression and self-criticism following binges (Root, Fallon, & Friedrich, 1986). Like those suffering from anorexia nervosa, self-evaluation of bulimics is unduly influenced by body shape and weight (American Psychiatric Association, 2000).

In contrast to anorexics, who maintain a lower than normal body weight, the binging–purging cycle of bulimics means that they maintain an average or above average body weight. Thus, bulimia and anorexia nervosa are generally considered to be separate and distinct syndromes. However, both groups also have been found to share many of the same family background factors (Emmett, 1985; Horesh et al., 1996; Root et al., 1986; Strober & Humphrey, 1987).

Binge eating disorder is a newly recognized condition that affects millions of Americans (NIMH, 2007). Individuals with binge eating disorder frequently eat large amounts of food while feeling a loss of control over their eating. The experience is often accompanied by feelings of depression, guilt, and disgust (USDHHS, 2000). The overeating or binging usually does not stop until the person is uncomfortably full. This disorder is different from binge–purge syndrome (bulimia) because people with binge eating disorder usually do not purge afterward by vomiting or using laxatives. The disorder usually begins in late adolescence or in the early twenties, often coming soon after significant weight loss from dieting (USDHHS, 2000). Current statistics suggest that as many as 3.5 percent of women and 2 percent of men will develop binge-eating disorder at some point in their lives, making this disorder more common than either anorexia or bulimia (Hudson, Hiripi, Pope, & Kessler, 2007). However, because less is known about the causes of this disorder, much of the discussion of family dynamics that follows will focus on anorexia and bulimia.

Most theories addressing the issue of anorexia (extreme weight loss) or bulimia (cycles of consuming large quantities of food followed by purging) identify numerous factors related to these increasingly common disorders typically found among young women. These include cultural factors such as a preoccupation with food and thinness (Emmett, 1985; Pike, 1995), biological predispositions (Strober, Freeman, Lampert, Diamond, & Kaye, 2000), and early trauma or unresolved psychological conflicts (Piazza, Piazza, & Rollins, 1980; Schwartz, Thompson, & Johnson, 1985). Psychological formulations emphasize the young woman's need for a sense of personal control; her incomplete sense of self; her preoccupation with her appearance and perfectionism; and her feelings of loneliness, abandonment, and unworthiness (Emmett, 1985).

Theories and research that have examined family factors often find family problems related to differentiation and individuation. The boundary between the family and the wider community is often rigid, with members protective of one another but isolated from the rest of society (Humphrey, 1986; Roberto, 1987). Loyalty to the family comes to be equated with maintaining the appearance of a harmonious, conflict-free home environment (Root et al., 1986). These families have been described as enmeshed and yet disengaged, meaning that they can vacillate between extremes of overinvolvement and abandonment (Humphrey, 1986; Meyer & Russell, 1998; Smolak & Levine, 1993). Often, conflicts between parents, siblings, or extended family members are avoided or triangled onto the young woman, who comes to serve an important role in protecting family members from unresolved issues. Family harmony and protection take precedence over individual members' needs for autonomy (Frank & Jackson, 1996; Minuchin, Rosman, & Baker, 1978; Stierlin & Weber, 1989).

Bulimic and anoretic families have been found to hold high expectations and standards of perfection for their children in such areas as academics, athletics, appearance, and fitness. These families, in other words, readily participate in defining and controlling the identities of their children. At the same time, true support for these accomplishments is often lacking (Horesh et al., 1996; Humphrey, 1986; Ordman & Kirschenbaum, 1986; Strober & Humphrey, 1987). Thus, in spite of feeling tightly bound to their families, many of these young women report feeling isolated in their families (Humphrey, 1986; Igoin-Apfelbaum, 1985).

When faced with the task of needing to individuate from the family and establish mature identities, these youth often find themselves caught in several developmental binds. Developing a personal identity in a family system that is emotionally invested in controlling and regulating one's identity places an individual in the difficult situation of either complying with the family, thereby giving up control over the self, or rebelling against the family. Such a rebellion carries with it a heavy price: being viewed as betraying the system and failing to repay one's debt and obligation to the family. In addition, because the family system often relies on these young people to stabilize the family when marital conflicts and family tensions arise, individuals are further bound to the family by subtle pressures not to disrupt the family's delicate equilibrium.

The development of problems around food and body image can be seen as a solution to these developmental binds. By not eating or by following the repeated pattern of binging and purging, the young woman is able to maintain the socially prescribed image of feminine attractiveness (thin and petite) and in so doing fulfill the family's expectation to keep up her appearance. Furthermore, her refusal to eat provides her with one clear area of control over her life. By having total and complete control over her body weight, she can assert a sense of separateness and autonomy. In a symbolic sense, the rejection of food and feeding can be seen as a rejection of her role as feeder and nurturer of the family. On the other hand, so long as she refuses to eat, and thus possibly risks her life, she is unable to assume a more adult role. She must remain someone who is dependent on the family and a focus of family concern. In so doing, she continues to play her role in maintaining the family's emotional equilibrium.

In the problems noted above—substance abuse and eating disorders—the family's interactional strategies can be thought of as inhibiting individuation. In each instance, the family appears to be conflicted and emotionally controlling, thereby limiting the young adult's ability to establish some sense of personal control over his or her identity and life. That is, adolescents must attempt to individuate from a system in which separation is discouraged and considered threatening to the family's stability. The problem becomes a solution by offering the young adult some psychological distance while not directly challenging the family's rigid rules for emotional closeness and overinvolvement.

Other problems may develop, however, when the family's strategies interfere with optimal development by prematurely pushing youth to separate from the family. Family systems with a high tolerance for individuality coupled with a low tolerance for intimacy allow children to separate from the family but fail to provide the nurturance, control, and guidance necessary for the development of a constructive identity and a mature capacity for intimacy. An example of a possible result of this problem is juvenile delinquency and antisocial behavior.

Juvenile Delinquency and Antisocial Behavior

Most children test the limits and boundaries set by their parents and other authority figures. As children reach adolescence, some rebelliousness and experimentation is typical. However, some adolescents engage in behaviors that exceed the limits created by organized society. **Juvenile delinquency** is a legal term for an antisocial act committed in violation of a law by a minor. A minor is someone under eighteen years of age. From a juvenile justice perspective, delinquent behavior is divided into two categories: status offenses and delinquency offenses. **Status offenses** are those acts that would not be considered offenses if committed by an adult. They include acts such as truancy (skipping school), running away, alcohol possession, or curfew violations. **Delinquency offenses** involve destruction or theft of property, commission of violent crimes against persons, possession of an illegal weapon, and possession or sale of illegal drugs (Snyder, 2005).

Mental health definitions of antisocial behaviors do not focus on delinquency directly. Instead, diagnostic categories such as oppositional defiance disorder and conduct disorder are emphasized. **Oppositional defiance disorder** is characterized by a pattern of negativistic, hostile, and defiant behavior that often includes losing one's temper; arguing with adults; defying rules; deliberately annoying others; blaming others for one's mistakes or misbehavior; and becoming easily annoyed, angry, resentful, spiteful, or vindictive. **Conduct disorder** refers to repeatedly violating the basic rights of others or major societal norms or rules. It may include aggression toward people or their possessions through bullying, threatening, intimidating, physical assault, mugging, purse snatching, shoplifting, armed robbery, or fire setting. Conduct disorder may also include cruelty toward animals and violations of rules and expectations such as lying and conning others, violating curfews, running away, or truancy from school (American Psychiatric Association, 2000).

Although many may think that juvenile crime is on the rise, it actually has been declining. According to a 2005 report by the Office of Juvenile Justice and Delinquency Prevention, the arrest rate of juveniles declined in 2003 for the ninth consecutive year, falling 48 percent from its peak in 1994. Violent crimes include murder, forcible rape, robbery, and aggravated assault. Juvenile arrest rates for property crimes also declined in 2003, reaching their lowest level in at least three decades. Between 1980 and 2003, juvenile arrest rates for property crimes declined 46 percent. Property crimes include burglary, larceny, motor vehicle theft, and arson. Although these statistics are promising, the reports also make clear that serious challenges remain. For example, between 1980 and 2003 juvenile arrest rates for simple assault increased 269 percent for females and 102 percent for males. During this same period, juvenile arrests for drug abuse violations increased 51 percent for females and 52 percent for males (Snyder, 2005).

As was the case for other adolescent problems, juvenile delinquency is recognized as a multidimensional problem including such factors as an individual's temperament (restless, impulsive), associations with deviant peers, poverty, disadvantaged neighborhoods, and poor school performance (Farrington, 2005; Kroneman, Loeber, & Hipwell, 2004). However, family factors have been shown to be an especially powerful risk factor in the prediction of delinquent and antisocial behaviors. Families of delinquent adolescents have been found to have high levels of family conflict and low levels of family cohesion and bonding (Farrington, 2005). The parents themselves may exhibit antisocial attitudes or behaviors. Backgrounds of parental divorce and separation, sometimes due to arrest or incarceration, are common among delinquent adolescents (Buehler, Anthony, Krishnakumar, Stone, Gerard, & Pemberton, 1997; Hawkins et al., 1998). When both parents are present, the marital relationship is often conflicted and distant. Delinquent youth are also more likely than other youth to have suffered child abuse, sexual abuse, or other kinds of victimization at the hands of family members or others in the community (Egeland, Yates, Appleyard, & van Dulmen, 2002; Hawkins et al., 1998).

The parent–child relationship within delinquent families does not promote the necessary tolerance for individuality and intimacy that is necessary for healthy adolescent development. One of the most significant predictors of delinquency among adolescents is a lack of parental supervision (Smith & Stern, 1997).

This is often described as poor parental involvement and a lack of monitoring of adolescents' activities, associations, and whereabouts (Voydanoff & Donnelly, 1999). Other factors related to adolescent delinquent and antisocial behavior are the use of harsh and punitive discipline and rejecting attitudes toward the young person (Haapasalo & Pokela, 1999; Smith & Stern, 1997).

A parenting strategy characterized by emotional abuse (disinterest, neglect, rejection, separation, and abandonment) and physical maltreatment (physical or sexual abuse, harsh or punitive discipline) that often begins during early childhood (Egeland et al., 2002; Farrington, 2005) may push the adolescent out of the family environment prematurely thereby interfering with the separation–individuation process. The family's individuation-inhibiting environment coupled with other negative influences in the adolescent's social environment are thought to result in hostile and aggressive behaviors being directed toward others or their property.

Other Problems of Forced Individuation

As noted earlier, some families may interfere with adolescents' successful individuation by prematurely pushing them to separate from their families. Stierlin (1981) described such family systems as "expelling," meaning that parents push their children out of the family orbit into autonomy before they may be developmentally ready. In these systems, parents may be preoccupied with themselves, their own projects, or their careers. They may also be occupied by marital conflicts to the extent that their children's needs are ignored or rejected (Gavazzi & Blumenkrantz, 1991; Mirkin, Raskin, & Antognini, 1984). The result is a lack of parental concern, involvement, or limit-setting (Crespi & Sabatelli, 1993; Stierlin, 1994). The child may come to be viewed as a nuisance or a troublemaker who is defiant, unreliable, or simply too mischievous to be controlled (Stierlin, 1981). Realizing that he or she is neither cared for nor wanted, the expelled youth may seek salvation in the peer group, a boyfriend or girlfriend, a gang, or the "runaway culture," which Stierlin defines as a counterculture, a temporary or lasting haven for early separators and runaways. Within the runaway culture, the adolescent finds a large, informal support network estimated to include 1,682,900 American youth who have run away from home or been thrown away (asked or told to leave) each year (Hammer, Finkelhor, & Sedlak, 2002).

When children are prematurely ejected and, therefore, do not experience nurturance, caring, and tenderness within their families, they often do not develop the necessary capacities and interpersonal skills they will need to engage in mature relationships. For example, runaways have been found to suffer from poor self-concepts; experience feelings of inadequacy, anxiety, and impulsivity; and display hostility and overly dependent behaviors (Crespi & Sabatelli, 1993; Jorgenson, Thornburg, & Williams, 1980). In their relationships, they have been described as shallow, manipulative, undersocialized, lacking in empathy for others, and unwilling to delay immediate gratification (Gavazzi & Blumenkrantz, 1991; Stierlin, 1994).

Another possible outcome for adolescents and young adults raised in expelling family systems is involvement in religious cults. Youth who have entered cults often report feeling alienated and isolated from their families, peers, religion, and community (Belitz & Schacht, 1992; Isser, 1988; Wright & Piper, 1986). Their relationships with their fathers are frequently described as weak or nonexistent (Marciano, 1982; Schwartz & Kaslow, 1982). In many instances, fathers were no longer living in the home (Steck, Anderson, & Boylin, 1992), and intense conflict with at least one parent is common (Wright & Piper, 1986).

Many researchers link the young adult's vulnerability to cult conversion to a sense of isolation within the family and an effort to compensate for unfulfilled familial needs (Appel, 1983; Marciano, 1982; Robbins & Anthony, 1982; Wright & Piper, 1986). They become easily influenced by the idealism, unconditional positive acceptance, and reinforcement for their anger against parents and society that the cult provides (Appel, 1983). Self-doubt about his or her abilities and pessimism about the future can undermine the young adult's clear sense of identity, making identification with a cult's powerful "father figure" attractive (Kaslow & Schwartz, 1983; Steck et al., 1992). Therefore, the cult can provide a strong parental figure and a "replacement family" in which the young adult can feel accepted and affirmed. Unfortunately, the price for this acceptance is unquestioning loyalty, conformity, and the loss of a separate sense of self.

Conclusions

This chapter has examined the relationship between a young adult's level of separation–individuation and the family's level of differentiation. The successful negotiation of this relationship during young adulthood requires a family environment that is tolerant of the young person's need for both separateness and autonomy as well as ongoing connection and affiliation. The well-differentiated family environment, in turn, requires its members (especially the parents) to have successfully negotiated their own separation–individuation efforts from their families of origin. Thus, the successful negotiation of separation–individuation during young adulthood is a multigenerational process, with each generation's individuation dependent on the successful individuation of each preceding generation.

The young adult's successful mastery of the task of separation–individuation is evident in the establishment of a clear sense of identity and the capacity for intimate relationships with significant others. Unsuccessful resolution of this transition has been associated with a host of problems, among which are substance abuse, eating disorders, suicidal gestures, running away from home, and involvement in cults. In each of these instances, the problem becomes an attempt to rebalance the individual's demands for both individuality and intimacy within a family system that has difficulty tolerating one or the other of these basic and universal needs. In the case of a too closely connected system, the problem becomes a way to establish distance without really individuating. In the case of an expelling or disconnected system, the youth may seek an alternative supportive environment but not have a sufficiently clear identity or the necessary interpersonal skills with which to establish satisfying intimate relationships.

Key Terms

Anorexia nervosa A condition characterized by the loss of at least 15 percent of body weight, refusal to gain weight, and a distorted body image in which one sees oneself as fat despite being dangerously underweight.

Binge eating disorder A condition characterized by episodes of excessive eating that does not stop until one is uncomfortably full. There are no efforts to purge afterward.

Bulimia A condition characterized by periods of binge eating followed by efforts to purge through self-induced vomiting, excessive exercise, or the abuse of laxatives.

Conduct disorder Repeatedly violating the basic rights of others or major societal rules or norms.

Delinquency offenses Acts that involve destruction or theft of property, violent crimes, or possession or sale of illegal drugs.

Differentiation The degree to which the family's patterns of interaction promote a sense of intimacy while tolerating the individuality of its members.

Emotional dependence The excessive need for approval, closeness, and emotional support.

Emotional reactivity The degree of conflictual feelings, including excessive guilt, anxiety, mistrust, resentment, and anger, toward one's parents or significant others.

Financial autonomy The ability to support oneself with one's own sources of income.

Functional autonomy The ability to manage and direct one's own personal affairs without help from family members.

Identity The basic feelings and knowledge about the self that come from defining one's place in the social order; those qualities and attributes accepted or internalized by the self that become relatively stable and enduring.

Individuation A developmental process through which one comes to see oneself as separate and distinct from others within one's relational (familial, social, cultural) context. The degree to which individuation has occurred is the degree to which the person no longer experiences himself or herself as fusing with others in personal relationships.

Intimacy The capacity to establish close, familiar, personally disclosing, and usually loving or affectionate relationships with others.

Juvenile delinquency A legal term for an antisocial act committed in violation of a law by someone under eighteen years of age.

Oppositional defiance disorder A pattern of negativistic, hostile, or defiant behavior.

Pseudo-individuation Efforts of an individual to separate from the family of origin that appear to have been successful but in actuality leave him or her dependent on the family.

Psychological autonomy The achievement of a sense of personal control over one's life while remaining free to act without worrying about what one's family will say or think about one's choices.

Status offense Acts committed by a young person that would not be considered offenses if committed by an adult (e.g., truancy, alcohol possession).

Tolerance for individuality The degree to which patterns of interaction in the family are enmeshing and interfere with the abilities of individuals to express their needs for autonomy and individuality.

Tolerance for intimacy The degree to which patterns of interaction in the family communicate respect, regard, and concern for individual family members and needs for support, responsiveness, and mutual-relatedness are met.

CHAPTER 7

Mate Selection and Family Development

Chapter Overview

This chapter examines the mate selection process by focusing on (1) the factors that influence our willingness to bond with another; (2) how family of origin experiences and developmental history affect this process; and (3) the factors that influence the patterns and dynamics of interaction found within these intimate relationships. In particular, both stage theories of mate selection and social exchange models of relationship development are discussed. Stage theories are essentially descriptive accounts of the different phases in a relationship's development. The social exchange approach highlights the intrapersonal and interpersonal factors that together account for a relationship's development. Key concepts within an exchange model of relationship development include interpersonal attraction, trust, commitment, love, dependence, and interdependence. The exchange model can also account for how family of origin experiences affect interpersonal attraction and mate selection processes by shaping the values and expectations we bring to relationships. In addition, our developmental history and, in particular, the way separation–individuation has been managed influence our attraction to others and our readiness to accept the responsibilities that accompany intimate adult relationships. The mate selection process can be thought of as a stage in the family life cycle in that the relationship strategies and rules established during this time have an effect on how subsequent family system tasks are managed.

Mate Selection and Family Development

From a contemporary perspective, the lives of young adults unfold in many different ways. Only a generation ago, it was expected that men, on leaving their families of origin, would settle into a job, get married, and raise a family. Women, conversely, were not expected to leave their families until they married and set up a household as a prelude to parenthood. Today, more and more young men and women are remaining single, delaying marriage, postponing parenthood, or choosing to remain childless (Teachman, Tedrow, & Crowder, 2000). For example, in 1970, the age at which someone typically married for the first time was 20.8 for women and 23.2 for men. By 2005, these figures had risen to 25.3 for women and

27.1 for men. Furthermore, one-third of men and nearly one-quarter of women have never been married when they reach age thirty-four, nearly four times the rates in 1970. Possible reasons for these demographic changes include young adults focusing more on education and careers and the easing of taboos about couples living together before marriage and having children outside of marriage. However, it is interesting to note that most Americans still do marry, eventually. In 1970, 8 percent of people sixty-five and older never had married; in 2005 only 4 percent never had married (U.S. Census Bureau, 2005a).

This variability, however, should not obscure the fact that all young adults experience similar underlying pressures to make commitments to adult roles and responsibilities (Allison & Sabatelli, 1988). For each individual, the transition from adolescence into early adulthood is accompanied by pressure to form a life plan (Levinson, 1986). During this period, individuals feel pressured by prevailing cultural forces, social expectations, and family norms to make a commitment to a lifestyle. In part because of these internal and external pressures, sooner or later the overwhelming percentage of young adults commit to what they hope will be a "lifetime relationship." This process of bonding with another or selecting a mate adds a new subsystem to the family system, forcing a realignment of identities, boundaries, hierarchies, alliances, and coalitions. The process of selecting a partner can be conceived as a stage in the family life cycle because it is a foundation for the patterns of interaction that will characterize future family relationships.

In this chapter, the processes involved in selecting a lifetime partner are discussed with acknowledgment of the complexity and diversity of the developmental paths available to young adults today. This will entail development of an understanding of (1) the factors that influence our willingness to bond with another; (2) how our family of origin experiences and developmental history affect this process; and (3) the factors that influence the patterns and dynamics of interaction found within these intimate relationships.

Selecting a Lifetime Companion

The decision to share one's lifetime with another is generally based on the belief that this relationship is special and unique. We expect that our partners will create with us a harmonious, joyous, and intimate union. We expect to be able to trust our partners, and we expect that, in spite of the difficulties that may lie ahead, our partners will remain committed to working with us to preserve the intimacy we currently experience in the relationship.

Because so much is expected of a lifetime relationship, selecting a partner is a complex and important decision. Over the years, two major approaches to the study of relationship development have evolved: stage theories of mate selection and social exchange models of relationship development (Brehm, Miller, Perlman, & Cambell, 2002). Stage theories can be characterized as largely descriptive accounts of the different phases in a relationship's development. The social exchange approach, in contrast, highlights the intrapersonal and interpersonal factors that, together, account for a relationship's development.

Stage Theories of Mate Selection

Stage theories of mate selection are largely based on the assumption that relationship formation is characterized by a developmental sequence. These theories speculate that a developing relationship goes through certain stages, such as initial attraction, establishing rapport (and checking out each other's values and attitudes), wooing and selective disclosure (getting to know each other—are we similar?), testing out the relationship (how well do we get along—are our needs being met?), disillusionment (he or she is irritating ... boring), and finally deciding whether to make a commitment to each other. If commitments are made, then a period of attachment may follow, involving warmth, security, and comfort. For example, Lewis (1972) proposes a six-stage model of dyadic formation (see Table 7.1). According to Lewis, relationships begin with attraction based on similarity, which contributes to the development of good rapport. The relationship then goes through the following stages: mutual self-disclosure, empathic understanding of the other person, role compatibility, and, finally, commitment to the relationship. Lewis highlights the importance of similarity and self-disclosure in fostering interpersonal attraction in the early stages of his model. In the later stages, identity tasks become more important as the partners establish a "dyadic crystallization" by developing mutually agreed upon roles and begin to define themselves as a couple.

Lewis's model, like all stage models of relationship development, is based on the assumption that relationships follow a similar and fixed sequence in their development. A number of investigators concluded, however, that the evidence for a fixed sequence of stages in the development of intimate relationships is quite weak (e.g., Leigh, Homan, & Burr, 1987; Stephen, 1987). On the contrary, research has found that relationships follow many different developmental trajectories; that is, not all couples experience the same stages, and the stages may even vary for males when compared to females (Brehm et al., 2002; Huston, Surra, Fitzgerald, & Cate, 1981; Surra & Huston, 1987). In addition, stage models often fail to consider the factors involved in moving the relationship to greater degrees

TABLE 7.1 Stage Models of Relationship Development

	Lewis's Theory of Dyadic Formation
Initial stages	Similarities
	Rapport
Intermediate stages	Mutual self-disclosure
	Empathy
	Interpersonal role fit
Later stages	Dyadic crystallization

of intimacy and involvement. This suggests that, in their efforts to describe the phases of a relationship's development, proponents of stage models do not examine the important processes within relationships that underlie the emergence of deeper levels of involvement and commitment. Furthermore, they do not provide a link between family of origin experiences and the process of selecting a partner. Finally, they do not help us understand the patterns of interaction found within developing relationships. Many of these issues are addressed by the social exchange approach to the study of relationship development.

Social Exchange Perspectives on Relationship Development

The social exchange framework, developed in the 1950s and 1960s (Blau, 1964; Homans, 1961; Thibaut & Kelley, 1959), has become one of the more dominant theoretical perspectives in family studies today (Sabatelli & Shehan, 1992). This perspective emphasizes an **economic metaphor** that views relationships as "extended markets." Individuals are seen as acting out of self-interest, with the goal of maximizing their profits and minimizing their costs. However, the goal of maximizing profits in an intimate relationship differs significantly from the marketplace due to the level of **interdependence** among partners in intimate relationships (Sabatelli & Shehan, 1992). In close personal relationships, one's own satisfactions generally depend significantly on the extent to which one's partner is satisfied as well. Acting in the best interests of the partner becomes one way of obtaining benefits for the self.

Interdependence can be thought of as the degree to which partners influence one another and are mutually dependent on the relationship (Kelley et al., 1983; Levinger, 1982). Within a close personal relationship, where the goal is to achieve and sustain a high level of intimacy, individuals cannot act out of self-interest alone, for such self-interested behavior undermines the experience of intimacy. It generates feelings of resentment and mistrust, and fosters complaints about the lack of reciprocity and fairness within the relationships.

A high degree of interdependence is achieved when both partners come to understand that acting in the best interests of the partner becomes one way of obtaining benefits for the self. Such an exchange relationship fosters trust and commitment that, if sustained over time, can lead to the belief that the relationship has many of the special and enduring qualities that define a lifetime relationship. In order to understand this process of selecting a partner more fully, the factors that lead to the development of an interdependent exchange relationship must be examined. Chief among these factors is a high degree of interpersonal attraction.

Interpersonal Attraction: Filtering the Pool of Eligibles

Exchange theories use the concepts of rewards, costs, outcomes, and comparison levels to understand interpersonal attraction. **Rewards** refer to the benefits exchanged in social relationships, and are defined as the pleasures, satisfactions, and gratifications a person derives from participating in a relationship (Thibaut & Kelley, 1959). There are many types of social rewards, including physical attractiveness, social acceptance and approval, the provision of services or favors, the bestowal of respect or prestige on another, and compliance with another's wishes (bestowal of power on another) (Blau, 1964). Still other rewards might include making positive verbal statements, listening to the other, offering self-disclosure, touching, giving gifts, or spending time together. Each of these rewards may be perceived as a positive benefit derived from the relationship. Each also serves as a reinforcement that increases the likelihood of a person being attracted to the relationship.

Costs refer to the drawbacks or expenses associated with a particular relationship. They can involve negative aspects of a relationship or rewards sacrificed as a result of engaging in the relationship. A partner's insensitivity or lack of a sense of humor may be perceived negatively, as might be the time and effort required to maintain the relationship and the real or imagined rewards available elsewhere were the individual not participating in the present relationship (Blau, 1964).

Rewards and costs can have a direct effect on the degree to which we are attracted to a relationship. Attraction is enhanced by the rewarding characteristics of the partner (e.g., physical attractiveness, sense of humor, social class standing) or the products of our interactions with the partner (e.g., the fun experienced, the ease of interaction, the love we feel for the partner). But rewards must be weighted against the costs incurred from participating in the relationship. This balance of rewards and costs is referred to as the level of **outcomes** available from the relationship. Higher levels of positive outcomes are, quite naturally, associated with a higher degree of interpersonal attraction.

The rewards and costs that we perceive to be available from a relationship function as filters narrowing the pool of eligible or potential partners. The filters employed in selecting a partner typically consist of the characteristics that an individual believes are desirable in a mate. The particular traits of others; their temperament, beliefs, attitudes, and values; their socioeconomic status; and their physical appearance are all factors associated with interpersonal attraction (Hendrick & Hendrick, 1992). In addition, researchers emphasize that attraction is facilitated by a high degree of similarity between individuals with respect to these characteristics. Similarity is important to attraction because it is directly reinforcing. It bolsters one's own sense of identity and esteem, and leads to an ease of interaction (Huston & Levinger, 1978). In this regard, research has shown a strong relationship between interpersonal attraction, similar economic backgrounds, personality characteristics, and levels of self-esteem (Berscheid, 1985; Berscheid & Reis, 1998).

However, an emphasis on similarity does not exclude the possibility that individuals will be attracted to individuals who are substantially different with respect to selected attitudes, values, or traits. Just as the filters that we employ to narrow the pool of eligibles may foster attraction to individuals who are similar to us in certain respects, they may also foster attraction to individuals who complement us with regard to other characteristics (Winch, 1958). For instance, a person with a strong need to take care of others may only be attracted to those who have a strong need to be cared for. The essential point is that these filters are important to interpersonal attraction. The filters that we employ to narrow the pool of eligibles reflect the characteristics that we believe are essential in a lifetime companion. We are most attracted to individuals who possess the unique combination of attributes and traits that enables them to pass through a large number of increasingly more particular and idiosyncratic filters.

Comparison Levels: The Uniqueness of Our Filters

The exchange model's explanation of interpersonal attraction would be strikingly simplistic if it did not consider two other important points. First, individuals vary considerably in terms of what they consider to be rewarding and costly. For instance, one individual may believe that a gift of flowers is a thoughtful and affectionate gesture, while another may assume that people give flowers only when they have done something wrong and are trying to make up for it. Second, individuals bring into their relationships different expectations of what they consider to be acceptable outcomes. For instance, one person may be willing to allow the partner as much time with friends as desired so long as Friday nights are reserved exclusively for the couple to be together. In contrast, another individual may expect much more time together as a couple in order to feel sufficiently rewarded in the relationship. Therefore, determining one's interpersonal attraction to another is highly subjective and very much determined by what the individuals involved consider to be rewarding, costly, or reasonable expectations.

Exchange perspectives refer to the unique values and expectations individuals bring to their relationships as the **comparison level (CL)** (Sabatelli, 1984, 1988; Thibaut & Kelley, 1959). These are the standards against which the relationship is judged. The CL can be thought of as a precursor to the critical identity images and role expectations that family members hold for one another. At this particular stage of early attraction, each prospective partner is measured against the other's CL, or against the image of what a prospective mate should offer. We tend to be more satisfied with, and attracted to, those partners who offer us the kinds of rewards that we value. We are also more satisfied with, and more readily attracted to, a relationship when its outcomes exceed our expectations. Conversely, when outcomes fall consistently below our expectations, the attractiveness of a relationship declines.

The specifics of each person's CL are influenced by (1) family of origin experiences; (2) information gained by observing peer relationships; and (3) the individual's own experiences in relationships. We will discuss the effect of family of origin experiences on the mate selection process in greater detail later in this chapter. For now, let it suffice to say that the characteristics of our parents' relationship with one another, the themes established within our families of origin, and our own developmental history all affect our CL and, thus, our mate selection process.

The characteristics, strengths, and weaknesses that we observe in other people's relationships and our own experiences in relationships have an effect on the CL as well. In general, observing or having successful and satisfying relationships tends to raise our expectations, while observing or having unsuccessful or dissatisfying relationships may tend to lower our CL. Furthermore, as our investment in a relationship increases, we may alter our expectations. While we may have been initially attracted to our partner because of his or her sexy demeanor and manner of dress, these attributes may become a problem for us as we become more invested in making the relationship more exclusive.

The concept of the CL helps to explain what makes the interpersonal attraction process so unique and, often, unpredictable. Personal experiences and history play an important role in the development of the generalized expectations that persons hold about the type and level of outcomes they desire from a relationship. Physical attractiveness, for example, may be an attribute of considerable importance to some people but relatively unimportant to others. In addition, the CL helps to explain why one individual can be intensely attracted to a person that another person finds personally repulsive. In other words, it is our CL, or the expectations that we hold for relationships, that determines who we find attractive and what qualities in relationships we find exciting.

In sum, exchange perspectives account for interpersonal attraction by focusing on the progressive and successive elimination of individuals from the pool of eligibles because they fail to conform to the standards we employ to screen out potential partners. Conversely, the individuals we are attracted to are those who pass through our screening filters; that is, we are attracted to those who meet the standards that we establish for a suitable and desirable partner.

Moving beyond Attraction

To move beyond interpersonal attraction and further understand the process of selecting a lifetime partner, we must examine the factors that encourage the emergence of trust, commitment, love, and interdependence. Being attracted to another is not sufficient to explain the willingness to spend the rest of one's adult life with a particular partner. This willingness requires the presence of a high level of trust in the partner, a strong commitment to the relationship, a deep affection and love for the partner, and a high degree of interdependence within the relationship.

Trust, Commitment, and Relationship Turning Points

Trust refers to the belief that one's partner will not exploit or take unfair advantage of him or her (Haas & Deseran, 1981; McDonald, 1981). Trust is important in relationship development because it allows individuals to be less calculating and seek longer-term outcomes (Burns, 1973; Scanzoni, 1979a). Put another way, trust allows us to become more future oriented by increasing our confidence and sense of security in the relationship (McDonald, 1981). For example, when trust is strong, we might become less inclined to take an offbeat remark by our partner as insulting because of the many times he or she has shown sensitivity or responsiveness to our feelings. We might conclude that in the future such occurrences are likely to be rare relative to the number of rewarding interactions we can anticipate. In the absence of trust, individuals need to attend more to their own self-interests. In so doing, they become less interested in attending to the needs of the other both in the present and in the future. The emergence of trust also contributes to a greater willingness to deepen our commitment to the relationship.

Commitment is reflected in the degree to which we are willing to work for the continuation of the relationship, and it is this willingness to work for the relationship that distinguishes an increasingly intimate and exclusive relationship from one that is casual and unchanging (Leik & Leik, 1977). As with increased trust, increased commitment to a relationship brings with it an abandonment of strict economic exchange principles in favor of a relationship in which rewards may be "future placed" (Leik & Leik, 1977). This suggests that individuals who experience a great level of commitment to a relationship feel a high degree of solidarity with their partners and are personally dedicated to the continuance of their relationships. Individuals who are personally dedicated to a relationship desire to maintain or improve it and thus are willing to sacrifice for it, invest in it, and link both personal goals and the partner's welfare to it. As these feelings of solidarity and dedication to the relationship emerge, no doubt as a result of the rewards each partner derives from the relationship, individuals are presumed to become progressively less attentive to alternative relationships (Leik & Leik, 1977; Scanzoni, 1979b).

This shift from a concern for or an awareness of alternative relationships to a cessation of such monitoring represents a significant turning point in the development of a relationship. That is, as attention to alternatives diminishes, individuals become increasingly reliant on the existing relationship for their identity and interpersonal needs (Leik & Leik, 1977). This absence of monitoring and this building of commitment result, in other words, in the relationship and the partner becoming an increasingly central aspect of one's life. That is, the greater our commitment to our partner, the more likely we are to anticipate the kind of future we want to have together.

This perspective on commitment makes it clear that relationships and the commitment that individuals feel to their partners and relationships evolve over time. A relationship can be thought of as going through critical periods, or **turning points**, when it either evolves to a deeper level of intimacy and involvement or dissolves (Bolton, 1961). It is at these junctures that trust and commitment either evolve to higher levels or dissipate. A deepening sense of trust and commitment requires a belief on our part that our partner shares our interest and investment in the relationship. In the absence of this type of reciprocity we become hesitant to trust and unwilling to make a stronger commitment to the relationship.

Turning points, therefore, seldom occur unless we make an effort to determine whether our partner's commitment to the relationship matches our own. These efforts to determine the status of the relationship involve us in **negotiations** with the partner. The goal of these negotiations is to reach a consensus on the extent of our "network of intermeshed interests" (Scanzoni, 1979b). That is, does our partner value the same activities and hobbies that we do? Does he or she have similar lifelong goals and aspirations? Is he or she as attracted to us as we are to him or her? Is he or she as interested in continuing the relationship as we are?

Negotiations on the status of the relationship may be direct, involving self-disclosure and "relationship talk" aimed at facilitating each partner's understanding and agreement about the relationship (Baxter & Bullis, 1986). That is, at certain junctures, we may sit down with our partner and openly discuss our level of interest in the other and the areas of the relationship we wish to develop further. Such negotiations provide direct feedback about how similar or dissimilar the partners' expectations are about the relationship. This information is important because it helps to determine how trusting each partner is of the other and how willing each will be to commit further to the relationship.

These negotiations may also be indirect, taking the form of "secret tests" (Baxter & Wilmot, 1984). Secret tests are indirect efforts on our part to determine whether our partner's level of commitment to the relationship matches our own. For example, a woman might tell a man that she really does not mind if he goes out with some of his friends. But, what she really wants to know is, "Does he want to be with me more than he wants to be with his friends?" If he goes out with his friends, he has failed the secret test. If he goes out with her instead, he has passed the test, and this increases her confidence that he is as committed as she is to the relationship.

The importance of these negotiations is that they provide us with information that we need to feel motivated to continue in the relationship. That indirect approaches to negotiating relationships are more prevalent than direct approaches (Baxter & Wilmot, 1984) demonstrates that people find it risky to talk directly about such issues. The prevalence of these indirect negotiations attests as well to the importance we attribute to the subtle and unconfirmed information that we are able to gather about how our partner views the relationship.

The Importance of Love

If persons are asked why they married, the most frequent response by far will include mention of the love that they feel for the partner. Despite all the attention that people give to love as a reason for commitment, love remains an elusive concept to define. The factors that contribute to the experience of love are equally hard to pin down. Hendrick and Hendrick (1992) maintain that "there is no one phenomenon that one can point to with certainty and say, 'that is love.' Love is at the very least a complex set of mental and emotional states. There also may be different types of love, and the types may be qualitatively different from each other" (p. 98).

In general, social scientists (as opposed to philosophers and poets) conceive of **love** as the emotion that is experienced in the presence of a heightened degree of physiological arousal combined with "relevant situational cues" (Berscheid & Walster, 1974). Relevant situational cues include the sense of intimacy, or connectedness and closeness, that we experience with the other, along with the sense of trust and commitment. Physiological arousal refers to the passion or excitement that we experience when we are with another. This includes, but is not restricted to, sexual desire (Sternberg, 1988). In short, love is the overarching term that we use to label the emotions that arise out of our rewarding and intimate interactions with another.

Within developing relationships, it seems reasonable to view love as both a cause for relationship development and an outcome derived from an intimate relationship. As a cause, feelings of love contribute to our attraction to the partner, our willingness to trust the partner, our commitment to the relationship, and our overall sense of intimacy in the relationship. Put another way, the positive feelings we have for our partner can reinforce our preoccupation and excitement with the partner (attraction); our confidence that we will not be exploited (trust); our sense of involvement and investment in the relationship (commitment); and our overall sense of closeness, well-being, and interdependence (intimacy). As an outcome, love is the emotion that emerges from the positive and intimate interactions we have with a partner. In a circular and cyclical fashion, the experience of love emerges from the intimate interactions between people, while also energizing these interactions and thereby contributing to the partners' experience of their relationship as unique and special (Sternberg, 1988).

From this later perspective, love and romance are among the major rewards derived from relationships. Such feelings fuel one's desire to continue investing in the relationship. However, as was the case with trust and commitment, it is important for feelings of love and romance to be perceived as reciprocal. When they are, we become more secure and committed to the relationship, more willing to trust the partner, and more motivated to act in a caring and altruistic way. When love and romance are not reciprocated, we may still choose to pursue the relationship, but we may be less secure and trusting, unless, that is, we can convince our partner to become as involved in the relationship as we are.

Before proceeding, we must emphasize that, for some individuals, the motivations for pursuing a relationship may have little to do with love, trust, commitment, or any of the other qualities of relationships that have been theorized as affecting the mate selection process. As a general rule, the experience of love is believed to be among the more important factors enhancing or inhibiting the development of a relationship. As love progresses, it builds, along with attraction, trust, and commitment, to increase the likelihood that the relationship will be experienced as special, exclusive, and enduring. For some persons, however, the most salient relational outcomes may be the avoidance of loneliness or the attainment of financial security. While the predominant cultural expectation is that relationships are based on a foundation of love, the mate selection process must be addressed on a more complex level.

Dependence, Interdependence, and Relationship Development

As we have seen, the willingness to form a lifetime relationship is based on the experiences of attraction, love, trust, and commitment combined with the perception that our partner's experiences of the relationship match our own. When these factors are present, partners can be considered to share a high level of dependence on the relationship. This shared dependence, or interdependence, is necessary for many of us to feel that a relationship will have the special and enduring characteristics of a lifetime partnership.

Interdependence, in other words, is the balance of dependence that exists within a relationship. **Dependence** can be defined as the degree to which we come to rely on our partners for relationship outcomes. Although most of us negatively react to the thought of being dependent on another, it is important to recognize the ways in which dependence works to inhibit or encourage the growth and development of a relationship. Dependence inhibits the development of a relationship when it is not balanced. Having a partner who is more dependent than we are creates stress and tension. When such an imbalance exists, the partner's neediness or jealousy can interfere with the rewards we derive from the relationship. These costs can, ultimately, lead us to look elsewhere for intimacy and companionship.

Being the more dependent partner is costly, as well, because we experience the relationship as being out of our control. The stress this dilemma creates is managed, typically, by using several strategies that are all geared toward rebalancing each partner's dependence on the relationship (Emerson, 1962). When one partner feels more dependent on the relationship than the other, for example, he or she may try to increase the other partner's dependence on the relationship by making the relationship more rewarding. He or she may try harder or seek new ways to please the less dependent partner and may even attempt to make the partner more appreciative by making him or her jealous, perhaps by threatening to go out with others. If these strategies fail, the more dependent partner may try to increase the other's dependence on the relationship by blocking access to alternatives.

Therefore, one way of understanding jealousy and possessiveness is as a reaction to the discomfort created by unbalanced levels of relationship dependence. If rebalancing strategies fail, the more dependent partner may choose instead to lower his or her own dependence on the relationship, by, for example, devaluing the relationship. When all else fails, the more dependent partner may even contemplate moving on.

The point is that stress and tension result when dependence on a relationship is not balanced and reciprocal. A relatively high level of mutual dependence, or interdependence, enhances our attraction to and trust in the relationship and our confidence that it will last. In addition, as noted, the presence of these factors enables each partner to act in accordance with the best interests of the other. Achievement of a high level of interdependence also enables each participant to derive a sense of psychological well-being and identity from the relationship (Lewis, 1972; Stephen, 1984).

According to the social exchange model presented here, the decision to form a lifetime relationship with another is contingent on the achievement of a high degree of interdependence. A summary of the factors that mediate the establishment of interdependence is presented in Figure 7.1. While all relationships, regardless of at what point they are in the developmental stage, are characterized by some degree of interdependence, the model posits that the high levels of interdependence that emerge at later stages of relationship development result from the perception that strong attraction, trust, commitment, and love exist within the relationship. A strong attraction to another and to the relationship originates from a favorable level of perceived outcomes. Our outcomes are determined in large part by the subjective filters that we bring to our relationships. The greater our attraction to the other, the more likely we are to consider becoming involved and committed to the relationship. Commitment, or our willingness to work for the continuation of the relationship, is further enhanced by the process of ongoing

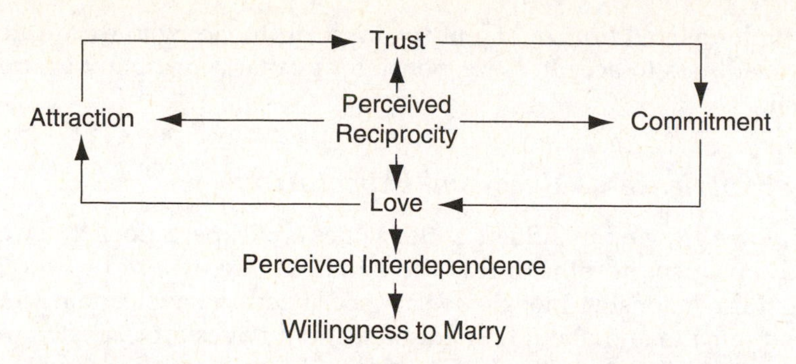

FIGURE 7.1 Interdependence Model of Mate Selection

negotiations with the partner. It is through negotiation that we clarify our expectations for one another and determine whether the partner shares a similar level of commitment to the relationship. The successful negotiation of a shared definition of the relationship increases the level of trust partners experience and their willingness to commit further to the relationship.

As the relationship evolves, and trust and commitment increase, so too does one's level of love for the partner. Although, admittedly, it is an elusive concept, it seems reasonable to assert that love is the emotion experienced as attraction grows and involvement in the relationship deepens. Love further reinforces our involvement in the relationship, strengthening the bonds of attraction, trust, and commitment toward the partner. The intensity of the attraction, trust, commitment, and love, in turn, fosters dependence on the relationship. Dependence is not experienced as a cost, however, so long as it is perceived that one partner's reliance on the other is reciprocated in kind.

The turning points that characterize the development of an intimate relationship are those negotiations occurring at critical junctures that help each partner to feel that attraction, trust, commitment, love, and dependence are balanced within the relationship. As interdependence is enhanced and the sense of identity and well-being derived from the relationship increase, the need for further negotiations about the relationship declines. It is at this point that partners generally come to believe that their relationship possesses the unique and enduring qualities of a lifetime relationship.

The Impact of Family of Origin Experiences on Mate Selection

To this point, the ways in which family of origin experiences influence the mate selection process have not been discussed at great length. The family of origin affects mate selection in two distinct and important ways. First, the family of origin experiences help to shape the values and expectations we bring to our relationships; that is, family experiences provide a foundation for our CL. Second, our developmental history, including our attachment history and the manner in which we have individuated from our family of origin, influence who we are attracted to and our readiness to accept the responsibilities that accompany intimate adult relationships.

Family Experiences, Values, and Expectations

The family we grow up in influences the values and expectations that we bring to our relationships with others. It is there that we are exposed to successful or unsuccessful relationship models. We are socialized to have certain views about males and females and about how husbands and wives are expected to behave. We are oriented to particular family themes, identity images, and myths that further delineate and define who is an appropriate intimate partner for us.

The characteristics and qualities that we admire (or do not admire) in our parents become elements of our CL. That is, they become a barometer against which we judge others. For example, perhaps an individual's parents had a successful relationship. One factor in this was the parents' ability to laugh at themselves and their faults. The result is a tendency for this person to attribute a great deal of importance to a sense of humor as a valued and rewarding characteristic of a potential partner. Conversely, when a potential partner has qualities that this same person did not approve of in his or her parents, these qualities may interfere with the development of attraction.

Our socialization experiences in the family of origin, as well as in the broader culture, also affect what we expect a husband and wife should be like. If we come from a traditional family, we may have learned that men are expected to be "good providers" or "occupational achievers," and that women are expected to be nurturing and supportive. If we were raised in a contemporary or nontraditional family, we may have learned that both men and women are expected to be "sensitive and caring parents" or "occupational achievers." Such values may become crucial to the evaluations we make of others as our relationships become more serious and exclusive.

The rules within our family of origin further help to define our expectations and attraction to others. We may feel more comfortable with those who come from families with rules similar to our own and less comfortable with those whose backgrounds are significantly different from ours. For instance, our family's rules for negotiating internal boundaries and communication may influence our comfort with and attraction to another. If our family valued openness and disclosure, we may experience tension with a partner who values privacy and silence over openness. On the other hand, we may feel uncomfortable with a partner who frequently and spontaneously interrupts when we speak if we came from a family that was quiet, polite, and honored the convention of taking turns in conversation.

Models for how to nurture others exist within our families as well. We will often find ourselves attracted to others whose intimacy rules match those of our family of origin. Some of us have observed marriages built on a foundation of respect, equity, and fairness, and this too influences our views of how we would like our relationships to be structured. Others may have observed marriages in which intimacy was expressed by one partner overfunctioning or caretaking for the other. Similarly, we ourselves may have become a "parental child" and been expected to act as caretaker for one or both of our parents. Having experienced such a background, we might become most comfortable in relationships in which our partner underfunctions in response to our "overfunctioning way" of nurturing. That daughters of alcoholic fathers often marry an alcoholic may be accounted for by such factors (Elkin, 1984). Women who expect, or at least tolerate, alcoholism in a partner may have been exposed to models for intimacy that left them feeling most comfortable in relationships dominated by an overfunctioning/underfunctioning complementarity.

Finally, we need to mention the ways in which the themes that exist in the family affect mate selection. Cultural and religious themes can act as filters that influence to whom we are attracted. A strong ethnic orientation within one's family may render intimate relationships with someone of a different ethnic heritage unacceptable. Similarly, forming a committed and intimate relationship with someone outside one's faith, race, or even class can be an issue if family of origin themes strongly endorse these as necessary prerequisites for prospective family members.

Attachment Theory and Mate Selection

How a relationship is formed, develops, and is maintained varies for each individual and couple. Many theories on how relationships develop and work have been proposed, tried, and tested. Although there are several prominent social psychological theories, attachment theory is presently among the most commonly cited for understanding interpersonal relationships in adulthood. As a theoretical framework, attachment theory gives us a basis for understanding the connections between early family of origin experiences and the ways adult partnerships are structured and experienced (Hazan & Shaver, 1994).

Attachment theory implies that the capacity to form emotional attachments to others is primarily developed during infancy and early childhood (Bowlby, 1979). Infants experience less anxiety when their adult caregivers are in close proximity. When the adult caregivers are nearby, this elicits feelings of security and love in the child. With this "felt security" the child usually displays a playful and more independent behavior that is best exemplified in an active exploration of the environment. If the child does not experience adequate attention, responsiveness, and proximity from caregivers, he or she may become less self-assured and less trusting of them and be at greater risk for developing insecure attachment relationships (Hazan & Shaver, 1994).

Put another way, the primary emotional experiences that children have with parents and caretakers form the basis of what Bowlby (1979) called the "internal working model." A child's internal working model includes expectations on how the caregiver will respond in certain situations. Attachment theory assumes that the expectations, beliefs, and feelings that an individual develops, because of the responsiveness of caregivers, are later transferred to, and displayed in, other close relationships (Hazan & Shaver, 1994). The internal working model that is formed during childhood reveals itself through an individual's beliefs of self, others, and the social world. When the emotional needs of the child are fulfilled, these individuals generally perceive themselves as being worthy of love and respect, see others as being trustworthy and dependable, and view the social world as being reliable and consistent. Conversely, when children's needs are not consistently met by caregivers, then as an adult, negative beliefs about such unworthiness, disrespect, distrust, and unreliability are more likely to guide their feelings and thoughts in most interpersonal relationships. This may result in insecure attachment relationships.

An extensive body of research has shown that the ways caregivers respond to a child's needs and expectations lead to three distinct attachment patterns: secure, avoidant, and anxious–ambivalent attachment (Bowlby, 1988; Feeney, 1999; Hazan & Shaver, 1987, 1994; Hazan & Zeifman, 1999). When parents and caretakers are responsive, attentive, and approving, the child is likely to become securely attached and exhibit less inhibited and more explorative behavior. Being inconsistent in responding and attention-giving leads to an anxious–ambivalent attachment that tends to try to reestablish contact, clings to the caregiver, and constantly checks to see where the caregiver is. Constantly ignoring or deflecting the needs and the attention of the child leads to an avoidant attachment style in which the child attempts to maintain proximity but avoids close contact with the caregiver (Hazan & Shaver, 1994).

For a long time, developmental psychologists have been interested in examining whether the attachment styles that individuals develop during childhood also affect their behavior as adults. Although longitudinal studies on the development of attachment styles have been mostly limited to middle and later childhood, recent research on adult attachment styles has shown that the attachment patterns formed in infancy and childhood seem to have equivalent counterparts in adulthood. That is, the three different attachment styles thought to exist in children have been shown to influence adult interpersonal relationships in profound ways.

Specifically, individuals who are characterized by a **secure attachment style** have been shown to have positive early family relationships and trusting attitudes toward others. Within their adult relationships, they are comfortable getting close to, and depending on, others. Their relationships are described as happy and trusting, and they view themselves as friendly and likable (Feeney & Noller, 1990; Collins & Read, 1990). They find it easy, in other words, to get close to others and are comfortable depending on others and having others depend on them. They usually do not worry about being abandoned or about others getting close to them.

Adults with an **avoidant attachment style** tend to view relationships as less satisfying and intimate compared to securely attached individuals. They are also less trusting of others and tend to avoid getting close to others (Feeney & Noller, 1990). Avoidant individuals are uncomfortable being close to others, find it difficult to trust others completely, and find it difficult to depend on others. They also become nervous when others get too close and often feel that their partners want them to be more intimate than they are comfortable being.

Adults with an **anxious–ambivalent attachment style** view others as unreliable and unable to commit. They also see their relationships as having less interdependence, trust, and satisfaction when compared to securely attached individuals (Simpson, 1990). That is, anxious–ambivalent adults often experience others as being reluctant to get as close as they would like them to be. They tend to worry that their partners do not really love them or will not want to stay with them. They want to become completely intimate with another person, but this neediness may scare the other away.

In sum, attachment histories in the family of origin have the potential to impact how adult partnerships are formed, structured, and experienced. This contention has been supported by two types of studies that look at adult attachment styles in interpersonal relationships: studies done with dating couples and studies done with married couples. Studies conducted with dating couples show that securely attached individuals are generally attracted to other securely attached individuals. Individuals characterized as having an insecure attachment style generally match up with others characterized as having an insecure attachment style (Simpson, 1990). Securely attached couples have also been shown to have longer and more satisfying relationships with one another (Simpson, 1990). Couples with insecure attachment styles, whether the relationship is anxious–ambivalent to anxious–ambivalent, avoidant to avoidant, or more commonly, avoidant to anxious–ambivalent, have been shown to have less relationship satisfaction and shorter-lasting relationships. The secure relationships tend to last because of the greater trust and self-confidence between the partners (Feeney & Noller, 1990).

Studies conducted with married couples have looked at how couples' communication and relationship quality are related to the different attachment styles. Not surprisingly, these studies found that securely attached couples, when compared to insecurely attached couples, reported higher relationship satisfaction, trust, supportiveness, and positive self-disclosure. Their communication was more open, and they utilized a more integrating or problem-solving strategy when dealing with conflicts (Feeney, 1999). In addition, securely attached individuals, when compared to insecurely attached individuals, reported compromising more with their significant others and were concerned for both their own and their partners' interests during conflicts (Feeney & Noller, 1996). They also tended to discuss conflicting goals openly and maintain constructive communication in the relationship (Kobak & Hazan, 1991).

Individuation Issues and Mate Selection

It should come as no surprise that developmental history has an effect on the mate selection process. In Chapter 6, it was suggested that individuation-enhancing family dynamics facilitate identity development and the capacity for intimacy, and that these "psychological resources" enable us to negotiate adult relationships and responsibilities maturely and competently. When we successfully individuate from our families, we have the ego and identity resources that enhance our capacity for intimacy with others. Under these circumstances, we form intimate bonds with others based on our genuine regard and affection for them. The absence of a mature sense of identity and capacity for intimacy, however, may lead us to bond with others to "complete our sense of self." In other words, we may become dependent on relationships for our sense of identity, and these fragile bonds can lock us into relationships that limit both personal growth and the quality of the relationship over time (Napier, 1988).

Individuation difficulties, therefore, set in motion processes that negatively influence mate selection and, potentially, the future health and adjustment of an intimate relationship. For instance, the family's boundary rules and tolerance for individuality can affect the freedom we experience when exploring outside relationships with others. When the family's boundaries fail to tolerate individuality, our identity and relationship choices may come to be controlled by the family of origin. The prospective mates of highly "fused" individuals may have to undergo intense family scrutiny and meet a fixed set of standards. Family approval can become the most salient and determining factor in the mate selection process.

Conversely, when an individual rebels against the family as a way of handling the developmental demands of individuation, he or she may deliberately select a partner of whom the family could never approve. The hurt, anger, and reactivity toward the family can fuel efforts to retaliate against the family by presenting them with the dilemma of an unacceptable mate. It is, of course, obvious that the long-term health and viability of a relationship built on this type of foundation are questionable.

When individuals cut off from the family as a way of handling individuation, they may attempt to fulfill their unmet needs by marrying into the family that "they never had." Finding a family to fuse with becomes the most salient factor mediating the mate selection process. Ironically, this partner is likely to be one who is also poorly individuated and fused with his or her own family of origin (Bowen, 1978). Therefore, the resolution of each partner's individuation dilemma is to find a partner who complements the other's needs and expectations. In this instance, the match is built on one partner's need to find a partner who will join his or her family, while the other partner is looking for a family to join (Wamboldt & Wolin, 1989).

In all of these instances, the main point is the same. Our developmental history and, in particular, the success with which we have managed the task of individuation influence to whom we are attracted and who we select as a prospective mate. In general, the health and viability of an adult intimate relationship are dependent on a clear sense of identity and the capacity for intimacy with others. The inability to negotiate the individuation process adequately increases the likelihood that our decisions about mate selection will be based on our own unfulfilled needs and emotional reactivity to our family of origin.

Mate Selection and Relationship Dynamics

The study of mate selection focuses almost exclusively on the factors that foster the willingness to bond with another. What can easily be overlooked from this perspective is that, during relationship formation, patterns and dynamics of interaction are established that will continue within the relationship over time. The patterns of interaction established during mate selection influence many of the strategies that couples employ for executing family system tasks. Once established, these patterns and dynamics of interaction play a part in determining the specific strategies that couples use to manage their household and finances, establish boundaries with friends and family, create family themes and identities, and nurture and support one another. Thus, it is important to view the mate selection process as a stage in the family life cycle because it is during this period that the foundation is established for the interactional dynamics that will organize the future family system.

There are two major determinants of the interactional strategies and rules that develop during the mate selection process: (1) the family of origin experiences and (2) each partner's relative attraction to, and dependence on, the relationship.

Family of origin experiences, including socialization experiences, birth order, and position within the family, do not directly create patterns and dynamics of interaction in intimate relationships. They do, however, influence our preferred styles of interacting with others in intimate relationships, or the rules we are comfortable with for managing issues like nurturance, conflict, power, and decision-making. This complex of strategies and rules is a precursor to the strategies and rules that couples will later establish for the execution of marital and family system tasks.

For example, women who have been socialized in their own families to be caretakers might find themselves paired with partners who expect women to assume such roles. Such women may find that they devote a considerable amount of their time and energy to supporting and nurturing a partner. Relationship dynamics such as these may function initially to enhance the comfort and attraction both partners experience with one another. Later, they can become the basis for how the couple nurtures and supports one another over time. That is, he will receive support, and she will be expected to be content providing it. Likewise, when men who have been socialized into traditional masculine values and orientations are paired with women who expect these traits in a man, the men may find that they are responsible for making decisions about how time and energy should be spent or what opinions, values, and identity the couple should maintain. Again, these preferred patterns of interaction become the harbingers of the strategies and rules that a couple will establish for managing their resources and establishing family themes and identities.

A second major influence on the patterns of interaction found within developing relationships is the relative balance of attraction and dependence that exists between partners. At any point, in any given relationship, one partner may be more attracted to, or dependent on, the relationship than the other. The relative balance of attraction and dependence has implications for the development of the couple's **power** and control (decision-making) strategies and distance-regulation patterns of interaction (Sabatelli & Shehan, 1992).

Power involves the control of another's behavior through the ability to elicit compliance or resist the other's influence (Blau, 1964; Thibaut & Kelley, 1959). Power dynamics within relationships are influenced by the complex interrelationship between resources and dependence. Essentially, our ability to control others or to resist their control efforts is based on the resources (attributes and characteristics) we possess relative to our partners. The more resources we possess, the more attractive we are to the partner, and the more dependent the partner is likely to be on the relationship for positive outcomes. In this situation, the partner with the fewer resources and the greater dependence tends to hold less power in the relationship (Emerson, 1962, 1976; Huston, 1983; Thibaut & Kelley, 1959).

Therefore, during the formation of a relationship and later on in the established relationship, the relative balance of resources and dependence that exists between partners influences how decisions are made and who has greater power in the relationship. When dependence is balanced, couples strive to involve one another in decisions. They are more likely to maintain an emphasis on equity and fairness in making decisions and feel mutually obligated to one another. This reciprocal sense of obligation fosters a system in which interactions are dominated by a concern for the happiness, interests, and needs of the partner (Greenberg, 1980).

When dependence and resources are not balanced, however, the less dependent partner is more likely to assert control within the relationship. The more dependent partner, because he or she has more to lose if the relationship ends, is more likely to defer to the partner. Inequities are tolerated because the costs of deferring to the partner do not outweigh the potential costs associated with conflict, that is, the loss of the relationship.

The balance of attraction and dependence found within a relationship also influences couples' patterns of distance regulation. As noted, distance regulation refers to the patterns of intimacy and autonomy observed within the relationship. The degree to which partners are attracted to, and dependent on, the relationship influences how closeness and distance are managed in the relationship. For example, asymmetrical patterns of attraction can result in the presence of a "pursuing–distancing" pattern of interaction in which the partner who is more attracted to the relationship pursues the relationship, while the less attracted partner distances from the relationship. In a similar vein, the partner who is more dependent on a relationship is more likely to pursue the other, while the partner with less investment in the relationship is more likely to demand greater autonomy within the relationship.

Not having power, or feeling as if one has to pursue the partner are, of course, undesirable positions to hold within a relationship. This explains why so much energy is invested in balancing dependence while relationships are forming. At the point at which one person commits to another for a lifetime, it can be assumed that most individuals are comfortable with the balance of attraction and dependence they have negotiated within the relationship. It can further be assumed that a sense of equity and fairness and a concern for the needs and concerns of one's partner are present within the relationship.

It is imperative, however, to emphasize that achieving an acceptable level of interdependence does not result in all couples being equally involved with or dependent on one another. Each of us holds different views about the degree of imbalance we are willing to tolerate. These views reflect our observations of other relationships, our previous experiences in interpersonal relationships, and our experiences in our own family of origin. Our views are further influenced by our level of individuation and self-confidence, and our perception of currently available alternatives. All of these factors help to determine the patterns of power, control, and distance regulation that develop during relationship formation and persist over time.

Conclusions

In sum, couples carry into their ongoing relationships the patterns of interaction that were established during the mate selection process. These patterns strongly influence the strategies couples employ in managing the future tasks of their relationship, and they inevitably change as the unfolding drama of the family life cycle alters partners' resources and their dependence on one another. These issues become increasingly relevant when we examine how family developmental transitions influence ongoing family patterns of interaction.

Key Terms

Anxious–ambivalent attachment style Adults with an anxious–ambivalent attachment style view others in a relationship as unreliable and unable to commit. They also see their relationships as having less interdependence, trust, and satisfaction when compared to securely attached individuals.

Avoidant attachment style Adults with an avoidant attachment style tend to view relationships as less satisfying and intimate compared to securely attached individuals. They are also less trusting of others and tend to avoid getting close to others.

Commitment The degree to which one is willing to work for the continuation of a relationship.

Comparison level (CL) The unique values and expectations individuals bring to their relationships. These are the standards against which the relationship is judged.

Costs The drawbacks or expenses associated with a particular relationship. They can involve negative aspects of the relationship or rewards sacrificed as a result of engaging in the relationship.

Dependence The degree to which one comes to rely on a partner for relationship outcomes.

Economic metaphor A term used in the social exchange framework to emphasize how relationships are viewed as "extended markets" in which individuals act out of self-interest with the goal of maximizing their profits and minimizing their costs.

Interdependence The notion that one's own satisfaction in a relationship depends on the extent to which one's partner is satisfied as well. Acting in the best interests of the partner becomes a way to obtain benefits for the self.

Love The overarching term used to label the emotions that arise out of rewarding and intimate interactions with another.

Negotiations Interactions with one's partner that have as their goal reaching a consensus regarding common concerns or interests.

Outcomes The balance of rewards and costs available from the relationship.

Power The control of another's behavior through the ability to elicit compliance or resist the other's influence.

Rewards The benefits exchanged in social relationships. The pleasures, satisfactions, and gratifications a person derives from participating in a relationship.

Secure attachment style Individuals who are characterized by a secure attachment style have reported positive early family relationships and trusting attitudes toward others. Within their adult partnerships, these individuals are comfortable getting close to and depending on others. They describe their relationships as being characterized by happiness and trust, and they view themselves as friendly and likable.

Trust The belief that one's partner will not exploit or take unfair advantage of the relationship.

Turning points Critical periods in the development of an intimate relationship during which it either evolves to a deeper level of intimacy and involvement or dissolves.

CHAPTER 8

The Transition to Marriage
The New Marital System

Chapter Overview

The marriage relationship forms a subsystem within a system of extended family members. This chapter examines the developmental tasks that confront this newly established family subsystem. The tasks of the marital system parallel those that must be executed by the larger family system. As such, newly married couples must deal with the identity transformations that accompany marriage and, in the process, establish marital themes, negotiate marital roles and responsibilities, and establish a congruence of conjugal identities. In addition, marital couples must establish boundary strategies that regulate distances with the extended family, friends, and work. Internal boundary strategies between marital partners also must be established such that a comfortable and satisfying balance of individuality and intimacy can be achieved. In addition, all couples must establish strategies for managing the household and finances. Finally, couples must enact strategies that effectively manage the emotional climate of the marriage. In particular, couples must establish intimacy and support strategies, develop a mutually satisfying sexual script, and evolve strategies for the management of conflict. It should be clear that, from a developmental perspective, the stress associated with the transition to marriage emanates from the wide range of strategies that must be negotiated over a short period of time.

A Postmodern Perspective on Marriage

In the 1980s an important book *American Couples* (Blumstein & Schwartz, 1983) was published that explored the experiences of individuals in intimate relationships. The study revealed the existence of a continuum of relationships within the United States. At one end of the continuum were traditional marriages, while at the other end were what Blumstein and Schwartz called "experimental forms" of marriage. They labeled the experimental forms "voluntary marriages" (based on love with the commitment to marriage periodically renewed), "trial marriages" (in which a marriage-like relationship is experienced as a prelude to formal marriage), "cohabitators who plan to never marry," and "same-sex couples."

It is fair to conclude that since the 1980s many of these so-called experimental forms of marriage have become more common. For example, census data demonstrate that over the past decades cohabitation rates have increased in America while marriage rates have declined. Specifically, the number of unmarried couples living together in the United States increased 72 percent between 1990 and 2000 (U.S. Census Bureau, 2005b). Over half of all first marriages are now preceded by living together, compared to virtually none fifty years ago (Bumpass & Lu, 2000).

Furthermore, although it is impossible to document whether the number of same-sex households has increased over the past decades, it is clear that there have been remarkable changes within this time period in the sociopolitical context surrounding lesbian and gay families (Laird, 2003). In the 1990s the visibility of gays and lesbians within the society increased in unprecedented ways (Walters, 2001). As a result of this increase in visibility, the rights of domestic partners to employer benefits and the rights of gay and lesbian couples to legally marry have now become prominent social and political issues.

This chapter applies a family systems theory and multigenerational perspective to the study of marriage and marital issues. The chapter embraces, as well, a postmodern perspective on marriage. For us, the term **marriage** refers to a specific family subsystem comprised of adults from two different families of origin who have bonded together to form what they intend to be a stable and long-term cohabiting relationship. A postmodern perspective on marriage assumes that all marriage-like relationships, regardless of their legal status, are similar when it comes to the relationship issues and tasks that they must manage. This generic definition of marriage allows us to discuss common tasks that must be managed within any intimate relationship during the transition to marriage—when this newly formed subsystem is integrated into an extended family system. Our decision to define all "lifetime relationships" as a marriage is based on the findings of the published research comparing couples residing in these various types of marriage-like relationships. As we will see, this research generally supports the conclusion that the different types of marriage-like relationships are similar in terms of the system issues and ordinary challenges that they must contend with. To illustrate how a generic, postmodern definition of marriage applies equally well to the patterns and dynamics found within diverse couple relationships, we will look more closely at gay and lesbian couples.

Gay and Lesbian Relationships

Intimate same-sex relationships have existed throughout history. It is estimated that about 1 percent of adult women self-identify as lesbian and 2 percent of adult men self-identify as gay, and it is estimated that about 40 percent of gay men and 50 percent of lesbians, between the ages of eighteen and fifty-nine, are currently living with a same-sex partner. In comparison, about 60 percent of heterosexuals within this same age group are living with an other-sex partner (Carpenter & Gates, 2008). The experiences of same-sex couples in the United States are influenced by the social stigma of homosexuality. Although social attitudes are becoming more tolerant, it is common for gay and lesbian couples to report incidents of social rejection, prejudice, and discrimination. In national polls, only half of Americans say that same-sex couples should be allowed to form legally recognized civil unions or domestic partnerships (Peplau & Fingerhut, 2007). Clearly the topic of same-sex marriage continues to be a source of heated controversy.

Despite the differing social contexts for same-sex and heterosexual relationships, there are many commonalities in the relationships of all couples. For example, the research of Blumstein and Schwartz (1983) reported the results of over 12,000 questionnaires and more than 300 interviews with gay, lesbian, married heterosexual, and cohabiting heterosexual couples on issues related to money, work, power, and sex. The Blumstein and Schwartz study provided one of the first opportunities to compare different forms of heterosexual and homosexual relationships. They essentially concluded that there were more similarities than differences among all of these relationship types in terms of (1) lifestyle patterns; and (2) the patterns of adjustment found within their relationships. This basic conclusion has been supported by the research done since the early 1980s. For example, the longitudinal research done by Kurdek and his associates with gay, lesbian, and heterosexual married couples (Kurdek & Schmitt, 1986a, 1986b) concluded that gay and lesbian relationships operate on essentially the same principles as heterosexual relationships and that the correlates of relationship quality are similar for heterosexual, gay, and lesbian couples. This is to suggest that lesbian and gay couples are no more likely to have good or bad relationships than are heterosexual couples (Peplau & Fingerhut, 2007).

Furthermore, the research comparing the patterns of communication and interaction within same-sex and heterosexual couples supports the existence, once again, of many similarities (Haas & Stafford, 2005). For example, according to Haas and Stafford, couples in heterosexual and same-sex relationships deal with a similar range of issues that create tensions and conflict within their relationships. Couples, in other words, regardless of their sexual orientation, fight about similar issues. In addition, Haas and Stafford report that couples, regardless of their sexual orientation, structure and maintain their relationships in similar ways. For example, they found that the most prevalent "maintenance behaviors" reported across both the heterosexual and same-sex relationships were shared tasks (e.g., paying bills, cooking meals, cleaning, doing laundry, and performing household maintenance). Clearly, couples, regardless of their sexual orientation, feel that such behaviors are one way of communicating their commitment to their partners and relationships.

This is not to suggest that there are no differences noted in the research comparing heterosexual and homosexual married partners (Blumstein & Schwartz, 1983; Kurdek, 2004; Peplau & Fingerhut, 2007). Compared to married partners, gay partners reported more autonomy, fewer barriers to leaving, and more frequent relationship dissolution. Compared to married partners, lesbian relationships reported more intimacy, more autonomy, more equality, and more frequent relationship dissolution.

Furthermore, the research of Gottman, Levenson, Seanson, Swanson, Tyson, and Yoshimoto (2003) suggests that conflict management processes may differ for heterosexual couples when compared to same-sex couples. Gottman and colleagues found that the start-up of conflict within homosexual couples was characterized by greater positivity and acceptance when compared to that of heterosexual couples. Specifically, homosexual partners, during the start-up of a conflict, were less belligerent and less domineering than heterosexual initiators. In addition, Gottman and colleagues found that there was less fear and tension, less sadness, and less whining in homosexual initiators than in heterosexual initiators. Their data also showed that homosexuals' throughout conflict situations demonstrated more positive emotions when compared with the heterosexual initiators: more affection, more humor, and more joy and excitement. Gottman and colleagues attribute considerable significance to these findings as the start-up of conflict is highly predictive of relationship stability within heterosexual married couples (Gottman, Coan, Carrère, & Swanson, 1998).

Lastly, Haas and Stafford (2005) found that partners within both same-sex and heterosexual relationships differed in the degree to which they engaged in open and direct discussions of the current state of their relationship. Haas and Stafford suggest that this finding may be a reflection of same-sex couples lacking a legal bond to hold the relationship together. Unlike heterosexual marriages, emotional commitment is the sole bonding force in same-sex relationships. It appears that to some degree heterosexual married couples may take for granted that they are bound together through legal marriage, whereas gays and lesbians must frequently "take the pulse" of the relationship to assess its status.

Given the available evidence, it is reasonable to conclude that intimate ongoing relationships, regardless of their form, have consistent issues that must be managed to promote the well-being of the relationship. While there are some differences in the patterns and dynamics found within same-sex relationships when compared to heterosexual relationships, it appears to be the case that there are more similarities than differences when it comes to how these relationships are structured and experienced. Furthermore, the differences that are noted have to do with the strategies employed within the relationships to manage conflict or promote cohesion and do not support the conclusion that the relationship issues confronted within these relationships are fundamentally different.

At the same time, it is important for us to point out that our endorsement of a postmodern view of marriage and our generic definition of marriage should not obscure the fact that the form of the marriage still has consequences for how married life is structured and experienced. The sociopolitical context of all of these marriage-like relationships differs. This means that the connections of the couples to the mainstream of the society and the degree of social support available to them will differ, which of course can have an impact on how married life is experienced (Laird, 2003).

Put another way, the different forms of marriage-like relationships that exist in the United States are more or less culturally endorsed and accepted. For example, the increase in the visibility of homosexual people within the society has been accompanied by a paradox that reveals an underlying ambivalence existing within the country when it comes to the acceptance of homosexuals. That is, while lesbians and gays are depicted as chic and pioneering, they are simultaneously depicted as a major sign of social deterioration and the source of the destruction of the family as we know it (Laird, 2003; Walters, 2001).

Furthermore, even among heterosexual couples there are varying degrees of social support and acceptance experienced by traditional couples when compared to those residing in less conventional types of marriage-like relationships. Couples who have been previously married and divorced operate within a society that seems to blame many of our societal problems on broken homes. Certainly, in the past, and perhaps still today, the support for and social acceptance of mixed race couples differed when compared to the support and acceptance of marriages among couples of similar races.

The point here is that the structure and experience of couples is influenced at any moment in time by a combination of micro- and macrolevel factors (Sabatelli & Ripoll, 2003). There is no doubt that cultural attitudes and the policies and practices found in the political, economic, educational, medical, and religious institutions of society play a role in how married couples experience their lives. Our inclination to adopt a postmodern view of marriage is based in large part on our belief that all married couples experience a similar range of issues and concerns. We nonetheless feel that it is important to note how the prevailing attitudes and policies found within the country at any point in time create a different set of realities for couples residing in less conventional or legitimate types of marriages as they then deal with the ordinary difficulties that all couples must manage.

The Tasks of the Newly Married Couple

The tasks of the newly formed marital subsystem parallel those that all families must execute. All marital subsystems must establish themes and identities, define their boundaries, maintain a household, and manage the emotional climate within the marriage. Clearly, what makes the beginning of a marriage challenging is that each couple must develop a broad array of rules and strategies for the execution of these tasks.

Establishing an Identity as a Married Couple

When we marry, our personal identity is altered. With marriage comes an acknowledgment that we are ready to assume the roles and responsibilities of adulthood (Rapoport, 1963). This critical identity shift changes how family members and friends relate to us. We are expected to have a "life plan," "have our act together," and be able to plan and organize our lives in a way that enables us to succeed as adult members of society.

Establishing Marital and Family Themes. Moving into the world of adult roles and responsibilities places pressure on newly married couples to develop marital and family themes. These themes reflect the ways in which the couple wishes to represent itself to the outside world. Themes provide the couple with a framework of meaning that serves to guide behavior and orient the couple to extended family, friends, and community. Therefore, the couple's themes become the blueprint for the establishment of basic values, priorities, and goals.

As mentioned in Chapter 2, the choice of family themes is not random but purposeful and goal-directed (Kantor & Lehr, 1975). Themes often reflect the ethnic, religious, and moral convictions of the family. They may also guide the couple's strategies for using its physical and psychological resources. For instance, a couple that wishes to be seen by others as upwardly mobile and achievement-oriented may establish a goal of owning a nice home and possessing quality furnishings as a means of communicating this identity. Couples who adopt a "working-class family" theme, in contrast, may rent a modest apartment when first married, buy used furniture, and set aside money for the future.

Marital and family themes also reflect the manner in which the couple maintains a sense of intergenerational connectedness with the families of origin (Hess & Handel, 1985). By adopting themes that have been central in the family of origin, the couple conveys a willingness to remain identified with and connected to past family experiences. Such themes might be reflected in the perpetuation of cherished holiday customs and traditions or in the reenactment of long-standing shared beliefs such as the "importance of children in families" or the "value of performing public service." Adopting the family's well-established ethnic or religious orientations also maintains intergenerational connectedness. The establishment of such themes not only solidifies the couple's ties to the families of origin but also defines the new couple's identity to family and the community.

Finally, themes also reflect ways in which couples see themselves as unique and different from family and friends (Hess & Handel, 1985). One factor here is the role or personal identity each partner developed within his or her family of origin. For example, the rebel within the family may detest his or her family's emphasis on materialism and adopt a counter-theme of "the simple and rustic life," which is then brought into the marriage. The rebel might, on the other hand, reject the "old world" ethnic values of the extended family in favor of a more modern approach to marriage and family life. Such shifts in themes and values can stress the relations between generations.

A major factor that can influence whether couples emphasize separateness over connectedness in relation to the family of origin is the extent to which each partner experienced their families as functioning successfully. Partners are generally more willing to incorporate major elements of their family's themes into their own marriages when they view their families as having successfully met their own and other family members' needs. When the family of origin is viewed as inadequate, flawed, or in need of repair, young couples are more likely to disengage from the family and reject its basic themes (Wamboldt & Wolin, 1989). In other words, the legacy each partner has incorporated from the family of origin also influences the themes that are (at least consciously) retained or rejected. Partners whose family legacy included themes of fairness, equity, and trust are more likely to remain intergenerationally connected with the extended family than are those whose family legacy involved themes of deprivation, mistrust, neglect, or exploitation (Wamboldt & Wolin, 1989).

Although some of the themes that are established in a new marriage are passed down from generation to generation, the establishment of these themes within the marriage requires considerable negotiation. Each marital partner seeks to integrate into the marriage the legacies that he or she brings from his or her respective family of origin. In some instances, these negotiations result in one legacy taking priority over the other. This occurs, for example, when spouses from different ethnic or religious origins assume the ethnic or religious identity of only one family of origin. In other instances, there is a blending and compromising of themes and identities that result in the emergence of novel themes. In still other instances, despite conscious intentions to the contrary, partners may reenact themes that perpetuate unresolved conflicts with the family of origin in the present marriage (Bagarozzi & Anderson, 1989; Napier, 1988).

The challenge confronted by newly married couples, therefore, is not only to establish themes but to integrate the legacies and themes from their respective families of origin. The pressures that couples may experience as they set about this task center around the need to negotiate their marital and family themes in ways that promote harmony both within the marriage and within the extended family system. This is a delicate negotiation, to be sure!

The Negotiation of Marital Roles. Marriage brings with it the acquisition of a new role, that of being a spouse or long-term partner. During the transition to marriage, couples must negotiate how they intend to act in accordance with this new role. This may seem like a relatively straightforward issue. After all, most heterosexuals have some idea of how husbands and wives are expected to behave. However, there is considerable ambiguity about what is expected of husbands and wives in contemporary society, and certainly even more ambiguity within same-sex relationships about how to organize these role relationships (Blumstein & Schwartz, 1983). This ambiguity amplifies the stress couples experience at the point of marriage.

It is useful at this time to discuss the concepts of roles, conjugal roles, and counter-roles. Simply defined, a **role** is the shared prescriptions for behavior associated with a social position (Heiss, 1981). A **conjugal role** is the prescriptions for behavior associated with the social position of a spouse. Individuals enter marriage with preconceived notions of how they and their partners should act as marital partners. Roles provide predictability and enable the occupants of social positions, and others with whom they interact, to anticipate behavior and maintain order or regularity in their social interactions (Turner, 1970).

Roles can be understood only in relation to complementary or **counter-roles** (LaRossa & Reitzes, 1992). The role of husband, for example, is complemented by the counter-role of wife. Each role carries with it expectations for behavior that superimpose expectations for behavior on the other in the counter-role position. When a man acts in accordance with his beliefs about how he is supposed to behave as a husband, he (1) assumes that his wife will share his expectations; and (2) anticipates that his wife will act in a particular way toward him in return.

To illustrate, when a man believes that husbands should not do housework, implicit in this set of expectations is the expectation that his wife (1) will agree that husbands should not have to do housework; and (2) will accept the responsibility for doing the housework. This expectation, and the behavior that follows from this expectation, does not create conflict in the relationship so long as there is a congruence of expectations and behavior (Burr, Leigh, Day, & Constantine, 1979). In other words, we are likely to be satisfied with our partner's behavior when that behavior is consistent with our own expectations. Conflict, stress, and dissatisfaction ensue, however, when one partner's expectations and behavior are not consistent with the other's expectations and behavior.

Our identities as marital partners are clearly embedded within our own unique conceptualization of how marital roles should be enacted. When expectations are shared, interactions flow smoothly, and we tend to feel satisfied with our partners and our relationship with them. We also tend to feel good about ourselves because the fit between expectations and behaviors confirms our own identities as individuals. In short, the fit between our expectations for our partner and our partner's actual behavior influences how we feel about our partner, our relationship, and ourselves. Thus, a primary task for newly married couples is the development of a relationship reality that makes concrete the expectations that we have for ourselves and our partner in the role of spouse (Berger & Kellner, 1985). Implicit in this process is the need to evolve a clear vision of the prescriptions for behavior associated with these conjugal roles. These transition times are clearly made easier when the norms for roles are clear and shared within the society (Burr et al., 1979; Wiley, 1985). Lack of role clarity and consensus about how roles should be enacted creates the stress of **role conflict**, which brings with it the need for negotiations.

Because family of origin and socialization experiences are different for men and women, it is likely that husbands and wives will have different views of how conjugal roles should be enacted. The stress experienced by newly married couples may be further amplified because the roles of husbands and wives within contemporary American society are undergoing change. The main point here is that conjugal roles are generally not altogether clear, nor is a consensus between partners guaranteed. For instance, if a woman views her marital role in terms of being a "financial provider" and her husband views her as a help mate and companion, there is bound to be tension.

It is important to note, in addition, how role ambiguity within same-sex relationships contributes to the stress experienced during the transition to marriage. Blumstein and Schwartz (1983) point out that gender prescriptions limit the amount of negotiation necessary when heterosexual couples contend with the organization of conjugal roles. For same-sex married partners, in contrast, greater role ambiguity increases the difficulty of arriving at a consensus regarding the allocation of role responsibilities. More negotiation and bargaining must accompany the initial transition to marriage within same-sex relationships. At the same time, however, Blumstein and Schwartz point out that this ambiguity provides a greater opportunity for innovation and choice than is often found within heterosexual couples.

In summary, at the point of marriage, couples embark on a process of constructing a marital identity that carries with it expectations for how the various role demands of the marriage will be enacted. Role-making and identity-bargaining activities tend to be more stressful when roles are not clear, when expectations are ambiguous, and when the partners' socialization experiences result in them developing different views of what marriage should be like.

Evolving a Congruence of Conjugal Identities. Every system must evolve a consensus about the identities of its members. During early marriage, couples face the task of negotiating a congruence of conjugal identities. **Conjugal identity** represents the unique attributes, traits, and characteristics associated with each individual as a spouse within the marriage. In any relationship, participants become identified as possessing unique attributes, traits, values, and characteristics. The conjugal identities that evolve during marriage influence both the manner in which spouses participate in the marriage and the ease of interaction that develops between spouses.

Arriving at a consensus regarding conjugal identities provides a foundation for the assignment of roles and responsibilities within the marriage. Responsibilities for various tasks are assigned, in part, according to each spouse's personal identity image (Bagarozzi & Anderson, 1989; Hess & Handel, 1985; Kantor & Lehr, 1975). For example, the "responsible spouse" becomes the one who pays the bills, keeps the schedule of appointments, and makes sure that the couple's other responsibilities are met. The "sociable spouse" becomes responsible for maintaining ties to extended family and friends.

Conjugal identities also facilitate the predictability and ease of interaction between marital partners. Knowing a partner's identity allows for assumptions about the values and attitudes the partner may hold or how the partner will act in various situations. We might assume that our "literary" spouse would be interested in going to the theater to see a play or would have no interest whatsoever in going to see the local professional football team play on a Sunday afternoon.

It is important to recognize that these identities are often context dependent. They can apply to an individual when interacting with a spouse but may not apply outside this system. For example, an individual might have established an identity within the marriage that includes being shy, withdrawn, and socially anxious. Yet, these same attributes may not apply to this individual in different contexts, such as at work or with friends.

It also is important to recognize that conjugal identities can constrain an individual's behavior or interests. Being identified as the "responsible spouse," for example, may prohibit one from acting in a carefree manner. Conversely, being identified as the "shy spouse" may limit one's opportunities to attend social gatherings. It is apparent that couples need to negotiate identities that support the full range of each member's interests and abilities, rather than constrain individuals from expressing their full potentials.

Finally, it should be apparent that establishing a congruence between each spouse's conjugal identity is only one element of the larger task of establishing a clearly defined **couple identity**. The couple's identity is further defined by the prevailing marital themes and specific conjugal roles adopted by each spouse. The couple's themes provide a framework of meaning that organizes the couple's basic values and beliefs, and offers guidelines for behavior. Conjugal roles prescribe the specific behaviors associated with the social position of husband or wife.

Defining Marital Boundaries

Marital boundaries must be established as couples make the transition to a newly married system. These boundaries involve the establishment of strategies and rules for (1) regulating distances with others outside the marriage; and (2) regulating patterns of separateness and connectedness within the marriage itself.

Regulating Distances with Family and Friends. Boundaries with both family and friends must be realigned at the point of marriage (McGoldrick, 2005b). Marriage typically carries with it the expectation that our primary loyalty will be to our partner and the marriage. One expression of this loyalty is the manner in which the boundary separating the marital couple from outsiders is established. The external marital boundary regulates the frequency and intensity of each partner's contacts with family and friends. Establishment of this boundary requires the development of rules for regulating such factors as how often we visit and call our families, how often we get together for dinner with friends, and how openly we discuss our problems or concerns with parents or friends rather than with the marriage partner. While there is clearly a need for ongoing connections with family and friends following marriage, these connections must be renegotiated such as not to interfere with the primacy of the marital relationship.

The strategies the couple establishes for regulating its external boundaries are influenced by two primary factors. One is the boundary rules that exist in each partner's family of origin, while the other is the manner and extent to which each partner has successfully individuated from his or her family of origin.

The family of origin's boundary rules and, in particular, its tolerance for individuality and intimacy have an effect on how the newly married couple structures its own boundaries. For example, extended families that emphasize personal space and privacy are likely to expect the newly married couple to establish formal, but somewhat distant and private, connections with them following the marriage. Such expectations might include calling parents once a month, talking in general about the weather and the health of family members, or visiting perhaps once or twice a year.

Conversely, the boundary between the extended family and the married couple will differ considerably if one or both partners come from a family that encourages enmeshment and overinvolvement. Here, the expectations might include eating at parents' homes two or three times a week; talking with parents daily; and spending all holidays, anniversaries, and birthdays with the extended family. Tension may result in this situation if both families of origin compete equally for attention from, and connection to, the newly married couple. In addition, an emphasis on extreme enmeshment or overinvolvement brings with it the risk of the extended family attempting to run the marriage. It may become difficult for the newly married pair to find its own identity as a couple while contending with the interference and demands encountered from the families of origin (McGoldrick, 2005b; Rapoport, 1963).

The second factor determining how newly married couples establish their external boundaries is the manner in which each marital partner has individuated from his or her family of origin. Well-individuated spouses can take personal responsibility for their own lives and marriages and also maintain closeness and intimacy with significant others. Such individuals can derive support and other coping resources from available outside relationships, while limiting the impact these significant others have on the overall quality and structure of the marriage.

In the absence of an adequate degree of individuation from the family, the likelihood increases that boundaries with the family of origin will be stressed. Individuals who are fused with their families may allow their continuing loyalty and sense of obligation to the family to interfere with the establishment of a secure and clearly defined marital relationship. Conversely, individuals who reactively cut off from their families may establish a rigid external boundary with the family that deprives the couple of the emotional, informational, and economic support, as well as the access to the intergenerational customs and traditions that could help to ease the transition into a new marriage (Friedman, 1991). In either instance, failure to resolve connections to the family results in the establishment of boundary patterns that interfere with the ability of the newly married couple to operate freely with both a sense of intergenerational continuity and a perception of autonomy and personal authority within the marriage.

The broader point here is that the external boundaries established by the newly married couple must be sufficiently permeable and open to allow for a comfortable interface with others outside the marriage. Newly married couples benefit from being embedded within a network of supportive relationships. At the same time, the boundaries must allow the couple to function as a couple without undue interference from others. All newly formed marriages are likely to experience a certain amount of stress during the establishment of these boundaries. Significant others may be disappointed by the frequency or intensity of contacts with outsiders. We may, in turn, feel guilty about disappointing those outside the marriage. In time, however, patterns generally become established that allow stable and satisfying connections to be made with both families and friends.

Regulating Distances within the New Marriage. When couples marry, they are not only faced with the task of establishing clear boundaries with extended family and friends but must also negotiate a comfortable and satisfying balance of individuality and intimacy for themselves within the marriage. The successful resolution of this task is aided by each spouse being aware of the emotional needs they bring into the marriage and having clear expectations about how the partner is to meet these emotional needs. The task of establishing clear internal boundaries is further enhanced by an openness toward communicating one's emotional needs to the other and a willingness by both partners to negotiate an equitable balance in meeting each other's needs. Finally, the task of establishing clear internal boundaries requires that each spouse be willing to make (and accept) an honest appraisal of the extent to which the partner may be unable or unwilling to meet some of the other partner's emotional needs. The boundaries established between spouses must also allow each to express his or her individuality and seek needed fulfillment through relationships and activities that do not involve the partner.

Marital boundaries, thus, reflect the tolerance for autonomy and individuality that exists within the marriage. In relationships that are characterized by relatively enmeshed boundaries, there is an emphasis on togetherness and mutuality. Couples expect to share time and activities. For instance, they seldom go out in the evening alone or with friends, preferring, instead, to do things together. They may feel that it is important to eat together every day. They will often go to bed at the same time. These boundary patterns should not be viewed as a problem unless the emphasis on togetherness interferes with the abilities of partners to act as individuals within the relationship. Marital partners who are overly enmeshed and involved with one another tend to fuse most of their physical, cognitive, and emotional energies within the relationship. These couples may expect to experience a total oneness with the other by mutually sharing all activities and tasks (Cuber & Harroff, 1972).

Often these overly enmeshed boundary patterns occur when individuals perceive the marriage as a way of meeting needs, such as the need for identity or a sense of belonging, that were unfulfilled within the family of origin (Napier, 1988). As Napier (1988) notes, we may unconsciously bring to marriage "a deep yearning for wholeness, for approval, for all the things we deserved as children and didn't get. . . . We all seem to believe that marriage will change our lives, will make us feel better about ourselves. . . . We dream of a fused, symbiotic union in which we feel nurtured, safe, profoundly valued, and all powerful" (p. 14). Because partners come to depend on the relationship to meet needs that were not met while they were growing up, any violation of the norms of togetherness can be perceived as eroding the foundation of intimacy experienced within the relationship.

At the other end of the continuum are relatively disengaged marital partners who tolerate a great deal of individuality or independent behavior. These couples may spend relatively little time in companionate activities and may maintain a cordial but impassionate connection to one another. Their boundaries permit considerable autonomy of thought, emotion, and behavior. For these couples, the disengagement that has been mutually negotiated emphasizes the primacy of individuality over connectedness. Such boundaries allow partners to pursue their own individual dreams and interests without interference from competing demands for companionship and togetherness (Cuber & Harroff, 1972).

It may seem odd to many that, after marriage, a couple spends little time together. However, it is important to emphasize that there are no right or wrong boundary patterns. What is crucial is that the boundary patterns that are established are mutually acceptable to both partners. Clearly, whether boundaries function in this way depends on whether they fulfill each partner's expectations. When boundary patterns are consistent with each partner's expectations, regardless of the form they take, they will tend to be satisfying. Conversely, when these boundary patterns violate one or both spouses' expectations, conflict ensues (Lewis & Spanier, 1979).

Boundary conflicts that arise during the early marriage period can be minimized to the extent that these issues have been negotiated during the earlier courtship period (Bagarozzi, Bagarozzi, Anderson, & Pollane, 1984). At the same time, it is important to recognize that the boundaries established during the courtship can differ from the boundaries that are established during early marriage. Married couples have different goals for their relationship than do courting couples. It is this shift in goals that characterizes the newly married couple's task of renegotiating its boundary strategies.

During courtship, boundaries are often structured to reinforce the exclusivity and uniqueness of the relationship. There is, therefore, a tendency for most couples to be somewhat overinvolved with one another as each partner invests a considerable part of his or her identity in the relationship. There is a strong tendency to idealize the relationship as well as a high degree of novelty and positive reinforcement in the relationship (Bagarozzi & Anderson, 1989; Jacobson & Margolin, 1979). Couples may spend most, if not all, of their free time with one another. They might not dream of doing something without the partner. Conversely, they may spend their time thinking about and planning their future together.

After marriage, however, the almost exclusive focus on the relationship tends to decline and be replaced with a greater interest in establishing boundaries that also enable each partner to maintain an identity and interests that are separate from the relationship (Napier, 1988). It may, thus, come as quite a shock to us that our partner is interested in going jogging without us, watching TV alone, going to a sporting event with friends instead of us, or going fishing alone on the weekend.

Stress and conflict often accompany this shift in the relationship's internal boundaries as the couple struggles to renegotiate a new, mutually acceptable level of individuality and intimacy. At the point of marriage, couples must work out boundaries that reinforce their identity as a couple and enable each partner to be comfortable with his or her identity as an individual. The particular boundary strategies established by couples can vary greatly, but they are always determined by the expectations that each brings to the relationship.

Managing the Household

The principal tasks associated with managing the household include managing housework and the family finances. While developing strategies for the execution of these tasks may seem straightforward, it is highly likely that couples will have different views about what these strategies should be. Arriving at a consensus about these strategies may require considerable negotiation.

Evolving Housekeeping Strategies. Completing housework is a reality of marriage. How it gets done, however, depends on the specific strategies each couple develops. There are several factors that shape the manner in which couples develop their strategies for completing housework.

One factor is gender socialization. Gender socialization affects many of the role responsibilities that men and women assume within marriage. Housekeeping strategies, as with many other aspects of the conjugal roles of husbands and wives, evolve from each spouse's engendered notions of what husbands and wives should be responsible for in a marriage. For example, traditional gender orientations assume that women should be responsible for cooking, cleaning, and laundry, while husbands should be responsible for yard work, minor indoor and outdoor repairs, painting, and care of automobiles.

The expectations held by both husbands and wives for housekeeping strategies evolve from a more general view of the roles and responsibilities of males and females within society. For instance, females are often cast in the role of caretaker within the broader society. This can easily account for the kind of housekeeping and caretaking roles and responsibilities that wives assume within the marriage. That is, the expectation for women to assume primary responsibility for housekeeping can be traced to socialization experiences that place a heavy emphasis on caretaking as the principal responsibility of women (Coltrane, 2000).

A second factor influencing the choice of housekeeping strategies is each spouse's unique abilities and areas of expertise. Housekeeping strategies depend on both spouses assessing their own abilities relative to the partner's. Each partner may be expected to assume responsibility for those tasks related to their areas of expertise.

However, being viewed as having a particular area of expertise can also be based on gender role stereotypes and earlier male and female socialization experiences. Most individuals are capable of mastering the knowledge needed to complete housekeeping tasks such as cleaning the bathroom; sorting and washing laundry; or ironing shirts, slacks, and skirts. In spite of this, however, women are often assumed to have more expertise in these areas because of their socialization into the caretaking and housekeeping roles. Consequently, because of this socialization, women typically end up taking responsibility for these tasks, even when employed outside the home. In one study, for instance, wives completed an average of thirty-two hours of housework per week compared to ten hours per week by husbands (Blair & Lichter, 1991). Although husbands' participation in household chores has risen dramatically in recent years, the majority of household labor is still done by women. For example, Robinson and Godbey (1999) reported that between 1965 and 1985, husbands' average contributions to routine housework increased from two hours per week to four hours per week (a 50 percent increase!). However, when this was contrasted with wives who completed an average of sixteen hours of housework per week, the differences are clear. Wives still do four times more housework per week than husbands.

Finally, management of the household involves the use of family resources (family members' time and energy and the family's finances). This means that issues of power and control also influence the evolution of housekeeping strategies. As a general rule, there is a positive and linear relationship between resources and power, and a negative and linear relationship between dependence and power (Sabatelli & Shehan, 1992). The individual who possesses the greater personal resources within the marriage, and who is the least dependent on the relationship, tends to be the one who has greater power in the relationship. This partner is more likely to delegate responsibility for tasks to others and is less likely to assume responsibility for "low-status" tasks. Some theorists have identified this as another factor that may explain the greater likelihood for wives to assume housekeeping responsibilities. They suggest that the culture's patriarchal system grants greater resources (e.g., higher status and better-paying jobs) to men, who then exert greater power and control in the marital relationship (Baruch, Biener, & Barnett, 1987; Hochschild & Machung, 1989). Men may then feel justified in leaving low-status household responsibilities to wives.

All three factors operate within each marital system to account for the strategies that couples use for executing housekeeping responsibilities. The strategies that evolve reflect the power and control dynamics that exist within the relationship. The more powerful spouse is less likely to assume principal responsibility for housekeeping tasks. Earlier gender socialization also contributes to the expectations that men and women bring to their marital relationships. Finally, responsibility for household tasks depends on each spouse's recognized areas of expertise.

The goal here is not to evaluate the adequacy or fairness of these strategies but to account for the factors that influence their development. The adequacy of these strategies is reflected in the satisfaction that spouses experience with respect to how these tasks are executed. Here again, satisfaction depends on whether the chosen strategies are congruent with each spouse's expectations. But when a wife, for example, assumes most of the responsibility for housekeeping tasks and expects to do this, she is likely to be satisfied with the strategy. But when a wife believes that housekeeping responsibilities should be shared equally, dissatisfaction is likely to result if her partner expects her to assume most of the responsibility.

Managing Finances within the New Marital System. Another important task for newly married couples is developing a strategy for managing finances. When couples marry, a great many decisions must be made, such as how checking and savings accounts will be established, who will be responsible for paying bills, and how discretionary income will be spent. Some couples may simply pool their incomes in joint checking and savings accounts, and designate one spouse as responsible for paying bills. They may also establish a rule that any discretionary expenditures must be agreed on by both partners. Other couples may set up separate personal bank accounts. This might provide each spouse with a greater sense of personal control over his or her own money but would require rules for how household expenses are to be shared. Still other couples might decide that they will alternate paying all the bills every other month or designate separate bills for which each will be responsible. Such arrangements might also include agreed-on rules for each spouse spending his or her discretionary money without the partner being involved in the decision. Clearly, there are many strategies for managing finances. Establishing these strategies early in marriage is important, because it is unlikely that the couple will have negotiated such decisions before they begin living with one another (Bagarozzi et al., 1984). There is also a great deal of symbolic significance associated with who controls and manages the family's finances. Negotiations around money management can come to reflect themes in the couple's relationship such as "dominance versus submission," "dependence versus independence," or "competence versus incompetence." Therefore, financial management strategies are closely tied to broader issues such as the successful negotiation of power and control, individuation issues, and each spouse's personal sense of competence and self-esteem. Successful strategies are those that leave spouses feeling satisfied that power and control have been equitably distributed and confident that finances are being competently managed. In this regard, it is reasonable to assert that, when couples fight about finances, it is the discomfort with the underlying issues of power and control, individuation, and competence that may be fueling this tension.

In sum, it is apparent that the tasks associated with setting up a household have the potential to stress couples during the transition to marriage. This stress emanates from the new strategies that must be developed to meet the full range of household tasks and responsibilities. Stress is amplified by the differing expectations that partners bring to the relationship (Sabatelli, 1988; Sabatelli & Pearce, 1986). This stress is further amplified since few couples actually discuss their expectations for how these tasks will be executed prior to living together.

Managing the Emotional Climate of the Marriage

When we marry, most of us expect that marriage will provide for our emotional needs and psychological well-being. We may expect marriage to provide us with a safe haven—one in which we can escape from the pressures and demands of life's hectic pace. We may expect that our partner will listen to us, share our concerns, and express the warmth and affection that we need on a day-to-day basis. Therefore, a critical task during early marriage is managing the emotional climate of the marriage. While strategies for managing the emotional climate of the relationship are established during courtship, these strategies will require adjustments when the couple makes the transition from courtship to cohabitation. Living together challenges spouses to balance their individual needs against those of the partner on a daily basis. New strategies will be needed for the expression of emotional support, sexual intimacy, and the management of conflict in a manner that promotes rather than inhibits intimacy.

Expressing Intimacy and Support. As was noted in Chapter 6, one of the developmental tasks of adolescence and early adulthood is the establishment of support networks that meet our needs for nurturance, support, and a sense of belonging. These needs are often met in our relationships with family and friends. However, when we marry, there is often the expectation that the partner will become the primary source of this type of support.

Although there may be little disagreement that meeting one another's needs for intimacy and support is a vital task of marriage, there is considerable variation in the strategies that couples employ for executing this task. Each of us comes from a family of origin that was likely to have employed somewhat different strategies for expressing intimacy, nurturance, and support. The challenge for the newly married couple is to consolidate these disparate legacies into a shared strategy that leaves both partners feeling supported and cared for.

For example, one spouse may come from a family in which feelings of affection and care were verbally expressed. Another might come from a family in which nurturance was expressed through actions rather than words. In such a family, doing little favors for others, providing for one another's physical needs, or performing household tasks such as cooking or cleaning might have been perceived as expressions of caring and support. When these disparate legacies are united, it is quite possible that each partner's expectations for how intimacy and support should be expressed might be violated by the partner's well-intentioned behavior.

The partner who expects feelings and affection to be openly expressed, for example, may not interpret the partner's well-meaning actions as supportive. Conversely, the partner who expects support to be expressed through actions may wonder why such supportive behaviors are not reciprocated. Intending to nurture and support a partner and having the partner actually feel nurtured and supported are quite different matters. The challenge for the new marital system, assuming that members truly intend to nurture and support one another, is to negotiate a set of shared perceptions and mutually satisfying strategies for the provision of nurturance and support. These negotiations must consider the different family legacies that each spouse brings to the marriage.

It is important, in addition, to consider how gender can affect the nurturance and support strategies established within new marriages. As a general rule, women are more socialized than men to take responsibility for caretaking in intimate relationships. The traditional socialization experiences of men often do not provide them with extensive training in how to attend to the emotional needs of others. These disparate socialization experiences are likely to affect the nurturance and support strategies that become established in marriage, with women assuming more responsibility than men for meeting the emotional needs of the partner.

There is a great deal of ambiguity and uncertainty associated with the transition to marriage (Boss, 1988). This ambiguity is evident in questions regarding how conjugal roles are to be defined and how strategies will be established to meet the wide array of necessary marital tasks. Given this uncertainty, it is likely, at least initially, that each spouse's socialization experiences will influence the emotional caretaking strategies that are established within the marriage.

Disparate caretaking responsibilities may or may not become a problem in marriage. Again, the degree of satisfaction with nurturance and support strategies depends on the degree to which each spouse's experiences are congruent with his or her expectations. It is also entirely possible, as will be discussed in greater detail in Chapter 9, that spouses' expectations for nurturance and support will change over time. It is when expectations change that communication processes become critical to the maintenance of marital stability and satisfaction.

Evolving a Marital Sexual Script. One of the expectations of marriage is that intimacy and support will be expressed through sexual ties. To do so, couples must evolve strategies for meeting the sexual needs of one another. The significance of sexuality lies in its ability to communicate symbolically the exclusiveness of the marital relationship. Sexuality is the means by which the couple establishes a special boundary and a special bond with one another. This important dimension of the marriage relationship becomes one way of communicating intimacy, nurturance, support, closeness, and concern for the partner.

One way to think of this responsibility is to consider how couples evolve a marital **sexual script**. A sexual script can be thought of as a blueprint for sexual activity. The script encompasses the wide range of motives and behaviors that guide how we act in sexual situations (Gagnon, 1977). Sexual motivations have to do with why we have sex. The behavioral aspect of the script addresses the range of sexual activities that are acceptable within the relationship. The script also prescribes where and when it is appropriate to engage in sex. For example, this might include at what times of day, where (in what rooms) in the house, and how frequently sex should occur. Finally, embedded within the script are guidelines for who takes responsibility for initiating sex.

When cohabiting, a mutually pleasing and satisfying sexual script must be negotiated. These negotiations are challenging because there are many potential disagreements around each of the various dimensions of the sexual script that can erode the intimate foundation of sexuality. For example, couples can disagree about the motives for having sex ("You are just interested in sex because you're tense, not because you love me!"); about which activities are appropriate expressions of nurturance and support ("Why won't you please me in the ways I want you to?"); about the frequency of sex; about who should take responsibility for sex; and even about where and when it is appropriate to have sex.

In other words, sexuality becomes one important means of communicating interest in and concern for the marital partner. The sexual scripts that partners establish are negotiated over time and, ideally, in a way that builds, rather than erodes, the foundation of intimacy. It should be clear, however, that evolving a script that fosters intimacy does not simply follow from good intentions. There are many opportunities for couples to misunderstand and disagree about different aspects of the sexual script. In each of these instances, open communication and negotiation are essential to set the script back on course.

Managing Conflict. Clearly, considerable potential for conflict exists within any close personal relationship. In fact, conflicts in relationships are inevitable (Sprey, 1978; Straus, 1979). **Conflict** can occur whenever one spouse's desires or expectations are incompatible with those of the other. What ensues is a struggle over differences in values, behaviors, powers, or resources in which one partner seeks to achieve his or her goals at the expense of the other (Scanzoni & Polonko, 1980).

In general, any source of stress has the potential to generate conflict. Stress may originate from a source external to the family, such as job pressures or a natural disaster. For example, a fight with a coworker may be brought home and displaced onto the spouse, who may be perceived as a safer target for anger. On the other hand, couples may find that they have very different ideas about how to alter the family budget to recover from the damage caused by a house fire. Stress may also originate from within the family due to each spouse's developmental changes or other internal changes, such as an unexpected illness or disability.

As noted in Chapter 2, stress can be thought of as the degree of pressure exerted on the family to alter the strategies it employs to accomplish its basic tasks. It is the alterations in the couple's established strategies that can often produce conflict. Couples generally tend to agree about the basic tasks of marriage. That is, most marital couples agree that establishing a clear couple identity, managing the household, and creating a supportive emotional environment for one another are important. What they often disagree about, however, is the exact manner in which these tasks should be addressed. Conflicts occur when partners disagree about the strategies that should be used to fulfill various system tasks (Kantor & Lehr, 1975).

Couples are constantly confronted by the need to negotiate and renegotiate their strategies for meeting marital tasks. To do this successfully, couples must develop effective strategies for managing conflict. The strategies that evolve are quite variable and are influenced, in part, by the models of conflict management to which each spouse was exposed in his or her family of origin. Some families yell. Other families go for walks and cool off before discussing conflicts further. Others deny that conflicts exist at all. Each spouse will bring into the marriage predispositions to manage conflict in certain ways based on his or her own family of origin experiences. These differing predispositions must be reworked into a shared strategy that is acceptable to both partners in the new marital system.

The exact strategies that we employ for the management of conflict are further influenced by the meanings associated with conflict. By meaning, we refer to the overarching interpretation and significance spouses attribute to the presence of conflict within the relationship. Some couples, for example, fear marital conflicts and may seek ways to avoid them (Storaasli & Markman, 1990). Others may readily accept that conflict is inevitable in relationships. Having this view is likely to lead to conflict management strategies that allow for the open discussion of conflicts and the negotiation of mutually agreed on solutions.

In other instances, the presence of conflict can be interpreted as a personal rejection. This can occur when the desires and expectations held for the partner are associated with the core elements of his or her personal identity. The greater the personal investment in a particular issue, the more emotional energy is likely to be invested, and the greater the potential for the ensuing conflict to shape feelings about the overall relationship. The emotional response is increased because, on some level, an unwillingness on the part of the partner to comply with a spouse's vision of how tasks should be managed can be experienced as a serious rejection of his or her sense of self.

A disagreement about a husband's unwillingness to clean the bathroom, for example, may be viewed by the wife as something more than a simple disagreement about how a common household task should be managed. She may view his unwillingness to clean the bathroom as expressing a view of her that she finds undesirable. In other words, embedded within this conflict may be the wife's deeper concern about her own identity and about her husband's view of her within the relationship.

When the meaning attributed to conflict lends itself to feelings of personal rejection, couples are more likely to get caught up in opinionated and defensive struggles with one another. These struggles are generally characterized by attempts to influence, convince, or coerce the spouse to adopt the other's point of view. The amount of emotion invested in these struggles reflects the underlying connection between our vision of how tasks should be completed and our vision of ourselves as individuals.

Spouses who experience conflict as personal rejection also may seek to form alliances or coalitions with others outside the marriage. The purpose is to obtain confirmation from others regarding the partner's view of the self as well as to gain outside support for how tasks should be managed. For example, if a husband talks with his parents about his conflict with his wife over his unwillingness to clean the bathroom, he is seeking support for his identity and his view of how men and women should act in marriage.

The broader point here is that all couples must manage conflict. How these conflicts are managed will affect significantly the level of intimacy and support experienced within the relationship. The strategies that spouses evolve for the management of conflict originate in the models they learned in their families of origin. Conflict management strategies are further influenced by the meaning that spouses attribute to the conflict. Conflict in relationships is inevitable. Understanding this and viewing conflict as differing views about which strategies to use to manage marital tasks, rather than as a personal attack upon the other's sense of personal identity, can facilitate the emergence of conflict management strategies that promote rather than inhibit intimacy.

Conclusions

From a developmental perspective, the transition to marriage is complicated by the need for couples to negotiate the many strategies necessary to execute the basic tasks of the new marital system. The demands placed on couples at this point are generally understood as ordinary demands. That is, most couples have the necessary resources and abilities to manage the stresses associated with this transitional period (McCubbin et al., 1980). At the same time, that the demands are ordinary should not undervalue the importance of the issues that must be addressed during this period. The strategies developed for executing system tasks influence how couples feel about their relationship and how they will deal with both the ordinary and extraordinary stresses and strains they will encounter over the life cycle of the family.

In general, adaptation to the demands and challenges of the early marriage stage is facilitated by the couple's ability to negotiate effective strategies. Each partner comes into the marriage having been exposed to a unique set of strategies and models for managing family systems tasks in their own family of origin. The challenge to couples is to merge these different legacies into a system of strategies and rules that foster family stability, the experience of intimacy, and a sense of belonging. Implicit in this process is the need for effective communication and negotiation skills.

Key Terms

Conflict Disagreements over values, behaviors, family strategies, powers, or resources during which one partner seeks to achieve his or her goals at the expense of the other.

Conjugal identity The unique attributes, traits, and characteristics associated with each individual as a spouse within the marriage.

Conjugal role The prescriptions for behavior associated with the social position of a spouse.

Counter-role The complementary expectations for behavior that are superimposed upon the partner as a result of the way an individual performs his or her own role.

Couple identity The framework of meaning couples establish to define themselves in relation to one another as well as to the outside world. This includes (1) each person's conjugal identity; (2) the marital themes that organize the couple's basic values and beliefs and provide guidelines for behavior; and (3) each partner's conjugal role, which defines the specific behaviors associated with the social position of husband or wife.

Marriage A specific family subsystem comprised of adults from two families of origins who have bonded together to form what they intend to be a stable and long-term cohabiting relationship.

Role The shared prescriptions for behavior associated with a social position.

Role conflict Disagreements between partners about marital roles and responsibilities.

Sexual script A blueprint for sexual activity; the full range of motives and behaviors that guide how we act in sexual situations.

CHAPTER 9

Communication and Intimacy

Chapter Overview

Communication is an essential feature of intimate relationships. This chapter provides an overview of the central assumptions and core constructs of communication theory. Specifically, the chapter provides an overview of the concepts of messages, metamessages, and framing as they relate to communication processes. Furthermore, the chapter outlines how conversational styles, that is, an individual's unique style of communicating with others, affect the experience of closeness and intimacy within ongoing relationships. The factors influencing the formation of conversational styles are discussed, with a focus on gender-based differences. Finally, the chapter underscores the elements of the communication process that facilitate the experience of intimacy. In this regard, confirmation, self-disclosure, and transaction management and their effect on the experience of intimacy are discussed in detail.

Communication and Intimacy

Establishing strategies for meeting the various tasks of marriage requires extensive negotiation. Couples, while not necessarily conscious of this need, will be required to establish rules for managing the household, handling the finances, and working out boundary patterns with friends and family. Internal boundaries must be negotiated, and mutually agreeable patterns of separateness and connectedness established. Couples must also establish themes and identities and negotiate marital roles and expectations. To accomplish all this, they will rely heavily on their abilities to communicate with one another.

A primary task of all newly married couples is to establish a **private message system** (Tannen, 1986). This is a system of rules for communication within an intimate relationship. The private message system gives the couple's relationship its distinctive quality and helps to organize the strategies that will be needed to face the many tasks and issues that will arise. The private message system also influences how couples feel about their relationship. As we shall see in this chapter, communication and, in particular, the couple's private message system are central to a couple's success at negotiating the tasks of marriage. Communication has the power to enhance or inhibit the experience of marital intimacy, which is why it is imperative to develop a grasp of this complex and important process.

Defining Communication

Communication can be viewed as a symbolic and transactional process through which we create and share meanings (Galvin & Brommel, 1991). Communication is symbolic in that, when we communicate with others, we employ symbols in the form of words and various nonverbal cues that have a shared meaning. The shared meaning associated with these various symbols is necessary to promote understanding. Communication is transactional in that, when people communicate, they have a mutual impact on one another (Galvin & Brommel, 1991). Both participants contribute to the patterns of communication that become established between them.

Communication, thus, can be thought of as a process involving the exchange of information through the use of symbols. When we interact with others, we participate in a "communicational system." To view communication as taking place within a system suggests that as individuals we do not originate communication but, rather, participate in it (Watzlawick, Beavin, & Jackson, 1967). A communication system, like all systems, is characterized by interdependence. Each participant's communication simultaneously influences and is influenced by the communications of others.

To illustrate, consider the situation in which a couple is disagreeing over the wife's unwillingness to do her share of the housework. As this conflict unfolds, the husband expresses his displeasure by nagging his wife, reminding her of what she is supposed to do and telling her how insensitive she is. The wife, in turn, responds by telling her husband what a nag he is and withdrawing from the interaction. As the wife withdraws, the husband only nags more. As the husband nags more, the wife tends to withdraw more.

This pattern of nagging and withdrawing illustrates the interdependent and systemic nature of communication. Clearly, each partner's communication influences the communication of the other and is, simultaneously, influenced by the communication of the other. The communication between this couple is structured by a conspicuous rule of relating: he nags and she withdraws. It is impossible to determine that one partner's behavior causes the behavior of the other, because, at any given moment, each partner's behavior is simultaneously a stimulus for and a response to the other's behavior (Watzlawick et al., 1967).

Within a communication system, all behavior is communication, and, thus, it is impossible not to communicate (Watzlawick et al., 1967). This means that, when interacting with another, everything we do and say (or do not do or say) conveys information and affects the course of interaction. How we say something, when we say it, what we are doing when we speak, and what we avoid saying are all behaviors that contribute to the meaning others derive from what we have said.

These behaviors also influence how others will, in turn, respond to us and how the interaction will proceed.

Basic Constructs: Messages, Metamessages, and Framing

The information that is exchanged when we communicate is conveyed in **messages**. Communication theorists highlight the complexity of conveying messages by suggesting that each message carries information at two levels—a **content level** and a **relationship level** (Watzlawick et al., 1967). The content level refers simply to the literal content of a message or *what* is communicated. The literal content of a message is evident in the statement, "I like your dress." The relationship level refers to how the content is communicated. The information contained in how the content is expressed is used to interpret the literal content of the message. For instance, the statement "I like your dress" when accompanied by snickering and frowning conveys a meaning different from the one conveyed by a pleasant smile and a sincere tone. It is difficult, if not impossible, to think of any message sent by one person to another that does not also carry a commentary on the relationship (Knapp & Hall, 2002). If someone insults our appearance, we might be inclined to think that they do not like us very much.

Metamessages: The Message within the Message. The information conveyed by how a message is expressed is also referred to as the **metamessage**, or "message about the message." Metamessages are conveyed in the behaviors and nonverbal cues that accompany our literal messages. Metamessages qualify how the message is to be taken, and convey information about how serious, how sure, or how honest we are about an assertion. For example, in the earlier example, the snicker, frown, smile, or voice tone comprises the metamessage. On the meta-level, the statement "I like your dress" can be reinforced, making it abundantly clear whether the speaker is being sincere or disingenuous.

Within a communication system, information about the self, the other, and the relationship is continually being exchanged on the meta-level. In other words, each communication can be thought of as conveying the following metamessages: (1) "This is how I see myself"; (2) "This is how I see you"; and (3) "This is how I see you seeing me" (Watzlawick et al., 1967).

Take, as an example, a rather innocent interaction that occurs countless times every day in American households. A husband and wife are about to sit down to dinner. A jar of pickles has been brought to the table, and the wife is sitting there struggling, trying to open the jar. The husband, seeing her struggling with the lid, turns to her while taking the jar and says, "Let me open that." In this example, are you able to recognize the information about the self, the other, and the relationship that can be conveyed?

By the manner in which he takes the jar and says, "Let me open that," the husband stakes a claim to a particular identity. If he takes the jar assuredly, unhesitatingly opens it, and gets a proud look on his face when the jar pops open, he is saying, "I am strong and capable." His behavior conveys a masculine and confident view of himself. He would, of course, convey a rather different view of himself if he only reluctantly took the jar and rather nervously attempted to open it. In this situation, his behavior could be viewed as calling into question not only his strength but his confidence in his ability to take on difficult challenges.

The way he takes the jar and says "Let me open that" also lets his wife know how he views her. If he has a look of impatience and disgust on his face while taking the jar, he is letting his wife know that he views her as weak, helpless, or, perhaps, even incompetent. He could, just as easily, let her know that her being unable to open the jar has nothing to do with her as a person. He might do this by not calling attention to the fact that she cannot open the jar but simply allowing his greater physical strength to be one of those things that really does not matter in the grander scheme of things!

At the same time, through this interaction, the husband is providing his wife with information about how he views their relationship. When he gently and willingly takes the jar and softly says, "Let me open that," he is letting her know that he is there to help her and that she can rely on him: he views their relationship as a supportive partnership. If he impatiently and aggressively grabs the jar and opens it with a look of disdain on his face, he is communicating a disdain for her and their relationship. He would then be saying in effect, "This relationship is such a bother—it annoys me to have to take care of you." (You probably never thought so much information was contained in the act of opening a jar of pickles!)

Metamessages and Nonverbal Symbols. Communication is largely about the assignment of meaning to the various **nonverbal symbols** and cues that are used when we interact with others. For example, gestures, body movements, facial expressions, eye contact, and posture are all symbolic and, hence, carry significant information. We use these symbols freely when talking with others to let them know how we view ourselves, them, and our relationships with them. We can express our trust and openness with another, for example, by making eye contact. Facial expressions can convey warmth, comfort, disgust, or indifference (Knapp & Vangelisti, 2005).

There is also symbolic significance associated with voice qualities, intonation, pacing, pitch, and loudness. Voice qualities can convey enthusiasm or indifference. Loudness and pitch can communicate seriousness or anger. Loudness, pacing, and intonation can also be used to establish or reinforce power and authority in a relationship (Pearson, 1985). Furthermore, social and personal space is used to interact with others to convey information on the meta-level. Intimacy, involvement, and interest are conveyed, in part, by our proximity to another when we interact with them. Patterns of power and authority can also be established and reinforced through the use of personal space. For example, touching can, in one context, convey closeness and solidarity, whereas in another it can convey superiority and authority. It can even be used to threaten or communicate hostility and anger (Pearson, 1985; Knapp & Hall, 2002).

By viewing all behavior as communication, we are alerted to the importance of nonverbal cues. Nonverbal cues have considerable impact on the communication process because they have symbolic significance. When we interact with others, we cannot help but gesture, make facial expressions, and employ other nonverbal signals. All of these various behaviors convey information and qualify the information that is being sent. They establish on the meta-level how the message is to be interpreted. Nonverbal behaviors convey a great deal of information about how we feel about ourselves, our partners, and the relationships that we share with them.

The Framing of Messages: How Messages Are Heard. In sending a message, we choose both words and behaviors that are intended to convey the information that we want others to "receive." However, what others hear when we communicate with them depends on their interpretation, or **framing**, of our messages. Framing refers here to the meaning attributed to the metamessages that accompany a literal message (Tannen, 1986). Clearly, the assignment of meaning to someone's metamessages is not an objective event but a personal, subjective process. As such, each person assigns meaning to a behavior that may differ from the meaning another would assign (Wilmot, 1975). That the framing of metamessages can vary explains how misunderstandings can occur whenever two people interact.

The complexity of communication is highlighted further when we consider that we cannot control what another will actually hear when we speak to them. For instance, you might put your arm around your partner in a candle-lit room as a way of conveying your caring and simple joy at sharing an intimate moment. However, your partner might interpret this behavior very differently. Your partner could frame your behavior as a sign that you are simply interested in sex. When this occurs, that is, when the intent of the metamessage and the manner in which it is framed do not match, even the most innocent of behaviors can lead to misunderstandings.

This example highlights two important points. First, the concept of framing is central to any discussion of the misunderstandings that people encounter when talking with one another. Second, as Tannen (2001) suggests, many misunderstandings result when individuals frame messages intended to promote connection as attempts to exert control. That is, every conversation involves creating a balance between connection and control. The same exact words and gestures can be expressions of connection or control—depending, of course, on (1) the message the sender intends to convey; (2) the particular ways the message is expressed; and (3) the way the message is interpreted or framed. Because the same messages can be an expression of connection or control, misunderstandings commonly occur when the intent of the message does not match the way it is framed. In the previous example, when you put your arm around your partner, you may have truly intended this as a message of caring and connection. However, because this same behavior could actually have been an effort on your part to control your partner (i.e., get your partner to fulfill your sexual needs), a misunderstanding occurred when the message was framed as a controlling rather than connecting message.

To further illustrate these points, consider how framing and the dimensions of connection and control result in a misunderstanding that commonly occurs when parents talk with their teenaged children. As an expression of interest and connection I might ask my sixteen-year-old son, "What are you doing after school today?" However, because the same question could be an expression of control (i.e., I could be asking him this question because I want to decide if I approve of what my son is doing), a misunderstanding could occur. My son might frame this message as having a controlling rather than a connecting intention.

Conversational Styles

Talking, like walking, is something we do without stopping to question how we are doing it. When we say something, we usually feel we are talking naturally, but what we say and how we say it are chosen from a great range of possibilities. Everything that is said, in other words, must be said in some way—in some tone of voice, at some rate of speed, and with some intonation and volume. We may consider what we want to say when we speak, but rarely do we consider how to say it unless the situation is emotionally charged. Rarely do we consider how loudly to speak or how fast, yet others use these signals to interpret meanings and decide what they think of the communication.

These differences in how we talk reflect the fact that each and every one of us develops a **conversational style**, a unique style of communicating with others (Tannen, 1986, 2001). This style is reflected in how we encode or shape messages—the words and manner we customarily use to convey information on the metalevel. Our conversational style also determines how we are likely to frame or interpret the messages we receive from others.

Obviously, it is hard to generalize about conversational styles because they are highly idiosyncratic. At the same time, conversational styles are thought to vary along certain general dimensions. One dimension is our degree of directness (Tannen, 1986). Some of us are quite comfortable communicating in a direct way. We say what we think and feel, looking people straight in the eye and telling them what we think of them. We do this, perhaps, because we were brought up to tell the truth. Similarly, our social experiences may have taught us that it is better to act this way with others. Regardless of our motives for adopting this style, we cannot necessarily control how others will frame our directness. To some, we may be perceived as insensitive to their feelings, while others might respect us for being honest.

Other individuals will evolve a conversational style that is decidedly indirect in nature. When using such a style, we tend to hint at what we really mean, think, or feel. We qualify our statements, only revealing information slowly, or we even attempt to get others to say for us what we intend to say. Indirect communicators do not make "I" statements such as, "I really like you and want to go out with you." They tend to use "it" or "you" statements such as, "Gee, it seems as if we have a nice time when we are together." They may then wait to see how the other might respond. If the other does not look totally disgusted in response to this statement, the indirect communicator might follow up this statement with another such as, "Do you think that we could do something together some time in the future, maybe?" This kind of statement might then be followed by another long pause, during which the effect of the statement is assessed (and during which it is hoped that the other will, in fact, acquiesce to the hint). After enough time passes, and only if forced into actually asking the question, the indirect communicator might say, "Well, I mean, what do you think? Do you think you want to go out sometime, or, perhaps, maybe even tonight?"

How we convey involvement with others is another highly personalized aspect of our conversational style (Tannen, 1986). Some individuals communicate in a way that makes it clear that they want to involve the other in the communication process. They may use nonverbal cues like touching or maintaining close physical proximity to the other to convey this interest. Others communicate in a more detached manner. They might use facial expressions and body postures to suggest to others that they keep their distance. Their tone of voice might convey the impression that they are indifferent to the feelings and ideas of others. The point here is that they may not, in fact, be indifferent to others' feelings and ideas although their conversational style may cause others to assume that this is the case.

A third element of conversational style is the extent to which one's messages are **congruent**. A message is congruent when all of its different components (verbal/nonverbal, content/relationship) convey the same meaning. Incongruent messages, on the other hand, are those in which contradictions occur between different levels of a communication. If I say, for instance, "I am cold," and begin taking off my jacket, the verbal and nonverbal elements of my statements contradict one another. Likewise, if I say, "You can decide, because I really don't care what movie we see tonight," and then I veto every suggestion you make until you mention the one I really want to see, the content and relationship levels of my statement are in contradiction. On the content level, I identify you as being in charge, but on the relationship level I am insisting that I actually want to be in charge. Incongruent messages tend to produce confusion and anxiety in the receiver, since it is difficult to know how to respond (Wilder & Collins, 1994).

Conversational styles also vary in terms of how messages are received and framed. Although most individuals tend to respond more to nonverbal than verbal cues (Watzlawick et al., 1967), some people are highly sensitive to the nonverbal elements of communications. They may engage in a process of constantly attending to this information to determine how others feel about them. Other individuals are less sensitive to the nonverbal elements of communication. They may attend to this information without interpreting it as a statement about their own personal worth. **Self-esteem**, or how positive individuals feel toward themselves, has been found to play an important role in determining how a person receives and frames messages. The greater the person's self-esteem, the more likely he or she is to be open to the verbal and nonverbal expressions of others and then to interpret others' communications accurately (Satir, 1972).

It is important to emphasize that there is no absolutely right or wrong conversational style. It is not possible to say that one way of shaping and framing messages is always better than another. This is not meant to imply, however, that conversational styles do not have an effect on interaction and our abilities to communicate with others. Conversational styles inevitably help to shape how social interactions proceed. Here it is interesting to note that people who share similar styles may communicate more successfully with one another than with people with different styles (Gottman, 1999). Sharing similar styles increases the likelihood of developing mutual understanding and intimacy, and decreases the possibility of misunderstanding, tension, and frustration.

Factors Influencing How We Shape and Frame Messages

Conversational styles reflect the idiosyncratic tendencies that individuals use when they send and receive messages. The highly personalized nature of conversational styles suggests that they are influenced by a number of different factors. For example, our communications with others are modified to accommodate different situations and circumstances. Whom we are speaking with, the nature of our relationship with the other, and the subject under discussion all affect the style employed. We may not feel free to be direct, for example, when communicating with our boss but may find it easy to be direct with our spouse.

The communication context is the physical and social environment within which communication occurs. The context influences how messages are shaped and framed. If a person's partner says, "I love you," in public, for everyone else to hear, he or she might attribute greater significance to this than when these same words are spoken in the context of sexual passion.

Interpersonal needs as well as the self-concept and self-esteem of an individual are all highly individualized factors that affect how communications are shaped and framed. When feeling confident and sure of ourselves, we are more apt to communicate directly. When feeling secure, we do not mind when others tease us, joke with us, or look at us in strange ways. These same behaviors, however, can take on a great deal of symbolic significance when we are not feeling confident and sure of ourselves. A joking comment might be framed as an insult, a glance as an expression of hostility.

As noted earlier, self-esteem, in particular, has a powerful effect on the communication process. The person with low self-esteem tends to frame messages negatively (Satir, 1972). When he or she is told, for example, "You look good today," the person with low self-esteem responds by asking, "Does that mean you don't like the way I look most of the time?" Similarly, if quietly and calmly prompted, "Let's go get something to eat," the insecure person frames the quiet demeanor as a lack of interest, enthusiasm, and sincerity, and responds, "Let's just skip it!" In other words, when people frame messages in consistently negative ways, the possibility that misunderstandings will occur is amplified and the potential for frustrating interactions substantially increased.

Culture and ethnicity also influence how messages are shaped and framed. Cultural rules for communication vary. Avoiding eye contact may be a way of showing respect for another in one culture, whereas the same behavior might be framed, in another culture, as an expression of indifference and disregard. Standing close to another can be, in one culture, an expression of interest, while in another culture this same behavior would be framed as an expression of hostility. The main point is that cultural and ethnic norms establish communication rules that are integrated into the conversational styles of individuals. When everyone is playing by the same rules, interaction tends to go more smoothly. When people do not know one another's rules, interactions are more apt to become frustrating due to the increased possibility of misunderstandings.

The family of origin also influences conversational styles. The family system establishes communication rules that become part of how we then shape and frame communications. Our family influences how we communicate many expressions, including support, intimacy, solidarity, and anger. In some families, support and solidarity are expressed by everyone talking at the same time and standing close to one another. In other families, solidarity is expressed through teasing and joking. Each of us grows up in a unique family context that provides us with models and rules for communication. The likelihood that others will share all the nuances of our models and rules is really quite remote.

Gender-Based Differences in Conversational Styles

We have discussed a number of factors that influence the conversational styles employed when interacting with others. Gender is another factor that is important to consider when discussing conversational styles. While researchers have made a case for the presence of gender-based differences in conversational styles (for an overview, see Dindia & Canary, 2006; Dow & Wood, 2006), it is important to address a couple of precautions before proceeding.

The first is that, while there are differences between males and females in conversational styles, the differences are often exaggerated. Pearson (1985), for example, when discussing gender and communication, notes that the clichés about the differences in the language of women and men appear to be stronger than are the actual differences. Pearson goes on to suggest that "because we live in a society which stresses differences between women and men rather than similarity, because of the nature of our culture which is based on competitiveness and power, we tend to perceive exaggerated differences in the verbalizations of women and men" (p. 178).

A second point is that, when we discuss the actual differences that exist between males and females in conversational styles, we need to be wary of the dangers of overgeneralizing. That some differences exist between males and females is important. It is important, as well, to consider that, in spite of these differences, substantial variations exist in the conversational styles of females when compared with "other females." Similarly, the conversational styles of males are quite variable as well. While it is important to discuss the differences that exist between groups, we do not want to lose sight of the variability that exists within a particular group. This can occur if we overgeneralize between-group differences. To do so will create the impression that the conversational styles of all men are similar, the conversational styles of all women are similar, and the conversational styles of all men differ from those of women. Nothing could be further from the truth.

The differences typically found in the conversational styles of men and women reflect different gender-based interpersonal orientations. This means that as a general rule, feminine communication differs from masculine communication

(Dindia & Canary, 2006; Dow & Wood, 2006; Wood, 2009). Extensive research has identified the following seven features of feminine communication:

- Disclosing personal information and learning about others
- Attempts to create equality between people
- Expressions of support, sympathy, empathy, and agreement
- Efforts to keep a conversation going by inviting others into interaction, asking questions, and encouraging others to elaborate on their ideas
- Highly responsive nonverbal expressions in the form of eye contact, head nodding, and facial expressions that show interest
- Include concrete details when describing events and experiences
- Likely to use hedges, qualifiers, and tag questions—all conversational styles that result in the communications appearing to be tentative.

In contrast, the following six features of masculine communication have been identified:

- Efforts to control the conversation
- Instrumentality in the form of attempting to accomplish objectives, solve problems, and devise strategies
- Attempts to dominate the conversation by talking more often and for longer periods of time
- Talking in a direct and assertive way
- Talking in abstract ways, relying on generalizations and conceptual levels of description
- The restricted use of emotion and disclosures

What these generalities illustrate is that when they are present in a couple's communication, they may very well have consequences for the conversational patterns that become established. As a general rule, women who adopt a feminine conversational style talk to connect. Men who adopt a masculine conversational style talk to inform, establish status, and assert their authority. That is, men often talk to give information or to report. Their conversational style tends to be direct, and they tend to talk about things—business, sports, and food—rather than people. They convey facts, not details. They are goal oriented. They focus on solving problems (and yes, it is true, they are less likely, even though they are problem solvers, to ask for help or directions).

Women, on the other hand, talk to get information, connect with others, or establish rapport. Their conversational styles tend to be indirect, and they often talk about people rather than things. They convey feelings and details. They are relationship oriented. As a result, they are more likely than men to encourage involvement and rapport by touching others when talking, smile more during interactions, and establish eye contact (Wood, 2009).

There are two primary explanations for the existence of gender-typed communication behaviors. The first explanation stresses the notion that these gender differences are a result of status or power differences between men and women.

The second explanation relies on gender-specific socialization as the basis for explaining gender differences in communication behaviors.

There is evidence that gender differences in communication behavior reflect the unequal status and power of men and women within societies (Dow and Wood, 2006; Wood, 2009). Specifically, studies reveal that people who hold subordinate social roles show more behaviors that are hesitant, supportive, and attentive to others' needs. People with less power speak more tentatively and indirectly, and they try to make others feel comfortable. Higher status people communicate in ways that emphasize their dominance and status. They are more likely to interrupt, talk for longer periods of time, and make direct assertions. As such, men's tendency to interrupt their partners, give directives, and talk longer can be seen as an expression of their higher status in society. In a similar way, some of the typical feminine communication behaviors, such as asking questions and using hedges, can be seen as reflecting women's lower status in society. The importance of status in this context is also underlined by studies that show status to be more important for explaining communication behavior differences than gender itself (Ellyson, Dovidio, & Brown, 1992; Johnson, 1994).

A second explanation for the existence of these gender differences focuses on the socialization experiences of males and females with respect to societal expectations and roles. The feminine gender role encourages women to exhibit expressive and social-emotional behaviors. Women are taught to be nonassertive, polite, kind, and socially responsive. Men, in contrast, are taught to act in instrumental and unemotional ways. These gendered expectations result in women and men adopting the specific conversational strategies outlined above. Gendered expectations may also place men and women in conflicting and incompatible situations. An example is when women are placed in a "damned if they do and damned if they don't" position because of gender-marked linguistic expectations. If they comply with social expectations by speaking softly and hesitantly, they are seen as trivial and behaving "just like a woman," and if they do not comply, women are seen as aggressive or masculine (Wood, 2009).

Here again, we emphasize the need for caution when addressing the differences in the conversational styles of men and women. Clearly, as mentioned previously, there is as much variation within gender groups as there is between them. In addition, the research is clear in demonstrating that gender differences in communication behaviors seem to depend on a number of other factors, including the gender of the interaction partners and the nature of the relationship between the interaction partners (e.g., coworkers as compared to intimate partners). For example, women and men use different modes of talking depending on whether they are talking to somebody of the same or opposite sex (Guerrero, 1997; Hall, 1984; Johnson, 1994; Moskowitz, 1993). In addition, Fitzpatrick, Mulac, & Dindia (1995) compared mixed-sex dyads that consisted of strangers with dyads that consisted of male–female couples. They found that men adjusted their behavior to a female partner with whom they had a relationship but not to a stranger. Women accommodated equally to partners and strangers.

In sum, the styles that men and women use to communicate have been described as "debate versus relate," "report versus rapport," or "competitive versus cooperative" (Tannen, 1990; Wood, 2009). Men often seek straightforward solutions to problems and useful advice, whereas women try to establish intimacy by discussing problems and showing concern and empathy.

Just as it was impossible to say earlier that one conversational style is always better than another, neither is it possible to favor the style of a man or woman over the other. The differences that exist in the styles of men and women, however, clearly have consequences for the satisfaction that they will experience when interacting with one another (Tannen, 1990). To illustrate this further, consider a wife asking her husband what he wants for dinner. Her goal in asking the question is to invite his participation and let him know that she is thinking of him. The husband, however, may not frame the question in this way. On the meta-level, using the style he is accustomed to, he may assume that this is a direct question that requires a simple and direct response. Therefore, he simply tells her, in a direct and authoritative way, what he wants for dinner. However, his wife may frame his directness as an attempt to be domineering and as a sign of his insensitivity to her feelings. These differences in communication styles can contribute to misunderstandings that, ultimately, work against the experience of intimacy.

Communication and Intimacy within Marriage

Marriage requires communication. In the course of a day, a marital partner may need to know if a spouse is going to stay at work late or is planning to go to a meeting or ball game that evening. A spouse may need to know what time friends are coming for dinner, who will do the shopping for the meal, and who will clean the house before the guests arrive. A typical day might also include negotiations about who will give the children baths, mow the lawn, clean the basement, wash the carpets, dust the furniture, or pay the bills. Married couples must arrange schedules, plan family get-togethers, or decide on their next major purchase. Obviously, couples rely on communication to convey a great deal of information. Without the exchange of this type of literal information, management of the various tasks of married life would be impossible.

However, communication is not only the vehicle through which basic information is exchanged, it is also the basis by which relationships are negotiated and defined. How we talk with a partner conveys information about how we feel about the relationship, how committed we are to it, and how comfortable we feel with our identity as a married individual. Our communications can convey and continuously reinforce the message that we care about a partner and our relationship, or they can just as easily convey detachment, indifference, and ambivalence about the relationship.

A primary task for marital partners is to establish a private message system or pattern of communicating that promotes mutual understanding and the experience of intimacy. The effectiveness of our marital communication system is dependent on our messages being clear and understandable. But because marriage is an intimate relationship, the goal of effective communication is broader than simply communicating clearly. It is also important that our communications promote closeness. That is, we must convey the message to our partner that they are cared for, esteemed, and valued.

It is clear, given its complex nature, that communication has the power to make or break a relationship (Tannen, 1986, 1990). It is useful, therefore, to examine some of the elements of the communication process that facilitate the experience of intimacy.

Confirmation

Within a communicational system, partners engage in a circular process of providing information and receiving feedback. Both partners simultaneously convey information, on the meta-level, about the self, the other, and the relationship. While doing this, each partner is also receiving feedback about the self, the other, and the relationship from the other. For example, when a man interacts with a woman, he reacts to (1) her portrayal of him; (2) her portrayal of herself; and (3) her portrayal of the relationship. His reactions constitute a form of feedback, which, in turn, influences how she feels about him and how she, subsequently, interacts with him (Watzlawick et al., 1967).

Confirmation occurs when we consistently provide our partners with the feedback that we value them, care about them, and share a deep concern for their welfare. Confirmation also involves conveying an enthusiasm for the relationship, an interest in its welfare, and a deep and ongoing commitment to making it work. Sieburg (1985) suggests that a message is confirming when it performs the following functions: (1) it expresses recognition of the other person's existence; (2) it acknowledges the other person as a unique being-in-relation, rather than simply as an object in the environment; (3) it expresses awareness of the significance (or worth) of the other; and (4) it endorses the other's self-experience as he or she expresses it. Confirmation, therefore, is a metamessage that is conveyed both verbally through our words and nonverbally through our behaviors toward the partner. When we act in a confirming way, the overarching metamessage that accompanies our interactions is one of acceptance, regard, concern, and involvement. When we attentively listen to our partners or gently hold their hand as they discuss their problems at work, we make it clear that we value their thoughts and feelings. Such actions send the message that both the person and the relationship are highly valued.

When we receive confirming metamessages, we are encouraged to feel good about ourselves and secure within the relationship. Enhanced self-esteem and feelings of security build intimacy. They enable us to trust the other, to act with our partners' interests in mind, to share our concerns and feelings more openly, and to take risks with anger and confrontation. We are better able to tackle the challenges of a marriage, secure in the knowledge that we share with our partners a deep and lasting bond (Montgomery, 1981).

"Feedback metamessages" are always a part of the interactions that occur between partners in a relationship. When feedback is confirming in nature, it builds a foundation for the experience of and the expansion of intimacy. When feedback is disconfirming, insecurity and mistrust function to erode the foundation of intimacy. Such disconfirming patterns occur when we ignore or discount our partners' thoughts and feelings, attack their self-concept out of anger, or completely ignore their interests in favor of our own. In acting and reacting to our partner in these ways, we provide the metamessage that we do not value them or our relationship with them.

It is important to be clear that the presence of confirmation does not mean that there is an absence of conflict in the relationship. Conflict is an inevitable part of any intimate relationship. When interactions are characterized by a confirming style of interaction, conflict does not do damage to the intimate foundation of the relationship. Partners are free to negotiate disagreements and resolve conflicts because the emotional environment surrounding the relationship promotes a sense of security and well-being. In other words, I can disagree with you, and even be quite angry with you, but I communicate this in a way that, on a meta-level, still conveys the message that you are valuable to me and that I care about our relationship.

Self-Disclosure

Self-disclosure is a communication process that involves revealing personal information about the self. Of course, this means that self-awareness and self-disclosure are closely linked. To the extent that we are aware of our actions; motivations; shortcomings; strengths; and what we see, hear, think, and feel, we increase our options for disclosing information about ourselves to others and thereby our chances for intimacy with others.

Disclosure operates on two levels to build intimacy. On the content level, the information that our partners reveal to us allows us to know them better and reduce uncertainty about the relationship. Through this process, we are better able to anticipate the others' needs and expectations. We are better able to predict their moods and feelings. There is, in other words, an empathy for and sensitivity to our partners that result from knowing them more fully.

Disclosure conveys a metamessage as well. It conveys a willingness to be open, honest, and trusting of the other and a desire to further the relationship (Montgomery, 1981). Self-disclosure delineates the boundaries of the relationship. On the meta-level, it communicates to the other that the relationship is special. After all, one does not share intimate personal information with everyone!

A **rule of reciprocity** exists with respect to disclosure. This rule demands that individuals must match the disclosures of others with disclosures of their own that are equally revealing. Recall in your own experience how you felt when someone revealed intimate and deeply personal information to you, but you had no interest in reciprocating. The discomfort that one experiences in such situations results, in part, from knowing that reciprocity is expected. So long as both partners abide by the rule of reciprocity, the act of disclosing personal information is likely to build intimacy. When disclosures are not reciprocated, however, the absence of reciprocity is likely to be framed as evidence that there is a problem in the relationship.

The rule of reciprocity is made even more complicated because women, in general, are more open and disclosing than men (Pearson, 1985; Tannen, 1990). This discrepancy increases the likelihood that the rule of reciprocity will be violated in interactions between women and men. Differences in male and female tendencies to self-disclose can once again be understood in terms of the differences in their socialization and respective interpersonal orientations. Male children are socialized to value their autonomy and independence, and to view revealing personal information as a sign of weakness. Such orientations discourage men from disclosing and abiding by the rule of reciprocity. Female children, in contrast, are socialized to value interconnectedness and involvement. For them, disclosure is a way of building connections with others.

It is not surprising that these differences can leave spouses feeling tense and frustrated with each other. From the woman's perspective, the unwillingness of a man to disclose is often framed as evidence that the partner does not care about her or the relationship. From the man's perspective, the pressure to disclose can be framed as an intrusion on his independence. He may well feel caught in a bind. On the one hand, he feels pressure to reciprocate by disclosing personal information, and, on the other hand, he may feel that such disclosures are evidence of personal weakness.

It is apparent how different styles of disclosing can add to the likelihood of frustrating interactions. Unfortunately, the tendency is for spouses to attribute the cause of this tension and frustration to their partners rather than to the differences in their respective conversational styles (Tannen, 1990). The wife of a nondisclosing husband might frame his behavior as evidence of his disregard for her and conclude, "He is a real jerk!" The husband might frame the pressure he experiences to disclose his feelings as an intrusion on his independence and conclude, "She's a demanding nag!" These frames can easily amplify the divisiveness and tension experienced within the relationship.

Transaction Management

In the course of a marriage, misunderstandings are bound to occur. Misunderstanding results when we receive or frame a message differently than the sender intended. This occurs, at times, simply because we read something into a behavior or glance that was not intended. It happens at other times because we have a conversational style that is distinctly different from that of our partner.

Just as misunderstandings will occur, so too will conflict. We will not always agree with our partners' opinions or about how various tasks should be executed. We may disagree about what they expect from us, about the ways in which they carry out their responsibilities, or about a myriad of other issues.

Couples must develop strategies for dealing with the inevitable misunderstandings and conflicts that they will encounter. In general, **transaction management**, the ability to manage misunderstandings and conflict, requires two primary skills: (1) the ability to establish realistic communication strategies and rules for interaction; and (2) the ability to exercise the self-control needed to keep the communication moving toward desired goals (Montgomery, 1981). Although all couples establish strategies for managing misunderstandings and conflict, not all strategies are equally effective. In addition, knowledge of effective strategies does not ensure their consistent use.

So what are some of the key factors related to the successful management of conversational transactions? Metacommunication, leveling/directness, listening skills, and situational adaptability are all key dimensions of transaction management. Each of these factors is a component of the communication process that enables couples to keep communication flowing toward the desired goal of intimacy and connection.

Metacommunication

Metacommunication involves communicating about communication (Watzlawick et al., 1967). Metacommunication is a conversational strategy that allows for the exploration with a partner of the meaning that has been attributed to his or her behaviors. When we metacommunicate, we engage in a process of talking about the metamessages that we "received." That is, we disclose just how we framed our partner's communications and seek clarification about what, in fact, our partner intended to convey. In doing this, the potential for misunderstandings is minimized in that each participant has the opportunity to correct the other's interpretation.

Furthermore, by seeking this clarification, an opportunity for more extensive and open dialogue is created. In other words, not only does metacommunication address the need for clarity in communication exchanges, but the process of metacommunication itself conveys a meta-level message of interest and involvement. Metacommunication is confirming in nature because it conveys a fundamental respect and concern for the other as a person (Tannen, 1990).

For example, a wife might come from a family in which others would never dream of intruding on a person's turn to talk. This would be considered rude and inappropriate behavior. Her husband, however, tends to finish her sentences, particularly when she is talking about things she has strong feelings about. Her tendency is to frame this behavior as an indicator of his disinterest and impatience. When he interrupts, she gets annoyed and feels hurt.

Her husband, in fact, finishes sentences as a way of communicating involvement and interest, but she would never interpret his behavior in this way unless both shared and discussed the different ways of framing this message. Metacommunicating allows us to explore misunderstandings and shift our frames in ways that promote intimacy rather than perpetuate disharmony and conflict.

Knowing that we should check out how we are framing our partner's metamessages, however, does not guarantee that this strategy will be consistently employed. When we are under stress, we are more likely to communicate in a defensive and less effective manner (Satir, 1972). Paradoxically, metacommunication is a more difficult strategy to use at precisely those times when it is most necessary! At the same time, as difficult as metacommunication is, the possible benefits gained from using this skill when confronted with the task of managing tensions cannot be overemphasized.

Leveling/Directness

While it may sound simple and self-evident, managing conversational transactions is easier when partners are able to talk in direct, open, and honest ways with one another—when they are able to level with one another, and be direct. Some people, however, have a difficult time communicating what they think and feel. If conversational styles are dominated by indirectness, individuals will only hint at what they think, feel, and want to have happen (Tannen, 1986). These indirect patterns of communicating do not promote intimacy and, instead, increase the probability of misunderstandings.

Indirectness contributes to the ineffective management of interpersonal tensions by placing the partner in the position of being solely responsible for deciphering what the problem is and what the solution should be. It is difficult to know if there is a problem, what the problem is, and what is expected when issues are broached in indirect ways. Individuals are in a much better position to respond to their partners when their partners level with them, that is, when they discuss issues, feelings, and solutions in a direct, open, honest, and straightforward way. When being direct, we communicate what the issues are, how we feel, and what we think the solutions should be. If done in a confirming and nonthreatening manner, this is likely to elicit the cooperation of the partner and promote an intimacy-enhancing solution.

Listening

Keeping communications flowing toward desired goals is enhanced not only by the partners' ability to level with one another, but also by their ability to listen to one another. The interdependent nature of marriage means that, to resolve any problem in a mutually agreeable way, the perspectives of each partner must be considered. However, when individuals are upset or under stress, listening also becomes more difficult. Anger and defensiveness can impede the ability to hear what the partner thinks and feels. Individuals then monopolize the conflict with their own feelings and thoughts, interrupting what their partners are saying. When listened to in these ways, partners feel discounted, which, in turn, influences how they listen in return.

Listening plays an important role in promoting intimacy and managing conflicts. When individuals actively and empathically listen to their partners, in spite of the accompanying stress, they are more apt to understand what is bothering the partner and what the partner would like to see changed. Listening in this way has the additional benefit of communicating a meta-level message of involvement and confirmation. It lets the other know that his or her partner is truly interested and values his or her perspective.

Situational Adaptability

While generally there are benefits associated with being direct and talking about issues as they occur, it is also important for couples to be able to make judgments about when and where to talk about important and sensitive issues. **Situational adaptability** refers to the ability of individuals to adapt their manner of communication to various social situations (Montgomery, 1981). Since the context of communication influences how interactions proceed, an important conversational skill is the ability to regulate when we talk about issues that are important to us and our relationships. For instance, there may be times when it is better to postpone an important conversation until both partners have the time to really talk. It is not reasonable, for example, to expect your partner to talk about an issue that you bring up just as he or she is about to leave for work. Similarly, there may be times when it is better to postpone talking about a complaint until both partners have sufficiently calmed down and are better able to listen objectively to each other's point of view.

In addition, saying something in public that is better said in private can intensify conflict and have a powerful negative impact on the relationship.

Suppose a couple is at a party, and the wife's behavior is getting on her husband's nerves. As his anger builds, he could criticize his partner in front of everyone, creating quite a scene and severely embarrassing both her and many of their friends who witness the confrontation. He could, alternatively, choose to talk with his wife later about his anger, because he recognizes that a party is neither the time nor the place to carry on such a confrontation. This latter strategy (1) still allows for the expression of conflict; (2) increases the probability of resolving the conflict; and (3) minimizes the potentially negative effect that this conflict will have on the couple's level of intimacy.

Although exercising this type of judgment becomes difficult when individuals are under stress, clear benefits can result from controlling when and where to react to conflict. Conflict is often a private matter. When conflicts spill out into the public domain, such as when couples fight in front of parents or friends, in church, or at a ball game, the destructive potential can amplify.

Conclusions

It is important for couples to realize the power of the meta-level of communication when it comes to understanding how communication processes impact on the experience of intimacy. How we talk, perhaps more so than what we actually say, has a powerful impact on how partners feel about their relationships. All of us need to feel confirmed, valued, and respected. It is particularly important for partners to feel that they are confirmed by the other. These messages are primarily conveyed through metamessages—through how we talk with our partners more so than through what we say. When we listen empathically, when we are patient with our partners, when we stay calm and talk in a thoughtful and direct manner, we convey a meta-level message of genuine respect for the partner and concern for the relationship. Such messages build intimacy even in those moments when tensions and conflicts are present in the relationship.

Furthermore, couples must establish communication strategies for dealing with conflicts. Conflicts, as will be discussed in greater detail in Chapter 10, are inevitable within intimate relationships. The presence of conflict is less a concern for a relationship than is the manner in which the conflicts are managed.

How we deal with misunderstandings, negotiate differences of opinion, and manage conflict are all governed by the rules and strategies that are unique to our relationship systems. These rules and strategies, like any rule or strategy, may be more or less effective. If they are effective, not only do they enable couples to resolve their differences, but they enable them to do so in ways that promote understanding and intimacy. In contrast, ineffective communication strategies are characterized by patterns that include hostile and disrespectful exchanges, a lack of empathy, conflict avoidance or uncontrolled conflicts, and ineffective problem-solving.

Key Terms

Communication A symbolic, transactional process that involves creating and sharing meanings through consistent patterns of interaction.

Confirmation A type of communication feedback that conveys the message to a partner that he or she is valued. Confirmation also involves conveying an enthusiasm for the relationship, an interest in its welfare, and a deep and ongoing commitment to making it work.

Congruent A message is congruent when all of its different components (verbal/nonverbal, content/relationship) convey the same meaning.

Content level of communication The literal content of a message or what is communicated.

Conversational style The unique ways in which individuals shape and frame messages when interacting with others.

Framing The meaning attributed to the metamessages that accompany a literal message. The assignment of meaning to someone's metamessages is not an objective event but a personal, subjective process. As such, each person assigns meaning to a behavior that may differ from the meaning another would assign.

Message The information that is exchanged when we communicate. Messages carry information at two levels: a content level and a relationship level.

Metacommunication Communication about the communication process—a process of talking about the communication process that can lead to greater clarity and the experience of intimacy.

Metamessage The information conveyed in how a message is expressed: the "message about the message." Metamessages are conveyed in the behaviors and nonverbal cues that accompany literal messages.

Nonverbal symbols Gestures and behaviors that accompany interaction that have symbolic value attributed to them.

Private message system A system of rules for communication within an intimate relationship. The private message system gives the couple's relationship its distinctive quality, helps to organize the strategies that will be needed to face the many tasks and issues that will arise, and influences how couples feel about the relationship.

Relationship level of communication The way in which the information contained in how the content of a message is expressed is used to determine how to interpret the literal content of the message.

Rule of reciprocity The tendency for individuals to match the disclosures of others with disclosures of their own that are equally revealing.

Self-disclosure The process of revealing personal information about the self.

Self-esteem The level of positive feelings individuals have toward themselves. The greater the person's self-esteem, the more likely he or she is to be open to the verbal and nonverbal expressions of others and to interpret another's communications accurately.

Situational adaptability The ability of individuals to adapt their manner of communication to various social situations.

Transaction management A part of the communication process that fosters intimacy and manages conflict; the ability to establish realistic communication strategies and rules for interaction, and to exercise the self-control needed to keep the communication flowing toward desired goals.

CHAPTER **10**

Conflict in Marriage

Chapter Overview

This chapter provides an overview of (1) common areas of conflict; (2) underlying sources of conflict; and (3) factors that shape the strategies couples use to manage conflict. Research indicates that couples commonly mention money, the distribution of household tasks, and sex as topics of disagreements. However, conflict is in no way restricted to these topics. A wide range of issues, some of them quite trivial, can become crucial areas of disagreement. The underlying sources of conflict include incongruent role expectations, tension between the competing needs for connectedness and separateness, and violation of relationship norms of fairness and equity. Factors that shape the choice of strategies for managing conflict include the goals individuals bring to the conflict situation, how disagreements and sources of tension are framed, and the conversational styles employed by partners when they engage in a conflict with one another.

The chapter ends with a discussion of marital violence, which is viewed as a conflict-management strategy that relies on the threat of punishment and the use of force as a way of controlling the other. In discussing marital violence, its incidence and the factors associated with its occurrence are outlined. In particular, the factors associated with wife battering are discussed, including (1) the presence of cultural norms that promote the use of violence; (2) a family legacy of violence; (3) personal characteristics that predispose men to use violence when confronted with conflict; (4) situational stresses that add to the tension and conflict present within the marriage; and (5) patterns of conflict management that escalate conflict within the relationship rather than adequately controlling or reducing it.

Conflict in Marriage

Conflict refers to overt opposition between partners that is identified by the partners as a source of difficulty in the relationship (Fincham & Beach, 1999). Conflict is inevitable in any ongoing intimate relationship. Within a marriage, the many tasks that must be executed provide ample opportunity for misunderstandings, disagreements, and conflict to occur. The presence of conflict signals the need for marital strategies and rules to be adjusted. Consequently, **conflict** can be viewed as a source of stress within the marital system. Like stress, conflict is neither good nor bad. Rather, how conflict affects an ongoing intimate relationship depends on how it is managed. Establishing strategies for dealing with conflict is a major aspect of managing the emotional climate of a marriage. Successful conflict-management strategies enable couples to communicate in ways that promote understanding, resolve differences, and foster intimacy. When managed constructively, the sources of the conflict and tension are renegotiated, and marital patterns of interaction are adjusted to bring about a corresponding reduction in frustration and tension. When managed destructively, marital patterns are rigidly maintained, resulting in escalating frustration, tension, and chronic marital discord.

Areas of Conflict

Conflict between spouses is among the most frequently investigated topics in marital research. This focus on conflict is understandable given its implications for mental, physical, and family health. Marital conflict, for example, has been linked to the onset of depressive symptoms, anxiety disorders, eating disorders, episodic and binge drinking, and male alcoholism. Although married individuals are healthier on average than the unmarried, marital conflict is associated with poorer health and with specific illnesses such as cancer, cardiac disease, and chronic pain—perhaps because hostile behaviors during conflict are related to alterations in immunological, endocrine, and cardiovascular functioning. Physical aggression occurs in over 25% of married couples in the United States, leading to a significant physical injury in a sizeable number of individuals. Marriage is also the most common interpersonal context for homicide, with more women being murdered by their partners than by anyone else. Finally, marital conflict is associated with important family outcomes, including poor parenting, poor adjustment of children, increased likelihood of parent–child conflicts, and conflict between siblings (Fincham, 2009).

Research over the past twenty-five years reports a relatively consistent list of issues that generate conflict in couples (Bradbury, Rogge, & Lawrence, 2001; Klein, Pleasant, Whitton, & Markman, 2006). These issues include the lack of quality time spent together as a couple; a real or perceived unfair division of labor; disagreements about child rearing; lack of sexual satisfaction for one or both partners; financial struggles over budget, spending, saving, and earning; difficulty with in-laws and other family members; and prior painful or traumatic events that are carried from childhood into adulthood. It is instructive to note that this list of issues occurs within gay, lesbian, and heterosexual couples (Kurdek, 2004). All lifetime partnerships are accompanied by common complaints and tensions.

While money, housework, and sex may be commonly mentioned topics of conflict, it is important to point out that these topics do not in any way reflect the full range of issues over which couples experience conflict. Social scientists have coined the phrase "tremendous trifles" to refer to this wide range of miscellaneous issues (matters pertaining to personal habits, preferences, and manners of conducting day-to-day living) that become areas of conflict in ongoing relationships. To be sure, individual couples disagree and even fight about such issues as where to go on vacation, what brand of tuna to buy, leaving the toothpaste cap off the tube, or the correct way to position the toilet seat! It is virtually impossible to list and discuss the specifics of what couples fight about.

Consequently, it could be argued that understanding the underlying sources of conflict is more important than understanding what couples disagree about. Knowledge of the underlying sources of conflict in a marriage helps us to place the specifics of what couples fight about into perspective, at which point we will be better able to appreciate the frustrations and tensions that accompany conflict and the importance of managing these emotions for marital intimacy.

The Underlying Sources of Conflict in Marriage

All couples are challenged to develop constructive strategies for the management of conflict. The successful management of conflict begins with an understanding of its underlying sources.

Role Expectations and Conflict

Each member of a marital dyad brings to the relationship a unique vision of how marital tasks should be allocated and executed. Couples are then faced with the task of negotiating a congruence of **role expectations**. That marital roles in contemporary society are in transition and no longer clearly prescribed adds to the difficulty of reaching a consensus on the assignment of these roles and responsibilities (Burr, Leigh, Day, & Constantine, 1979). As a result, the potential for role conflict at the beginning of a marriage is quite high.

For example, a man might come into marriage with traditional role expectations. He might expect to do yard work but not housework. He might expect that his wife will be responsible for maintaining ties with both her and his extended family (e.g., sending cards and gifts on holidays and birthdays). He might also expect that he will be responsible for financial decisions and that he and his wife will share equal responsibility for initiating sexual contact.

His wife, however, may come into the relationship with a more modern set of role expectations. She may agree that both she and he should share equal responsibility for initiating sexual contact. She may not agree, however, with her husband about how the finances should be managed. Furthermore, she may expect him to do housework as well as the yard work. Consequently, conflicts will likely develop in those areas in which expectations vary. The management of conflict requires the couple to reach a consensus regarding the allocation and distribution of marital tasks.

Even when couples agree about the allocation of tasks, disagreements may stem from differences regarding how tasks should be executed (Burr et al., 1979). A husband who expects the bathroom to be cleaned twice a week will be upset with a wife who believes that the bathroom needs to be cleaned every two to three weeks. A wife who expects dirty pots and pans to be cleaned and put away immediately after dinner will be upset with a husband who believes that the right way to clean them is to let them soak in the sink overnight.

Quite clearly, these differing expectations regarding role tasks can be a nagging source of tension and conflict within the relationship (Sabatelli & Chadwick, 2000). Of course, not all role conflicts will necessarily generate conflict. Complaints of these types force couples to enter into a process of negotiation that involves, in essence, a discussion of the legitimacy of one partner's expectations and the other partner's behaviors (Sabatelli, 1988; Scanzoni, 1979a). The "complaining partner" wades into this negotiation, typically, by calling attention to the manner in which the "offending partner" is acting inappropriately—meaning the offending partner's behaviors are not consistent with the complaining partner's expectations. If the offending partner views the offense he or she is being accused of as being genuine and legitimate, then the negotiation process is a rather simple one. Not all complaints, in other words, involve protracted negotiations. When complaints are viewed as legitimate, the offending partner simply makes an effort to shift his or her behaviors to pull them in line with the complaining partner's expectations.

For example, a wife who is balancing her career and parenthood might complain to her partner that he does not do enough housework. She justifies this complaint by calling attention to all the demands placed on her at home and at work. She further justifies this complaint by documenting how the work he does around the house does not measure up to the work that she is required to do. Implicit in her discussion of his behavior is the fact that she views his behaviors as failing to conform to what she expects is a reasonable amount of housework on his part. Though this complaint generates tension in the relationship, if her partner acknowledges the legitimacy of her complaint and makes an effort to adjust his behaviors to conform to her expectations, the basis for the complaint is neutralized and harmony is restored in the relationship.

The so-called offending partner, however, may not concur with the complaining partner's construction of reality. An offending partner might view the partner's assessment of his or her behavior as being wrong. Or an offending partner might view the partner's expectations as being unrealistic. When either of these occurs, the negotiations surrounding such complaints become more complex. Both partners hold to the view that their partner's construction of the reality of the situation or the relationship is distorted and wrong. Each partner stakes a claim for the legitimacy of his or her respective position. The complaining partner insists that the offending partner change the way he or she acts. The offending partner counters by insisting that the complaining partner make an adjustment in his or her expectations. Such negotiations are time consuming, often resulting in deadlocks and impasses. And while these protracted negotiations can be peacefully resolved, it is a distinct possibility that these protracted negotiations will evolve into conflicts accompanied by an escalation of emotional tensions and negativity (Gottman, 1994).

The Competing Needs for Connectedness and Separateness

To suggest that everyone has individual needs comes as no great revelation. Among the more basic of needs are the needs for intimacy, closeness, togetherness, companionship, and sexual fulfillment—needs that reflect the importance we attach to feeling connected to others. This need for connectedness is met through participation in primary relationships with family, friends, and other loved ones. For adults, marriage serves as one of the more important primary relationships. This relationship can provide a sense of security and belonging and fulfill the needs for companionship and sexual fulfillment. At the same time, each person has needs for privacy, autonomy, and independence—needs that reflect the importance attached to the experience of separateness. Periodically, everyone needs time for themselves, time to act independently and autonomously in work or play, without having to answer to the needs or demands of others.

Therefore, the need for connectedness coexists with a need for separateness. These needs peacefully coexist so long as one partner's needs do not compete with the other's. It is when the needs for connectedness and separateness compete with one another that the potential for conflict is enhanced. One partner's desire to be alone, for example, might compete with the other's desire to go on a walk together. One partner's desire to go out with friends may compete with the other's desire to spend a quiet and romantic evening together at home. The challenge for all couples, then, becomes one of balancing these competing needs (Kantor & Lehr, 1975).

Conflicting needs for connectedness and separateness produce a problem for the relationship that is not easily resolved in a mutually beneficial way. Because marital partners comprise an interdependent system, one partner's need for connectedness imposes, quite literally, demands on the other partner. Needing to talk with a partner about a problem experienced at work requires that the partner be willing to listen. If the need to talk catches the partner at a time when he or she does not want to listen because he or she needs to spend time alone, "zoning out," or watching television reruns, the partners will wind up being at odds with one another.

In such situations, both partners experience the other as unwilling to meet their needs. Each is likely to feel as well that he or she is being asked to act in a way that is contrary to his or her own needs. Therefore, the source of conflict is twofold: (1) the partners' needs are not being met; and (2) to resolve the conflict, one partner must forgo his or her own needs or convince the other partner to relinquish his or hers. The process of managing these competing needs is complex, because it requires each partner to balance self-interest with a concern for the well-being of the other.

It is interesting to note how these contradictory and conflicting needs help to establish patterns of interaction. Essentially, patterns of distance regulation are influenced in large part by the manner in which the coexisting needs for connectedness and separateness are managed. When these needs remain balanced, couples comfortably move between patterns of closeness and separateness. When connectedness and separateness needs compete, the partner who desires connectedness is likely to feel lonely and isolated. This partner is then likely to act in an increasingly demanding manner. The partner who desires separateness will often react to this increasing pressure by distancing even further from the partner. The more he or she distances, however, the more the other partner pursues. The more the other partner pursues, the greater the pressure to distance. These pursuing–distancing patterns of interaction produce tension and frustration in the relationship.

Both partners will experience the relationship as unfulfilling and be likely to blame the partner for the problem (Napier, 1988).

The tension that results from competing needs for connectedness and separateness can be thought of as another source of stress within the marital system. This stress again signals the need for the couple to renegotiate their competing needs and find a way to restore harmony within the system. It is not the presence of conflict over competing needs for closeness and separateness, per se, that threatens the system, but the strategies employed to manage this stress that either fosters intimacy or escalates distress.

Fairness, Equity, and Conflict

The patterns and dynamics that occur within a marriage are governed by the partners' cognitive orientations—the themes, values, and comparison levels—that delineate acceptable and appropriate behavior. We expect our relationships to be structured in ways that conform to these orientations. Among the more prominent of the orientations that couples bring to their marriage relationship is an emphasis on **fairness** (Blau, 1964; Homans, 1961) and **equity** (Walster, Walster, & Berscheid, 1978). The violation of these norms serves as a fundamental source of conflict within ongoing intimate relationships.

In the American culture, a relationship is perceived to be fair when the rewards derived from it are proportional to the costs. A relationship is perceived to be equitable when the benefits or rewards derived from it are comparable to those the partner derives. Relationships are experienced as inequitable when one partner derives greater benefits from the relationship than the other. Thus, fairness and equity are two interrelated, but subtly different, relationship orientations. This means that all relationships are characterized by a degree of fairness and a degree of equity. Some relationships, clearly, will be perceived as being both fair and equitable. Under these circumstances, the benefits a partner derives from the relationship favorably compare to what he or she puts into the relationship and to what the partner derives from the relationship.

Other relationships will, however, be perceived as both unfair and inequitable. Within these relationships the potential for conflict is high in that the benefits a partner derives from the relationship do not favorably compare to what he or she puts into the relationship, and the partner is perceived as having a better deal.

It is possible, in addition, that a relationship will be perceived as unfair and, nonetheless, equitable. This occurs when an individual feels that he or she is working hard at the relationship for little return (this is what makes the relationship unfair), but perceives that the partner, too, is working hard for little return (this is what makes the relationship equitable). Furthermore, a relationship can be experienced as fair but inequitable when the input is comparable to the outcome, but the partner's benefits appear to be greater.

While these distinctions may seem unnecessarily complex, keeping the distinctions between these concepts clear is important in understanding how they function as sources of conflict in marriage and how they influence marital interactions. The experience of injustice or inequity generates stress and tension. The stress and tension influence patterns of interaction as individuals act to restore fairness and equity within their relationships. These efforts to restore fairness and equity can involve actions designed to (1) decrease the costs of the relationship; (2) increase the benefits derived from the relationship; or (3) decrease the partner's benefits derived from the relationship.

Suppose, for example, a wife works hard around the house, cleaning, shopping, preparing meals, and taking care of the kids, and feels as though she gets few benefits in return. In response to the frustration and stress she experiences as a result of this injustice, she acts to make the relationship fairer. This could be accomplished by reducing what she puts into the relationship. For example, she could simply stop some or all of the tasks that contribute to her experience of injustice (but now this is likely to create a problem for her partner and perhaps decrease his benefits from the relationship). She could, on the other hand, attempt to increase the benefits she derives from the relationship, thereby making the work she puts into it more worthwhile. She might do this by demanding more from her partner, which might include a weekly dinner out alone together or more free time for hobbies and personal interests (note again how this affects the partner's experience of the relationship).

Therefore, the experience of injustice or inequity serves as a basic source of conflict, and the efforts to resolve this conflict often result in the alteration of existing patterns of interaction. The new patterns that emerge reflect the couple's efforts to manage the stress brought on by perceived injustices or inequities. Quite obviously, the efforts employed to restore fairness or equity can be either constructive or destructive to the relationship. When one partner changes his or her role behavior or expects the partner to change, these changes or demands reverberate throughout the marital system. If changes are made without regard for the partner, this only amplifies the potential for distress within the relationship. If changes are negotiated and they reflect the cooperation of both partners, the potential for distress is reduced.

The Dynamics of Managing Conflict

Given its pervasiveness, it is clear that how conflict is managed is chief among the factors determining the level of intimacy experienced within a marriage. Conflict in and of itself is not necessarily bad for relationships. Conflict is often necessary to encourage the changes and reorganizations that are required to make the relationship optimally responsive to both partners' needs. When managed constructively, conflict brings about changes that are helpful, but, when managed destructively, conflict erodes the foundation of intimacy, setting in motion patterns of interaction that contribute to ever-increasing levels of frustration, tension, and conflict.

Attempts to manage conflict reflect a choice of strategies. Each individual develops his or her own unique strategies, which vary considerably from one person to another. Where do these strategies come from? How do they evolve? Clearly, a number of factors shape the strategies that individuals employ to manage conflict.

Conflict-Management Goals

Conflict resolution strategies are determined, in part, by our goals for the interaction. This is another way of saying that behavior is purposeful, that our actions reflect particular goals and objectives. This is especially true in conflict situations. While we may not always be consciously aware of our **conflict-management goals**, we nonetheless tend to act and talk in ways that reveal our underlying motives and objectives. In some marital systems, conflict is managed with the goal of coping with stress and maintaining or enhancing the experience of intimacy. The objectives of other couples may differ considerably. Some may hope to eliminate all sources of conflict, while for others conflict is a type of competition dominated by the goal of winning and controlling the partner.

Maintaining Intimacy. When restoring harmony and maintaining intimacy are the goals of conflict management, strategies tend to emphasize the importance of compromise and cooperation (Mace, 1983; Sanders & Suls, 1982). Individuals tend to be open to talking about their experiences and negotiating with their partners to make the relationship more responsive to the needs of both. The behaviors used and the approach to managing conflict convey the metamessage of involvement, interest, concern, and support for the partner.

These metamessages help to establish patterns of interaction that are more likely to elicit the cooperation of the partner. When a conflict situation is approached in an open, honest, and nondemanding way, one partner is less likely to react negatively or defensively and more likely to work with the other to find a mutually agreeable solution. By drawing the partner into the conflict in a cooperative way, he or she is provided with an opportunity to respond to the feelings and needs of the other. There is no guarantee that this will always succeed, because the partner may not be in a receptive mood. However, approaching the situation in this way provides more opportunity for this to occur than other, more destructive strategies offer.

For example, a husband is at home, taking care of the kids, getting meals, and feeling all of this is somewhat unfair. His wife calls to let him know that she will be home from work late because some of her coworkers are getting together later for drinks. In this situation, the husband not only feels that what he has to do is unfair but also that his wife has a much better deal. The way he deals with his wife when she returns home will be determined by the goals that he brings to the situation. If the goal is to restore harmony and promote intimacy, even though he is hurt and angry, he will talk with her in a way that will make his feelings clear and provide her with an opportunity to be responsive to his needs. By being nonreactive and conveying a sincere interest in cooperating to resolve this tension, he increases the potential for an intimacy-enhancing resolution to this conflict. If instead, he sets out to "get even" by making his wife's life miserable, he will sulk around until his partner gets home ("So, you're finally home!") and then proceed to complain to her about her insensitivity. In the process, he calls her a few names, repeatedly mentions that he hates being married, and speculates how much better off his life would be if he were to get a divorce. Living "happily ever after" becomes increasingly more difficult when strategies such as these are employed.

Eliminating Conflict. When the elimination of conflict becomes the goal for managing conflict, the denial of conflict, the avoidance of conflict-inducing situations, and the repression of anger become the themes that dominate the couple's choice of strategies. In such relationships, couples are often under the impression that conflict and the expression of anger will do irreparable damage to the relationship. The couple establishes patterns of interaction that maintain a facade of mutuality, or **pseudomutuality**, at all costs. These relationships are, however, often devoid of true intimacy, because the fear of conflict makes the experience of getting close to another too risky to undertake (Wynne, 1988).

Couples who organize themselves around the avoidance of conflict or themes of pseudomutuality tend to avoid situations that might induce conflict and repress any anger that does occur. When this is the underlying objective, topics that might stress the relationship are avoided, actions that might upset the partner are refrained from, and any anger that does occur is minimized. One partner might quickly agree with the other's point of view, volunteer that he or she was at fault, and apologize or promise never to "behave that way again." In short, he or she does whatever is necessary to diffuse anger and avoid a confrontation.

It must be emphasized, however, that, in the process of avoiding conflict, a metamessage is communicated about the partner and the relationship that is, in reality, quite uncomplimentary and antithetical to the experience of intimacy. That is, by avoiding conflict and being unwilling to risk the consequences of anger, it is suggested that the relationship does not possess the necessary foundation of respect and concern that would enable it to endure such intense emotions. Partners indirectly acknowledge that they are neither sufficiently skilled to manage conflict constructively nor secure enough in their commitment to one another to risk the destabilizing effect that conflict can temporarily have on a relationship.

If the question, "What's wrong with avoiding conflict?" comes to mind, consider the following. Conflict is the vehicle by which spouses alert one another to the unresolved stresses in their relationship. Relational growth and interpersonal intimacy require a willingness to make adjustments in response to the unfulfilled needs and expectations of the other. When we set out to minimize conflict and repress our feelings, we establish rigid patterns of interaction that are not only devoid of conflict but also unresponsive to the needs of the partner. Intimacy requires a willingness to risk conflict. For a relationship to change to accommodate the ongoing demands of family life, couples must be open to adjusting their patterns of interaction in response to the stresses and conflicts they encounter. The maxim "no pain, no gain," applies to many facets of life!

Winning at All Costs! For some couples, the goal of conflict is to assert power and dominance, that is, defeat the partner and force him or her to concede. On a broader level, the goal of winning can be understood as an effort to control the other. When winning becomes the objective, power and control strategies tend to dominate the relationship.

When discussing **power**, a clear distinction must be drawn between legitimate and nonlegitimate power (Emerson, 1976; Scanzoni, 1979b). Within any marriage, power must be distributed; that is, partners must take control over different aspects and domains of the marriage. One partner may be responsible for working out the monthly budget and, in so doing, control how money is allocated and spent. One partner may take control of shopping, planning meals, and housework and, therefore, control the daily management of the household. The control that these individuals have is not experienced as a threat to the relationship, however, because the expression of power within these domains has been legitimized.

Power is legitimized when the authority of a partner is negotiated within the relationship (Scanzoni, 1979b). Legitimate power is not experienced as a problem because both partners have agreed that this is an appropriate and acceptable expression of control. The nonlegitimate expression of power, on the other hand, is manifested in efforts to control the partner or the relationship without the authority to do so having been agreed on by both parties. It is the nonlegitimate expression of power—the attempt to dominate and control the partner without concern for his or her input, needs, or interests—that characterizes the conflict-management strategies associated with winning. An attempt to win is an attempt to control the partner in ways that satisfy the needs of one partner while discounting the importance of the other's needs.

When a wife tries to control her husband, for example, he is left with two fundamental options: comply or resist. When he complies, he participates in a process of discounting his own authority and importance. In essence, he gives his wife control over him. Consequences of this decision often are the harboring of resentment and feelings of being controlled, taken for granted, and undervalued.

On the other hand, when a husband in this situation actively resists his partner's attempts at control, he engages in a power struggle. He takes a position in opposition to his wife and makes counterefforts to control her. In other words, in a power struggle, each partner maintains a rigid position that is nonnegotiable; each resists acknowledging the position of the other. This symmetrical pattern of resistance is likely to result in the escalation of conflict and erode the foundation of intimacy (Watzlawick et al., 1967).

There are, clearly, a number of different strategies that individuals can evoke when the goal is one of control. Take the situation in which the needs for connectedness and separateness are in conflict. Suppose it is a quiet Saturday afternoon, and a husband is interested in having sex with his wife. The wife, however, having had a hard week at work, is interested in being alone, reading, and taking it easy. If the goal for the management of this conflict is to foster intimacy, the husband will seek a compromise, that is, a cooperative resolution of this conflict. If the goal is winning, however, he will attempt to get his wife to meet his needs while forgoing her own.

He could, for example, tell his wife that he misses her and hint that he finds it a bit selfish for her to be so wrapped up in her own needs. In this manner, he may be able to induce guilt and use it to his advantage. Similarly, he could attempt to foster feelings of obligation and indebtedness in an effort to make his wife abandon her own needs and attend to his. He could, alternatively, become more and more insistent and demand that his needs be met.

In other words, a variety of coercive and controlling strategies can be employed in conflict situations to control the partner. These strategies will not always be aggressive. Once a power struggle is begun, however, the patterns and dynamics can escalate and become increasingly aggressive. Partners insult one another, call one another names, and threaten one another, symbolically and literally, sometimes even physically abusing one another in an effort to assert control. In such a scenario, neither will give in to the other. Ironically, both partners' needs remain unfulfilled.

When recognized for what they are, regardless of the specific tactics employed, controlling strategies set in motion patterns of interaction that undermine the relationship. When a partner attempts to win by defeating, dominating, and controlling, the other feels personally undervalued, discounted, and taken for granted. The foundation of trust and intimacy is progressively eroded.

Framing: The Attribution of Causality

The strategies employed to manage conflict also depend on the meaning and significance attributed to a partner's behavior. Since conflict is inevitable, how it is framed influences how it is managed. Take for instance the case when partners have differing expectations for one another. A partner who understands a mate's failure to conform to expectations as a willful and deliberate effort to make him or her unhappy may threaten to leave the relationship in order to win compliance. If these discrepancies are understood as expected and ordinary aspects of married life, however, partners are more apt to negotiate compromise solutions calmly.

It is only natural to search for causes when conflicts erupt. As a general rule, everyone tends to believe that they have justifiable reasons for their own behavior. In contrast, people tend to hold their partners responsible for whatever goes wrong in the relationship and attribute negative and permanent qualities to their behavior (Christensen & Jacobsen, 2000; Fincham & Beach, 1999). For example, a husband who fails to call his wife to let her know that he will be home from work late will attribute this behavior to the particularly hectic day he is having. When his wife fails to call, however, he may be likely to attribute this behavior to her chronic insensitivity and indifference to his needs.

It is this tendency to hold partners responsible for the negative aspects of the relationship and to attribute bad and permanent qualities to their behavior that often sets in motion conflict-management strategies that erode the foundation of marital intimacy. Partners attack each other, criticize each other's behavior, call each other names, or threaten each other as a result of attaching causal motivations to one another's behaviors. These reactions tend to amplify conflicts and detract from the overall quality of the relationship.

It is clear, as well, that the attributional process is influenced by generalized feelings about the relationship. The general emotional tone of a relationship acts as a filter for one partner's perceptions of another's behavior (Fincham, 2000; Fincham & Beach, 2002). When partners are satisfied with a relationship, they tend to amplify the meaning of positive behaviors and reduce the meaning of negative behaviors. When they feel dissatisfied with the relationship, there is a tendency to amplify the meaning of negative behaviors and reduce the meaning of positive behaviors.

In other words, there is a strong relationship between how behavior is framed and how the partners feel about a relationship, and both of these are importantly linked to how conflict is managed. Conflict introduces stress to the relationship and, unfortunately, when individuals are under stress, there is a tendency to increase the negativity of attributions and amplify the significance of the conflict. This negativity tends to result in the use of less constructive strategies for the management of conflict, which, in turn, erodes the quality of the relationship. As the quality of the relationship erodes, attributions become increasingly more negative and conflict-management strategies become more ineffective. A "negativity cycle" is established that becomes increasingly more difficult to break.

Interactional Patterns Leading to Marital Success and Failure

We now turn our attention to what the research on conflict management tells us about how couples manage conflict in constructive and destructive ways. In our view, by far, the most influential researchers in this area are John Gottman and his colleagues (Gottman, 1994; Gottman, Coan, Carrère, & Swanson, 1998; Gottman & Levenson, 1999a, 1999b; Gottman & Silver, 1999). Gottman's research explores the notion that there are styles of conflict management that differentiate distressed from nondistressed couples. In the following sections we present an overview of the factors found by Gottman to differentiate successful from unsuccessful couples.

The Four Horsemen of the Apocalypse

Four negativity processes, labeled the **Four Horsemen of the Apocalypse**, characterize the management of conflict in unsuccessful couples. Although everyone engages in these negative communication patterns some of the time, distressed couples do them more, and couples who do them a lot are on the fast track to divorce. These patterns include the following:

- *Criticism.* "What kind of person are you?"
- *Defensiveness.* "Yeah? Well what about what *you* did?"
- *Contempt.* "I would never be so low as to do something like *that*!"
- *Stonewalling.* Shutting down, associated with high physiological arousal and efforts to self-soothe with thoughts such as "I can't *believe* she's saying this!"

Criticism involves attaching someone's personality or character, rather than a specific behavior, usually with blame. Criticisms can be thought of as complaints that turn personal. These criticisms are directed at the partner's self-concept and identity. Instead of saying, "I am unhappy when you leave your clothes on the floor when you get home from work," a person prone to the use of criticism personally attacks the partner saying things such as, "you are so inconsiderate of me," or "you are such a slob." Such personal attacks evoke emotionally reactive responses such as defensiveness, contempt, and possibly withdrawal.

Defensiveness comes from an attempt to fend off criticisms without taking responsibility for one's own problem behaviors. Defensive reactions include making excuses, giving "yes-but" responses, repeating oneself, and taking anxious or rigid body postures. Another defensive response is counter-criticizing the partner (meeting a criticism with another criticism). In general, criticisms within unsuccessful couples tend to be accompanied by defensive reactions on the part of partners that further the cascade of negativity.

Contempt is the intention to insult and psychologically abuse the partner, and includes insults, name-calling, hostile humor, mockery, and various forms of nonverbal derision. Gottman's work makes it clear that criticisms and defensive reactions can build negativity to the point where couples develop deeper and deeper levels of contempt for one another. This growing contempt for the partner represents an important turning point in the undoing of the relationship. At this point, couples increasingly focus on only those aspects of their partners that bother them. They tend to develop rather inflexible and negative views of their partners. As this pattern unfolds, it becomes increasingly more difficult for partners to believe that there is hope for the relationship.

Stonewalling occurs when communication breaks down completely. The stonewalling spouse just turns off, ignores the other, withdraws, or minimizes communication. When distancing behaviors become the norm, the marriage becomes fragile.

Emotional Disengagement

While the Four Horsemen are detrimental to intimate and ongoing relationships, it is also damaging for couples to display emotional disengagement (Driver, Tabares, Shapiro, Nahm, & Gottman, 2003). Emotionally disengaged couples do not enact extreme levels of negativity and are unlikely to use the Four Horsemen. They instead show a complete lack of positive affect. They generally demonstrate little of the interest, affection, humor, and concern that characterizes happy couples. Emotionally disengaged couples appear fine on the surface but are actually highly distressed as they try to keep their problems from poisoning the entire relationship. However, the cost of this avoidance is the erosion of intimacy and absence of shared positive feelings in their interactions. These relationships slowly atrophy as the partners become more and more distant.

Flooding

When conflicts are tainted by the Four Horsemen or by emotional disengagement, it is common for one or both partners to become emotionally and physically overwhelmed (Gottman, 1994). At the point when individuals are emotionally and physically overwhelmed, they are in a state that Gottman calls **flooding**. At the point of flooding individuals' palms begin to sweat, their heart rates increase to over ninety beats per minute, and their breathing becomes shallow or irregular. With these physiological symptoms, the partner is unable to think clearly or participate in constructive conversation. The primary focus of the flooded individual is self-preservation, accompanied by thoughts such as, "I can't stand this anymore" or "Why is she attacking me?" At the point of flooding, it is impossible for individuals to take in information or respond to others.

In other words, flooding is an emergency state that can occur during conflict (Driver et al., 2003). Although it is more common in men than women, flooding can happen to either partner during arguments. Gottman and his colleagues find that successful couples treat flooding with respect and concern. In this regard the best antidote for flooding is to take a break from the conflict for at least twenty minutes. These time outs are followed by a return to the conflict in a timely manner. If the couple does not return to the argument, these breaks to avoid flooding can become a way to stonewall and damage the relationship over time.

Negative Reciprocity

Negativity, according to Gottman, is not necessarily damaging to relationships. All individuals within intimate relationships occasionally react in negative ways toward their partners. A pattern of negative escalation, however, in which negativity is responded to with increased negativity, is harmful to relationships. These reciprocally negative patterns are characterized by each partner using a more hurtful or severe response to the other. It is as if each partner is trying to get back at the other by trying to win. This type of negative escalation is often found in conjunction with the Four Horsemen. That is, negative affect from one partner will be reciprocated with contempt, defensiveness, or criticism.

The Conflict Styles of Happy Couples

Gottman's research makes it clear that adaptive couples are not necessarily those with fewer complaints. Those couples within "regulated" or more successful relationships have complaints and often do not deal with their complaints in ways that many professional therapists and family life educators would suggest are constructive. Gottman identifies three styles of marriage that fit into the regulated type: the **validating couple,** the **volatile couple,** and the **conflict-minimizing couple**. The styles are based on the couple's predominate style of managing conflict (Gottman, 1994).

The validating couple style is generally the style of managing conflict that most professionals would agree represents a constructive style of conflict management. These couples show a low level of negative expressed emotion. These couples tend to listen respectfully to one another and confirm the partner's feelings. They tend to use metacommunication and feeling probes to take the "emotional temperature" of their partner (Gottman, 1994). And, while not necessarily passionate, validating couples are in fact quite happy with their life together and demonstrate a great deal of support and empathy for one another.

The volatile couple is characterized by intense emotion. They confront each other and argue persuasively in their efforts to get the "offending partner" to comply with the "complaining partner's" point of view. According to Gottman, high levels of passion, romance, and satisfaction characterize this volatile group. These couples are passionate about their relationship, and this passion spills over into their conflicts. And, in spite of the fact that they often have bitter disputes characterized by attacks, counterattacks, and fits of rage, they manage to maintain a sense of connection and genuine intimacy.

The conflict-minimizing couple tends to minimize or avoid conflict. They live with the pain of unsolved, yet solvable problems. According to Gottman, these are couples who lack the skills necessary to work through conflict. Although their style of managing conflict may not be ideal, they still manage to avoid having their relationships dominated by pervasive levels of negativity and distancing. Hence, they can sustain a sense of cohesion and intimacy.

So the question arises, how can couples who do not manage conflicts in ways we would call constructive manage to avoid divorce? Gottman has found that successful couples maintain a higher proportion of positive to negative interactions when compared to distressed couples. Furthermore, successful couples are more likely than distressed couples to have compatible styles of conflict resolution.

Gottman's research has shown that satisfied couples, no matter how their marriage stacks up against the ideal, maintain a five-to-one ratio of positive to negative interactions. Maintaining a sufficiently high balance between positive and negative interactions allows relationships to overcome the times when destructive and ineffective conflict management threatens the overall health of the system. In other words, successful couples manage enough of their critical conflicts in positive ways, even if they do not always do it perfectly.

A second way in which happy couples differ from distressed couples has to do with the fit between or compatibility of their styles of fighting. Simply stated, successful couples have matching styles of fighting. They agree on the ways in which they will disagree with one another. In contrast, couples who fail to maintain a sufficiently high ratio of positive to negative interactions tend to have different styles of fighting. One partner pursues, for example, while the other distances. One partner needs to process feelings and probe solutions. The other finds it difficult to talk about such issues.

Why are matched conflict-management styles associated with better relationship outcomes? Mismatched styles of fighting are more likely to result in mismatched interpretations of the other's behavior. Both partners are likely to be left feeling that their personal identities have been devalued or that the relationship is not important. For example, actively trying to engage a partner who prefers to avoid conflict can easily become a source of frustration for both partners: "I chase after you and try to engage you in a discussion about my complaints. I then feel discounted when you distance yourself from me. Furthermore, as I yell at you and you withdraw, I feel that you do not value our relationship. You, in turn, feel discounted by my complaining about you and by my unwillingness to respect how you prefer to deal with our conflicts. You also feel that I do not value our relationship (if I did why would I insist on fighting?)."

In contrast, matched styles of fighting communicate a meta-level message of involvement, connection, and a fundamental respect for each partner (cf. Watzlawick et al., 1967). This is because matched couples are more likely to focus on the issue to be resolved rather than the partner. Mismatched couples, on the other hand, are more likely to move away from a focus on the issue (e.g., housework) to a discussion of the inadequate (meaning different) ways in which the partner approaches the management of conflict. Matched styles do not necessarily mean that conflicts will always be managed constructively.

However, matched styles are less likely to contribute to the escalation of tensions and negativity.

Solvable versus Unsolvable Problems

Gottman maintains that a myth about happy couples is that they are able to resolve all their disagreements. What Gottman has found is that both happy and unhappy marriages have unsolvable as well as solvable problems. Solvable problems have a solution, whereas unsolvable problems are ongoing issues that may never be resolved. These perpetual problems often arise from fundamental personality, cultural, or religious differences, or essential needs of each spouse. One partner may love to go boating and fishing, whereas the other enjoys cultural events and city attractions.

What differentiates successful from unsuccessful relationships is that those in successful relationships seem to understand and respect the distinctions between the two types of problems and they handle them differently. Successful couples deal with perpetual problems by learning to accept them. The aim in discussing a perpetual problem is to create an atmosphere of acceptance of the partner's viewpoint rather than creating a condition of gridlock. So the goal is not to solve the problem, but for the couple to find a way to discuss it openly and to gain some degree of peace around it (Driver et al., 2003).

Partners who are gridlocked are firmly planted in their respective positions. As a result their discussions include very little positive affect. Over time, these couples feel rejected, overwhelmed, and hopeless about ever reaching any sort of compromise or peace.

Accepting Influence

One of the ways that successful couples deal with conflict is by accepting influence from each other. Gottman uses this term to describe each partner's willingness to yield during an argument in order to win in the relationship (Driver et al., 2003). Yielding to win, however, should not be mistaken as surrendering to the other's whims. Instead, accepting influence is the ability to find a point of agreement in the other's position. It is reflected in the ability to see the partner's point of view, understand the partner's position, or understand why the partner might feel the way he or she does. Although accepting influence is difficult at times, it has a tremendous and positive impact on the relationship. When partners yield on certain points in a conflict, they realize that they can cooperate as a couple. The problems become an issue they can conquer as a team.

Repair Attempts

In addition to accepting influence, happy couples also manage conflict and miscommunication with what Gottman refers to as "repair attempts." **Repair attempts** are defined as interactions that decrease negative escalation. The ability to repair the cohesion and connection that is disrupted by conflict is essential to the well-being of an ongoing relationship. Examples of repair attempts include apologies, humor, affection, and changing the subject. These interactions are not necessarily related to the content of the argument, but may simply provide a brief reprieve from it.

It is interesting to note that successful couples use repair attempts more often throughout conflicts, and earlier in conflict situations, than do unhappy couples. Using the repair attempt earlier is one way of preventing a conflict from becoming too negative. In contrast, unhappy couples may wait until the argument is heated and divisive before making any attempt at a repair. In addition, unhappy couples frequently respond to attempts at repair by interpreting the overture in a negative way (Driver et al., 2003).

Turning Toward

Besides studying how couples manage conflicts, Gottman and his colleagues studied the ongoing, everyday interactions that occur between intimate partners. Everyday interactions between intimate partners are characterized by what Gottman and his colleagues call **emotional bids** (Gottman, 1999). An emotional bid occurs when a member of a couple initiates contact with the partner through ordinary conversation. The partner can respond to these emotional bids by "turning toward" the partner, "turning away" from the partner, or "turning against" the partner. For example, I might say to my partner, "look at the birds on the birdfeeder," or initiate an interaction with my partner by saying, "you will never guess who I saw today." These conversational bids create opportunities to interact and help to define the couple as a couple. When these conversational bids are responded to positively, these interactions reinforce the sense of connection between the members of the couple. When such bids are not responded to or are negatively reacted to ("Why are you bothering me about birds on the feeder?"), they undermine the experience of intimacy.

Needless to say, in happy couples, partners rarely ignore emotional bids. Having an eagerness to interact creates more interactions and increases a sense of connection and friendship. In particular, playful bidding is a characteristic of happy couples—this takes the form of good-natured teasing or physical sparring. For example, a husband might throw a crumpled napkin at his wife in response to her teasing him about an improper use of grammar. In many respects, these daily interactions can contribute to the level of affect present in the relationship. Hence, the overall quality of the relationship is affected by these minor moments.

Rewriting the Past

Gottman and his colleagues have found that couples' descriptions of their past are good indicators of the future of their relationships (Driver et al., 2003). What they have found is that couples who are entrenched in a negative view of their partner and their relationship often revise the past, such that they remember and talk only about the negative things that have happened in their relationships. Happy couples, in contrast, highlight their good memories. They look back on their early days with fondness. They emphasize the joy that they have experienced in their relationship over time.

That is, most couples enter marriage with high hopes and great expectations. When a marriage is not going well, history gets rewritten for the worse. The wife, for example, will recall how her husband was thirty minutes late to the engagement party. The husband will recall how the wife disappointed him on his thirtieth birthday. In addition, along with remembering the worst, unhappy couples find the past difficult to remember. Such negative characterizations of the past are, according to Gottman, highly predictive of an unhappy future.

Positive Sentiment Override

The relationships of successful couples are characterized by what Gottman refers to as **positive sentiment override (PSO)**. This refers to the emotional climate created by successful and happy couples that enables them to override the negative effects that conflict creates in the relationship. PSO is built on a foundation of fondness and admiration and a good knowledge of the partner's life and world. PSO can be thought of as a filter that colors how couples remember past events and view new issues. Have you ever heard the saying, "If you dislike someone, the way they hold their fork will make you furious. But if you like them, they can turn their plate over in your lap and you won't even mind." That's because of PSO.

It is important to point out that PSO and conflict management reciprocally influence one another. As such, the effective management of conflict creates an emotional climate that fosters PSO. In turn, the presence of PSO results in couples approaching conflict in a more constructive way. They are more likely to soften the startup of a conflict by bringing up issues tactfully and more likely to accept influence and make repair attempts. That is, it is not possible for us to know whether it is the effective management of conflict over time that creates PSO, or if PSO results in successful couples effectively managing conflict over time. Both of these factors are present in successful couples, and clearly these factors are interdependently connected to one another.

It goes without saying that the relationships of unhappy couples are characterized by cascading negativity and negative sentiment. Within unhappy couples this negative sentiment overrides positive events when they occur. That is, positive events are minimized and framed as irrelevant and unimportant as couples hold on to their negative views of the relationship. Couples under these circumstances tend to rewrite their history together in less complimentary ways, have a hard time remembering what brought them together, become easily flooded, use the Four Horsemen, and emotionally disengage from one another.

Gender, Conversational Styles, and the Management of Conflict

The discussion of compatibility in conflict-management styles and its relationship to distress also calls our attention to the research on gender differences in the management of conflict. If it is the case that men and women generally differ in terms of how they manage conflict, then this gender-driven incompatibility must be examined as it relates to overall levels of satisfaction and distress in relationships.

As was noted earlier in Chapter 9, extreme care should be taken when making generalizations about males as compared to females. We would not want to give the impression that all men deal with conflict in certain ways and all women deal with conflict in different ways. Obviously, this would be misleading. When talking about gender differences in conflict-management styles we clearly do not want to overstate the differences between men and women, particularly when this can result in a polarization of men and women in relationships!

We balance these concerns, however, against the "weight of the evidence" that suggests that there are, indeed, important differences in the conflict-management styles of men and women that can impact on how they experience their intimate relationships (cf. Gottman, 1994; Tannen, 1990, 1996). The research suggests that men and women often differ in terms of how they express intimacy. And, when dealing with conflicts, they often employ different strategies for the management of interpersonal tensions (Gottman; 1994). These stylistic differences can contribute to the escalation of tensions between men and women in lifetime partnerships.

Men and women often differ in terms of how they define intimacy and in terms of its critical indicators (cf. Bem, 1993). Specifically, there is a tendency for women to define intimacy in terms of verbal communication. Women express closeness through talking. Women create connections through conversations, sharing feelings, talking about personal issues, and having in-depth conversations.

On the other hand, men are less likely to use conversation as a way to achieve closeness. Men often connect by doing things together, participating in team sports, or working on a project. In the "rough and tumble" world many boys grow up in, relationships revolve around activities. When you like someone, you express this through shared activities (Bem, 1993).

Thus, while men desire intimacy in their lifetime partnerships just as much as women do, the different preferences for how to express this connection can result in complaints and disaffection. When a wife asks her husband to spend some time talking about feelings, she is showing her preference for intimacy, as is a husband who asks his wife to take a walk with him or go fishing with him. A problem for the relationship exists if these different preferences result in husbands and wives feeling as if their partners fail to fulfill their expectations around the expressions of intimacy.

The negotiation of these complaints is made difficult by the fact that each partner's construction of how intimacy should be expressed is tied to his or her gender and, thus, his or her personal identity. Men and women often are genuinely surprised when their partners have difficulty understanding "the right ways" to express closeness. Men cannot understand why their partners are not content doing things together. Women cannot understand why their partners are so uncomfortable just talking with them. If these differences are not constructively negotiated, the potential for an emotionally charged showdown exists.

Furthermore, the research on gender and conflict-management styles suggests that when conflicts arise interpersonal tensions are often amplified by the fact that men and women can differ with respect to (a) how they respond to potential or anticipated conflicts and (b) how they actually manage conflicts (Gottman, 1994; Tannen, 1990). When women go into a conflict-management mode, they pursue a dialogue around the issues. Talking is the solution to the problem. When men go into a conflict-management mode, they limit their choices concerning intimacy because they are overly focused on preventing conflict from erupting. They prefer to avoid or withdraw from it—sometimes at all costs.

As a result, a common mismatched pattern of conflict management fuels an amplification of negativity within many relationships. Women pursue; men distance. Women interpret the distancing as a lack of interest. Women voice concerns about withdrawn, avoidant husbands who will not open up or talk. These women feel shut out and begin to feel that their husbands do not care about the relationship. For these women this lack of talking equals a lack of caring.

On the other hand, men complain that their wives get upset too much. They feel hassled by their partners chasing after them to get them to talk. Men want peace and harmony. They distance themselves from their partners during times of conflict in an effort to minimize the emotional tensions that seem to be at the heart of the crisis in the relationship. As a result of these different approaches to the management of conflict, each partner can come to view his or her spouse as being the problem. This sets in motion patterns of criticisms and negativity that can, ultimately, become a foundation for contempt and distress. In point of fact, however, the problem really lies in the relationship—that is, it results from the lack of fit in the strategies that men and women use when dealing with interpersonal tensions.

With respect to these different modes of solving interpersonal tensions, it is interesting to note that Gottman (1994) has come to the conclusion that men tend to withdraw from conflict situations simply because they are not equipped to handle conflict as well as women. Quoting Gottman, "In a sea of conflict, women swim and men sink" (Gottman, 1994, p. 140). To account for this observation Gottman calls attention on both cultural and biological factors.

Culturally, it is relatively easy to identify the ways in which socialization practices result in boys and girls growing up with different abilities to manage emotion-evoking situations. From early childhood on, girls are encouraged to manage a complete range of emotions and to manage conflicts through talking about their feelings. Boys, in contrast, are socialized to suppress their emotions. Talking (particularly about feelings) are activities that girls participate in. Boys grow up in a developmental niche that would ridicule them if they were to "act like a girl" (Kupers, 1993). That is, "You are acting like a girl!" may be the worst thing that you can say to boys and young men.

Not surprisingly, by the time many boys and girls grow up and enter into lifetime partnerships, they are at opposite ends of the spectrum when it comes to the importance they place on expressing feelings. A man is more likely to equate being emotional with weakness or vulnerability whereas women have spent their early years learning how to verbalize their emotions (Gottman, Katz, & Hooven, 1997). As a result, there is a tendency for men and women to approach conflicts in very different ways and a tendency for men to be more easily overwhelmed by having to deal with emotion-evoking situations.

In addition, Gottman and Levenson offer physiological reasons for why men, more than women, are likely to withdraw from emotion-evoking situations (cf. Gottman & Levenson, 1992; Levenson & Gottman, 1983). This work highlights the greater physiological vulnerability of males as compared to females and uses this vulnerability to argue that it may be more adaptive for men to avoid conflict situations. Gottman, in addition, suggests that the autonomic nervous system of males differs from that of females. Males, physiologically speaking, are more sensitive to emotion than women. They have stronger reactions to emotions and take longer to recover from emotional upset than women do. Once they are aroused, men stay aroused longer than women and take longer to settle down. This means that they spend more time being reactive than women do.

Taken together, these cultural and biological factors can explain why men, in the final analysis, are much more likely than women to be what Gottman calls "stonewallers" when tensions build (Gottman, 1994). Women, while not invulnerable to stress, experience conflict less intensely than men. Women typically have better skills than men for dealing with situations where emotions flood or take over otherwise rational thinking. Men, in contrast, get flooded much more easily than women by emotion-evoking situations. Their tendency is to shut down and withdraw. Unfortunately, their withdrawal often only serves to increase interpersonal tensions.

It is important here for us to emphasize that the fact that cultural and biological forces result in men being less equipped than women to manage conflict cannot be used to hold men responsible for the escalation of tensions that accompanies the mismanagement of conflict. Conflicts escalate not because men are less equipped to handle emotions than women are but because there is a "lack of fit" in the preferred styles of men and women for the management of conflicts. It is this lack of fit that leads to cascading negativity within the relationship.

Marital Violence

No discussion of either the sources of conflict or the management of conflict within marriage would be complete without a discussion of marital violence. The use of violence can be viewed as a conflict-management strategy, one that relies on the threat of punishment and use of force as a way of controlling the other. It is important to point out that coercive and power-driven conflict-management strategies take many forms, including the use of physical aggression, verbal abuse, and other forms of psychological violence.

Incidence

As with other forms of family violence, such as child abuse, actual data on spousal abuse are impossible to obtain. These events take place in private and are often kept private because of the shame or fear victims feel. Furthermore, the data available on spousal abuse are often unreliable because they come from self-report surveys, and people often do not admit to socially unacceptable behavior even when a survey guarantees anonymity and confidentiality. In addition, knowledge of spousal abuse is also limited because much of what we know about it comes from those victims who have sought help or from perpetrators who become known to the criminal justice system. We have no way of knowing how representative of all victims and perpetrators these populations are.

The difficulties in obtaining reliable data suggest that all calculations of the incidence of spousal abuse probably underestimate its actual occurrence. Along these lines, Kaufman and Straus (1990) estimate that less than 7 percent of marital assaults are officially reported. Although the statistics may be imprecise, they nonetheless reveal that spousal abuse is a common practice. Consider the following:

- In a national survey of households representative of the general population in 1985, Straus and Gelles (1986) found that 16 percent of American couples experienced at least one act of violence in the year preceding the survey. Three percent of all husbands admitted to severe wife-battering (kicking, biting, hitting with the fist or some other object, threatening with a knife or a gun, or actually using a knife or gun). Interestingly, 4.4 percent of all wives admitted to severe acts of violence toward their husbands.
- In contrast, the National Crime Victimization Survey found that 91 percent of spousal violent crimes were attacks on women by their husbands or ex-husbands. Furthermore, 32 percent of assaulted wives were assaulted by the husbands again within six months (Langan & Innes, 1986).
- In another nationwide sample of couples, 28 percent were found to have experienced violence at some point in their history (Sugg & Inui, 1992).
- Severe, repeated violence occurs in one in fourteen marriages (Dutton, 1988), with an average of thirty-five incidents occurring before it is reported (Avis, 1992).
- A longitudinal study of aggression in marriage found that over 50 percent of the couples in the sample reported some form of physical aggression in their relationship before they were married (O'Leary, Malone, & Tyree, 1994). This suggests that the use of violence as a strategy for managing conflict begins very early in many relationships.

While it is true that physical violence by wives also exists, the violence directed by wives toward husbands is less likely to result in physical harm. When husbands and wives engage in a violent exchange, wives are far more likely than husbands to be injured (Barnett, Miller-Perrin, & Perrin, 1997). Indeed, Straus and Gelles (1986) caution that wife-beating tends to be hidden more often than is husband-beating and that wives are, in fact, far more often victims than are husbands. Men are more likely than women to minimize and underreport the frequency and severity of their violent actions (Dutton & Hemphill, 1992; Riggs, Murphy, & O'Leary, 1989).

Factors Associated with Marital Violence

Perhaps because women are victimized by violence more often than men, much more attention has been focused on the factors that lead to wife-battering. What follows is a summary of the factors that social scientists believe contribute to the likelihood of wife-battering, including (1) the presence of cultural norms that promote the use of violence; (2) a family legacy of violence; (3) personal characteristics that predispose men to use violence when confronted with conflict; (4) situational stresses that add to the tension and conflict present within the marriage; and (5) marital patterns of conflict management that escalate conflict within the relationship rather than adequately controlling or reducing it.

Cultural Norms. The prevailing values and attitudes of a society influence the patterns of interaction found within families and, thus, help to define the acceptable strategies employed within family systems to manage conflict. Straus (1974, 1977), for example, believes that the causes of wife-beating are to be found in the very structure of American society and the family system. In his view, the following combination of societal factors is responsible for the presence and prevalence of wife-beating:

- The United States is a nation that is fundamentally committed to the use of violence to maintain the status quo or achieve desirable changes.
- The child-rearing patterns typically employed by American parents train children to be violent.
- The commitment to the use of violence as a way of dealing with conflict and the use of physically aggressive child-rearing patterns (1) legitimize violence within the family; (2) build violence into the most fundamental levels of personality and establish the link between love and violence; and (3) reinforce the male-dominant nature of the family system, with a corresponding tendency to use physical force to maintain that dominance when it is threatened.
- The sexual inequalities inherent in the family system, economic system, social services, and criminal justice system effectively leave many women locked into a brutal marriage. They literally have no means of seeking redress or even of leaving such a marriage.

A Family Legacy of Violence. Social scientists have long asserted that a major contributing factor to violence in a family situation originates from a family of origin that was itself prone to violence. Husbands who batter their wives often come from homes in which they were beaten by their parents or in which they had observed their own fathers beating their mothers (Doumas, Margolin, & John, 1994; Hotaling & Sugarman, 1990). It is important to point out, however, that while there is a relationship between a family legacy of violence and marital violence, this does not predetermine that all children who experience violence will grow up to be abusers. Clearly, those who have been exposed to violence are more likely than those who have not been exposed to violence to employ violent strategies to manage conflict, but only a minority of those who have been exposed to a legacy of violence act in violent ways toward their spouses (Gelles & Straus, 1988).

The Personal Characteristics of Abusers. In summarizing the research on husbands identified as wife abusers, Gelles and Straus (1988) assert that "perhaps the most telling of all attributes of the battering man is that he feels inadequate and sees violence as a culturally acceptable way to be both dominant and powerful" (p. 89). Not surprisingly, batterers have been found to suffer from a variety of psychological problems, such as depression, low self-esteem, poor communication (self-assertion) and problem-solving skills (Dutton, 1995; Holzworth-Munroe & Stuart, 1994). They also display extreme jealousy, emotional dependence, and fears of abandonment (Dutton, 1995; Holzworth-Munroe, Stuart, & Hutchinson, 1997). Furthermore, it appears that batterers' feelings of inadequacy are amplified when their wives surpass them in status or prestige (Gelles & Straus, 1988). Apparently, as a way of compensating for their lack of power and authority, men who feel inadequate are increasingly likely to use verbally and physically aggressive conflict-management strategies.

Situational Stress and Marital Violence. Factors that add to the levels of stress found within family systems are associated with marital violence. As a general rule, research has noted a tendency for factors such as low employment status, low educational attainment, and low income to be associated with both high levels of marital conflict and an increased incidence of marital violence (Dibble & Straus, 1980; Gelles & Straus, 1988; Hoffman, Demo, & Edwards, 1994). Although official reports of abuse indicate that poor families are more likely to be violent, these data, according to Gelles and Straus (1988), probably distort the actual incidence of marital violence found within low-income households. This is because the poor run the greatest risk of being publicly identified and labeled as abusers. In other words, while it is true that marital violence is more common among the poor, the degree to which the level of abuse among the poor differs from that found in higher income groups is probably exaggerated.

Age has been associated with wife abuse, with young women between the ages of eighteen and twenty-four being the most likely to be beaten (Barnett et al., 1997; Straus & Sweet, 1992). It could be argued that couples who marry early, particularly in their teens, face a more stressful transition to marriage than those who marry at somewhat later ages. This greater stress increases the likelihood of the mismanagement of conflict.

Finally, the excessive use of alcohol is often associated with wife abuse. Alcohol intoxication alters one's behavior by producing impaired judgement, mood fluctuations, and the disinhibition of aggressive impulses (Nace & Isbell, 1991). Such behavioral alterations increase the potential for violence to occur. The excessive use of alcohol is also a stress-engendering factor that, indirectly rather than directly, contributes to wife abuse (Edelson, Miller, Stone, & Chapman, 1985). In this sense, the excessive use of alcohol increases the stress between husbands and wives because it becomes one of the principal issues of their fighting. Conflicts over drinking, particularly when the husband has been drinking excessively, increase the potential for the use of violence as a conflict-management strategy.

Marital Dynamics and the Escalation of Conflict. Marital violence is more likely to occur within those relationship systems in which conflict-management strategies escalate the level of conflict rather than contain or resolve it. Such patterns of interaction are often referred to as symmetrical patterns of interaction (Watzlawick et al., 1967). Within **symmetrical relationships**, neither partner is willing to give in to the other. The relationship is dominated by a power struggle, in which each partner's goal is to prove the other wrong. In such a system, stress and the aggressiveness of each partner easily escalate because neither partner backs down from the other. Verbal attacks become increasingly aggressive and offensive. If the pattern continues and the conflict escalates further, this can lead to the use of violence (Babcock, Walz, Jacobson, & Gottman, 1993; Burman, John, & Margolin, 1992).

It has been found that the patterns of interaction and conflict management associated with marital violence follow an identifiable cycle (Walker, 1979, 1984). This cycle begins with an accumulation of frustration and tension in the relationship. The conflict can develop around any number of issues. If the relationship pattern at this point becomes dominated by symmetrical patterns, this accumulation of tension can escalate quickly to an explosion or crisis phase. It is during this explosion phase that injuries occur. For example, the husband sets out to teach his wife a lesson. He may want to put her in her place or see her as a source of all of the problems in his life. In many cases, there are repeated incidents of hitting, involving one or both spouses (Walker, 1984).

This explosion of aggression and violence is followed by a honeymoon phase (Walker, 1984), during which the batterer often becomes apologetic and asks for forgiveness. He will often promise never to do it again. Unfortunately, many women believe their spouses. After a period of time, however, the cycle begins again and eventually becomes a recurring strategy for the management of conflict within the relationship.

It is important to point out that, on many occasions, rather than symmetrically fighting with her husband, the wife will attempt to curb the violence by forming a **complementary relationship** with him. That is, she will try to please the batterer and keep things calm by giving in to his demands (Walker, 1979). Levels of conflict can be kept in check for a while by resorting to such complementary patterns of conflict management. However, when the levels of frustration and conflict build in spite of this strategy, the wife may eventually take a symmetrical stance with respect to her spouse. That is, she may reach a point at which she can no longer submit to her partner or strive to please him. When this occurs, an explosion of violence can quickly follow. Alternately, the wife may maintain her complementary position only to find that the batterer erupts into violence in spite of it.

The unfortunate outcome of this process is that many women come to believe not only that it is their responsibility to prevent the abuse, but that they are responsible for the abuse (Andrews & Brewin, 1990; Walker, 1984). They believe that, if only they were more skillful at handling their husbands, the abuse would never occur. The husband colludes in this process. Asking for forgiveness is one way the man acknowledges the inappropriateness of his behavior, but it is interesting that this apology is often accompanied by excuses and justifications for his behavior (Wolf-Smith & LaRossa, 1992). These excuses and justifications can be viewed as signals of an unwillingness to take responsibility for the behavior. In other words, when he says, "I'm sorry, but you shouldn't have argued with me," he is attempting to hold his partner responsible for his behavior.

This focus on the marital dynamics found within abusive relationships demonstrates that a number of factors coalesce to enhance the likelihood of marital violence. That women can be viewed as participating in a system that leads to violent outcomes should not, however, be construed as holding women responsible for the abuse. In all ways, men should be held responsible for being unable to control their violent behavior. It is important at the same time, however, to be aware of the dynamic rules and patterns of interaction that characterize violent marital systems.

Conclusions

Much attention has been devoted to the issue of conflict in marriage due to the important relationship between the successful management of conflict and the experience of intimacy. Conflict is inevitable in marriage in that there are simply too many potential sources for it to be avoided. One of the challenges encountered in all marital systems is evolving successful strategies for its management. Some strategies are ineffective and undermine the quality of the relationship. Ineffective strategies for managing conflict can amplify tension and stress, build antipathy, erode trust, undermine commitment, and lead to marital violence. The effective management of conflict, in contrast, fosters understanding and intimacy. It enables couples to differ while remaining comfortably connected to one another.

In many ways, communication and the management of conflict are synonymous. To manage conflict successfully, couples must employ effective communication skills. However, to assert simply that couples must communicate well to manage the stress of incompatible expectations, contradictory needs for connectedness and separateness, or discordant perceptions of injustice or inequity successfully is a gross oversimplification of a complex process. All too often educators advise couples, married or not, about the importance of good communication. We believe this counsel should be taken a step further to alert couples to the importance of communicating openly about the underlying sources of conflict in their relationship.

Talking openly about partners' expectations for one another, for example, can be framed as an essential part of the negotiation process that must occur in any personal relationship. The successful management of conflict begins with a willingness to talk in an open, direct, and honest way about personal and relational sources of conflict. It requires remaining nondefensive and nonreactive when discussing problems, and resolve to resist falling into rigid, unrewarding patterns of interaction that can erode the foundation of intimacy. To do this, partners must be willing to disclose their own needs, reveal how they are framing their partner's behavior, and be willing to metacommunicate about the process that is occurring between them. Finally, partners must be willing to negotiate and compromise in order to construct a relationship in which they can peacefully coexist rather than destructively compete or passively avoid one another.

Key Terms

Complementary relationships A pattern of interaction characterized by the willingness of one partner to defer to the other. One partner asserts a position and the other agrees.

Conflict The tension between family members that results from competing goals or strategies; like stress, conflict is neither good nor bad, but, rather, signals the need for a readjustment of patterns of interaction.

Conflict-management goals The goals that individuals bring to a conflict situation that influence their choice of conflict-management strategies.

Conflict-minimizing couples Couples who live with the pain of unresolved problems due to minimization or avoidance of conflict and yet are able to remain close and intimate.

Emotional bids When a member of a couple initiates contact with the partner through ordinary conversation. The partner can respond to these emotional bids by "turning toward" the partner, "turning away" from the partner, or "turning against" the partner.

Equity When the benefits or rewards one partner derives from a relationship are comparable with those the other derives. Relationships are experienced as inequitable when one partner derives greater benefits from the relationship than the other.

Fairness When the rewards derived from a relationship are proportional to the costs. That is, what partners get out of the relationship is comparable with what they put into it.

Flooding An "emergency state" resulting from an individual being emotionally and physically overwhelmed by conflict. At the point of flooding, it is impossible for individuals to take in information or respond to others.

Four Horsemen of the Apocalypse Patterns of interaction characterized by criticism, defensiveness, contempt, and withdrawal that result in increasing negativity and possibly the end of the relationship.

Positive sentiment override (PSO) The emotional climate created by successful and happy couples that enables them to override the negative effects that conflict creates in the relationship. PSO can be thought of as a filter that colors how couples remember past events and view new issues.

Power Distinguished by a degree of legitimacy, power refers to an individual's efforts to control the behavior of another or the relationship. Power is legitimized when the authority of one partner is negotiated within the relationship. Nonlegitimate expressions of power are manifested in efforts to control the partner or the relationship without the authority to do so having been agreed on by both parties.

Pseudomutuality A pattern of interaction that maintains a facade of mutuality and harmony that is often devoid of intimacy because the fear of conflict makes the experience of getting close to another too risky to undertake.

Repair attempts Interactions that decrease the negative escalation of conflict. Examples of repair attempts include apologies, humor, affection, and changing the subject. These interactions are not necessarily related to the content of the argument but may simply provide a brief reprieve from it.

Role expectations The expectations that people bring to relationships regarding how role tasks should be either allocated or executed.

Symmetrical relationships Patterns of interaction characterized by an unwillingness of either partner to give in to the other.

Validating couples Couples who maintain closeness and intimacy by listening respectfully to one another and confirming each other's feelings.

Volatile couples Couples who can maintain a sense of connection and intimacy despite bitter arguments characterized by attacks, counterattacks, and fits of rage.

CHAPTER 11

Families with Young Children
The Transition to Parenthood

Chapter Overview

This chapter focuses on the transformations that occur within family systems during the transition to parenthood. Consistent with the multigenerational developmental perspective outlined in earlier chapters, this chapter will present an overview of how the arrival of children affects the structure of the family system. The view taken within this chapter is that all families with children must negotiate changes in the same basic tasks that have been discussed in earlier chapters. The arrival of children brings with it the need to renegotiate family themes and rework personal identities as parents take on the roles and responsibilities of parenthood. The transition to parenthood requires a reworking of the family's external and internal boundaries. Families with children must devise new strategies for maintaining the family's physical environment. Lastly, because the presence of children changes the emotional climate of the family, the strategies for maintaining intimacy and family cohesion and reducing the destructive consequences of conflict will need to be refined.

Parenthood as Just One Developmental Pathway

Before discussing how children affect family systems, several points need to be raised. First, contemporary American families follow a wide and diverse range of developmental pathways. Thirty years ago nearly 95 percent of newly married couples wanted to have a child at some point (Glick, 1977). Today, many couples question this traditional family developmental course. For example, estimates suggest that just under 20 percent of women in the United States will end their childbearing years without having children. This is nearly twice as many as in 1976 (U.S. Census Bureau, 2003b).

For a significant percentage of these women, childlessness is a matter of personal choice. Decisions not to raise children, or voluntary childlessness, have been associated with changes in the attitudes and values regarding the importance of children in contemporary society. New societal norms are emerging based on individualism; equal opportunity for men and women (in education, income, etc.); and freedom of choice in sexual behavior, fertility, and family formation (Gold & Wilson,

2002). These evolving cultural value orientations provide women with choices that were not present in the past.

The Changing Context of Parenthood

It is clear, as well, that the social environment confronted by those who become parents is decidedly different today from what it was thirty years ago. Social attitudes toward marriage and parenthood have markedly changed. For example, emerging value orientations emphasizing success, excitement, and independence can be disruptive to parenting because they often involve interests and activities that directly compete with parenting responsibilities (Simons, Whitbeck, Conger, & Melby, 1990). In addition, changing cultural value orientations may make the transition to parenthood more difficult by eroding the foundation of support traditionally extended to new parents.

Furthermore, the many social changes that now define contemporary life have also dramatically influenced the course of family development even in those families headed by two parents. Many contemporary couples delay parenting often because of a desire to complete their education and establish a career before raising a family. In addition, the traditional roles of husband as breadwinner and wife as homemaker and mother have been replaced by a host of possible role arrangements, all with their own set of potential satisfactions, stresses, and demands. A majority of women are now engaged in paid employment outside the home, which requires them to negotiate a delicate balance among the demands of work, marriage, homemaking, and parenthood. These changes also have impressed on some men the need to rethink and renegotiate their own roles as husband and father.

The Structural Diversity within Families with Children

It is also important to be aware of the structural diversity found within families with children and not to assume that only individuals residing within nuclear family systems become parents. When parenthood is discussed only from a traditional nuclear family perspective, the unique system challenges confronted by families comprised of alternative structures can be obscured. Consider, for example, the following facts: In 2001, 26 percent of American children lived in single-parent households. Seventy-eight percent of these children lived with their mothers (U.S. Census Bureau, 2005a). Some of these women were unwed teenagers; others were cohabiting with the child's father, out of marriage; and still others were adults who had chosen to raise the child alone (Seltzer, 2000). Another 4 percent of American children were living in homes with neither parent. These children were most likely to be living with grandparents (48 percent), other relatives (33 percent), foster parents (9 percent), or other nonrelatives (9 percent) (U.S. Census Bureau, 2005a). Quite clearly, each of these family arrangements is accompanied by its own unique set of potential satisfactions, stresses, and demands as the challenges posed by the presence of children are confronted.

The essential point is that all families must make adaptations that are shaped and constrained by the family's unique composition, structure, and circumstances. To be sensitive to these issues, this chapter discusses the basic challenges confronted by the nuclear family with young children. In Chapters 16, 17, and 18 the challenges confronted by divorced, single-parent, and remarried family systems will be covered in greater detail.

The Challenges Confronted by the Family with Young Children

From a multigenerational developmental perspective, the effects of the transition to parenthood reverberate throughout the entire family system. Parenthood marks the transition of the family from a two-person to a three-person system, which involves the addition of a parental subsystem to the already established marital subsystem. There is for the first time in the family a generational boundary between the child and parental generations. New interactional patterns must be established to account for these basic changes in the system's structure. Spouses must add the parental role to their already established marital roles, and renegotiate how their time and energies will be divided among the differing responsibilities of these roles. The family's basic tasks will take on new dimensions, and previous strategies will have to be revised to account for these changes.

Identity Tasks Accompanying Parenthood

Altering Family Themes. The themes that had governed a couple's earlier marital relationship will undergo change as the family moves developmentally from an adult-focused to a child-focused system. However, families can differ widely in their views of children and the importance they place on the parenting experience. Some may view raising children and passing on the family name as one of their "primary reasons for being." Others may view raising children as "necessary but inconvenient," and still others may view it as "an intolerable curse." Naturally, the particular child-related themes that predominate in a given family have implications for how much children will be valued and how they will be treated. Some families place a high priority on children, placing their needs above all others. Others place a low priority on children, choosing instead to focus on other interests and activities. Others attempt to balance the needs of children with their own personal needs and those of their spouses and extended families. Families also differ widely in how they define children's needs and in the strategies they implement for meeting these needs.

As noted earlier, the kinds of parenting and child-rearing themes that the family establishes are heavily influenced by the themes and legacies each parent experienced in his or her own family of origin. Parents who were valued, affirmed, and treated with equity and fairness are more likely to establish similar themes with their own children (Curran, Hazen, Jacobvitz, & Feldman, 2005; Serbin & Karp, 2003). Those who experienced rejection, alienation, conflict, and hostility are more likely either to perpetuate these themes in their own families or to become highly invested (at least consciously) in ensuring that their own children do not experience a similar fate. This latter option can lead to the kind of child-focused system in which intense parent–child emotional bonds develop, children are overly indulged, and the marriage or other extended family relationships are ignored (Carter, 2005).

Defining a Parental Role Identity. It has been said that the beginning of parenthood, rather than marriage, is the most accurate marker event for achievement of adult status in our society. Marriages can end, but once one becomes a parent, under most circumstances, there is no turning back (Rossi, 1968). Parenting a child is a long-term, intensive, and, for most, a lifelong commitment. Parenthood also provides a kind of validation to adults that they are moving through the life cycle in a way that is normatively expected.

It is clear that the identity transformations that accompany the transition to parenthood are far-reaching. It should be clear, as well, that this transitional period is potentially very stressful. From the moment a child is born, parents are required to make a number of important decisions about how they intend to fulfill the role responsibilities accompanying their identity as parents. Parents must establish goals for their children, develop a perspective on what the needs of their children are, and enact strategies to facilitate the fulfillment of these needs.

As a general rule, four factors influence the ease with which the transition to parenthood is accomplished: (1) the degree to which parents want to be parents; (2) the amount of anticipatory socialization or training that they have received for the role; (3) the clarity of the role demands of parenthood; and (4) the amount of support available to them while they are making the transition (Steffensmeier, 1982). For decades, family social scientists have noted that the amount of anticipatory socialization, or formal and informal training in meeting the needs of children and the techniques of child care, that most adults receive is quite limited (Rossi, 1968). This can place parents in the stressful position of having to learn about parenting by experimenting on their newborn baby.

Furthermore, parental roles are not clear. The roles of mothers and fathers are affected differently today by the competing role demands of work and marriage than they were in the past. Parents must find ways, often without the presence of role models, to balance commitments to full-time employment, marriage, and parenthood. In addition, they must do so within a social context that is increasingly seen as indifferent to children and unsupportive to parents.

As a result of a combination of factors, including a lack of information, a lack of support, and a lack of contemporary models, parents are often confronted by unexpected demands. Therefore, it is not surprising that many parents are stressed by the sudden role changes that accompany the birth of a child. Researchers studying the transition to parenthood from the late 1950s to the present have consistently documented a series of stresses associated with this event. Those most commonly reported for both men and women have included disruptions in their routine habits, fatigue, excess work, increased money problems, and, for some, interference from in-laws. New mothers also have reported feeling edgy or emotionally upset and having concerns about changes in their appearance.

Mothers, regardless of racial background, have consistently been found to experience more difficulties during the transition than fathers (Florsheim et al.,

2003). An especially serious risk factor is postnatal depression, which has been found to affect between 8 percent and 15 percent of new mothers (Feeney, Alexander, Noller, & Hohaus, 2003). Other studies indicated that parents complain about a "lack of time," difficulties in balancing parenting and work demands, problems arranging for adequate child care, financial issues, and struggles over the division of household labor (Arendell, 2000; Helms-Erikson, 2001; Kluwer & Johnson, 2007).

However, during the transition to parenthood, a parent's experience is not simply the sum of his or her complaints. New parents often experience a great deal of discomfort and stress while still viewing this time as positive and special (Demo & Cox, 2000). In general, children bring a sense of meaning, purpose, fulfillment, commitment, and value to one's life. For women, the sense of purpose is based on feeling needed by, and essential to, their children (Arendell, 2000). Children also provide a continuity between the past and the future, ensuring that the family's name, traditions, and legacy will be represented in succeeding generations. In similar fashion, they can provide parents with stronger links to their extended families. Children are a continuous source of affection and companionship. Parents take great pleasure in watching their children grow and develop. Children bring change and stimulation to life. Successfully raising a child is a source of accomplishment and achievement. Parenthood also provides the opportunity to guide, teach, and pass on values (Demo, 1992).

In sum, the roles and responsibilities of parenthood require a reworking of one's adult identity. Furthermore, investment in this new role inevitably affects other personal interests and role responsibilities. In one study, parents were asked to provide descriptions of themselves during pregnancy, before the birth of their child, and again two years later by using a pie cut into three sections: self as partner/lover, self as worker, and self as parent. Not surprisingly, the proportions of self as partner/lover declined from 28 percent to 21 percent for men and from 30 percent to 18 percent for women. Men's sense of self as parents increased from 5 percent to 24 percent, while women's increased from 11 percent to 38 percent. Women's sense of self as workers declined from 19 percent to 11 percent, while men's increased from 28 percent to 33 percent (Cowan & Cowan, 2000). These findings not only document, once again, the differences between the experiences of men and women, but also emphasize the dramatic changes that occur in personal identity during this critical period of the family life cycle.

The Child's Evolving Identity. Parents are confronted with the task of shaping and molding the identities of their children. Parents bring to the parenting experience their own idealized image and expectations for each child that enters the family system. How each child is seen depends on several factors. For instance, the sex of the child; the child's physical appearance; the child's position in the birth order; the parent's hopes, dreams, aspirations; and the parent's unresolved personal conflicts all play a part in the construction of each parent's image of a particular child (Bagarozzi & Anderson, 1989). In addition, specific role expectations accompany each parent's image of the child. Children are expected to fulfill a particular role and play out their unique part in order to fit with the parent's image of how the broader family should operate.

However, it is highly unlikely that both parents will share an identical image of each child or the same image of how the entire family should operate. Some disagreement and conflict are inevitable. The probability of successfully resolving these differences and forming a consensus identity for each child is dependent on how successfully parents have developed effective communication and negotiation skills. When parents are able to agree on their expectations for the child, the child can be clear about the rules for discipline and the guidelines for appropriate behavior.

If parents are unable to resolve their differences concerning their expectations for the child, the child can find himself or herself caught in the middle of a parental power struggle. Under such conditions, the child can come to symbolize a number of things. The child may become the "battleground" upon which the family's civil war is fought. The child may become the "prize" that goes to the victorious parent. In such cases, the child is likely to become the ally of one parent by conforming more closely to this parent's image of the child. In exchange for this conformity, the child may gain support, power, and leverage in the family. In other instances, the child may become an arbiter or referee in the parents' struggles. Frequently, a child who attempts to conform to both parents' conflicting and contradictory expectations can develop psychological symptoms or other adjustment difficulties. Whatever action he or she takes is likely to be approved by one parent but disapproved by the other (Bagarozzi & Anderson, 1989).

The Transformation of Family Boundaries

Renegotiating Distances with Family and Friends. The addition of children to the system is generally accompanied by changes in the family's external boundaries. The relatively closed boundary that previously differentiated the couple from others and helped them to consolidate a new family system and couple identity must now be renegotiated to allow for greater involvement of each spouse's family of origin. Support from extended family, especially from the new parents' own parents, has been found to be an important factor in managing the transition to parenthood (Best, Cox, & Payne, 2002). Although the amount of time available to spend with friends may be in short supply due to the demands of raising a child, contacts with friends, who are perhaps also new parents, can offer another important source of adult contact. This may be especially important to women who remain at home to care for their children. Although many new parents may have received preparation for the actual birth of their child, many remain relatively unprepared for the tasks they will face. The extended family and friends are important sources of emotional support and guidance for new parents.

The beginning of parenthood can be thought of as requiring a realignment of the parents' connections to the family system's past and future. The addition of children means that parents' own parents become grandparents and their siblings become aunts and uncles. As will become apparent in later chapters, one of the major developmental issues for older adults is the continuity of the family and the passing along to future generations the knowledge, traditions, and skills that have been learned over a lifetime. Therefore, the couple's system boundaries must be altered to accommodate to the increased stake that the older generation has in the growth and development of the family's newest members (Carter, 2005).

However, the involvement of friends and extended family must be balanced with the parents' own stake in their family. Too much reliance on the extended family and friends can undermine the couple's sense of autonomy and competence as parents. Overinvolvement with one or both spouses' family of origin or friends can also result in the neglect of children as the parents' emotional energies can remain invested in these relationships at the expense of the child's needs. In some cases, marital conflicts may develop as one spouse begins to resent the intrusions of the other's parents (Florsheim et al., 2003). The addition of children also creates the opportunity for three-generational conflicts to develop. Grandparents may align with the child against one or both parents. In extreme cases, such conflicts can lead to emotional separation from the extended family.

On the other hand, too little involvement with the extended family and friends risks the loss of guidance and support, and a discontinuity with the extended family's past history and traditions. Limited involvement with the extended family may also result in an overly child-focused family in which one or both parents become highly enmeshed with their children at the expense of the marital relationship (Carter, 2005; Coltrane, 2000; Feinberg, 2002).

Couples who are able to successfully negotiate a balanced boundary between the nuclear family and the extended system of family and friends are more likely to maintain a sense of integrity as a family unit along with a free flow of interaction with significant others. Such a system is characterized by minimal conflict between and within generations, a sense of intergenerational continuity, and a satisfying level of support and guidance. Marital relationships, free from excessive unresolved conflicts with earlier generations, are more capable of meeting the individual needs of both spouses and children.

Realigning Marital Boundaries. Married couples with children are challenged to maintain their own marital relationship while being responsive to the needs of the child. Young children place strong physical demands on parents for caretaking, monitoring, feeding, diapering, and clothing. They also elicit powerful emotional reactions such as feelings of love and attachment, anxiety over their health, and concern regarding how best to respond to their needs. The net effect of these circumstances is that spouses spend less time together and more time with children (MacDermid, Huston, & McHale, 1990). This is especially true for women, who, regardless of the child's age, are typically more invested and involved in their children's daily lives than are men (Feinberg, 2002).

Research has consistently documented that early parenthood is a time of reduced quality of marital interaction and declining marital satisfaction for many couples (Belsky & Kelly, 1994; Helms-Erikson, 2001; Kluwer & Johnson, 2007). Although the average level of decline is not large, its consistency makes it noteworthy. In addition, although many reasons have been postulated for this decline, one factor is the demands placed on spouses to devote more time to their children rather than to each other (Cowan & Cowan, 2000). Those couples who are most successful at managing this phase of the family life cycle are those who are able to balance their parenting responsibilities with the needs in their marital relationship for ongoing adult companionship, intimacy, and communication (Paley, Cox, Kanoy, Harter, Burchinal, & Margand, 2005; Van Egeren, 2004).

Couples also must balance their responsibilities as parents and spouses with their personal needs for separateness and individuality. As demands and responsibilities in one's marital and parental roles increase, the interests and activities that one typically carries out alone, or at least separate from significant others, may be adversely affected. However, one's needs for separateness involve more than being able to engage in separate activities. They also involve the extent to which one values that individual and separate part of the self as important to one's personal development (Grossman, Pollack, Golding, & Fedele, 1987). When new parents are able to acknowledge and affirm these personal needs, both for themselves and for their partners, it bodes well for the successful negotiation of the parenthood transition. Negotiating a system that acknowledges each spouse's needs for individuality may be especially important for women, who typically experience the greatest demands on their time for child care (LaRossa & LaRossa, 1981).

Balancing the Boundary between Work and Family. The boundary between work and family for most families, but especially those in which both parents work, is altered by the presence of young children. Most families, whether or not the wife works, experience an increase in financial stress following the birth of a child. In addition, it appears that men are more affected by the financial concerns of parenthood than women. Most men believe that being a good father means being a good provider, and this often translates into them working longer hours. In some cases, men have reported changing jobs to support their families better or to compensate for the income lost when their wives stay home to care for a child (Coltrane, 2000; Sanchez & Thomson, 1997).

When women become mothers, many face the challenge of balancing their time between working and parenting. Many mothers report that they would prefer to stop working outside the home or cut back on their hours (Cowan & Cowan, 2000). This is likely due to their greater involvement in child-rearing compared to fathers and to their concerns about affordable, quality child care (Arendell, 2000). Thus, while men are moving more deeply into the work world, women are moving more toward the home. In the process, women may forgo a valued source of satisfaction and social support. Women's absence from the work force can mean a loss of personal and financial autonomy and fewer social contacts with other adults. In fact, research has shown that working can be a positive source of social support and autonomy for many women and can translate into improved mental health and psychological well-being (Arendell, 2000; Hochschild, 1997).

Although many mothers would prefer to cut back on their commitments to work outside the home, it is clear that this is not the reality for most women, at least over the long term. Approximately 80 percent of women are employed before the birth of their first child, and about one-third of them are back at work within six months after giving birth (Bianci, 2000). However, the majority return to work within a year. In addition, a quarter of the women who were not employed during their pregnancy enter the work force within one year after giving birth (Smith, Downs, & O'Connell, 2001).

When mothers continue to work outside the home, they usually bear primary responsibility for providing child care when at home and arranging for child care when they are away (Coltrane, 2000; Duxbury, Higgins, & Lee, 1994; Singley & Hynes, 2005). This high level of demands confronted by working parents, especially working mothers, increases the potential for role conflict between spouses. **Role conflict** exists when partners disagree about marital roles and responsibilities. That is, they disagree about (1) who should execute various tasks; or (2) how tasks should be performed. It is possible that couples, because of the compression of time and the expansion of demands associated with parenthood, will find themselves in animated confrontations and negotiations. Couples may fight, for example, about who should clean the house, make dinner, and mow the lawn more than before now that parenting tasks need to be executed as well.

Balancing the demands of work and marriage can also produce role strain. **Role strain** exists when husbands or wives have a clear idea of what their family role responsibilities are, but they are not able to fulfill them in a way that satisfies their own expectations (Burr et al., 1979). Role strain is often accompanied by feelings of guilt. That is, when one fails to live up to one's personal role standards, the results can be feelings of guilt about one's role performance.

Parents and partners in dual-worker relationships are especially vulnerable to role strain and guilt, because the demands of work can become so great as to interfere with their ability to meet their marital and familial roles. The research literature clearly suggests that employed mothers, in particular, are likely to experience role strain (Barnett & Shen, 1997; Milkie & Peltola, 1999). Because of women's socialization to assume primary responsibility for family tasks, they are likely to fall short of their own expectations for family caretaking. Working mothers often want to spend more time with their children and be more directly involved with their care. The inability to do so, however, amplifies their feelings of role strain and guilt.

The competing demands of work and family life can also result in spouses, and women in particular, experiencing **role overload** (Menaghan & Parcels, 1990). Overloaded individuals feel that it is impossible to meet all of the competing demands they face. Role overload is often accompanied by feelings of anxiety and loss of control over one's life. Individuals may also begin to feel a sense of hopelessness and helplessness when trying to cope with these excessive and competing demands.

Role overload, role strain, and role conflict are obviously interrelated. An overloaded individual is also usually less able to enact many of these roles in accordance with his or her internal standards, which, in turn, contributes to the experience of role strain. An overloaded individual is also likely to attempt to reduce the experience of overload by shifting responsibilities to the partner, thereby increasing the potential for role conflict. Making the distinction between these concepts is important, because it highlights the complexity of the issues that must be dealt with when couples balance the demands of work, married life, and parenthood.

Quite clearly, a contemporary challenge to married couples is to develop novel and fair ways of balancing the demands of work and family. Without the benefits of successful role models, many of these couples must try to discover a satisfactory way of balancing these competing demands by trial and error. This effort can strain the family with young children as couples strive to enact strategies that both reduce the burden on individuals and enhance the experience of intimacy within the relationship.

Many reviews of research on mothers' employment assert that spousal support is the key to the success of these dual-earner family systems (Arendell, 2000; Glade, Bean, & Vira, 2005; Perry-Jenkins, Repetti, & Crouter, 2000). This suggests that it is not maternal employment per se that affects marital satisfaction but "the law of husband cooperation" (Bernard, 1974). Husband cooperation includes positive attitudes toward maternal employment and cooperation with household and child-care tasks (Bernardo, Shehan, & Leslie, 1987; Gilbert, 1988). Mothers who receive little or no spouse support clearly are more stressed by their multiple roles than women who receive such support (Glade et al., 2005; Perry-Jenkins et al., 2000).

It is obvious that some of the work burden on women could be lessened if men took greater responsibility for the execution of family tasks. While some recent research suggests that men are becoming more involved in household chores and home life (Blair & Lichter, 1991; Robinson & Godbey, 1997; Singley & Hynes, 2005), it does not yet appear to be sufficient to offset the experience of overload and strain for many women.

In sum, the family with young children, like any family, can be viewed as an interconnected, interdependent system. The addition of children to the system and the additional demands they bring to the system mean that previous relationships must be renegotiated. The needs of the extended family to have greater involvement must be balanced with the needs of the nuclear family to maintain a sense of coherence and stability. The closeness between husbands and wives must be renegotiated to consider the physical and emotional needs of the child as well as those of the spouses for one another. Furthermore, each spouse's need for a sense of individuality and separateness must be balanced with the responsibilities that accompany being a parent and a marital partner. Finally, how parents manage their work responsibilities will affect and be affected by the couple's strategies for maintaining the marital relationship, meeting the child's needs, and respecting each other's needs for closeness and support as well as separateness and individuality.

Managing the Household

Renegotiating Housekeeping Strategies. The addition of children to the family brings with it an incremental increase in the tasks of managing a household, not including the added tasks of child care. There is more laundry, more meal preparation (formulas, special baby foods), more cleaning (baby bottles, diapers, etc.), and more shopping (for baby food and child-care items) to be done, to name only a few of the additional chores. Despite contemporary images of egalitarian marriages in which men participate as equal partners in parenthood, studies of parents with young children continue to show a different picture. Regardless of how much husbands helped out around the house prior to the child's arrival, they tend to do less afterward, relative to the increased work load. This phenomenon has been referred to as the "traditionalization of sex roles." Essentially, this means that there tends to be a growing separation of male and female roles with the entrance into parenthood (Glade et al., 2005; Johnson & Huston, 1998; MacDermid et al., 1990; Van Egeren, 2004).

LaRossa and LaRossa (1981) have speculated that sex-role socialization of men and women is such that women tend to embrace the mother role, whereas men react with "role distancing." Another explanation is that, because of the increased demands on couples at this time, it becomes inefficient to share all tasks and responsibilities. Traditionalization may result because each spouse's background and training give him or her greater skill and training in traditional domains. Naturally, women's involvement in pregnancy, childbirth, postpartum recovery, and, possibly, breast-feeding also serves to differentiate their experience from that of men.

Still another possible explanation involves the changes occurring with regard to the boundary between work and family. For women who remain at home to care for their child and men who increase their workforce participation, there is a restructuring toward the traditional man-as-breadwinner and woman-as-homemaker division of labor. Negotiations regarding the division of household labor may be based on the relative time allocations of each partner to these separate spheres. Research has shown that the total number of hours men and women spend as workers (combined paid and family work) is about the same. However, women shift their time and investment back and forth between paid and family work more than men. It is women who generally feel responsible for ensuring that family life is maintained (Singley & Hynes, 2005).

Despite these overall statistics of equal time spent working, mothers do more *in the home* than they did before the arrival of children and continue to do more than their husbands. The overall participation of husbands in the household tends to increase only slightly over their participation prior to the child's arrival (Belsky & Kelly, 1994). Therefore, mothers continue to do three or four times more household work than their husbands; only now there is more of it to do (Coltrane, 2000; Hochschild, 1997). In addition, the nature of the work continues to vary considerably between men and women. Women do most of the repetitive and routine work such as cleaning, doing dishes, making the beds, cooking, shopping, washing clothes, and straightening up, whereas men tend to take on more infrequent and irregular tasks such as making household repairs, taking out the trash, mowing the lawn, and gardening (Johnson & Huston, 1998; MacDermid et al., 1990).

Managing Family Finances. By any estimate, raising children is expensive. Because actual dollar figures quickly become outdated by inflation, we can use a general rule of thumb to determine just how expensive it is. We can calculate the average **direct costs** of raising a child from birth to age eighteen as three or four times the family's annual income (Miller & Myers-Walls, 1983). Direct costs include out-of-pocket expenses for childbirth, food, clothing, housing, and education. The actual expense of raising a child may be even higher if one considers **indirect costs** as well. Indirect costs are the potential income forgone by women who stay at home to raise children or the added costs of child care for those who do work. Child care has now been estimated to be the fourth highest family expense after housing, food, and taxes (Allegretto, 2005).

It is clear that the addition of these new expenses to the family will tax many couples' existing resources, requiring a reevaluation of their priorities and a renegotiation of strategies for managing the family's finances. Discretionary income may become scarce, affecting couples' and individual spouse's leisure activities. The movement of wives out of paid employment into the home and of men into the primary provider role may alter the balance of power and control that existed earlier in couples' relationships. Decision-making strategies may be altered due to the changes in wives' self-esteem, sense of competence, or feelings of dependence on their husbands for emotional and financial support. These are common reactions that frequently accompany a wife's departure from the workforce (Cowan & Cowan, 2000).

As noted, financial concerns appear to be more keenly felt by husbands than by their wives, although financial concerns are obviously important to both. This difference may, at least in part, be related to the increased responsibilities men experience as primary family providers. Research has shown that increased financial pressures can result in men becoming depressed and more likely to perceive their children as "difficult" (Simons et al., 1990). Such pressures, may, in turn, lead men to disengage both from their wives and from their children (Belsky & Kelly, 1994). Successful resolution of these changes depends, in part, on how successfully the couple established a satisfactory system of communication and decision-making during the preceding courtship and early marriage periods.

Managing the Family's Emotional Climate

Maintaining the Quality of the Marital Relationship As noted, research has established that many couples experience a clear and discernible decline in the quality of their marriage after becoming parents (Belsky & Kelly, 1994; Helms-Erikson, 2001; Kluwer & Johnson, 2007). In general, changes in the quality of marriage can be attributed to changes in communication patterns, the level of intimacy, and the amount of shared companionate activities that couples experience after the arrival of children. In addition, as we have seen, communication, intimacy, and shared time are all affected by a host of factors, including how couples negotiate their external and internal family boundaries, differences in husbands' and wives' socialization for the role of parent, the amount of time and energy required to meet the needs of children, the conflicting demands of multiple roles (spouse, parent, worker, homemaker), and the economic pressures of parenthood (wives' departure from paid employment, the added expenses of raising children). To this list can be added the temperamental differences between children and the extent to which they are calm, healthy, and regular in their eating and sleeping cycles versus unhealthy or irregular in their daily rhythms (Belsky & Kelly, 1994).

However, as Belsky and Rovine (1990) noted, "even though, on average, marital quality deteriorates modestly—but ever so reliably—across the first three years of the infant's life, changes in marriage are much more variable than the consideration of central tendency suggests" (p. 18). That is, not all marriages deteriorate as a result of spouses becoming parents. Some couples experience a great deal of distress, others a moderate amount, and others very little, if any. Some experience many of the demands noted above while still maintaining a positive appraisal of their relationship, whereas others find their marriage highly unsatisfying in the face of these added pressures. How are we to differentiate these couples? What is it that enables couples to survive this developmental period relatively intact?

In general, those couples who have a satisfying marriage after the birth of a child are those who had more positive relationships prior to the arrival of children (Belsky & Kelly, 1994; Helms-Erikson, 2001; Kluwer & Johnson, 2007; Van Egeren, 2004). The relationships of couples who fare the best are characterized by the same qualities described in earlier chapters. These couples are more likely to have achieved a sense of closeness, commitment, and intimacy; a shared sense of power and decision-making; and an appreciation for the individuality and uniqueness of one another.

Another critical factor is the expectations partners bring into their parenting experience. Spouses who have a realistic appraisal of how parenthood will affect the marriage tend to be more satisfied later than those who do not accurately anticipate what is to come. That is, when parents accurately anticipate the kinds of demands (diapering, feeding, washing clothes, erratic sleeping patterns, diminished opportunities for adult social interactions, less leisure time) that children bring, they tend to remain more satisfied with their partners (Belsky & Kelly, 1994; Kalmuss, Davidson, & Cushman, 1992). Accurately expecting what is to come appears to be even more critical for women, since they generally experience the greatest demands from parenthood and the greatest decline in marital satisfaction (Belsky & Kelly, 1994; Cowan & Cowan, 2000).

Finally, another critical factor seems to be the extent to which husbands and wives share a similar orientation to their roles and responsibilities as spouses and parents. For example, couples who share nontraditional sex-role attitudes tend to be satisfied with one another so long as the partner's actual involvement in the home (especially the husband's) matches the other's expectations (MacDermid et al., 1990). However, as noted, this can be a relatively infrequent experience in that most men do not participate equally in housework and child care. Women who hold nontraditional sex-role attitudes and values are more likely to become dissatisfied because their husbands may not actually measure up to their expectations. On the other hand, women with a more traditional orientation may actually prefer that their husbands not assist them with housework or child care. Some women perceive this to be their own area of expertise and competence, and prefer not to share it with their husbands. Others believe that encouraging their husbands to participate and then having to monitor their efforts may be even more work than simply doing the work themselves. Still others appear not to want to accept assistance from their partners because they are reluctant to "pay the price" for his "helping out." That is, the husband may demand some favor in return (e.g., sex, an expensive purchase) that she is unwilling to supply (LaRossa & LaRossa, 1981).

Therefore, the critical factor again seems to be the extent to which couples have adequately planned for the parenting role and are committed to its added demands (Belsky & Kelly, 1994). The greater the couple's openness of communication and the more clearly they have negotiated their expectations for one another prior to the arrival of the child, the more likely they are to remain satisfied with one another throughout the transition. Furthermore, research has consistently shown that harmonious marriages tend to be associated with more sensitive parenting and warmer parent–child relations. In contrast, less supportive relationships appear to render parents unable to provide consistent direction, guidance, and discipline to their children (Gable, Belsky, & Crnic, 1992).

In sum, it appears that it is the couple's ability or inability to negotiate their expectations, and to bring their expectations and experiences into alignment with one another, that is a key to understanding how children affect the marriage relationship (Sabatelli, 1988). This suggests several critical points to keep in mind when considering the impact of children and parenting on marriage. First, the presence of children and the demands of child-rearing have a definite impact upon parents' efforts to manage the emotional climate within the marriage. Children clearly change the family system. Second, spouses will often change what they expect of their partners in response to the increased demands of parenthood. A decline in satisfaction will result if partners are unresponsive to these changes in expectations.

At the same time, it is important to emphasize that children do not cause spouses' marital satisfaction to decline. They can, like other stresses, introduce demands on the marriage that increase the likelihood of conflicts around expectations. Thus, satisfaction declines when couples fail to discuss their expectations and constructively manage differences of opinion. In this regard, it is important for couples to take responsibility for how their marriage is experienced, rather than simply blame their children, as this is the first step in maintaining a vital marriage throughout these years.

Maintaining a Satisfying Sexual Relationship. The strategies couples have evolved for meeting one another's sexual needs generally undergo changes with the arrival of children. The shift from a marital- to a child-focused system, along with the general decline in the overall quality of marriage experienced during this period, inevitably affects the couple's sexual relationship. The frequency of sexual interactions tends to decline throughout pregnancy, only to increase again weeks and sometimes months after childbirth. Although there is less agreement in the research literature on the determinants of postpartum sexual activity, most research suggests that parenthood transforms the sexual lives of most couples (Francoeur & Noonan, 2004). A recent statistical analyses involving a large number of studies found that parents tend to report lower levels of sexual satisfaction than nonparents, but the precise reasons for these changes in sexual behavior and satisfaction are still largely unknown (Harvey, Wenzel, & Sprecher, 2004).

However difficult or discouraging these changes in the sexual relationship are to couples, most appear to be able to accept them as understandable (Cowan & Cowan, 2000). For many, these changes are only temporary and limited to the later stages of pregnancy and to the first few months after the child's birth.

As noted in Chapter 8, the primary significance of sexuality is its ability to symbolically communicate the specialness of the marriage relationship and define a special bond between partners. With the arrival of children, this special bond must be modified to account for the newly forming emotional bonds between parents and child. Couples who are able to alter their sexual relationship temporarily to account for these competing emotional and physical demands are more likely to resume a satisfactory sexual relationship after the initial transition is passed.

Such couples are also more likely to experience new feelings of closeness that come from sharing the experience of being parents and enjoying their baby's growing responsiveness (Cowan & Cowan, 2000).

Managing Leisure Activities. The additional time and effort required to manage a household with young children mean that not much time is left for leisure activities. Still, the viability, strength, and quality of the couple's marriage and each partner's personal well-being are often dependent on a sufficient amount of time spent together as a couple in companionate activities, in addition to time spent alone engaging in personal interests and activities. The family must devise strategies that consider these needs for leisure while also balancing the demands placed on the system from paid employment, housekeeping, and child care.

Unfortunately, most women report that, after the birth of their children, marriage becomes more of a partnership than a romance and that their husbands do not pay enough attention to them (Belsky & Kelly, 1994). That is, most of the time spent together as a couple is spent engaging in instrumental tasks such as housework and parenting, rather than in leisure activities such as going out to dinner or the movies, watching television together, or just spending intimate time alone (MacDermid et al., 1990). Many factors can account for these changes. One may be the lack of energy and enthusiasm for more activities after completing one's necessary work, household, and parenting responsibilities. Leisure activities require time away from children, which may be experienced as an unwanted sacrifice, especially for women who work full-time outside the home. Finally, leisure activities are expensive, requiring money for the activity as well as babysitters. The added expenses of raising children may make expenditures for leisure activities more of a luxury than some couples can afford.

Managing New Areas of Conflict. It should be apparent by now that the entry into parenthood is fraught with numerous sources of potential conflict. One potential source of conflict involves relationships with the extended family. The addition of children to the family system has an intergenerational effect on the family system. Parents and in-laws experience changes as they assume the role of grandparents. Spouses may disagree about the role grandparents will be expected to play in their family. Similarly, grandparents may have different expectations for their role in the family than their adult children have for them. For instance, parents and in-laws may increase the frequency of their visits to help out with the children, or they may have "helpful advice" for the new parents that is perceived as intrusive by one or both spouses. Alternatively, new parents may expect more attention and help from grandparents than they actually receive, leaving them feeling rejected, ignored, or unimportant. That research has consistently identified problems with in-laws as a source of stress during the transition to parenthood points to the importance of new parents renegotiating a mutually acceptable level of involvement with extended family members (Carter, 2005).

Success in these negotiations will be determined, in part, by the degree of individuation each spouse has achieved from his or her family of origin. Unsuccessful individuation efforts can lead to intensified conflicts with parents or in-laws. Unresolved dependency needs and feelings of anger, rejection, or alienation toward parents can be displaced onto the marriage, where these earlier conflicts are then reenacted. Alternatively, children may come to be viewed as sources of potential problems, which also may reflect earlier unresolved conflicts in the family of origin. For instance, it is not uncommon in clinical interviews to hear parents report that a particular child "was a problem from day one" or that "this child always had the same irritating characteristics as his (or her) mother (or father)." These images of the child, formed very early in life, can become reinforced over time and become key elements of the child's identity and a precursor to parent–child conflicts later in the child's development.

Conflicts also can develop over how the couple is to balance best the demands of maintaining an intimate and supportive marital relationship with the demands of raising children. Too much focus on the marriage, to the exclusion of children's needs, or too much focus on the children, to the exclusion of the marriage, can severely disrupt the family's emotional environment by provoking further feelings of rejection, anger, or alienation.

The transition to parenthood also demands a renegotiation of each spouse's need for individuality and separateness with his or her need for connectedness to family. As noted, prevailing social and cultural values and socialization experiences can fuel potential conflict by placing greater demands on women to assume family responsibilities while men remain more free to engage in individualized tasks, leisure activities, or responsibilities outside the home. To the extent that one or both spouses perceive their needs for separateness or connectedness to be unfulfilled, this becomes another potential source of family conflict. LaRossa and LaRossa (1981) suggested that a major source of conflict between spouses during this period is the scarcity of free time and the differences that emerge regarding how this scarce commodity will be allocated. They propose that young children, because of their total dependency on adults for survival and their need for "continuous coverage," demand a large amount of time. This demand, when coupled with the demands on the system to allocate time to paid employment, household management, leisure activities, or social activities, means that conflicts with regard to spousal interests are inevitable.

Finally, spouses may differ in their images of a given child or of what common values to pass along to each child. One may want a son or daughter to be a doctor, a star athlete, or an accountant, while the other wants him or her to take over the family business or become president of the United States. One may view the child's behaviors as humorous, while the other may see the same behaviors as disrespectful or sarcastic. If spouses are from mixed ethnic or religious backgrounds, conflicts may emerge over which set of values children will be expected to follow. Parents also may differ in their preferred style of parenting, with one preferring a more permissive style and the other preferring a more authoritarian style. Here again, the strategies and rules that spouses have established earlier in the marital career will greatly influence their degree of success or failure in renegotiating their competing images and expectations for their children.

Conclusions

The patterns and dynamics established during the newly married stages of the family life cycle are all affected by the presence of children. The demands of children on family systems require a reworking of family and personal identities, external and internal boundaries, and household maintenance strategies. The stresses and strains associated with parenthood also affect the marital relationship. Couples must make space for their children and keep space available for their own relationship. Leisure time is affected. Patterns of companionship and sexual intimacy must be adjusted. Couples must negotiate tensions and conflicts in ways that facilitate intimacy rather than erode the foundation of the marriage.

It must be emphasized, however, that these stresses are ordinary in the sense that they confront the system with common, everyday difficulties. It is the coping strategies that couples select to deal with these ordinary demands that has important implications for the future adaptation of the system. Family systems rich in resources, as discussed in Chapter 2, may be able to accommodate the demands of parenthood with a minimum of discomfort and distress. Conversely, systems lacking in coping resources—systems, for example, lacking a legacy of cohesion and supportiveness, or comprised of individuals lacking self-esteem or self-efficacy—are more apt to be overwhelmed by the accumulation of demands that accompanies the entrance of children into the family system. In fact, our attempt to outline, throughout this chapter, the challenges encountered by the family system with young children is motivated by a belief that knowledge of these challenges will serve to help couples cope better with this stage of the family life cycle.

Key Terms

Direct costs Out-of-pocket expenses for raising a child that include childbirth, food, clothing, housing, and education.

Indirect costs The potential income forgone by women who stay at home to raise their children or the added costs of child care for those who do work.

Role conflict Disagreements about marital roles and responsibilities and who should perform various tasks or how they should be performed.

Role overload The experience of finding it impossible to meet all of the competing demands one faces. It is often accompanied by feelings of anxiety and a loss of control over one's life.

Role strain The tension experienced when one has a clear idea of one's role responsibilities but is unable to fulfill them in a way that satisfies one's own expectations.

CHAPTER 12

The Parent–Child Relationship System

Chapter Overview

Raising children requires development of strategies for (1) nurturing children; and (2) controlling their behavior. Nurturance strategies communicate support, warmth, acceptance, and encouragement. Control strategies are essential for protecting children from harm and socializing them to act in socially appropriate ways. The strategies parents select for providing nurturance and control are evident in their parenting style.

An authoritarian style is highly controlling but generally lacking in warmth. A permissive style lacks control and can be either overly indulgent or neglectful. An authoritative style blends warmth and control in a manner that sets clear parental guidelines for the child's behavior while recognizing the child's unique thoughts, feelings, and abilities. The parenting style is determined by three key factors: (1) the parents' own developmental history and psychological and interpersonal resources; (2) the child's unique qualities, including temperament, gender, age, and developmental status; and (3) contextual sources of stress and support available to the family.

The effectiveness of a parenting style is ultimately determined by the ability of parents to nurture and control their children appropriately. In this respect, child abuse and neglect can be viewed as examples of ineffective parenting styles.

The Parent–Child Relationship System

Attention is now directed to the patterns of interaction found in the relationships between parents and their children. There is no debating that there is great variation found in the interactions between parents and children. In order to understand this diversity, however, it is necessary to keep in mind the relationship between system tasks and strategies. Parents and children comprise a subsystem within the family system. Within this subsystem, parents are charged with the tasks of attending to the emotional, physical, social, and psychological needs of their children. Parents must evolve strategies to accomplish these tasks, and the strategies they select are evident in their particular parenting styles.

Dimensions of Parenting Style

Each of us, on becoming a parent, must develop strategies for meeting the demands and responsibilities of the parental role. Quite clearly, parenting is a complex activity that includes many behaviors that work individually and together to influence child outcomes. Although specific parenting behaviors, such as spanking or reading aloud, may influence child development, looking at any particular behavior in isolation may be misleading. Many authors have noted that individual parenting practices are less important in predicting child well-being than is the broad pattern of parenting (Darling & Steinburg, 1993; Maccoby & Martin, 1983).

The concept of parenting style is central to understanding the dynamics that occur in parent–child relationships. The construct of parenting style denotes normal variations in parents' attempts to nurture, control, and socialize their children. In describing parenting styles, many researchers rely on a typology of parenting styles created by Baumrind (1991a). Two points are critical in understanding Baumrind's way of classifying parenting styles. First, parenting style is meant to describe normal variations in parenting. In other words, the parenting style typology Baumrind developed should not be understood to include deviant parenting, such as might be observed in abusive or neglectful homes. Second, Baumrind assumes that normal parenting centers on issues of control. Although parents may differ in how they try to control or socialize their children and the extent to which they do so, it is assumed that the primary role of all parents is to influence, teach, and control their children (Darling & Steinburg, 1993).

Parenting style captures two important elements of parenting: **parental responsiveness** and **parental demandingness** (Maccoby & Martin, 1983). Parental responsiveness (also referred to as "parental warmth" or "supportiveness") refers to "the extent to which parents intentionally foster individuality, self-regulation, and self-assertion by being attuned, supportive, and acquiescent to children's special needs and demands" (Baumrind, 1991a, p. 62). Parental responsiveness and warmth are evident in the ways parents physically and verbally interact with their children. For example, physical expressions of acceptance include hugging, fondling, caressing, and kissing. Expressions of verbal warmth include praising, complimenting, and saying other nice things to or about the child (Rohner, 1986).

Parental demandingness (also referred to as "behavioral control") refers to "the claims parents make on children to become integrated into the family whole, by their maturity demands, supervision, disciplinary efforts, and willingness to confront the child who disobeys" (Baumrind, 1991a, pp. 61–62). Parents are charged with the task of protecting their children from harm. Parents also must teach their children to act in socially appropriate ways. Children need to learn to control their impulses, respect the rights of others, and be responsive to the dictates of social norms and customs. In short, parents must evolve parenting strategies for teaching their children to act in age-appropriate ways.

Four Parenting Styles

Categorizing parents according to whether they are high or low on the dimensions of parental demandingness and responsiveness creates a typology of four parenting styles: **indulgent**, **authoritarian**, **authoritative**, and **uninvolved** (Maccoby & Martin, 1983). Each of these parenting styles reflects different naturally occurring patterns of parental values, practices, and behaviors (Baumrind, 1991a, 1991b).

Indulgent parents (also referred to as "permissive" or "nondirective") are responsive but not demanding. They are lenient, do not require mature behavior, and avoid confrontation (Baumrind, 1991a, 1991b). Indulgent parents may be further divided into two types: democratic parents and nondirective parents. Of these two, the democratic parents, though lenient, are more conscientious, engaged, and committed to the children than are the nondirective parents (Lamborn, Mounts, Steinberg, & Dornbusch, 1991). That is, the democratic parents are more likely than the nondirective parents to at least make an effort to make their children aware of family rules and explain the rationale for them.

Authoritarian parents are highly demanding and directive, but not responsive. "They are obedience- and status-oriented, and expect their orders to be obeyed without explanation" (Baumrind, 1991a, p. 62). These parents provide well-ordered and structured environments with clearly stated rules. They tend to favor the use of punitive and forceful disciplinary methods. Their intent is generally to curb the child's self-will whenever the child acts or thinks in a manner that conflicts with what the parent thinks is appropriate. Authoritarian parents have been found to differ in the degree to which they are intrusive (Darling & Steinburg, 1993). That is, some authoritarian parents are directive but not intrusive or autocratic in their use of power, whereas other authoritarian parents are highly controlling, directive, and intrusive.

Authoritative parents are both demanding and responsive. "They monitor and impart clear standards for their children's conduct. They are assertive, but not intrusive and restrictive. Their disciplinary methods are supportive, rather than punitive. They want their children to be assertive, socially responsible, self-regulated, and cooperative" (Baumrind, 1991a, p. 63). These parents, in other words, tend to be nurturing and rely primarily on positive reinforcement rather than punishment in an effort to control their children. They are willing to direct and exert control over their children, but in a manner that displays awareness of the children's thoughts, feelings, and developmental capabilities. They demand mature, responsible, and independent behavior from their children and will explain the rationale behind their discipline or choice of family rules.

Uninvolved parents are low in both responsiveness and demandingness. In a sense, these parents can be thought of as being both neglectful and permissive (Lamborn et al., 1991). Children are given no clearly defined rules for behavior, and they receive little or no attention. They are not monitored and are deprived of acceptance and affirmation. The absence of both acceptance and clear guidelines or standards for self-control can leave children confused, anxious, and unable to internalize standards for self control (Baumrind, 1991a, 1991b).

In addition to differing on responsiveness and demandingness, the parenting styles also differ in the extent to which they are characterized by a third dimension: psychological control. **Psychological control** refers to control attempts that intrude into the psychological and emotional development of the child through the use of parenting practices such as guilt induction, withdrawal of love, or shaming (Barber, 1996, 2002). One key difference between authoritarian and authoritative parenting is in the dimension of psychological control. Both authoritarian and authoritative parents place high demands on their children and expect their children to behave appropriately and obey parental rules. Authoritarian parents, however, also expect their children to accept their judgments, values, and goals without questioning. In contrast, authoritative parents are more open to give and take with their children and make greater use of explanations. Thus, although authoritative and authoritarian parents are equally high in behavioral control, authoritative parents tend to be low in psychological control, while authoritarian parents tend to be high.

Consequences for Children

Parenting style has been found to predict child well-being in the domains of social competence, psychosocial development, instrumental competence (i.e., academic performance), and problem behavior. Numerous studies have documented that a parenting style characterized by warmth, support, logical reasoning, clear communication, appropriate monitoring, and involvement is associated with positive developmental outcomes for children (Darling & Steinburg, 1993). This research, based on parent interviews, child reports, and parent observations, consistently finds that children and adolescents whose parents are authoritative (responsive and appropriately demanding) rate themselves and are rated by objective measures as more socially and instrumentally competent than those whose parents are nonauthoritative. In contrast, the detrimental effects of uninvolved parenting are evident as early as the preschool years and continue throughout adolescence and into early adulthood (Darling & Steinburg, 1993).

Research also has shown that high levels of psychological control are associated with negative outcomes for children. Most notable are internalizing problems, such as anxiety, depression, loneliness, and confusion. Furthermore, when inadequate behavioral control is combined with high levels of psychological control, externalizing problems such as acting out, drug use, truancy, and antisocial behaviors are common. It appears that psychological control, including parental intrusiveness, guilt induction, and love withdrawal, undermines psychosocial development by interfering with children's ability to become independent or develop a healthy sense of self and personal identity (Barber, 2002).

In conclusion, in reviewing the literature on parenting style, one is struck by the consistency with which authoritative upbringing is associated with both instrumental and social competence and lower levels of problem behavior in both males and females at all developmental stages. Clearly, parenting style provides a robust indicator of parental functioning that predicts child well-being across a wide spectrum of environments and communities. Both parental responsiveness and parental demandingness are important components of good parenting. Authoritative parenting, with its emphasis on clear parental demands balanced with emotional responsiveness and support for child autonomy, is one of the most consistent family predictors of positive youth development from early childhood through adolescence.

Determinants of Parenting Style

Parenting styles reflect the unique strategies adopted by parents in their efforts to fulfill the tasks associated with the parental role. Belsky (1984) has proposed a conceptual model that addresses the determinants of the style of parenting adopted by mothers and fathers. Within his model, the many determinants of the style of parenting are organized into three primary dimensions: (1) parents' personal psychological resources; (2) the unique characteristics of the child; and (3) contextual sources of stress and support.

The Parents' Contribution

Parents' own developmental histories or family legacies have a profound effect on the resources they bring to their parenting style. More specifically, earlier experiences with the family of origin influence the individual parent's psychological health and personality, two critical resources related to one's parenting style. In this regard, it can be argued that the psychological health, personality, and parenting practices employed with one's own children are all affected by the level of differentiation found within one's family of origin. Well-differentiated family systems, characterized by a high tolerance for autonomy and intimacy, encourage individuals to speak for themselves, take personal responsibility for age-appropriate tasks, be sensitive to the needs of others, and communicate confirmation and respect for one another. These dynamics provide individuals with the psychological and interpersonal resources necessary to deal with the demands of parenthood. These individuals are more likely than those from relatively poorly differentiated families to possess the patience, communication skills, empathy, and sensitivity necessary to nurture and control their children effectively.

According to Belsky, effective parents are capable of decentering and accurately appraising the perspective of others. They are able to empathize with others and take on a nurturing orientation. Only by possessing such abilities would one be able to respond to the demands of parenting without abdicating responsibility (as in neglectful or indulgent-permissive parenting) or relying on absolute power (as in child abuse or authoritarian parenting). Furthermore, to function in this way parents will need to experience a sense of control over their own lives and destinies as well as feel that their own psychological needs are being met. Since the essence of parenting, especially in the childhood years, involves giving, those who have been exposed to confirming and individuation-enhancing patterns of interaction while growing up are more likely to be able to relate to their children in a sensitive, individuation-enhancing manner (Belsky, Steinburg, & Draper, 1991).

The Child's Contribution

Not only do parents influence children, but children influence parents. Factors such as the child's gender and age or developmental status are among those that may elicit different responses from parents. For example, girls are often encouraged to maintain close family ties and be more dependent, while boys are encouraged to explore more, achieve more, and be more competitive and independent (Bates & Pettit, 2007). Each of these orientations toward children helps to determine the manner in which boys and girls are nurtured and, more specifically, controlled. In addition, the child's temperament, which includes such characteristics as mood, activity level, distractibility, attention span, adaptability to new situations, intensity of reactions, pattern of approach–withdrawal, and fluidity of bodily functions, also influences parenting styles.

However, it is not sufficient to consider only the direct effects of children's characteristics on adults' parenting styles. Children's influence on their parents' behavior is actually bidirectional and interdependent. This suggests that parenting styles are influenced not only by the temperament of the child, but by how the child's temperament influences the parents, whose own personal traits, in turn, influence how they are likely to respond to the child's requests. Thus, a critical factor in determining effective parenting is the "goodness of fit" between the child's characteristics and those of the parent. For instance, the emotionally expressive child may require a great deal of physical stimulation and comforting in order to feel secure. Such a child would respond well to a parent whose preferred method of expressing affection also involves physical gestures. But the child would be less responsive to a parent who relies on verbal expressions of support and comfort rather than physical gestures. Likewise, such a parent is likely to respond more positively to a child who shares his or her preferred mode of expression than to one who does not. Here again, the critical factor is not only the temperament or individual traits of the particular child but how well the child's traits interact with the parent's own temperament and traits. The better the fit between parent and child, the greater the likelihood of quality parent–child interactions (Belsky, 1984).

Contextual Sources of Stress and Support

The ordinary demands of parenthood require the establishment of patterns of nurturance and control and care and responsiveness that protect children and attend to their evolving physical, social, emotional, and psychological needs. As a general rule, stressed parents tend to be less responsive to their children (Belsky, Youngblade, Rovine, & Volling, 1991). That families with children comprise a "continual coverage system" (LaRossa & LaRossa, 1981) means that parents experience a considerable amount of ordinary stress in their efforts to adapt continually to the ongoing demands of their children. Thus, success at managing these ordinary demands of parenthood will be influenced by contextual sources of stress and support.

Belsky highlights the importance of the marriage relationship, social networks, and the work environment as critical contextual sources of both potential stress and support. These contextual factors serve as stressors when they complicate or compound the ordinary tasks of parenthood. They serve as coping resources when they help parents to adopt patterns of interaction that enable them to fulfill the tasks of parenthood. It should be clear that these contextual factors are always operating in ways that help to determine the adopted style of parenting.

Marriage and Parenting. If one views the marriage as a parental support system, it is apparent that marriage provides two basic forms of support: emotional and instrumental. Emotional support communicates to the parent that he or she is loved, esteemed, and valued, and this, in turn, influences the degree of patience that a parent brings to the caregiving role. Instrumental support involves the provision of goods and services that can free energy the parent can use in this role. Thus, for women who generally assume the primary caregiving role, their relationship with their husbands becomes an important source of support that can strongly influence their enjoyment of parenting. At the same time, the quality of the marital relationship is itself a function of the developmental histories and personalities involved in the relationship.

Belsky and Kelly (1994) review a number of studies supporting the important link between the qualities of the marriage relationship and parenting attitudes and behaviors. In general, this research suggests that parents with poor marriages tend to have more negative attitudes toward parenting and act in less warm and supportive ways toward their children. In other words, marital stress and conflict can reverberate throughout the system, affecting parent–child patterns of interaction. In some instances, for example, parents may attempt to cope with marital strife by using their children as a source of emotional support, which involves them in a cross-generational coalition. In other instances, parents may blame their children for the marital stress. In either instance, the abilities of parents to attend to the needs of their children effectively are compromised by the manner in which the marital stress is mismanaged.

Not surprisingly, interparental conflict has been found to have a negative impact on children's development. Specifically, when interparental conflict is more frequent, intense, and long-lasting, studies show that children are at increased risk for emotional and behavioral difficulties (Cummings & Davies, 1994). Living with marital conflict also increases the risk of children displaying poor interpersonal skills and low levels of social competence (Cummings, Davies, & Campbell, 2000). Finally, although no clear patterns have consistently emerged across studies, some interesting findings have begun to appear with respect to interactions between sex of parent and sex of children. There are some indications that marital conflict may be more likely to affect opposite-sex parent–child relationships than same-sex parent–child relationships (Cox, Paley, & Harter, 2001).

Social Networks and Parenthood. If the marital relationship is the primary support system for parents, the interpersonal relations between parents and their friends, relatives, and neighbors function as the second most important system of support. A great deal of evidence demonstrates the relationship between the availability of support from others and effective parent–child relations. Social support has been associated with enhanced parental competence, greater verbal and emotional responsiveness, reduced reliance on punishment for parental control, increased self-esteem, and greater patience with and sensitivity toward one's children (Belsky, Youngblade, et al., 1991).

These findings are understandable in view of the ways in which social networks serve as coping resources for parents. Social networks, as can marital partners, serve as a source of both instrumental and emotional support. For example, family, friends, and neighbors may provide parents with information. This could be anything from information about what to expect at different developmental phases, suggested discipline strategies, ideas for helping children with school work, to the schedule of community activities. These same individuals may also provide assistance with child care, relieving some of the burden of having to provide "continual coverage." In addition, emotional support can be gained from these social contacts. All parents could occasionally use adult companionship and conversation to help them deal with a particularly hard day.

Work and Parenting. For most parents, balancing the demands of work, marriage, and parenthood poses a considerable challenge. In this regard, the context of work can function for parents as a source of either stress, further complicating the challenges of parenthood, or support, assisting them in their efforts to balance the many competing demands of work and family life. For example, corporate-sponsored day care provides parents of preschool-aged children with an affordable and secure child-care arrangement. This can help reduce some of the anxiety associated with finding quality, low-cost child care. Similarly, employers who allow parents to alter their work schedules to deal with a sick child or a child who has the day off from school can help reduce the additional stress that these ordinary demands produce.

In addition, parents' attitudes toward their work, that is, how much they enjoy it and whether their work contributes positively to their self-concept, can influence how parenting roles and responsibilities are approached. The incidence of child abuse is higher, for example, among unemployed men who would prefer to be working than among working fathers. Furthermore, work absorption, or devotion of a great deal of time and energy to work, has been associated with men becoming more irritable and impatient with their children. For women who work, the degree to which they are satisfied with their employment status has important consequences for their experience of parenthood. Women who are not satisfied with their work situation, for example, have been found to perform less competently in the parenting role and have more poorly adjusted children than those who are more satisfied with their work status (Belsky, Youngblade, et al., 1991).

In sum, the demands of parenting are many and diverse. It is clear, as well, that a number of factors help to determine the particular strategies parents select to meet these demands. Belsky (1984) believes that personal and contextual resources have the greatest effect on the style of parenting that is adopted. This suggests that the stresses and demands of parenthood may be reasonably managed when parents' personal adjustment is positive and when the marital and other support systems are readily available. In contrast, the absence of strong marital and extended support systems or the presence of persistent psychological problems between parents increases the likelihood that parents will not effectively meet the emotional, physical, social, and psychological needs of their children.

Gender and Parenting Styles

As with all roles, men and women often approach the responsibilities of parenthood differently. Couples must negotiate these differences to arrive at a consensus regarding (1) how each parent will address parenting tasks; and (2) how parental responsibilities within the family system will be allocated.

The extant research supports the existence of gender differences in parenting styles. For example, the research on parents with young children suggests, not surprisingly, that mothers provide most of the continuous coverage that children require and generally sacrifice their free time to do so, unless they are occasionally relieved by their husbands. More than fathers, mothers provide care and attend, respond to, protect, hold, soothe, and comfort their children (Darling-Fisher & Tiedje, 1990; Johnson & Huston, 1998; Marsiglio, Amato, Day, & Lamb, 2000).

Fathers' participation with their children is qualitatively different. They are rarely alone with their children, and when both parents are present, mothers typically manage and monitor what takes place between a father and small children (Pleck, 1997). Fathers are more likely to engage in play or other types of activities that are less repetitive, redundant, or boring (Lamb, 2004; Marsiglio et al., 2000). In one study, fathers were found to spend 50 percent of the time they spent with their children in play, compared with mothers, who spent less than 10 percent of such time in play (LaRossa & LaRossa, 1981). Play is a cleaner, less demanding, and more novel activity than some of the more repetitive day-to-day tasks of child care. In addition, when men do participate in child care, they tend to view their involvement as helping out their wives rather than sharing equally in the responsibility (Blain, 1994; Coltrane, 1996; Hawkins, Roberts, Christiansen, & Marshall, 1994).

Earlier socialization experiences appear to play an important role in men's and women's different approaches to parenting. Most men lack role models for parenting because they have come from families in which their fathers did not participate in the care of young children (Palkovitz, 2002). There are indications, however, that changes in men's approach to fathering may be taking place. Recent studies, for example, have pointed out that men younger than age thirty with preschool children do more child care. This is especially true when wives work long hours (Almeida, Maggs, & Galambos, 1993; Demo & Acock, 1993; Greenstein, 1996) or partners' work schedules do not overlap. In addition, most men report that parenting is an important role for them. However, they still consider their primary parental responsibility as being a good provider (Perry-Jenkins et al., 2000).

Whether and to what extent women expect their partners to assume parental responsibilities are also a function of socialization experiences. Because women are identified within our culture as being more responsible for parenting than men

(Simons et al., 1990), many women still do not expect men to do much around the house or to be highly involved in child care (Demaris & Longmore, 1996; Lennon & Rosenfield, 1994; Marsiglio et al., 2000). When women do expect their partners to be actively involved in parenting, however, men clearly become much more actively involved (Simons et al., 1990). That is, men will typically defer to their wives in matters of child-rearing unless their wives believe that their participation is important. It is interesting to note that, when men do participate more equally in the responsibilities of child care, men and women experience parenthood in similar ways. Men enjoy the close, rich fulfillment of relationships with their children just as women do, and they also report the same frustrations, boredom, exhaustion, and worry that accompany this involvement (Thompson & Walker, 1989).

It is fair to conclude that fatherhood is changing. That is, the norms regarding father involvement are clearly changing, and fathers are expected to be more involved with their children today than ever before. Although the norms have changed, it is also clear that family factors are an important determinant of father involvement. Apparently, mothers can either facilitate or inhibit fathers' involvement through their role as gatekeepers. In addition, the quality of the marital relationship is a further determinant of father involvement—when the marital relationship is positive, the level of father involvement is higher (Parke, 1996).

Ethnic and Minority Parenting

As the Belsky model suggests, parenting takes place in various contexts. Much of the early research on parent–child relationships investigated white middle-class families, neglecting the cultural and structural diversity that characterizes contemporary families. Today it is recognized that culture, ethnicity, and minority status can shape both the structure and the experience of parenthood (Parke & Buriel, 2002).

Culture can influence the parenting styles of parents by shaping the values, attitudes, beliefs, and goals that parents bring to their relationships with their children. Child-rearing, in addition to being influenced by culture, is also a vehicle by which culture is transmitted from parent to child (Harkness & Super, 2002). This is to suggest that parents from cultures that are outside the dominant culture of the United States may have distinct beliefs, attitudes, values, and parenting behaviors that overlap with, but are also unique from, those of the dominant culture. These unique features refer to basic issues such as the definition and roles of the family in the life of a child. They also refer to parental beliefs about the determinants of a child's development, including what and who may foster or hinder development, and how and which aspects of development are most important (i.e., discipline versus intelligence), and how competence is defined in each of these areas. For example, some cultural groups value education, and therefore attempt to instill a respect for teachers and knowledge in their children. Other groups value creativity and spontaneity in their children, while still others value respect and obedience. The varied values and beliefs are what ethnic and minority parents consider to be in the best interest of their children (Garcia-Coll and Pachter, 2002).

It is, of course, important to note that culture is not deterministic; that is, the influence of culture on the parenting process will obviously vary across people and situations. The metaperspective presented in Chapter 5 reminds us that not all members of a particular group behave in the same way. There will be individual differences among members of a group with respect to how strongly they identify with the culture. This can be partially attributed to varying degrees of acculturation.

It should be also emphasized from the start that there are as many areas of overlap as there are differences between parenting processes observed in minority populations and in the dominant society. The basic parenting processes are shared by most families, regardless of their ethnicity, race, and minority status (Garcia-Coll & Pachter, 2002). However, there are certain unique factors within families that may be shaped by culture. Unique parenting traditions can create tension between members of the cultural groups and those within the dominant culture when culturally specific patterns of parenting are viewed as deviant or dysfunctional rather than simply different.

For example consider the following vignettes reported by Garcia-Coll and Pachter (2002, p. 1):

> *Rosa is a 4-year-old girl who recently immigrated with her family from the Dominican Republic. She and her 5-year-old sister sleep in their parents' bedroom, often sharing the same bed with their parents. A church member was concerned when Rosa drew a picture of herself sleeping next to her father as part of a Sunday School project, and spoke with the parents. Rosa's parents were angry and did not understand the church member's concerns. The family questioned whether they really belonged in the church after all, even though worship and church community had always been important to them.*
>
> *Marvin is a 7-year-old African-American boy who is disruptive in the classroom and aggressive toward young children on the playground. He is being reared by his mother and grandmother in a Chicago public housing project where drug-related violence occurs frequently. The family's disciplinary practices include spanking and withholding meals, which are described as necessary given the potentially high price of misbehavior around the project. Teachers are frustrated by the family's apparent dismissal of Marvin's school behavior as "nothing to worry about" and "just practice for the real world." (p. 189)*

These examples demonstrate that parenting styles are rooted in the cultural context of the family, and yet judgments of parenting styles are sometimes based on whether parents conform to the dominant norms of the society. Tension can obviously exist between the cultural traditions of minority or immigrant parents and those of the dominant culture. Certainly the knowledge of how culture, ethnicity, and minority status inform approaches to parenting is necessary to understand parenting styles and to make judgments of parenting effectiveness.

In sum, the particular attitudes and behaviors that any given minority or ethnic group espouses can be thought of as standardized formulas developed to promote children's competencies and socially adaptive behaviors within a given societal context (Garcia-Coll, 1990; Ogbu, 1981, 1987). Certainly, then, it is important to have a basic understanding of the traditional child-rearing attitudes, values, and practices that characterize various ethnic and minority groups.

What follows is an overview of some of the predominate parenting values and beliefs found within African American, Hispanic American, and Asian American families. Again, before presenting these views we need to include another cautionary note urging restraint against overgeneralizing about different ethnic and minority groups. We need to be ever mindful of intragroup variability and individual differences. By examining a group's history, roots, and parenting norms, however, it may be possible to delineate which aspects may be congruent or incongruent with the parenting norms espoused within the dominant society. This may provide insight regarding what areas of parenting may be most likely to create conflict and incompatibility between the group's traditional practices and the majority practices within the country. That is, this overview of the traditional attitudes, values, and parenting practices found within different cultural groups can serve as a guidepost not only for the parents but also for clinicians, social workers, and researchers who strive for sociocultural sensitivity.

African American Parents

Because of their history of being subject to prejudice and discrimination, many African Americans recognize the importance of a positive racial identity and kinship networks. Thus, for example, African American child-rearing priorities might emphasize both fostering children's sense of personal identity and self-esteem and promoting their awareness of their cultural heritage and membership in the broader kinship network and community (Thomas, 1993). Socializing priorities often include enhancing the African American consciousness and identity of children, which can enhance their feelings of pride and competence as members of society (Billingsley, 1974). Family members and other responsible people in the community often come together to provide children with care, protection, guidance, and discipline. This communal effort can be particularly adaptive given the challenges, and real dangers, of rearing children in inner-city settings. Emphasis may be placed on providing children with opportunities to play and be young, rather than demanding that they assume adult responsibilities before they are ready. Children's effective learning of obedience and respect for elders is also generally encouraged (Willis, 1992).

A wide range of disciplinary practices is found in African American families, but the tendency to be restrictive and to expect immediate obedience has been noted by several researchers (Julian, McKenry, & McKelvey, 1994; Peters, 1985). Such disciplinary practices of parents, particularly those of low socioeconomic status, have been posited to be necessary, in part, due to the consequences of growing up in dangerous neighborhoods where violence and the risks of antisocial activities are relatively commonplace (Kelley, Power, & Wimbush, 1992). In addition, discipline has been described as serving to teach African American children to understand how to follow rules in society (Willis, 1992). Suffice it to say that there is considerable variation in contemporary disciplinary practices, which may be influenced by socioeconomic status, social support, the level of safety and violence in neighborhoods, and religious affiliation (Kelley et al., 1992). Providing racial socialization and teaching children how to cope with discrimination, racism, and prejudice are also of importance to many African American parents (McAdoo, 1991).

Hispanic American Parents

Hispanic American families tend to be nurturant, warm, and egalitarian toward their children. Young children are often indulged, and parenting practices appear quite permissive (Vega, 1990). The attitude toward young children is often to placate them, rather than to emphasize early achievement or attainment of developmental milestones (Zuniga, 1992). Although parents may be permissive and indulgent with infants and younger children, an emphasis on obedience as children grow older may lead to a more authoritarian style. Strictness in the context of high nurturance is guided by a desire to protect children and instill respect of adults (Garcia-Preto, 2005).

Within Hispanic American families, emphasis is typically placed on close mother–child relationships, interpersonal responsiveness, and the development of a proper demeanor and sense of dignity (Harwood, 1992). It is not unusual for Hispanic children to share the parental bedroom and/or bed, reflecting a combination of extended family living arrangements and family interdependence and intimacy. That is, these approaches to child-rearing are consistent with cultural values encouraging family member interdependence rather than independence and individuation (Roland, 1988). A well-educated child is generally considered to be *tranquilo, obediente, y respetuoso,* that is, calm, obedient, and respectful toward adults (Briggs, 1986). Parents, thus, are likely to place particular emphasis on encouraging their children to master skills in human relationships and to understand the importance of interacting and relating to others with respect and dignity (Zuniga, 1988).

Asian American Parents

In general, the primary parenting goals in families with Asian roots include proper development of character (Ho, 1981) and formal academic education (Dung, 1984). During infancy and early childhood, parents tend to be highly lenient, nurturant, and permissive, because young children are generally believed to be incapable of understanding the difference between right and wrong (Chan, 1992). However, once children reach the "age of understanding" (three to six years), they are less likely to be indulged by their parents, who then might impose stricter behavioral expectations. For example, early mastery of emotional maturity, self-control, and social courtesies might be viewed as priorities for young Asian American children. They may be taught in various ways that their actions will reflect not only on themselves but also on the larger family (Suzuki, 1980), thus inculcating a sense of moral obligation and primary loyalty to the family (Chan, 1992).

As noted, considerable emphasis can be placed on academic effort as a means to achieve personal advancement, higher social status, wealth, and family respect, and to overcome discrimination (Lum & Char, 1985). These values and socialization priorities of Asian American families are compatible with several mainstream values (e.g., academic achievement and hard work) and may facilitate the bicultural identification or promote the assimilation of Asian American families into the broader American society (Garcia-Coll & Pachter, 2002).

The Effectiveness of Parenting Styles: Child Abuse and Neglect

The effectiveness of a parenting style is ultimately determined by the ability of parents to nurture and appropriately control their children in a manner that supports their emotional, physical, social, and psychological development. By attending to these needs, parents communicate a concern for and an acceptance of their children. As a result of the confirmation that is communicated through effective parenting strategies, children regard themselves positively, believe in their own competence, develop a positive attitude toward work and life, and believe that they are worthy of being loved and capable of loving others (Parke, 2004).

Not all parenting styles are equally confirming, and, therefore, not all parenting styles are equally effective. Ineffective parenting styles place children at risk for physical, social, or psychological injury (Kandel, 1990). One way to think about child abuse and neglect is to view them as examples of ineffective parenting styles—strategies adopted by parents that fail to nurture and control children appropriately, and that leave children at risk for physical, social, or psychological injury.

There are no fully agreed upon definitions of child abuse and neglect. In general, the term **abuse** is used to refer to those situations in which the nonaccidental injury of a child by a parent or other responsible caretaker occurs (Rohner, 1986). **Neglect** refers to harming a child through the lack of either proper care or adequate supervision. It is virtually impossible to know how many American children are maltreated, but recent estimates from public records suggest that 12 out of every 1,000 children in the United States have been victims of some form of child maltreatment. Of the documented cases, it has been estimated that approximately 63 percent involve neglect, 17 percent involve physical abuse, 9 percent involve sexual abuse, and 7 percent involve emotional abuse (Cicchetti & Toth, 2005; Cicchetti & Valentino, 2006). Once again, however, it is important to note that because the vast majority of child abuse incidents involve victims who cannot protect themselves and remain hidden from police and social service agencies, many researchers think that actual figures are much higher.

Determinants of Abusive Parenting Styles

Conceiving of child abuse and neglect as the results of ineffective parenting styles suggests that they are determined by multiple causes. In general, following the Belsky model, the psychological resources of parents, characteristics of children, and contextual sources of stress all contribute to the adoption of an abusive or neglectful style of parenting. To this list of factors can be added the presence of patterns of interaction within the family system that predispose parents toward the scapegoating of children.

Parental Characteristics. The factors most frequently cited as predisposing parents to act in abusive ways toward their children are a history of having been abused themselves as children and certain individual traits. The three most identified individual traits of abusive parents are depression, anxiety, and antisocial behavior (Gelles, 1998). Others include anger-control problems, low frustration-tolerance, poor self-esteem, deficits in empathy, and rigidity (Barnett et al., 1997; Wiehe, 1998). Earlier studies identified abusive parents as likely to have psychiatric disorders, but recent studies have found that only a small percentage of abusive parents have diagnosable psychiatric disorders (Gelles, 1998). In other words, it is not a sufficient explanation in and of itself to suggest that most parents who abuse children are psychologically impaired.

Researchers have contended that a developmental history dominated by parental maltreatment is a major reason for child abuse (Ayoub & Willett, 1992; Milner & Chilamkurti, 1991; Whipple & Webster-Stratton, 1991). However, having been abused does not inevitably mean that an individual will abuse his or her own child. Recent studies suggest that the intergenerational cycle of abuse is found only in a limited number of families. Specifically, while parents who were abused as children are three times more likely to abuse their own children than parents who were not abused as children; only about 30 percent of those parents who were abused as children in fact abuse their own children (Kaufman & Zigler, 1993).

Studies of abusive parents further reveal that these parents often have unrealistic expectations of what children can do or lack effective child-management strategies (Milner & Chilamkurti, 1991; Wiehe, 1998). These parents often become easily upset with their children and frame their ordinary behavior as willful disobedience or evidence of deliberate malice. In these situations, the unrealistic expectations and the inability to manage the child's behavior contribute to the escalation of tension within the parent–child relationship, thus contributing to the potential for abuse.

Child Characteristics. There is speculation that selected characteristics in children may trigger abuse. Clearly, although the research on the existence of the "abuse-provoking" child is not yet conclusive (Ammerman, 1990), research suggests that some children may provoke frustration to the point that they elicit abuse. For example, parents are more likely to abuse children whose temperaments make them difficult to control or nurture. Low-birth-weight babies who are hard to handle and calm may be more likely to be abused than other infants (Ayoub & Willett, 1992; Weiss, Dodge, Bates, & Pettit, 1992). Similarly, children with special needs, who demand more attention (e.g., children with mental retardation, physical handicaps, or developmental deviations), may also be more likely to be victims of abuse (Barnett et al., 1997).

What is critical to keep in mind, however, is that the characteristics of the child are not responsible for the abuse. Parents are responsible for their choice of parenting strategies. That certain characteristics in children may provoke abuse attests, more than anything else, to the relationship between stress and parents' style of parenting.

Contextual Stress and Abuse. Contextual sources of stress and the absence of social support are among the factors believed to contribute to abusive parenting styles. Researchers have found that child abuse often occurs when parents are overburdened with the responsibilities and stresses of life (Whipple & Webster-Stratton, 1991). Abusive parents are often separated from sources of support (Milner & Chilamkurti, 1991). For example, they often have few community ties, relatives, or close friends from whom to seek assistance (Garbarino & Kostelny, 1992). In addition, abusive parents are more likely than nonabusive parents to be poor or unemployed, to abuse alcohol, to be experiencing legal problems, and to be in marriages dominated by discord and conflict (Ayoub & Willett, 1992; McLoyd, 1990).

Again, it is important to note that stress is not responsible for the abuse but can contribute to the frustration that parents experience with their children. In addition, stress can diminish the ability of parents to control hostile impulses or to monitor their children's behavior. Imagine, for example, a parent who is late for work, whose car has broken down, whose boss has been critical lately, and who has no one in the neighborhood to call for assistance in getting to work or transporting the children to their day-care center. Under these conditions, parents are more apt to overreact to their children's misbehavior and less likely to monitor their children's safety. The children may not be fed, or they may not be as carefully supervised as they would be under less stressful circumstances.

Family Dynamics. Throughout this text, the view has been maintained that one of the basic tasks that the family must fulfill is the management of its emotional environment. Managing the emotional environment requires that families evolve strategies for managing the interpersonal stresses and strains that accompany marital and family life. Within abusive families, often the strategies for managing stress and conflict place children directly at risk (Silber, 1990). This occurs when marital conflict, for example, is detoured onto the child (Minuchin, 1974). In this situation, husbands and wives, rather than dealing directly with the tension that exists between them, direct their hostility for one another toward the child. The child becomes, in essence, a family scapegoat (Pillari, 1991; Vogel & Bell, 1968). This scapegoat is held responsible for the stress within the family.

In other words, children can easily be held responsible for tension and conflicts within the family. When the strategies for managing conflict project the blame for family tensions onto the child, the child is often treated in physically aggressive and emotionally rejecting ways. This scapegoating helps the family system maintain an emotional equilibrium. It is done, however, at the expense of the child's physical and emotional well-being.

Consequences of Child Abuse

It may be useful to conceive of child abuse and neglect as ineffective parenting styles that are adopted due to the presence of a variety of factors. However, it is important to remember that the effectiveness of any particular style of parenting can be thought of as existing on a continuum. All parenting styles, and not only abusive parenting styles, can be judged in terms of their effectiveness. And, while some styles are clearly not as effective as others, not all of these less-than-optimal styles would be labeled as abusive or neglectful. When discussing the effectiveness of parenting styles, we are dealing with subtle distinctions. As a general rule, more effective parenting styles optimize the potential for child development. Children in these systems develop the personal and psychological resources that will assist them in adjusting well to the demands of childhood and adulthood.

Children exposed to abuse and neglect, however, develop within a context that is indifferent to or rejecting of their needs. It is difficult for these children to feel confirmed and valued. As a result of their exposure to repeated and consistent rejection, their behavior is apt to become less and less adaptive. For example, the absence of warmth and nurturance and the persistent rejection of children have been found to be related to children becoming emotionally unresponsive, hostile, and aggressive (Barnes & Farrell, 1992; Cassidy et al., 1992; MacDonald, 1992). These children are more likely to develop low self-esteem and a poor sense of their own self-adequacy. They are more likely, as well, to develop a negative world view and become emotionally unstable (Chu & Dill, 1990; Rohner, 1986; Shearer, Peters, Quayman, & Ogden, 1990; Swett, Surrey, & Cohen, 1990). Abuse, in other words, can establish a family legacy that impedes the functioning of successive generations.

Key Terms

Abuse The nonaccidental injury of a child by a parent or other responsible caretaker.

Authoritarian parenting A style of parenting that attempts to shape, control, and evaluate the child's attitudes and behaviors according to a preestablished and fixed set of standards. Authoritarian parents value obedience to their authority and tend to favor the use of punitive, forceful disciplinary methods.

Authoritative parenting A style of parenting that is nurturing and relies primarily on positive reinforcement rather than punishment to control the child. Direct control over the child is achieved in a manner that displays awareness of the child's thoughts, feelings, and developmental capabilities. In addition to being loving as well as controlling, authoritative parents tend to demand mature, responsible, and independent behavior from their children.

Indulgent parenting A style of parenting that exerts little or no control over the child's behavior. Children are given a great deal of personal freedom and few restrictions.

Neglect The harming of a child through the lack of either proper care or adequate supervision.

Parental responsiveness A dimension of parenting style (also referred to as "parental warmth" or "supportiveness"). This refers to the extent to which parents intentionally foster individuality, self-regulation, and self-assertion by being attuned, supportive, and acquiescent to children's special needs and demands.

Parental demandingness A dimension of parenting style (also referred to as "behavioral control"). This refers to the expectations parents have for their children to become integrated into the family whole, by their maturity demands, supervision, disciplinary efforts, and willingness to confront children who disobey.

Psychological control Refers to a parenting strategy characterized by attempts on the part of the parent to control the child by intruding into the psychological and emotional development of the child through the use of practices such as guilt induction, withdrawal of love, or shaming.

Uninvolved parenting A parenting style characterized by neglect and permissiveness. Children are given no clearly defined rules for behavior and receive little or no attention.

CHAPTER 13

Family Tasks during Middle Adulthood

Chapter Overview

This chapter provides an overview of the challenges and demands confronted by married couples, parents, and children during the middle-adult years of the family life cycle. The marital system must continually adjust to the ongoing and changing demands of parenthood, including the changes brought on by the launching of children. In addition, married couples must grapple with the ongoing need to balance the competing demands of work and marriage.

The individuation process is discussed in this chapter as a lifelong developmental process that has consequences for how parent–child relationships are structured. During the middle-adult years, parents and children are challenged to transform their relationship as children move through adolescence and are launched from the family. These transformations are complicated because many contemporary children leave home temporarily in their twenties, only to return home again, a phenomenon referred to as the renested family. Once children are launched and no longer reside in the parents' household, parents and children face the task of developing an adult-to-adult relationship. How this particular task is managed has consequences for the intimacy experienced between parents and their adult children.

Family Tasks during Middle Adulthood

The middle-adulthood period is generally defined by the ages of parents and extends roughly from the mid-forties to the mid-sixties. This is also the time when children complete the developmental tasks of adolescence and early adulthood, leave the family of origin, establish their own occupations, and possibly marry and have their own children.

While the middle-adult years may not be dominated by the rapid and dramatic changes of the early-adult years, the challenges confronted by the family system during this period are nonetheless many and decidedly stressful. Once again, the family must alter its strategies for meeting its basic tasks. The family's internal and external boundaries must be flexible enough to accommodate to the adolescent's increasing individuation; the young adult's launching from the family; the introduction of sons-in-law and daughters-in-law and grandchildren into the system; and changes in the relationships between middle-aged adults and their own aging, and sometimes frail, parents. The family's identity, emotional climate, and household management strategies must be altered to account for the declining focus on parenting responsibilities and the reemergence of the marriage as the primary subsystem.

Increased life expectancy and declines in the size of the average family mean that contemporary couples will spend more years than previous generations in the post-child-rearing stage of the family life cycle. The middle-adulthood phase of the family life cycle highlights in a rather dramatic way the interdependence among parenthood, marriage, work, and relationships with extended family and friends. As the amount of time and energy devoted to raising children declines, relationships with spouses, work, parents, and friends must be altered to fill the void. Husbands and wives must develop new strategies to nurture their marriage, fulfill changing job-related responsibilities, and rework relationships with their parents. Even though the many stresses confronted during this time are ordinary in nature, as they increase, they can overwhelm even the most resourceful of family systems.

The Marriage Relationship during the Middle-Adult Years

The marital subsystem is a fluid and dynamic system that lies at the heart of the broader family system. Any stressor experienced by the family system will be channeled through the marital subsystem, requiring frequent adaptations on the part of the marital partners. It is during the middle-adult years that married individuals can find themselves particularly challenged by their multiple responsibilities toward their spouses, children, extended family members, and employers. These multiple responsibilities are a source of constant stress on the marriage. In addition, although this stress, like any stress, is neither good nor bad, the manner in which it is managed will affect the quality of the marriage relationship.

Launching Children: The Effect on the Marriage

It has been suggested that married couples currently spend about half of their married lives in the postchild phase of the family life cycle. This means that the **launching** of children marks a significant turning point in the life of many married adults. When they no longer have to deal with the demands of parenthood, many married couples begin to refocus their attention and energy on marital concerns (Carter & McGoldrick, 2005a).

While there has been much speculation over the years about the degree of crisis associated with the "**empty nest**," the research literature largely supports the conclusion that the launching of children is experienced by women as a relief, an opportunity for growth, and a period of heightened marital satisfaction and fulfillment (Blacker, 1999; Mitchell & Helson, 1990). The exit from the child-rearing stage of the family life cycle is thus *not* accompanied by a profound sense of role loss on the part of mothers. On the contrary, mothers look forward to their increased freedom and the challenges of this second half of their marital careers (Devries, Kerrick, & Oetinger, 2007; Gorchoff, Oliver, & Helson, 2008; Proulx & Helms, 2008).

Less is known about the reactions of fathers to the empty-nest phase. While some studies have found that fathers seem to have few difficulties with the shift in their parenting responsibilities (Proulx & Helms, 2008), some research suggests that fathers may be less emotionally prepared for the empty nest than mothers (Gorchoff et al., 2008). It is interesting that the fathers negatively affected by the launching of children are those who feel that they have lost an opportunity to be involved in their children's lives. Fathers' involvement with their children prior to launching, in other words, may predict how they adjust to the launching.

The overarching conclusion drawn from this research is that both mothers and fathers evaluate the nest-emptying experience positively more often than negatively (Gorchoff et al., 2008; White & Edwards, 1993). It would be a mistake, however, to conclude that all couples adjust well to the launching of their children. For instance, in one study, 10 percent of the parents reported negative reactions to the departure of their oldest child (Anderson, 1988). Apparently, how the marriage is affected by the launching of children depends on how central children are to the functioning of the marital system. The clinical literature is particularly useful in helping us to understand how the launching of children affects what are, admittedly, less functional family systems.

The launching of children will constitute a significant crisis for those couples who rely on their children to provide a sense of meaning and purpose to their daily lives. Parents who live vicariously through their children or who overidentify with them can be left with a significant void in their lives when the children leave home. The child's launching can represent an existential crisis for some couples. With the child gone and the child's need for the parent reduced, life loses its meaning.

Similarly, those couples who rely on their children to stabilize marital conflict will be distressed by the launching of children. Within these marriages, children have been involved in regulating the emotional distance between spouses (Byng-Hall, 1980). They may have performed the role of referee during conflicts or misbehaved when marital tensions were high in order to deflect attention to themselves, or they may have become involved in cross-generational coalitions and triangles and be expected to support one parent against the other (Anderson, 1990). For these couples, the departure of children means that they may have to deal directly with their conflicts or find another distance-regulator (e.g., another person, a hobby, extra hours at work) to maintain the triangle (Bowen, 1978; Byng-Hall, 1980).

In both instances, parents may invest considerable effort and energy into blocking the departure of their children. They might communicate metamessages that equate leaving home with disloyalty, thereby creating feelings of guilt. Alternatively, they may precipitate a crisis within the family that encourages the child to stay. Mother might have a nervous breakdown, or father might become ill.

Similarly, parents might encourage their children to remain emotionally or financially dependent on them as a way of avoiding a complete psychological separation (Anderson & Fleming, 1986). By the same token, in true systemic fashion, children may sabotage their own efforts to leave home (Haley, 1980). They might develop a problem like substance abuse, depression, or suicidal ideation that postpones their separation.

Another distinction can be drawn between those couples who have relied on the presence of their children to provide them with meaning and purpose or to buffer their conflicted marriage, and those who have remained married for the sake of the children. Those couples who have remained married for the sake of the children can be thought of as "parents on a mission" (McCullough & Rutenberg, 1989). These parents may not have a particularly difficult time launching their children. In fact, they may even look forward to it. Having completed their mission, they are free to renegotiate their unsatisfactory marriage relationship, often by divorcing.

While divorce is most common among couples during the early years of adulthood, it also affects a sizeable number of midlife couples. Recent data published by the U.S. Census Bureau (2007b) suggest that in the United States 27 percent of divorces in a given year involve men between the ages of forty-five and sixty-four, while 18 percent involve women between the same ages. In addition, the data suggest that the divorce rate in midlife is increasing as it has doubled since 1971.

There are two factors that might help to explain the high rate of divorce that has been found among couples in midlife (Shapiro, P. G., 1996). One is the newfound freedom when one is relieved of the day-to-day responsibilities for children. Increased time, energy, and financial resources may offer the necessary ingredients for making a change. The other is that one or both spouses may become motivated to seek a divorce because of the unpleasant prospect of spending one's remaining years alone with a stranger or an adversary (Blacker, 1999).

It is virtually impossible to talk about how a marital couple will adapt to the challenges of launching their children without considering the role children have played within the marital relationship. Most couples are ready to move on to the challenges of the postparenting years as their children move through late adolescence. However, if couples rely on their children to give sole meaning and purpose to their lives or to stabilize their marriage, the emptying of the nest can create a crisis for the family system.

Balancing the Demands of Work and Marriage

The interface of work, marriage, and family life is an issue for couples at every stage of the family life cycle. The middle years are no exception. Here, as in other stages of the life cycle, strategies must be modified such that couples can continue to fulfill their responsibilities to employers while also executing the basic tasks that are essential to the effective functioning of the marriage and family as a whole. A number of factors that emerge during this period can either facilitate or interfere with a couple's capacity to balance work and family.

One consideration is that many couples reach their maximum earning potentials during the middle years. For instance, the age group between forty-five and fifty-four has been found to have the highest mean household income of any age group (U.S. Census Bureau, 2001a). For those who still have children at home, this increase in earnings may be offset by the added expenses of raising late adolescents or launching young adults (e.g., clothing expenses, allowances, college tuition, wedding costs). For those who have reached the empty-nest period, higher earnings may contribute to the greater sense of freedom and excitement couples frequently report. There may be more money for travel, recreation, or a special purchase that was previously sacrificed for the sake of the children. The stresses that develop when spouses are no longer able to relate to one another in their parental roles may be soothed by the introduction of new shared activities formerly prevented by a lack of finances.

The middle years are also a time when men's work demands frequently change. While some may continue their occupation with the same intensity as in earlier stages, many men will have either achieved their occupational goals or accepted their present job as the highest level they are likely to attain (Levinson, 1986). Most major promotions go to younger men. Physical signs of aging (e.g., fatigue, slower recovery from illness) may contribute to men's realization that they do not have the time, ability, or opportunity to accomplish all that they had once planned (Aldous, 1978). As corporations reorganize and downsize, older men at the higher income ranges also become vulnerable to becoming unemployed or forced into early retirement. Some men may decide to shift their attention to new activities. Others may decide to try an entirely new career.

Whatever the actual demands men face at this time, many will bring these stresses into the marital relationship (Barnett, Marshall, & Pleck, 1992). The capacity of the marriage to manage these stresses is dependent on the kind of relationship the couple has been able to establish during earlier stages in the family life cycle. A stable, intimate, and supportive marriage has been found to be one of the strongest predictors of men's adjustment to the stresses of the middle years (Gottman et al., 1998; Gottman & Levenson, 1992; Pasch & Bradbury, 1998). Those men without the support of a strong marital relationship may attempt to cope through having extramarital affairs, becoming preoccupied with material possessions such as a sports car or boat, or pursuing some other form of diversion (McCullough & Rutenberg, 1989).

The stress of balancing work and family life is also greater when women enter the workforce for the first time during the middle years. Within these marital systems, wives are taking on the stresses and challenges of a new job at the same time that their husbands may be beginning to shift their focus away from work and toward family or other interests. The perception that partners have different goals and interests at this point in their lives may increase the levels of conflict within the marriage. It may not be until the later middle years that these couples are able to balance their investments in work or shift their focus to other shared activities.

Of course, most women enter the workforce prior to midlife. These women may experience less role strain and overload during the middle years because they no longer have to balance the demands of work with parenthood and have already established themselves in their chosen line of work. Decreased role strain and overload combined with the positive benefits of working—a greater sense of challenge, control, self-esteem, and social connection—can contribute to the middle years being a time of increased personal satisfaction for women, unless demands from other sources, such as tending to an ailing, aged parent or supporting an adult child through a crisis, compound the situation (Blacker, 1999).

It is important to note, however, that not all women love their work. Many women work because they feel they have to in order to make ends meet. Many women find themselves in low-status, low-paying, monotonous jobs that combine high demands with little autonomy and personal control (Baruch, Biener, & Barnett, 1987). The stresses that these environments create have been found to produce fatigue and irritability and interfere with the completion of routine household tasks, thereby contributing to arguments and conflicts between husbands and wives (Hughes, Galinsky, & Morris, 1992; Spitze, 1988).

Therefore, it is not a question of whether men or women work that affects the quality of their marriage. The effects of work on the marriage are determined more by the overall quality of the marriage established during earlier stages of the life cycle, how satisfied men and women are with their work, and how the couple negotiates the changes that may be occurring in their work experiences during the middle years. This can be a time of declining role strain and role overload and an opportunity to invest more time and energy into the marriage. This can also be a time when new demands fill in the void left by reduced parenting responsibilities (new or increased work demands, demands from aging parents, new outside interests), leaving the couple's relationship relatively unchanged. Finally, this can be a time when husbands and wives move in separate directions. One may want to reinvest in the marriage, while the other wishes to pursue experiences outside the family.

Parent–Child Dynamics during Middle Adulthood

A substantial portion of the middle adult years is devoted to completing the task of parenthood and launching children. The goal for most parents is to produce mature and responsible children—children capable of caring and thinking for themselves, acting in socially appropriate ways, and competently assuming the various roles and responsibilities of adulthood. Because children are not born with these abilities, parents are charged with the responsibility of devising strategies that guide their children's physical, social, emotional, and psychological development throughout childhood and into adulthood.

Individuation and the Lifelong Challenges of Parenthood

As noted in Chapter 6, individuation can be thought of as a lifelong developmental process (Allison & Sabatelli, 1988; Anderson & Sabatelli, 1990). As such, children, soon after they are born, begin the process of establishing their individuality within the context of their relationships with parents and other family members. The task for parents is to support these expressions of individuality while also providing a foundation of support, nurturance, and guidance that ensures their children's safe development. Ideally, parenting strategies will help children to develop the confidence and skills necessary to cope with the demands of childhood and develop the social and psychological maturity necessary to function as adults.

As a general rule, the stress that exists in the relationships between parents and children originates from two principal internal sources: (1) the children's changing perspective on their own developmental needs and abilities; and (2) the changing developmental demands that parents place on their children. At various points in time, children come to feel that they should be able, because of their advancing age and abilities, to express greater control over their lives. At other times, parents will alter their own expectations of their children. They may expect their children to assume greater responsibility over some aspect of their lives than they have yet to assume. In either case, existing patterns of interaction must change in response to these developmental stressors.

For example, as children's cognitive abilities mature throughout middle childhood and early adolescence, they become increasingly aware of the norms and pressures for conformity that exist within their peer relationships (Dodge, Pettit, McClaskey, & Brown, 1986). For a ten-year-old daughter, this may mean pressuring her parents to allow her to use makeup. A twelve-year-old son might decide that he would not be caught dead wearing jeans that have not been washed two hundred times and have gaping holes in the knees. Parents may decide that their ten-year-old son is now old enough to get up on time for school on his own without repeated efforts by parents.

Thus, during the middle adult years, parents and children are continually challenged to alter the rules and strategies that regulate how they interact with one another as previous strategies become obsolete. That is, previous strategies are no longer appropriate for the current age, abilities, or needs of the child. In negotiating these changes, strategies are established that are, like all strategies, more or less effective. In some instances, the chosen strategies will undermine the confidence and evolving competence of children. Parents may maintain tight control over the child, but at the expense of the child's psychological and emotional development. In other instances, children may not be given the proper guidance and support that they require. These individuation-inhibiting patterns of nurturance and control ultimately interfere with the abilities of children to make mature commitments to adult roles and responsibilities.

In other instances, strategies are developed that foster the evolving autonomy and confidence of children. Children are progressively given more autonomy and responsibility in accordance with their ages and abilities. Parents trust the child, and the child works to maintain the parents' trust and approval. Under these conditions, the parent–child relationship tends to be dominated by experiences of intimacy and satisfaction. Children feel nurtured and supported, and parents feel gratified and satisfied within their role of parent.

In sum, it is important to have an overarching perspective on how the developmental needs of children and the tasks of parenthood mutually affect the patterns of interaction found within the parent–child relationship. In this regard, to understand the dynamics that govern the relationship between parents and children, it is useful to view children, from birth on, as being engaged in a process of individuating from their parents. Developmentally, children strive to express their individuality in age-appropriate ways. From a system's perspective, these developmentally appropriate expressions of individuality require ongoing adjustments in parenting strategies. Ultimately, as children move through their individual life cycles, both the parents and the children influence the patterns of interaction that become established in their relationships with one another.

The Parent–Adolescent Relationship

The family with adolescents is involved in preparing and assisting children to begin their adult lives. During this time, the major developmental tasks for the family system center around increasing the flexibility of family boundaries to enable children to move in and out of the family system (Carter & McGoldrick, 2005a; Preto, 2005). Adolescents need to explore their identities and develop a sense of individuality separate from parents and other family members. They need to develop their social skills and capacity for intimacy through exploring relationships outside the family. As they undertake these tasks, they will push for greater autonomy and control over their lives. At the same time, parents will resist their children's demands for autonomy unless the children show that they can take greater responsibility for themselves. These pushes and pulls of the ongoing individuation process require further transformations of the parent–child relationship (Allison & Sabatelli, 1988; Youniss & Smollar, 1985).

Alterations in parenting strategies during adolescence are accompanied by stress and potential conflicts. At the same time, however, overestimating the amount of stress and conflict between adolescents and parents should be avoided. The mass media and popular literature have typically portrayed relationships between parents and adolescents as being dominated by intense conflict and adolescent rebelliousness. Even in the social sciences, the prevailing view for much of this century was that adolescence was marked by greater turmoil (storm and stress) than the preceding and subsequent stages of life (Gecas & Seff, 1990). In fact, over half of the articles in the major journals on adolescence were found to still focus on problem behaviors such as delinquency, substance abuse, school problems, and mental health (Furstenberg, 2000). However, reviews of research have typically found that this view of adolescence as a time of excessive conflict is untenable. To be sure, a percentage of youth do experience severe conflicts and a host of problem behaviors during this period. However, the adolescent transition has been found to be relatively trouble-free for about three-quarters of young people and their families (American Medical Association, 1990; Helsen, Vollebergh, & Meeus, 2000; Henricson & Roker, 2000). Furthermore, many adolescents who do engage in problem behaviors do so experimentally and for a limited amount of time (Coie, 1996; Furstenberg, 2000; Jessor, 1993).

In other words, parent–child relationships are marked by a certain continuity. When the family system has been individuation-enhancing throughout childhood, there is no reason to expect that adolescence will be dominated by excessive tension and conflict. Despite their quest for autonomy and independence, most adolescents have deep love, affection, and respect for their parents—reciprocating the feelings that their parents have for them. In fact, there is no evidence suggesting that family problems are worse during adolescence than at any other stage of development (Steinberg, 2005).

This is not meant to dismiss the inevitable conflicts that will occur between parents and adolescents. Usually, the underlying source of these conflicts will be the tension that results when adolescents push for greater control over their lives. Attempts at greater control include a host of factors including who they hang out with, where they go and when they come home, how they dress, how they style their hair, when they date, who they date, and where they go on dates. However, as with all conflicts over personal control throughout childhood, these issues are eventually worked through as parenting strategies are adapted to accommodate to the changing developmental needs and abilities of adolescents (Collins, Laursen, Mortensen, Luebker, & Ferreira, 1997; Steinberg, 2005).

While most parent–adolescent relationships may not be characterized by excessive conflict, there appears to be little doubt that this is a stressful time for parents with adolescents. Adolescent autonomy (pushing for more freedom than parents were willing to grant), failure to adhere to parental advice, and deviant behavior (behavior that deviated from parental norms) are the main reasons for parental stress (Furstenberg, 2000; Henricson & Roker, 2000). These research findings highlight that allowing their children to express their independence during adolescence is somehow experienced by parents as being qualitatively different from supporting their individuation prior to adolescence. This perception results, in part, because the consequences of allowing adolescents to take control of their lives may appear greater than the consequences associated with allowing a younger child to act in an age-appropriate manner. Somehow the potential consequences of allowing a five-year-old to dress himself or herself for school do not seem as great as allowing a sixteen-year-old to take the car out on a date!

Transforming the Parent–Child Relationship during Launching

The transition from adolescence to young adulthood is marked by the launching of children. During this time, children will physically separate from the family and take on adult roles and responsibilities. The challenge to parents throughout this time is to accept the separation of the child (Anderson, 1988, 1990; Anderson & Fleming, 1986a; Carter & McGoldrick, 2005a). In this regard, it is clear that the transition from adolescence to young adulthood is a stage of development not only for the child but also for the parents. Parents must participate in the individuation process by transforming their own roles and identities (McCullough & Rutenberg, 1989; Stierlin, Levi, & Savard, 1971).

The ability of parents to accomplish this shift is tied to their own developmental legacy. Specifically, parents' success or failure at individuating from their own parents is critically tied to their ability to accept the transformation of their relationships with their own children (Framo, 1976, 1981; Stierlin, 1981). Our experiences with our own parents establish an individuation legacy. When we have successfully individuated, we are more likely to be comfortable with our own children's separation. In contrast, parents who have not successfully individuated often reenact their own unresolved conflicts with their separating children, thereby creating greater tension. In these instances, parents tend either to expel their children from the family prematurely or interfere with their separation by fostering ongoing dependence.

Thus, as children move through their adolescent years, the transformations that optimally occur in the parent–child relationship facilitate not only the physical health of the child, but also his or her social, emotional, and psychological health and well-being. The demands of the individuation process compel parents to encourage and support their children's autonomous actions and expressions of individuality. Parents must accept the inevitable and necessary separation of their children. The ability to accept this transformation is influenced heavily by the intergenerational legacies that parents inherited from their own families of origin. High levels of anxiety, emotional reactivity, and unresolved anger toward their parents interfere with parents' ability to accept the adult status of their own children. A generational cycle is perpetuated in poorly differentiated families, which places children at risk.

The Renested Family. A recent trend has added to the complexity of transforming the parent–child relationship during the launching period: Many children today leave home temporarily in their twenties, only to return home later. The popular media has coined the phrase "boomerang kids" to refer to these young adult children. The most recent census figures show that 56 percent of males and 43 percent of females between eighteen and twenty-four come back to live with their parents at least once before making it on their own (U.S. Census Bureau, 2005a). In addition, according to the National Survey of Households and Families, the number of boomerang kids is on the increase and has doubled over the last fifty years. This means that 30 percent of all parents with children in their twenties will have at least one (perhaps more) of their young adult children living at home (Aquilino, 1990). Usually this **renested family** is a temporary arrangement, brought about when adult children divorce, lose a job, or change career objectives (Goldscheider, 1997; Mitchell & Gee, 1996).

Interestingly, researchers William Aquilino and Khalil Supple (1991) found that most parents whose adult children, ages nineteen to thirty-four, live at home are happy with things the way they are. They noted, however, two important factors that caused problems. First, the child's unemployment or financial dependence on the parent increased the chances of parent–child conflict. Second, having a divorced or separated child—especially one with a baby in tow—move back home reduced the parents' satisfaction with the entire living arrangement.

In addition, researchers have become interested in how boomerang kids affect parental marital satisfaction. Studies show that although the mere presence of adult children in the household is not always related to a reduction in marital satisfaction, conflicts between parents and children do tend to spill over into the marital domain (Suitor & Pillemer, 1987). In other words, high levels of parent–child conflict tend to be associated with higher levels of marital conflict. It appears, as well, that parents are able to maintain their marital satisfaction when children return home one or two times but are less satisfied when children continue to leave and return (Mitchell & Gee, 1996).

That this trend is expected to continue for a few decades (Goldscheider, 1997; Schnaiberg & Goldenberg, 1989) means that we may be witnessing a major transformation in the family life cycle. The degree to which this transformation stresses families will depend on whether both parents and children are able to revise their expectations regarding when launching will occur. In any event, even if parents get to the point where they expect a delayed launching, the presence of adult children in the home will clearly challenge the relationship between parents and children. Parents will need to find a way to support their adult children's needs for autonomy and psychological independence, despite their lingering functional and financial dependence.

The Parent–Child Relationship in the Postparenting Years

Once children are launched and no longer reside in their parents' household, parents and children are confronted with the task of developing an adult-to-adult relationship (Blacker, 1999). This transformation, as with the ones that precede it, takes place gradually. At stake is the level of intimacy to be experienced between parents and their adult children over the years to come.

Intimacy between adult children and their parents, as in other relationships, is based on acceptance and mutual respect for one another. Within individuation-enhancing families, children feel accepted and respected because they are allowed to control their own identities and lives in age-appropriate ways. The individuation-inhibiting family, in contrast, is characterized by patterns of interaction that do not communicate support and respect. The residual resentments and lingering antipathies that these interaction patterns produce can carry on throughout the adult years, creating barriers to ongoing, intimate parent–child relationships (Boszormenyi-Nagy & Krasner, 1986).

Put another way, the parent–child relationship is the primary architect of the developmental legacy that children bring with them into their adult years. In individuation-enhancing family systems, the authority relationship between parents and children is continuously renegotiated to allow children to express their autonomy in an age-appropriate way. The progressive, age-appropriate, and successful reworking of the personal authority relationship promotes maturity and adjustment in children and fosters ongoing mutuality and connection among family members.

This focus on personal authority in the relationship between parents and adult children is the cornerstone of Williamson's (1981) intergenerational developmental theory. As developed by Williamson (1981, 1982) and colleagues (Bray, Williamson, & Malone, 1984), personal authority involves terminating the hierarchical parent–child relationship and establishing a symmetrical, peer-like relationship in its place. This transition is considered an individual as well as a family system task for both individuals and their families (Bray et al., 1984; Williamson, 1981).

At the heart of this transition is a redistribution of the power in the parent–child relationship. Accomplishing this shift in power is a complex developmental task that is not generally completed until the adult child is in the fourth or fifth decade of life. In order to achieve this shift, Williamson (1981) states that the adult child needs to have mastered a variety of issues. For example, the adult child must see the parents not as parents but as human beings. Seeing the person behind the parent role helps the adult child relate to the parent as one fellow human being to another, instead of as a child to a parent. The adult child needs to give up any unmet expectations of the parents and accept them just the way they are. This also involves giving up the need to be parented and managing the fear of being free from parental guidance. Feelings of intimidation must be addressed as when the adult child fears parental rejection or disapproval. The adult child needs to be able to make decisions without fearing the parent's reaction.

For this transition to go more smoothly, parents also need to see their adult child not as a child but as a human being. The parents must look behind the child role and see the person that is there. The parents will need to give up any unmet expectations and accept the adult child just as he or she is. This process also requires the parents to overcome the need to parent. When they no longer exert parental authority, parents may fear that their adult child will not voluntarily choose to be with them. Thus, parents will need to resolve any fears of abandonment that come from being an equal with one's child. Lastly, both the adult child and the parents will need to deal with the anxiety of relating to each other as equals.

What emerges, then, as the parent–child relationship is renegotiated is an internal psychological shift in how the parent views the child and how the child views the parent. This also will require shifts in the patterns of interaction within the relationship. On a systemic level, the development of personal authority involves a radical redistribution of the power between the two generations (Bray et al., 1984). The reworking of the authority hierarchy enables the adult child to gain a sense of emotional freedom, remaining in close contact with the parents without experiencing overwhelming emotional costs (Williamson, 1981). Termination of the hierarchical parent–child relationship establishes relational equality between the self and the parents (Bray et al., 1984; Williamson, 1981). Feelings of affection and trust may emerge as they do between close friends. True intimacy, which is defined as emotional closeness consisting of affection, altruism, openness, honesty, and respect for each other, may occur.

From an intergenerational perspective, the relationship that an adult child experiences with his or her parent is a manifestation of the patterns of interaction experienced in the family over time. For optimal functioning, the personal authority transition is experienced as a normal and expected shift in the power dynamics between parents and children. The adult child in this type of family is likely to describe this shift as evolving easily over time. However, in less optimally functioning families, this shift is more likely to be fraught with difficulties. Parents and their adult child are likely to struggle unsuccessfully to achieve a peer-like relationship with each other and will often remain in a hierarchical parent–child relationship.

The ongoing failure to resolve the reworking of the personal authority relationship inhibits the ability of the adult child to be in contact with his or her parents without easily becoming overwhelmed by feelings of anxiety, guilt, or anger. This high level of emotional reactivity may lead them to conform to their parents' demands or expectations. Alternatively, highly reactive individuals may rebel and temporarily distance themselves emotionally and/or physically from their parents. Typically, these two reactions, sacrificing one's own needs or rebelling, are experienced as the only options to reduce the level of anxiety experienced in the relationship.

In sum, parents' control and dominance of their children can foster intimacy only so long as the parents' power is accepted as legitimate by both parents and children. Within most parent–child relationships, there comes a time when children no longer tolerate the controlling efforts of their parents, and parents no longer tolerate their children's lingering dependencies. It is at this point that the relationships between parents and children must be reconstituted on a more adult-to-adult level.

When parents or adult children agree about the legitimate degree of power and control that each should hold in the relationship, acceptance and mutual respect ensue. When disagreements arise over the legitimacy of power, conflicts develop, interactions become framed as rejecting, and each side views the other as attempting to control the identity of the other. When these opposing positions become fixed, rigid, and nonnegotiable, power struggles occur, and the relationship will be devoid of intimacy.

While all children and their parents are challenged to develop an adult-to-adult relationship during the middle years, it is difficult to generalize about the timetable for this development. This is because culture, gender, class, and ethnicity are all factors that can affect the degree of parental authority that is accepted as legitimate in the relationship. In the patriarchal Italian family, for example, fathers expect their children, even their adult sons and daughters, to listen and obey (Giordano et al., 2005). So long as the authority of the father is accepted as legitimate, his power and control do not undermine the potential for intimacy in the relationship.

In other words, relationships between adult children and their parents can be structured in a variety of ways and still be experienced as intimate. As a general rule, however, we can expect that there will come a time when both parents and children expect their relationship to be reconstituted on a more mutual and equal level. The timetable for this transformation will vary considerably and will not necessarily occur during later adolescence. Perhaps, even more normatively, such transformations will not take place until adult children have children of their own and are entering their forties (Williamson, 1981).

It should be clear that a continuity exists in the tasks confronted by the parent–child relationship over time. The parent–child relationship system is challenged by children's need to individuate at each stage of development. A parent–child subsystem characterized by warmth, sensitivity, empathy, and flexibility—all characteristics of the well-differentiated family system—enables children to act in increasingly mature and autonomous ways. In a reciprocal manner, the support and encouragement that children receive help them to develop intimate relationships with parents and others.

In addition, it should be clear that the establishment of an adult-to-adult relationship between adult children and their parents reverberates throughout the family system, creating a ripple effect that influences how subsequent family developmental transitions are handled (McCullough & Rutenberg, 1989). For example, when parents have renegotiated their relationship with their child on an adult-to-adult level, they are less likely to interfere with their child's choice of marital partner or with the newly forming marital subsystem (McGoldrick, 2005b). The quality of the parent–adult child relationship also can influence the kind of relationships permitted between grandparents and grandchildren. Adult children who lack intimacy with their parents may prohibit their children from having a positive relationship with their grandparents. By the same token, these grandparents may reject their grandchildren outright or attempt to form a coalition with them against the parents.

The Demands of Being in the Middle

While the launching of children may appear to reduce the demands on the middle-adult generation, it actually signals the beginning of a series of changes that require systemwide adaptations. To begin, not all children are launched at the same time. While one child is still at home or in the process of leaving home, another child may be getting married. While one child is marrying, another child may be having a child. While one child is becoming a parent for the first time, another child may be getting a divorce. There is an ongoing flow of exits and entrances that require family boundaries and relationships to be continually reworked during this period of time. Adapting to this multitude of exits and entrances is one of the key challenges confronted by the family system during middle adulthood (Carter & McGoldrick, 2005a).

This period is made even more complex in that middle-aged adult children are connected to a network of increasingly aging family members who may require their support and assistance. In every family system, there will come a time when the frail elderly will require assistance and care. When this occurs the family system must evolve strategies for dealing with the demand that frailty places on the system. While these issues will be discussed in greater detail in Chapter 14 dealing with later-life families, we note here that meeting the needs of elderly family members for assistance and support will often fall on middle-aged adult children.

Because family transitions do not occur independently of other transitions, the issues confronted by the middle-aged couple can easily accumulate. The middle-aged couple faces one set of demands from their children and another set from their aging parents. They must also manage to meet their own individual and couple needs at the same time. The realities of this **generational squeeze**, of being caught between the developmental demands of the older and younger generations of the family system, places a great deal of stress on the middle-adult generation (Marks, 1996, 1998). When this occurs, resources and support tend to be directed toward those who have the greatest need (Aldous & Klein, 1991; Ward, Logan, & Spitze, 1992).

In conclusion, from a broader family systems perspective, the middle-adult years of the family life cycle are accompanied by multiple family developmental transitions. The launching of children does not completely release middle-aged adults from their family system responsibilities. There is a continual demand placed on the middle generation to evolve strategies and rules for meeting the needs of both the younger and older generations within the family. These demands will stress even the most resourceful of families and perhaps require greater adaption than in any of the other phases of the family life cycle. Yet, the middle years also offer families many challenges and opportunities that have the potential to enrich marital and parent–child relationships in new and diverse ways.

Key Terms

Empty nest A period of the family life cycle occurring after all children have left home to live on their own.

Generational squeeze The situation in which middle-aged adults are responsible for simultaneously meeting the needs of their own dependent children and those of their aging and frail parents.

Launching A period of the family life cycle that begins with the departure of the first child from the home and ends when all children have left home to live on their own.

Renested family The situation that results when adult children who have been launched from the family return home to live with their parents.

CHAPTER 14

The Family in Later Life

Chapter Overview

Middle-aged adults and their families face many changes as they move into their later-adult years. Consistent with the framework presented in earlier chapters, the challenges of aging can be viewed as stressing patterns of interaction found within and among the various subsystems of the family. Within the marital subsystem, marital strategies and rules will require readjustments as individuals retire. Furthermore, the changes associated with aging challenge married couples to adjust their patterns of recreation, companionship, and support.

From an intergenerational perspective, grandparenthood is discussed in the context of the later-life family because of how the birth of grandchildren symbolically signifies a shift in centrality and power from the aging generation to the middle generation within the family hierarchy. As the aging process proceeds, aging parents and adult children face the task of transforming their relationship in order to accommodate the changing developmental needs and abilities of the aging generation. In this regard, the parent–child relationship must accommodate aging parents' evolving dependency and eventual frailty. Relationships must be restructured such that the needs of both generations can be met and the experience of intimacy can be fostered.

The Family in Later Life

Technological advances in medicine and nutrition have extended the lives of family members. Life expectancies, for example, have risen from 67.1 for males and 74.7 for females born in 1970, to 75.2 for males and 80.4 for females born in 2004. By the year 2030, the United States will have more old people than children, with the number of people over eighty-five being the fastest growing segment of the population (U.S. Census Bureau, 2008).

The result of more family members living into old-old age is that many more adults will be members of three-, four-, and even five-generation families. This means that family members will have opportunities to experience a variety of roles and relationships for a longer time than ever before. For example, more than 60 percent of all older adults in the United States are married and approximately

90 percent have living children. Of those with adult children, about 94 percent have grandchildren and 60 percent have great-grandchildren (U.S. Census Bureau, 2008).

The availability of aging family members brings opportunities for greater family continuity, stability, and support across generations. Put another way, it is virtually impossible to separate the issues faced by individuals from those experienced by the family system over the course of its development. The individual and the family are interdependently connected. As individuals grapple with developmental issues tailored to their age and stage in life, the family system is pushed to evolve strategies and rules that take into account these changing developmental agendas. This interdependence between the individual and family is present at all stages in the life cycle. It is not surprising, then, that this meshing of developmental issues and agendas is again present within the family system comprised of older adults.

This chapter examines the changes that occur within family systems as middle-aged adults move into their later-adult years. Consistent with the framework presented in earlier chapters, the later years of the family life cycle are characterized by continuity and change. That is, the patterns of interaction found between spouses and between parents and children during these years are based on the patterns of interaction that were established long before this particular period of time (Allen, Blieszner, & Roberto, 2000; Roberto, 2006). At the same time, the unique challenges confronted by the family system during this period will stress these established patterns of interaction, requiring a reorganization of existing strategies and rules.

Marriage during the Later-Adult Years

The marital relationship is challenged by the changes that spouses experience during their later-adult years. Marital partners experience the aging process in unique but predictable ways. That is, there are predictable or normative developmental changes and role transitions that accompany the aging process. Individuals retire. They slow down as a result of aging and eventually become frail. While these events can be thought of as altering the individual's roles, personal identity, and health, the marital system also must accommodate to these changes by reorganizing its strategies for fulfilling its basic tasks. The marital subsystem's boundaries, identity, emotional environment, and approach to managing the household all undergo change as spouses age.

Rebalancing the Boundary between Work and Family Life

It should be apparent by now that the boundary between work and family life must be renegotiated at each stage of the marital life cycle. During the later-adult years, the balance between family and work is altered due to **retirement**. Retirement refers to both a physical withdrawal from paid employment and a psychological reorientation of the importance of work to one's identity. While it is obvious that not all individuals retire, quite clearly the number of retired individuals and the length of time spent in retirement are increasing. Because life expectancy continues to increase, those retiring at age sixty-five, on average, can expect to spend eighteen to twenty years, or 25 percent of their life, in the role of retiree (U.S. Census Bureau, 2007a). Because women tend to live longer than men, it is reasonable to expect that employed women will spend an even higher percentage of their lives in retirement.

As a general rule, most workers appear to look forward to retirement and have relatively little difficulty adjusting to it. At the same time the research suggests that in retrospect, many retirees come to realize that their preparation for retirement should have included more emphasis on the psychosocial aspects of this change rather than focusing exclusively on its financial impact. Retirement is a major life change, and those who cope successfully with it tend to remain optimistic, active in confronting new challenges, and physically active (Rosenkoetter & Garris, 2001; Sharpley & Yardley, 1999). Those individuals whose identity is highly invested in their work, or who are forced prematurely into retirement, have the greatest difficulties (Szinovacz & Washo, 1992; Zimmerman, Mitchell, Wister, & Gutman, 2000).

While retirement has largely been thought of as requiring a change in the individual's personal identity, it clearly has an effect on the marital system as well. The marital subsystem's emotional environment can be altered, for instance, by changes in the couple's patterns of negotiating separateness and connectedness. There may be more opportunities to do things together as a couple. Some couples may welcome this opportunity, whereas others may experience tension because they do not share the same expectations for shared companionship.

Those couples who have relied on work as a distance regulator or as a means of mediating tension and conflict within the relationship will be the most affected by retirement. Working provides some couples with a way of keeping a distance from one another that is essential if they are to coexist peacefully. Retirement can destabilize this delicate balance of separateness and connectedness.

Furthermore, retirement can alter the organization and operation of the household. Financial priorities may have to be changed, and spending patterns reorganized. This period of reorganization may be accompanied by an increase in stress and the potential for conflict within the marital system (Szinovacz & Schaffer, 2000).

While retirement provides time to share in activities around the house, the research literature suggests that husbands do not substantially increase their participation in household activities. Rather, they continue the patterns (many of which are traditionally divided) they had established before retirement. This is to suggest that, although some sharing of less traditional household tasks may occur in elderly marriages, for the most part, older couples continue to follow household division-of-labor patterns established earlier in their marriages, even though they expect to share the workload more evenly after they retire (Szinovacz, 2000).

Despite the popular notion that retirement creates multiple marital problems, there is considerable continuity in marital relations over the retirement transition (Allen et al., 2000). Put another way, retirement tends to reinforce the patterns of marital satisfaction and quality that were present in the relationship prior to retirement. Most couples tend to profit from retirement. Improvements in postretirement marriages are linked to decreased stress and more time for companionship. Lowered marital satisfaction often results if the husband retires prior to his wife and the couple abides by traditional gender role attitudes. Not surprisingly, problems can also arise when spouses approach retirement with unrealistic or different expectations about how they will structure their lives after retirement (Moen, Kim, & Hofmeister, 2001; Myers & Booth, 1996; Vinick & Ekerdt, 1991).

Lastly, it is interesting to note that the attractiveness of retiring is also influenced by the quality of the marital relationship. Spouses who enjoy a close relationship, have joint hobbies, or desire more time with one another are more inclined to retire. Couples in conflict-laden relationships may dread spending more time together and hence delay retirement. Some husbands also fear that retirement could undermine their power position in the marriage and postpone retirement for that reason (Szinovacz & DeViney, 2000).

Coping with the Physical Changes of Aging

Although the aging process affects individuals in different ways, there are distinct physical changes that accompany the aging process. All adults age and must cope with the physical changes that aging brings. From a family system's perspective, these physical changes also represent challenges to the marital system.

Behavioral slowing (reduced speed in responding to stimuli) and sensory changes in vision, hearing, taste, touch, and smell accompany the aging process. These physiological changes have the potential to alter dramatically the emotional climate within the marriage. Leisure and recreation and companionship and sexuality can all be affected by the physical changes that accompany aging (Carter & McGoldrick, 2005b).

For example, the stereotypical notion is that older adults lose their interest in sex. However, although sexual activity apparently declines with aging, most older adults remain sexually active throughout their later-adult years (Alline & Johnson, 2002; Mezey et al., 2001). At the same time, however, the physiological changes that accompany the aging process challenge couples to alter their sexual scripts. Men, for example, often need increased time and stimulation to produce an erection. Women may need to use artificial lubricants due to the declining ability of vaginal tissues to remain self-lubricated as aging occurs. In order for these physiological changes to be integrated into the couple's sexual script, partners must be able to discuss these changes and talk openly about their changing expectations and needs.

Shared leisure and recreational activities also may change. The effect these changes have on the marital relationship will be determined by the symbolic significance attributed to them. For example, a couple who is fond of attending plays and musical performances together may have to alter this activity should one of the spouses develop a hearing loss. Some couples might adjust to the partner's hearing loss with good humor and grace. Others might frame this change as a deliberate effort on the part of the hearing-impaired spouse to undermine the harmony of the marital relationship, that is, as an expression of hostility toward the spouse. Being able to attribute the source of the stress to the aging process rather than the partner is one factor that enables couples to maintain a sense of marital vitality and harmony.

The broader point here is that interest in sexual and recreational activities during the aging years will be based on previous patterns of interest. While interest follows a continuous path, the physiological changes associated with aging will require couples to renegotiate marital patterns of interaction. The very same communication skills and abilities needed during earlier stages in the family life cycle are needed during the aging years as well.

Coping with Frailty within the Marital System

By the time most married couples reach the later-adult years, their children have generally left the home and established independent households. The typical older family in our society is composed of a husband and wife. About two-thirds of all elderly couples live alone (U.S. Census Bureau, 2007a).

Within these aging households, temporary illness, chronic illness, and **frailty** are all issues that will be encountered. People living to advanced age must often rely on assistance from other family members as their primary caregivers for social, psychological, and physical support. The research literature is clear in pointing out that women are the primary caretakers for family members with a chronic illness or functional impairment. About three-quarters of caregivers are women who tend to provide hands-on care, compared to men, who provide care management. Studies, in other words, clearly document that women more so than men and wives more so than husbands serve as the primary caregivers of the frail elderly. While it is possible to perceive these differences as being an outgrowth of gender roles (the emphasis of caregiving within the female role), these differences are not solely accounted for by a differential willingness on the part of husbands and wives to fulfill the caregiving role. Husbands and wives generally respond equally to the needs of their dependent partner. Wives, however, are more likely to be caregivers because of age and longevity differences; that is, women generally live longer than men and tend to be younger than their husbands (Roberto & Jarrott, 2008; Walker, Manoogian-O'Dell, McGraw, & White, 2001).

Older couples, as discussed in Chapter 13, typically experience an increase in marital satisfaction after the launching of children. They generally value the companionship and support of the partner. The frailty of a partner represents a major stressor within the marriage relationship because the strain of needing to provide care is combined with the loss of companionship and support. In general, spouses who serve as caregivers miss the way their spouses were, worry about what would happen if they became ill, have a tendency to feel depressed, and find it physically difficult to perform care-related tasks (Bedford & Blieszner, 1997). In one study, for example, the rate of depression found in spouses who were caregivers was six times higher than the rate occurring in noncaregivers (Cannuscio, Jones, Kawachi, Colditz, Berkman, & Rimm, 2002). Although husbands and wives tend to report similar levels of burden associated with caregiving, wives report more depressive symptoms and a greater decline in marital satisfaction (Beach, Schulz, Yell, & Jackson, 2000).

In other words, there is a suggestion within the research that wives find the caregiving role at this stage in life more stressful and restricting than do caregiving husbands. It may be that women come to resent having to fulfill this caregiver role in their later years after having had to fulfill it during earlier stages in the family life cycle. Alternatively, social norms that suggest that husbands should be emotionally and physically stronger than their wives may increase the discomfort that both dependent husbands and caregiving wives experience. In addition, as wives in later life tend to expand their social relationships, they may experience the loss of social ties and opportunities that accompany caregiving as a greater source of personal distress than husbands, who tend to rely, with age, more heavily on their spouses for social support. That many women reduce their work hours or quit their jobs altogether in response to their partner's frailty may contribute to their feeling a loss of social ties and support (Bedford & Blieszner, 1997; Roberto & Jarrott, 2008).

The important point is that the demands of caregiving constitute a significant stress on the marital system. Couples must negotiate new patterns of relating that take into account the changing needs and expectations of partners as they become frail and in need of care. Patterns of dependency and power shift. Patterns of affection and support change. At the same time, there is a fragility to these caregiving arrangements because the caregiver is vulnerable to age-related health problems as well. Caregiving spouses often focus on the spouse's illness and neglect their own health needs. In the process, they become vulnerable to social isolation (Beach et al., 2000; Friesen, 1996). Coping with frailty is not just a matter of managing the care of the spouse, but of managing to have one's own social and health-related needs met as well. Clearly, this can challenge the resourcefulness of most marital couples.

Intergenerational Dynamics during the Later Years

Intergenerational ties between parents and children shift according to the developmental agendas of each generation. For middle-aged adults, as discussed in Chapter 13, the launching of children is accompanied by a renegotiation of the marital system and a shift in attention to the needs and concerns of elderly family members. The middle-adult generation within the family can be thought of as the hub of the family wheel—activity, energy, and resources flow around them. Family cohesion and stability are maintained when they assume a position of leadership and authority within the system.

At the same time, in the normative course of the family life cycle, aging family members must accept their shifting roles within the family system (Carter & McGoldrick, 2005a). To make space for the centrality of the middle generation, they must be willing to give up their previously central role within the system. This shift in the later-adult generation's centrality is marshaled in by a number of changes in intergenerational roles and relationships. The identities of older adults are transformed as they become grandparents. Furthermore, financial, functional, and emotional patterns of support and interconnectedness shift as aging family members retire and cope with the physical changes of aging.

Grandparenthood

While typically discussed as a later-adult issue, it is clear that grandparenthood is first experienced by most adults during their middle-adult years. It is a role transition that is discussed in the context of the later-life family, however, because **grandparenthood** is symbolic of the shifting generational ties that occur within the family. The grandparent role, from a normative family developmental perspective, symbolically releases the older generation from the position of primary caregiver and places it in a secondary, less responsible position in relation to the younger generation. Grandparenthood signifies a shift in centrality and power from the aging generation to the middle generation within the family hierarchy.

Interestingly, of children born in 1900, only one in four had all four grandparents alive, and by the time they reached fifteen years, only one in fifty still had all four grandparents alive. In comparison, approximately one-third of those who were twelve years old in the early 1990s had all four grandparents alive, and approximately 70 percent had at least two of them alive when they reached adulthood (Szinovacz, 1998). This means that more older adults than ever before will have contact with their grandchildren, and because of longer life expectancy, they will experience a longer period of grandparenthood.

In contemporary society, the role of grandparent is ambiguous. It is often unclear what this role means and how it functions in the family system (Cherlin & Furstenberg, 1986). This ambiguity results in considerable variation in how the grandparent role is enacted. A principal developmental challenge for grandparents is to define for themselves the meaning of the role and then to evolve the necessary strategies to enact it.

For example, some grandparents may define their role as that of being a "reserve parent" (nurturing children and providing care when necessary), the "family arbitrator" (mediating family conflicts), or "family historian" (Cherlin & Furstenberg, 1986). Each of these different ways of defining the role has implications for how the role is enacted. For example, reserve parents fulfill the popular image of contemporary grandparents. Reserve grandparents are viewed as loving older persons who do not interfere with the relationship that the grandchild has with his or her parents. These grandparents see their grandchildren frequently, care for them when care is needed, and provide them with opportunities for fun and recreation. Family arbitrators attempt to maintain a more central role within the extended family by keeping abreast of the issues facing various family members and offering themselves as a resource when problems occur. Family historians assume the role of passing on to the younger generations the family's identity, traditions, and legacies.

Although the styles and types of grandparenting relationships vary, generally grandparents value the relationships they have with their grandchildren and derive satisfaction from the role. The flexibility the culture affords grandparents in defining their role, however, is not without potential complications. As noted in earlier chapters, conflict and strain develop in relationships when family members have different views about how roles should be enacted. The grandparent role is no different. The level of stress, conflict, and intimacy experienced between the generations will depend on whether the grandparents' definition of their role fulfills the expectations of their children and grandchildren (Szinovacz, 1998).

Clearly, intergenerational patterns of interaction involving grandparents are influenced by the degree to which adult children and their aging parents have succeeded at negotiating an intimate, adult-to-adult relationship. When this has not occurred, cross-generational coalitions become more likely. Parents may attempt to undermine the relationship between grandparents and grandchildren by forming a coalition with their children against the grandparents. Similarly, grandparents and grandchildren may form a coalition against the parents, viewing them as the "common enemy."

The point is that the family's historical patterns of interaction have consequences for how the relationships between the multiple generations of the family are structured. Roles and relationships are interlocking. The manner in which the grandparent role is structured within the family is inevitably influenced by the historical patterns of interaction found between aging adults and their spouses and between aging parents and their adult children. At the same time, the ongoing patterns of interaction found within and between these generations contribute to the family system's ever-evolving legacy (Walker et al., 2001).

Transforming the Parent–Child Relationship: Individuation and the Aging Years

A fundamental tension exists within the parent–child relationship over the entire course of the family life cycle. This tension has to do with balancing the developmental needs of each generation for autonomy and dependence and separateness and connectedness. The individuation process and the reworking of the personal authority relationship push parents and children to continually renegotiate their financial, functional, and emotional connections throughout childhood, adolescence, and early and middle adulthood. The asymmetrical dependency that characterizes the parent–child relationship during childhood gradually shifts throughout the adolescent, early-adult, and middle-adult years toward a more symmetrical and mutually independent relationship system. As this occurs, children develop a mature identity and capacity for intimacy. Successful individuation enables the parent–child relationship to be characterized by genuine mutuality and respect.

During the later-adult years, the parent–child relationship is challenged by the gradual and increasing needs for support and assistance that accompany the aging process. This shift in self-sufficiency and dependency pressures aging parents and their adult children once again to modify the symmetrical patterns of interconnectedness that were established during early and middle adulthood.

In their place, somewhat asymmetrical patterns of interconnectedness reappear. These asymmetrical patterns differ from those of the past, however, as now it is the aging parents who require more care and the adult children who are called on to assume the role of caregiver.

The successful transformation of the parent–child relationship throughout the aging years thus requires aging parents to accept their evolving dependency and to allow their children to meet their needs. Adult children, in turn, need to adjust their perceptions of their parents and to accept their changing role in their parents' lives. The extent to which these transformations are satisfactorily renegotiated determines the level of intimacy and mutuality that will exist within the relationship.

Intergenerational Patterns of Contact and Support

The research literature is clear that, as a general rule, elderly parents and their adult children restructure their relationships in ways that are satisfying for both. For example, studies show that elderly parents and children maintain regular contact with one another even when geographical distances are considerable. Furthermore, research has shown that adult children provide a wide range of instrumental (e.g., help with chores, shopping, and transportation) and emotional support for their aging parents (Silverstein, Giarrusso, & Bengston, 2005).

It is important to point out that the patterns of support and care between generations during this time are dominated by a theme of reciprocity. Older parents continue to provide support of various kinds to their adult children and are not only the recipients of support (Silverstein et al., 2005). As such, the research on intergenerational relationships in the later years supports the conclusion that older adults are neither abandoned by, nor alienated from, their adult children. To the contrary, parents and children engage in mutually supportive exchange patterns. Their contact is frequent, and a variety of personal services and forms of assistance are exchanged.

Frailty and the Changing Parent–Adult Child Relationship

Most of the elderly within the United States are neither chronically ill nor frail. Today's elderly are living longer than ever before and are capable of carrying out daily routines. For the most part, they appear to be self-sufficient and enjoy their lives.

However, advancing age often brings the need for assistance in day-to-day living. Because the provision of assistance and caregiving is an extension of the ongoing patterns of contact and support that occur among family members, it is difficult to estimate the prevalence of family caregiving. In 2005, the National Family Caregiver Survey, sponsored by the National Alliance for Caregiving and AARP, reported that nearly one in four U.S. households was involved in helping care for an individual fifty-years-old or older and that the number of informal caregivers in the United States tripled from 1988 to 2005. This report goes on to conclude that a conservative estimate of the prevalence of caregiving falls between 23.6 million and 27.4 million caregivers in 2005. All indications are that these shifting patterns of involvement and care will need to increase in years to come (National Alliance for Caregiving & AARP, 2005).

There is no doubt that frailty represents a critical family system stressor. It is clear, as well, that the responsibility for providing care for the frail elderly further transforms the parent–child relationship when adult children are called on to provide this care. That is, as suggested, when a spouse is not present to perform these necessary caregiving tasks, the caregiving role shifts to adult children, especially to daughters. As would be expected, unmarried children, and particularly unmarried daughters, are expected to provide more help than married children. The expectation that adult daughters will provide care for their aging parents is an extension of the caregiving and expressive role that women are generally expected to fulfill within the family. It also is not surprising that the involvement of sons in caregiving is most often limited to "instrumental tasks" (providing financial assistance, handling paperwork, and paying bills). As a result, daughters typically provide the bulk of direct hands-on services such as chores, meals, and assistance with personal care, and spend more hours than men in caregiving activities. Because of their greater involvement, they tend to have greater difficulty emotionally detaching themselves from these tasks (Barusch, 1995; Fingerman, 2001; Roberto & Jarrott, 2008).

Becoming a caregiver is difficult in that (1) there is no prior training for the role; (2) the role itself is often unclear; and (3) the role is highly idiosyncratic—that is, each caregiver confronts a unique set of demands and expectations due to the particular health and care needs of the frail parent. In addition, assuming the caregiver role is complicated in that adult children not only must find a way to meet the needs of their aging parents, but they must do so in the context of continuing to meet the needs of their spouses, dependent children, and, perhaps, grandchildren. Caught in the middle, adult daughters, in particular, typically respond by trying to fulfill all the demands that their roles in different generational subsystems require of them. This results in the increased potential for role strain, conflict, and overload. When a caregiver, for example, identifies her primary loyalty as being to her husband and children, she may experience guilt over the level of care she is able to provide to her parents. Conversely, meeting the needs of aging parents may result in tension between husbands and wives or guilt over failing to provide for the needs of children (Fingerman, 2001). There is no simple solution to being caught in the middle.

Apparently, many adult children prefer to define the caregiver role in terms of being a coordinator of services rather than a direct service provider. Socioeconomic status is a primary factor in determining whether children become a care provider or a care manager. Lower-income daughters are more likely to be direct care providers. Children in higher socioeconomic brackets, in contrast, are more likely to identify service needs and manage the assistance provided to their parents by others. In the latter instance, adult children attempt to meet the parents' needs while maintaining some physical and psychological distance (Qualls & Roberto, 2006; Szinovacz & Davey, 2008).

Taking on the caregiver role apparently comes with personal reservations and costs. The instrumental and emotional demands of caregiving can tax even the closest of parent–child relationships, and caregivers often experience a considerable amount of burden (Fingerman, 2001). A number of factors influence the type and level of burden that is experienced by caregivers. Rolland (1994) suggests that four factors, in particular, influence the burden associated with caregiving:

- Onset—in other words, whether the illness begins gradually, as in Alzheimer's and Parkinson's diseases, or suddenly, as in stroke
- Disease course—of which there are three types: progressive, as in Alzheimer's disease and cancer, with increased severity and continual adaptations over time; constant, as in stroke, where an initial acute event stabilizes and persists over time; and relapsing/episodic, as in severe and persistent mental illness, in which periods of remission for acute illness provide relief for caregivers only to be followed by repeated, acute episodes
- Outcome—in other words, whether the illness diagnosis carries a prognosis of fatality or shortening of the life span
- Incapacitation—in other words whether the ill family member experiences short- or long-term cognitive, speech, or physical impairments as well as the degree of the impairment or incapacitation

At the same time, caregiving can have positive effects for the caregiver as well (Beach et al., 2000). Adult children who are caregivers to elderly parents report that they find caregiving gratifying because they can pay back the care that their parents provided to them when they were young. In addition, caregivers report that being a caregiver helps them gain inner strength, learn new skills, aid their personal growth, and increase their understanding of family problems.

In sum, the frailty of aging parents forces a reorganization of the relationship between aging adults and their adult children. For adult children, the caregiver role represents a significant identity and role transformation. The stress engendered within this role is amplified in that adult children have other role demands and responsibilities that compete for their time and energy. Stress, strain, and broader family tensions can occur when adult children find themselves confronted with the task of finding a way to balance these competing demands. At the same time, adult children often feel it is their responsibility to assume this role. Providing care is one way of extending to aging parents the care and concern that the parents themselves expressed for their children in earlier stages in the family life cycle. While the role of caregiver is obviously stressful, it can be satisfying and gratifying as well.

Family System Dynamics and the Caregiving/Care-Receiving Relationship

Throughout this text, it has been maintained that the parent–child relationship is influenced by the intergenerational legacy found within the broader family system. It is, thus, reasonable to theorize that the ability of adult children and aging parents to transform their relationship to accommodate the demands of the aging process is tied to the family's intergenerational legacy. Caregiving takes place within a historical context.

That is, both caregivers and care-receivers enter the relationship with a history of interactions that may either facilitate or impede the caregiving relationship. In other words, family life is characterized by both change and a continuity of relationships that can assist or inhibit adjustment to these changes. As health difficulties increase, other family members are often expected to provide assistance. Often, this assistance is based on patterns of interaction that were established long before health became problematic (Szinovacz & Davey, 2008; Walker et al., 2001).

In the following section, we turn our attention to an understanding of the various ways in which caregiving might be structured and experienced by adult children. In doing this, a typology of caregiving relationships will be presented (Holmes & Sabatelli, 1997). Within this typology, the structure and the experience of the caregiving relationship are based upon the unfolding and ongoing manner in which parents and children resolve their personal authority relationship.

Personal Authority and the Caregiving/Care-Receiving Relationship

How care for the frail parent is structured and how adult children experience the caregiving role will depend on the extent to which the personal authority relationship has been reworked. In general, it is reasonable to expect that caregiving will be radically different for those children who experience a peer-like relationship with their parents as compared to those who experience that relationship as hierarchical. That is, the legacy of the parent–child relationship constitutes one of the principle mediators of, first, whether a child is willing to assume the caregiver role, and, second, how caregiving is approached and experienced (Holmes & Sabatelli, 1997). The proposed model posits three primary types of possible relationships, as described below.

Type I: The Mutual Relationship. The tolerance for individuality and intimacy that has characterized the family system all along will affect how the relationship between a frail parent and adult child is transformed. In well-differentiated and individuation-enhancing family systems, intergenerational relationships are dominated by respect, empathy, and sensitivity to the needs of one another. Parents and children are able to rework the personal authority relationship, and, as such, their relationships are based on mutual respect and trust.

Within these mutual systems, caregivers confirm the dignity and worth of the elderly and frail by attending to their needs without overfunctioning for them (Carter & McGoldrick, 2005b). In such relationships, the integrity and individuality of the elderly are preserved, and intergenerational intimacy enhanced. Each is able to be emotionally close to the other while maintaining autonomy. Conflict is not to be avoided at all costs but is dealt with openly and positively. Both aging parents and adult children are able to tolerate anxiety, see the other's point of view, and solve problems productively. Children no longer fear their parents' disapproval but are able to see them as separate individuals with their own opinions. Parents no longer try to have parental power over their children but treat them as equals.

In the mutual relationship, a context of acceptance, mutual respect, and genuine concern for each other prevails. For those children who are able to maintain a high level of personal authority, caregiving is more manageable in the sense that this role does not create intense emotions stemming from feeling like a child in relation to one's parent. They are helping not a powerful parent but a benign aging person in need.

Caregiving strategies that these adult children develop are likely to be positive and productive, balancing the needs of both the adult child and the parent in a healthy manner. Children are able to provide care in a respectful manner, enhancing their parents' independence as much as possible without assuming emotional responsibility for their welfare and happiness. Children in this type of relationship also are able to set healthy limits on what they are able to do as caregivers without feeling overwhelmed by guilt, anxiety, or resentment. Their parents are able to see these limits as necessary instead of a sign that their child is being disloyal or unloving (Holmes & Sabatelli, 1997).

Type II: The Hierarchical—Passive Relationship. Clearly some parents and children are unable to rework their personal authority relationship. This inability can result in parents maintaining (or attempting to maintain) a position of parental authority within the family system and adult children resigning themselves to and accepting their child-like position within the family system (Holmes & Sabatelli, 1997).

In this type of relationship, the adult child continues to play the good son or good daughter role, while the parent continues in the role of powerful parent. Parents relish their authority and can actively attempt to sabotage their children's efforts to rework their relationship. That is, any effort on the part of adult children to change their role may be quickly thwarted by the parents through the use of disapproval and intimidation. Parents also may attempt to make their children feel guilty as a way of keeping them in line. They may fear that giving up their hold over their children may result in the children choosing not to care for them.

Children in this type of relationship typically respond to their parents' disapproval with overwhelming guilt, often feeling as if they are letting the parents down. Instead of being able to manage their feelings of guilt and anxiety, adult children may believe that their only choice is to give in and do what their parents want, even if this means sacrificing their own personal and family needs. For example, a daughter may want to spend Sunday afternoon relaxing with her husband, yet her mother expects her to visit every Sunday afternoon. Because of being intimated by the power of her mother, the daughter cannot imagine even telling her mother that she would rather spend a relaxed Sunday afternoon at home with her husband. The very thought of confronting her mother fills her with fear and guilt. She fears creating a "huge scene" with her mother, feeling that her mother would become very upset if she did not come over. She fears that her mother would never accept "no" as an answer and fantasizes that her mother would actually cut off contact with her until she acquiesced to her mother's wishes. Thus, she may feel stuck in a child-like role with her mother. And, as a result, she is likely to sacrifice her own needs and those of her husband and children by giving in to what her mother expects.

The important difference between the mutual relationship and this relationship is in how the children respond to emotion-evoking situations that arise as parents age and become frail. In a mutual relationship, children respond by managing their own feelings so that they are not overwhelmed by them. Even if they feel anxiety or guilt, they are still able to express their wishes as an adult, and their parents are able to accept these wishes. In the Sunday afternoon example, the daughter would be able to empathize with her mother's disappointment, while the mother would be able to understand her daughter's needs.

In a hierarchical–passive relationship, children respond to emotion-evoking situations by sacrificing their own autonomy in order to reduce their anxiety and the level of conflict in the relationship. When a daughter thinks about changing the power dynamics in her relationship with her mother, for example, she may feel that her mother is incapable of seeing her side of an issue and of treating her as an adult. She may become overwhelmed with anxiety just thinking about acting autonomously toward her mother. Without the ability to maintain a high level of personal authority, she is unable to initiate any changes in the power distribution with her mother. In effect, she continues to feel intimidated by her mother. She may feel that the only way to continue her relationship with her mother is to continue the long-established patterns of interaction whereby she sacrifices her own needs in order to reduce her level of anxiety when relating to her mother.

Caregiving within these relationships, thus, is dominated by the children feeling compelled to care for their parents—caregiving is not a choice but an obligation. Caregiving is likely to focus on fulfilling the parents' expectations regardless of what may be in the parents' or the children's best interest. These adult children are often unable to separate their own needs and feelings from those of the dependent older person. Ironically, when this occurs, the ability of caregivers to manage caregiving tasks is impeded. They become paralyzed by their grief or anxiety. Their ability to make rational decisions and mature judgments is impaired. They are unable to set healthy limits on what they can and cannot do for their parents, and may sacrifice their own needs, and the needs of their husband and children, in order to fulfill their parents' expectations and minimize intergenerational tensions.

In other situations, dysfunctional overfunctioning and underfunctioning patterns are established that rigidly lock both caregivers and care-receivers into roles that undermine the health and welfare of the elderly. Because of the need to please the parents and the overwhelming feelings of guilt and obligation, these children may overfunction for their frail parents, stripping them of any responsibility for their own care. Paradoxically, thus, the children wind up treating the parents like children, and their dependency is encouraged. Occupying such a position for an extended period of time is likely to undermine the competence of the elderly, and, ultimately, contribute to impaired physical and/or mental health.

Type III: The Hierarchical—Rebellious Relationship. In some instances, when parents and children fail to resolve their personal authority struggle, the adult children, instead of sacrificing their own needs in order to reduce the tension in the relationship, will become angry and emotionally cut off from their parents. Similar to the children in the hierarchical–passive relationships, these adult children feel trapped into a child-like position within the family and believe that their parents will never accept them as adults. These children, however, instead of avoiding the conflict and accepting their child-like position of authority, engage their parents in a fight for power (Holmes & Sabatelli, 1997).

The power struggles that characterize the hierarchical–rebellious relationships represent the children's efforts to get their parents to see and treat them as adults. Put another way, anger and resentment predominate in the interactions found within these dyads, with both parents and children feeling invalidated and disrespected by the other. These children, however, when compared to those who maintain peace at the expense of personal authority, refuse to give in to the parents' authority, and become angry, reactive, and often cut off from them. As such, these children are not likely to be willing to choose to be caregivers in the first instance. That is, these are the children who will pressure siblings and other family members to provide the care that the parents require.

However, some of these adult children do become caregivers. When this occurs, the relationships are dominated by themes of anger and resentment. Neither the caregiver nor care-receiver feels validated and respected by the other. For example, daughters who continue to struggle for authority in their relationships with their mother may find that their efforts to provide care are criticized or challenged by their mothers. Daughters respond to such criticisms by becoming defensive and attacking the mother. In other caregiving relationships, mothers might refuse to allow the daughters to provide care. The daughters, of course, feeling invalidated and angry, may attack the mothers as a way of defending their own personal integrity. Mothers and daughters, consequently, can get locked into an ongoing power struggle, with neither acknowledging the other, and each holding the other responsible for the difficulties in the relationship. Locked into such a struggle, the only way to avoid stress is to avoid the relationship.

The bottom line here is that the ordinary stresses and demands of caregiving generate defensive and conflicted patterns of interaction. This pattern of interaction is best understood as emanating from the children's ongoing effort to claim what they view as their legitimate right for personal authority in their relationship with the parents. Neither the children nor the parents view their own actions as contributing to the problems in the relationship. Simple disagreements are viewed as rejections rather than just differences of opinion. Conflicts within these volatile relationships can easily escalate.

Caregiving, then, may become an arena for power struggles in which the children are trying to assert their power as adults, while the parents are trying to assert their power as parents. In such a relationship, even the simplest task may easily become a power struggle. It should be clear, thus, that these volatile relationships are probably the least responsive to the needs of the frail parents.

Furthermore, it is theorized that these types of relationships, because of their volatility and high levels of conflict, are more likely than the other types to be dominated by emotional and/or physical abuse. Adult children who continue to struggle for authority within the family system are likely to resent the intrusion of the parents into their lives and project all of the responsibility for the problems that exist within the family on to the parents. This projection of blame and a legacy of ongoing resentments and tensions can result in elderly parents being scapegoated and, consequently, neglected and/or emotionally or physically abused.

The abuse of the elderly represents the dark side of intergenerational caregiving. These abuses take many forms including neglect, verbal and emotional abuse, physical assault, physical neglect, and financial exploitation. Currently, it is estimated that over one million elderly Americans suffer maltreatment each year at the hands of a family member. This figure is expected to rise in the years to come (Barnett et al., 1997; Pillemer & Suitor, 1998).

The existing research on elderly abuse is relatively sparse. What researchers know is that the perpetrators of elderly abuse are experiencing role overload as well as some kind of personal crisis, such as substance abuse, illness, financial problems, or marital troubles. However, it is the elderly parents and the problems in the parent–child relationship that are most often cited as the reason for these personal and marital crises. In other words, relationship issues and the ongoing struggle between parents and children are factors that contribute to the problems in the lives of adult children that in turn cause them to be abusive in their relationships with their frail parents (Krause & Rook, 2003; Pillemer & Suitor, 1998).

In summary, America is graying. It is estimated that, by the year 2030, one in four Americans will be age sixty-five years or older (U.S. Census Bureau, 2008). This will result in an ever-increasing percentage of families confronting the challenges of transforming the parent–child relationship to one capable of meeting the needs of the frail elderly. While most families will readily respond to the needs of aging family members, it is also clear that the demands of caregiving can easily stress the family system. It will become increasingly important for American society to provide the resources that families will need to confront successfully the challenges of caregiving. One way of helping families cope with the demands of caregiving is to increase the coping resources available to them. Social policy initiatives and the creation of community-based support services that assist families dealing with these particular challenges are examples of such contextual resources. The presence of such resources increases the likelihood that the frail elderly and their adult children will evolve a mutually rewarding and adaptive pattern of interaction during the later adult years.

It should also be clear, however, that in some instances the best way to assist the elderly is to help the aging parents and their adult children finally resolve their authority struggles with one another. Caregiving is an extension of intergenerational patterns of connection and support. Obviously it is going to be more responsive when a relationship based on mutuality, respect, and trust exists between parents and children. Thus, it appears that for some families, underlying intergenerational issues and tensions must be addressed in order to help parents and children successfully negotiate the demands of caregiving.

Conclusions

Readers are encouraged to refrain from viewing the family life cycle as a linear process. The family life cycle does not consist of a beginning, middle, and end, although it has been discussed as having separate and age-graded stages. The family in later life is just one subsystem within the broader family system. How the family manages its tasks during this period is dependent on and influenced by how other generational subsystems within the family managed their tasks as well.

The stresses and strains confronted by the family in later life are many and varied. Examination of these stressors should clarify that there is an intergenerational and systemic continuity that characterizes the family system regardless of its stage in the family life cycle. Certain basic tasks must be executed by all systems, regardless of their stage of development. All systems must evolve strategies for the successful execution of these tasks. Underlying all these strategies is the fact that effective families are characterized by patterns of interaction that support each member's individuation process and foster positive, nurturing, and identity-enhancing bonds within and between generations. Within such systems, a healthy tolerance exists for the expression of uniqueness and individuality. The irony is that it is only through the fostering of individuality that true intimacy is achieved.

Key Terms

Behavioral slowing The reduced speed in responding to stimuli and the sensory changes in vision, hearing, taste, touch, and smell that accompany the aging process.

Frailty A condition brought on by a decline in health status that stresses the relationships between aging spouses and between adult children and their aging parents.

Grandparenthood A role transition that is discussed in the context of the later-life family because the birth of grandchildren symbolically signifies a shift in centrality and power from the aging generation to the middle generation within the family hierarchy.

Retirement Both a physical withdrawal from paid employment and a psychological reorientation of the importance of work to one's identity.

PART IV

Alternative Family Developmental Pathways

Many factors influence a family's patterns of interaction over time. As we have seen in previous chapters, the family's strategies for managing its basic tasks must continually shift in response to individual family members' developmental changes and other family stresses. The family's success in making these adaptations has a profound impact upon the health and well-being of individual family members and the family system as a whole.

Each family follows its own developmental course. This is shaped, in part, by the unique characteristics of individual family members; the family's particular cultural, ethnic, and social context; the intergenerational legacies the family inherits from previous generations; and the extent to which the family follows the typical developmental course prescribed by the norms of the dominant culture. However, there is also an unpredictable, random quality to family life. Not all changes can be anticipated, and not all families follow the normative course of family development.

It would be impossible for any text to examine all of the potential variations and contingencies a family might encounter over the course of its development. However, it would be a major oversight to ignore the fact that not all families follow a normative developmental pathway. In the following chapters, we discuss some of the most common events that can dramatically alter a family's development. They all share several characteristics. First, they all deal with the addition and/or loss of family members to the family system. As such, they precipitate major changes in the family's structure and organization. Second, all these events can dramatically alter how the family executes its basic tasks. This, in turn, can precipitate major alterations in the family's interactional strategies. Third, all provide serious challenges to the family system and have the potential, if managed poorly, to have negative effects upon the health and well-being of family members.

In addition, each of the events highlighted in this part of the text also presents unique challenges to the family system. The experiences of death and loss, for example, are universal. Every family must contend with this issue over the course of its development. However, the nature of the death, its timing, the family's history of previous losses, the family's cultural attitudes about death, and other circumstances surrounding the event make each a unique experience. Not all families experience divorce, single parenthood, or remarriage, but these events are becoming increasingly common in our culture. Each presents the family with a unique set of challenges that must be faced.

In the next four chapters, we outline these challenges in greater detail and discuss what researchers and theorists have determined to be the particular stresses associated with each challenge. We will also examine the factors that may lead to successful or unsuccessful adaptation. We refer to these stressor events as "alternative developmental pathways" to emphasize the frequency with which they occur in contemporary family life and also their potential to alter the family's trajectory permanently.

CHAPTER 15

Death, Loss, and Bereavement

Chapter Overview

The death of a family member can disrupt a family's equilibrium, producing major changes in the family's structure and requiring alterations in the family's strategies. There is no common response to the death of a family member. Rather, the response of each family member and the family system as a whole is influenced by the particular context of the family. This context includes a number of factors, such as the nature of the death; the position the deceased family member held in the family; the family's history of previous losses; the family's unique societal, cultural, ethnic, and religious orientations; and the timing of the death in the family's life cycle. It is important to consider the family's stage in the life cycle and other contextual factors, because a death never occurs in isolation. Other normative and non-normative stresses can pile up and affect the magnitude and intensity of the loss. Furthermore, when previous losses remain unresolved, the impact of the present loss can have an even greater effect on the family's interactional strategies. Successful resolution generally depends upon the family's capacity to master several important tasks. These tasks include how able family members are to accept the reality of the death, share their experiences of pain and grief, reorganize the family system in response to the loss, and move toward the future by investing in other relationships and new life pursuits.

Death, Loss, and Bereavement

Although the developmental trajectory of a family can be altered in many ways, some of the most profound alterations occur when family members experience loss. For many of us, our first reaction to the topic of loss is to think of the death of a close family member or friend. And although the death of a family member has powerful and wide-ranging repercussions throughout the family system, many other kinds of losses also can produce a significant impact upon the family's development and choice of strategies. The loss of a parent's job, the loss of the family's home due to a poor economy or a natural disaster, the loss of a family member's physical health, and the loss of one's physical mobility or the capacity to carry on a favorite activity or hobby are all examples of losses that can alter a family's developmental course and require adjustments in the family's preferred strategies for managing its boundaries, identity, emotional environment, daily maintenance, and ability to cope with stressful changes.

Loss and bereavement are an inevitable part of one's individual and family life. Many stressor events encountered by the family over time have embedded within them one or more experiences of loss. Take for instance, the experience of divorce, which will be discussed in Chapter 16. Divorce entails the separation of the marital partners and the end of the relationship as it was previously organized. Divorce also includes the loss of each partner's identity as a "married person." For some family members, or perhaps all, it means the loss of the shared family home. It may mean the loss of a particular standard of living, the end of relationships with in-laws, or the termination of some of the couple's friendships. For children, it may mean the loss of regular contact with one parent or the loss of a sense of security and family cohesion.

Or, consider, for instance, the loss of a parent's good-paying job. Such an event can alter the family's standard and style of living. Favorite (and perhaps expensive) activities may have to be forgone. The loss of a carefree view of life may be replaced with worry and concern about how the rent will be paid or how food will be purchased. The loss of income may mean that the family will miss a planned vacation or that college-aged family members will lose valued financial support. For the parent, the loss of a job may be accompanied by a loss of self-esteem and a "success" identity. Thus, losses of many different types are encountered by all families as they move through time, and every experience of loss has the potential to alter family strategies and functioning.

In this chapter, we focus specifically upon the impact of death on the family system. Consistent with the focus of this text, we will examine its impact from a multigenerational, developmental perspective. It is assumed within this perspective that the death of a family member can disrupt a family's equilibrium, produce major changes in the family's structure, and require alterations in the family's strategies. As such, the death of a central family figure can produce **emotional shock waves** that reverberate throughout the entire extended family, perhaps even creating changes in individual family members who may have had limited or no direct contact with the deceased member (Bowen, 1976).

Death within the Family System

A multigenerational, developmental perspective on the death of a family member calls our attention to several general points. First, how a family system responds to a death is importantly influenced by the unique context of the family. Second, the death of a family member affects each family member in a unique and individual manner. There is no one prescribed way to mourn the death of a loved one. Third, the death of a family member reverberates throughout the entire family system, altering the family's structure, organization, and interactional strategies. Fourth, although we generally accept that death will occur during old age, it can in fact occur at any age. Fifth, the death of a family member requires the family to manage a number of additional tasks along with the ones it must typically address.

Family Tasks in Response to a Death

Adapting to the death of a family member requires both immediate and long-term reorganization of the family system. The family's reorganization is enhanced when the family is able to complete the necessary tasks of mourning. When these tasks are not managed well, the continued health and development of family members and the family as a whole can be adversely affected. Four tasks have been identified as critical for successful adaptation. Although it is impossible to predict a family's particular coping style or the timing of their unique response to the grieving process, these tasks are typically thought to be sequential and overlapping (Walsh & McGoldrick, 2004).

1. *Shared acknowledgement of the reality of the death.* The management of the emotional shock waves created by a death requires that all family members acknowledge the reality of the death. This is typically facilitated by (1) the sharing of clear information and open communication throughout the family system about the death; (2) the participation of all family members in funeral and burial rites; and (3) visits by family members to the grave or other final resting place of the deceased. Questions asked by children or other family members, for example, need to be answered in a direct and open manner. Efforts to protect children or other vulnerable family members by keeping secrets or withholding information are likely to inhibit resolution of the loss and may lead to the development of ineffective coping strategies such as denial, minimization, and avoidance.

2. *Shared experience of the pain of grief.* The management of a death within a family system requires an acceptance of family members' pain and grief as well as a tolerance for the full range of emotions that might accompany the loss of a loved one. Family members may experience a broad range of mixed emotional responses, including ambivalence, anger, disappointment, helplessness, guilt, relief, or abandonment. When coping strategies or family loyalties prohibit certain feelings from being expressed, problems in adaptation may occur in the form of symptomatic behavior, physical health problems, or psychological symptoms.

3. *Reorganization of the family system.* The death of a family member necessitates a reorganization in family members' roles and in the family's strategies for managing its basic tasks (e.g., maintenance, identity, boundaries, emotional climate, and adaptability). The roles and responsibilities of the deceased must be reassigned in order for the family to carry on with life. The turmoil and distress that accompany the transition to a new family organization may prompt families to hold on to old strategies that are no longer effective. For example, if no one in the family were to assume the deceased member's responsibilities for the repair and upkeep of the home, the general condition of the home would eventually deteriorate. Alternatively, the family may prematurely seek replacements for the deceased so that family stability can be regained. In such instances, the member recruited to fulfill the role of the deceased may not have the necessary skills or inclination to perform it, resulting in role dissonance; conflict; and feelings of guilt, coercion, or disconfirmation.

4. *Reinvestment in other relationships and life pursuits.* The successful adaptation of a family system to the death of a member is signified by the gradual and eventual ability of family members to reinvest in other relationships and life pursuits. The process of mourning is likely to last at least one or two years. Each new season, holiday, anniversary, or special occasion can rekindle feelings of loss and can keep the family's focus on the past rather than on the future (Becvar, 2001; Walsh, 1998). The formation of new attachments and commitments may be further obstructed if the deceased has been idealized, or if moving on with life is viewed as a form of disloyalty to the deceased. Fears of additional losses also can impede the family's capacity to move on. Eventually, however, the family must put the past (and the deceased) to rest and move on with new relationships and commitments. This is not to suggest that the deceased is forgotten or ignored. Rather, the successful resolution of the tasks of mourning results in family members feeling free to discuss the deceased and to recall memories of the deceased. However, their energy is no longer tied to the past but rather is available for new activities and experiences.

Factors Mediating the Family System's Response to Death

In view of the legacy of connections among family members, it is apparent that death has the potential to stress the family system significantly. Death reverberates throughout the system and directly touches many of the reciprocal relationships found within it. Death challenges family members to grieve the loss of loved ones. Death also forces a restructuring of the family system and alters its patterns of interaction. The family system's adaptation to these challenges is influenced by a number of factors, including (1) the nature of the death; (2) the position of the deceased in the family; (3) the family's history of losses; (4) the openness and adaptability of the family system; (5) the family's societal, cultural, ethnic, and religious context; and (6) the timing of the death in the family's life cycle (Brown, 1989; McGoldrick & Walsh, 2005; Walsh, 1998).

Furthermore, the discussion of the impact of death on the family would be incomplete without attention to the family's broader experiences with loss and other stresses. The family's efforts to cope with a death are profoundly influenced by both the vertical and horizontal stresses that accompany a death. Although the most immediate impact of a loss is felt in the present, and is often accompanied by a period of confusion, disorganization, and intense feelings of pain and anxiety, these vertical stresses are deeply affected by the family's horizontal stresses. Over time, the impact of repeated losses that are not fully resolved or worked through can lead to a pile-up of unresolved losses that can disrupt effective family functioning.

The Nature of the Death

The nature of the death of a family member refers to (1) whether the death was expected; and (2) the reasons for the death. Both of these factors affect the amount and type of stress and support encountered by the family system in response to the death. Both of the factors have consequences for how a family system adapts in response to the death of a family member.

As a general rule, unexpected deaths are thought to be more stressful than expected deaths. In part, this is because when a death occurs suddenly and unexpectedly, there are no opportunities for family members to engage in anticipatory mourning. In such cases, the intensity and duration of grief tend to be greater (Becvar, 2001; Walsh & McGoldrick, 2004).

In contrast, when a death is expected, family members may be able to deal with the eventual death through a series of smaller losses. Such is the case when a family member first becomes ill, resulting in the loss of a healthy family member, the loss of the customary patterns of everyday living, and the loss of the person's ability to perform particular roles or specific tasks. It is important to point out, however, that prolonged illnesses produce a series of additional stresses that can have a pronounced impact on the family system. For example, the time commitments required to care for the ill member, financial costs, lost employment, career disruption, emotional exhaustion, lost time for other family members, and an ensuing sense of social isolation can severely deplete the family's coping capacity (Murray, 1994).

In addition, the reasons for the death affect the stress and support encountered by grieving family members. Certain kinds of deaths are more likely to be viewed by others in such a way as to make grieving more difficult for family members. Family members may feel less support from others when the cause of death was a stigmatizing illness such as AIDS. Fear of contagion or the fact that AIDS primarily affects select groups such as homosexuals and intravenous drug users can leave family members feeling uncomfortable about sharing their emotional reactions with others. Suicide is another example of a death that carries stigma in our culture, provoking feelings of shame, guilt, and anger. The resulting secrecy and blame can distort family communication, isolate family members from one another, and interfere with efforts to seek social support outside the family (Becvar, 2001; Calhoun & Allen, 1991; Murray, 1994; E. R. Shapiro, 1996).

The Position of the Deceased in the Family

The impact of a death on the family system is further influenced by the position the deceased occupied within the family system. Families are comprised of interdependent networks of people, and a multigenerational, developmental perspective on death calls attention to the fact that each death involves multiple losses. The deceased was generally many things to many people. For instance, he may have been a brother, son, parent, husband, in-law, uncle, ex-spouse, and stepfather. This distinctive constellation of relationships influences the sense of loss experienced by each individual, every generation, and the entire family system (Becvar, 2001; Walsh & McGoldrick, 2004).

It is also important to note that within a given family system, selected individuals tend to occupy positions of greater centrality or importance than others. This significance to the family can be understood in terms of (1) the person's functional role within the family; and (2) the degree of emotional dependence the family has had on the individual (Brown, 1989). As a general rule, the death of a person occupying a more central position in the family network is likely to have a greater impact on the functioning of the family system than the death of a person occupying a less central position (Brown, 1989; McGoldrick & Walsh, 2005).

The position of the deceased in the family system is also governed by the level of conflict that other family members experienced with the person. Although, as we have seen in earlier chapters, conflict is an inevitable part of family life, unresolved conflicts can complicate the grieving process (Walsh & McGoldrick, 2004). For example, when conflict with the deceased has resulted in emotional cutoffs or estrangement, the death means that efforts to repair the relationship become impossible. Family members may experience a greater sense of guilt when the relationship with the deceased has been ambivalent or difficult.

The Family's History of Losses

The family's history of previous losses and how these losses have been dealt with are among the factors that also influence a family's response to death. A history of coping effectively with losses builds a legacy that in turn positively affects current coping efforts. Such a legacy can be one of empowerment in which family members accept their vulnerability to being hurt while at the same time view themselves as survivors who will not be defeated (Murray, 1994). Conversely, the inability of families to cope with prior losses may create a pile-up of stressors that overburdens the family system. An overload of past losses and a history of difficulty in dealing with losses will often impede a family's ability to handle a current loss (Brown, 1989; Walsh & McGoldrick, 2004). Such an outcome can produce a legacy of trauma from which the family is cursed or unable to rise above (Murray, 1994). Difficulty in accepting earlier losses can reduce the openness of the family system and create an unwillingness to tolerate the intense and powerful emotions that can accompany a loss.

The Openness and Adaptability of the Family System

According to Brown (1989), many of the long-term adjustment difficulties that occur within families confronted by death originate in the lack of openness in the family system. In essence, this discussion of openness speaks to the level of differentiation found within the system. Well-differentiated systems are better able to maintain their integrity and ability to function in the presence of stress. These systems are characterized by a level of adaptability and permeability that fosters effective communication and the open sharing of personal feelings. Family members are able to support and nurture one another, even in times of crisis. Stress, tension, and conflict are all dealt with directly and managed in ways that maintain cohesion and support the integrity of the system.

Perhaps one of the best indicators of the emotional response of the family to a death is the quality of emotional support present in the family prior to the loss. When families have established strategies that nurture and support family members, build family cohesion, effectively manage conflict, and resolve tensions, the individual adjustment of family members to the loss can be fostered and the functioning of the family system maximized. The family is able to acknowledge the pain of the loss and tolerate a wide range of feeling expressions, such as delayed reactions; quiet reflection; intense crying; and expressions of guilt, anger, emptiness, or physical distress.

An absence of openness in the family system means that rigid patterns of interaction have become established that are difficult to change. The role responsibilities of the deceased may not be easily accepted by other family members, thus leaving critical tasks left undone. Or, another family member may be recruited to fulfill the vacated role, even though he or she may have neither the interest nor the ability to do so. Rules for secrecy may develop, making it difficult for family members to share their feelings with one another. Memories of the deceased may be discouraged or distorted due to an inability to discuss them openly. Such reactions are a form of denial because the family is unable or unwilling to accept the loss and the changes in the family's structure that have occurred. Although denial and minimization can be effective coping strategies in the short run, giving family members time to accommodate to the loss, they can become dysfunctional if the family is prevented from making needed changes in its strategies over time.

The Family's Societal, Cultural, Ethnic, and Religious Context

In general, a family's coping strategies are influenced by the societal, cultural, ethnic, and religious value orientations toward death. For example, losses that are generally unrecognized by society are typically more difficult for family members to resolve. We noted earlier the complexity created when the cause of death is one stigmatized by society, such as AIDS or suicide. Societal expectations also affect who is expected to grieve the loss of a loved one. **Unrecognized or unsanctioned grief** is grief that exists even though society does not recognize one's need, right, or capacity to grieve (Pine et al., 1990). Examples of such unrecognized family relationships include former spouses, cohabitors, or extramarital lovers; foster children; stepparents or stepchildren; partners in gay or lesbian relationships; stillbirths, miscarriages, or elective abortions; or a companion animal (Murray, 1994). In such instances, norms for grieving do not apply, thus leaving the grieving person with a greater sense of isolation and uncertainty about how to express his or her feelings. Social support from extended family members, friends, or acquaintances may be unavailable as well (Shapiro, 1994).

The family's cultural, ethnic, and religious values influence many aspects of its response to death. These factors include the rituals families establish for dealing with death, the need to see the dying relative, the openness of displays of emotion, the appropriate length of mourning, the importance of anniversary events, the role of the extended family, beliefs about what happens after death, and the established roles of men and women (Shapiro, 1996; Walsh, 1998).

Well-defined rituals that provide an important social network of support during times of grief will assist family systems in their efforts to reorganize in response to a loss. Jewish families sit shiva for seven days following a family member's death. This is a period of mourning when the family refrains from normal activities. The family receives visits from extended family and friends, and together they exchange stories about the deceased, resurrect cherished memories, and share feelings of loss. In contrast, the absence of such rituals and traditions for dealing with death may increase the vulnerability of families during these times of crisis (van der Hart, 1988; Walsh & Pryce, 2003). The lack of such rituals, combined with cultural value orientations emphasizing social autonomy and emotional self-sufficiency, may impede the abilities of white Anglo-Saxon Protestants to cope with the death of a family member. Within such families, the inability to acknowledge and share the grief of death openly and the preference for quick and efficient funerals that require little inconvenience (Walsh & McGoldrick, 2004) increase the potential for further disruptions in family life, such as divorce, suicide, or serious illness (Brown, 1989).

In other words, cultural rituals influence the manner in which a particular family responds to a death and, possibly, the amount of social support available to the family during this time of crisis. For example, in African American families it is accepted and expected that grief will be expressed freely and openly, and the extended community is openly supportive of families during times of loss. In Irish families, in contrast, grieving friends of the family are apt to get drunk, tell jokes, and treat the wake as a party with little or no expressions of grief or overt support to grieving family members (Walsh & McGoldrick, 2004).

It is, of course, important to remember, as noted in Chapter 5, that generalizations such as these cannot replace a careful examination of each family's unique social and cultural context. Variations between families within a given cultural, ethnic, or religious group can be as great as those between different cultural, ethnic, or religious groups. As such, it is important to consider the fact that societal, cultural, ethnic, and religious factors are among a broader constellation of factors, and not the sole determining factors, affecting how a family manages the stresses and demands accompanying the loss of a family member.

The Timing of the Death

Timing in this instance refers to two interrelated factors: (1) the age and generational position of the deceased; and (2) the normative developmental stressors that accompany the death (Walsh & McGoldrick, 2004).

The Age and Generational Position of the Deceased. In general, the death of older family members tends to be viewed as a natural process and, as a result, engenders less stress than the death of younger family members (Brown, 1989). This is not meant to imply that it creates no stress. However, the emotional shock waves experienced by the family when an elderly member dies are typically less intense than those experienced when a younger or middle-aged family member dies in the prime of life. This may stem in part from the fact that the "generational torch" has been passed.

Expected deaths are contrasted with "off-time" deaths—deaths that defy the accepted views on life expectancy. Such deaths, like the early death of a parent, of a young spouse, or of a child, tend to evoke a greater sense of rage and a search for an explanation (Becvar, 2001; Murray, 1994). The death of a member of the middle generation may have important consequences for the caretaking of both children and aging parents. The deaths of young and adolescent children are especially traumatic, because they defy our expectations of the natural order of life and death. For this reason, family members can be easily overwhelmed by the emotional grief that accompanies such losses. This overwhelming grief can resonate throughout the family system, potentially affecting its functioning and adaptation.

The Broader Developmental Context of the Death. Death generally occurs within the broader developmental context of the family. That is, death usually takes place along with other normative stressors, such as the birth of one child, the leaving home of another, or the marriage of a third. The co-occurrence of these other normative stressors complicates the family's grieving process and capacity for reorganization.

In the next section, we will examine in greater detail the importance of timing in determining the family system's response to death. We will pay particular attention to the family's broader developmental context and the impact of death on multiple generations within the family.

A Multigenerational, Developmental Perspective on Death

A multigenerational, developmental perspective assumes that the death of a family member sends an emotional shock wave throughout the entire family system. Just how the family system responds and adapts to this crisis is influenced by the various factors discussed previously, including the nature of the death, the position of the deceased in the family, the family's history of losses, the family's openness and level of adaptability, the family's broader cultural context, and the particular timing of the death.

Because no two family systems are the same, it is hard to predict how a death will affect the multiple generations of a family. Despite this uniqueness, family scholars have identified certain "systemic regularities" that tend to characterize a family's adaptation to death at different life-cycle stages (Shapiro, 1994; Walsh & McGoldrick, 2004). In the following sections, we examine how the response of a family system to the death of a member is influenced by the interaction between the age and generational position of the deceased and the broader family developmental context. Although it is difficult to capture the complexity and diversity that define each death, placing a death within a developmental context is useful in organizing some of the tasks that are critical at each stage of the family life cycle.

Transition from Adolescence to Adulthood

Sometimes a death occurs to a child, parent, or grandparent while the family is simultaneously adjusting to the launching of adolescent family members. When the death is that of an adolescent who is in the midst of being launched, the event is clearly off-time. Furthermore, the stress engendered by a death at this stage is exacerbated by the fact that it is often caused by sudden and/or traumatic events, such as auto accidents, drug overdoses, suicide, homicide, or terminal illness. Consider, for example, that in 2002, unintentional injury was the leading cause of death and accounted for approximately 52 percent of all deaths among adolescents fifteen to nineteen years of age. Just over half of these unintentional deaths were the result of motor vehicle crashes. Alcohol was a significant contributor to these auto-related deaths. Nearly one-third of adolescent drivers killed in crashes had been drinking. Firearms were the next leading cause of death due to unintentional injury, accounting for 23 percent of deaths in this age group. Besides unintentional injury, other leading causes of death among adolescents were homicide and suicide, accounting for 14 percent and 11 percent, respectively, of all deaths reported (Child Trends, 2006). When deaths occur in these unexpected and dramatic ways, parents, in particular, may experience profound feelings of guilt over not monitoring the adolescent's behavior more carefully. Both siblings and parents may experience conflicting feelings of anger at the deceased adolescent's impulsive actions as well as sadness over the senseless loss.

Should the death be that of a parent, the adolescent's developmental focus on individuation from the family can complicate the grieving process. The adolescent's efforts to individuate from the deceased parent may have included ambivalent and conflicting feelings toward the parent that are now left unresolved. The adolescent's wish to be out of the parent's control may lead to feelings of guilt. The adolescent's reluctance to share his or her feelings with others may result in feeling cut off or alienated from the family. Rather than express their feelings directly, adolescents may choose instead to act on their feelings by becoming involved in drugs, stealing, misbehavior at school, fighting, or sexual activity (Lehman et al., 1989).

If the young adult has already left home, the death of a parent can challenge the successful resolution of the just-completed launching phase. The young person may experience a pull to slip back into a more dependent relationship with the surviving parent and other family members. Those who have been overly close to the family or who have had to cut off emotionally or physically in order to leave home may be especially reluctant to reenter the family system at this time. Returning home to grieve the loss or to support a dying family member through a prolonged illness may hinder the young adult's efforts to deal with age-appropriate tasks such as managing his or her own household, pursuing a career, or entering into new relationship commitments.

Although the loss of a grandparent at this stage of the family life cycle may be perceived as on-time, such a loss can be complicated by prior unresolved issues within the family system. This is particularly the case when unresolved issues remain between the grandparent and their own adult children. If the parent is conflicted or ambivalent about the loss of a parent or unable to accept the loss, it may be one of the adolescents in the family who act out these unresolved feelings by misbehaving (Becvar, 2001). The adolescent's misbehavior may, in effect, represent the parent's own inability to come to terms with the loss.

Transition to Marriage

Clearly, one of the most traumatic losses during this family developmental stage is the loss of one's spouse. Although relatively uncommon, such losses are likely to be sudden and traumatic. Not only does the widowed spouse have to cope with the loss of the partner, but he or she must also adjust to the loss of the marriage role (Walsh & McGoldrick, 2004). There is often an expectation within the family for a young widowed spouse to move on quickly with his or her life, which can have the effect of denying that person's pain. The surviving spouse's relationships with in-laws may be complicated by the fact that they have not been as fully defined at this stage as they would have been later in the family life cycle, when the presence of children would have helped define the in-laws' role as grandparents.

During the young-adult stage, the death of a parent may actually be less difficult following marriage than it is prior to marriage. This is especially so if the spouse left home on good terms with the parent (Walsh & McGoldrick, 2004). The partner can provide an important source of emotional support that can foster the grieving process, especially if the partner has survived the death of a parent. However, the pain of the loss can also produce strain in the marriage if the bereaved is unable to fulfill his or her family and work roles or unwilling to communicate with the partner about the loss (Guttman, 1991; Umberson, 1995). Complications can also arise at this stage if the spouse is called on by the extended family to play a caretaking role with the dying parent or the surviving parent, a role more likely to be fulfilled by daughters as opposed to sons. This can strain the marriage if the partner feels that the bereaved spouse's primary loyalty is no longer to the marriage. Such caretaking burdens at the early stage of marriage can shift the focus back toward the family of origin, thus complicating the couple's adjustment to the new marital subsystem.

Other losses during the life-cycle stage can also impact the marriage. The loss of grandparents at this stage may be less traumatic than at earlier stages because young adults who have just recently married have had the opportunity to know their grandparents throughout their childhood and early adulthood. However, the overall impact of such a loss is highly dependent on the factors noted earlier, including the nature of the death, the grandparent's position in the family, and the centrality of the grandparent in the young adult's life.

Miscarriages, stillbirths, and abortions are especially difficult for young couples to grieve, particularly because society does not generally recognize them as serious losses. Women generally experience these unrecognized or unsanctioned losses more intensely, since they have carried the baby during pregnancy. Men, in contrast, may be more interested in moving on, possibly by having more children

(DeFrain, 1991; Stinson, Lasker, Lohmann, & Toedter, 1992). The trauma will often challenge the newly established boundary around the new marital system, requiring it to loosen in order to receive support from others outside the system. If support is not available or if the couple turns inward, two negative outcomes become possible. First, the couple may develop an "us against the world" mentality. Second, they may blame each other for the death or for not being able to relieve their sense of loss (Walsh & McGoldrick, 2004).

Families with Young Children

The death of a child is one of the most difficult to deal with, since it is generally unexpected. Because the child has not yet fulfilled the promise of his or her young life, the loss is especially difficult to comprehend and the emotional responses are especially strong. The loss of a child involves the loss of the parents' hopes and dreams (Walsh & McGoldrick, 2004). Bereaved parents of children suffer from a number of physical and mental health problems, including depression, anxiety, lost self-esteem, increased alcohol consumption, and various somatic symptoms (Rando, 1986). They may blame themselves or turn their anger, depression, or guilt toward one another, with each holding the other responsible for the death (Farnsworth & Allen, 1996). This can have a negative effect on the parents' marital relationship. Although some couples may become closer, many bereaved parents experience a distancing from each other (Lehman et al., 1989). This distancing may be due to the differing coping styles of men and women. The mother's need to express her emotions and the father's need to withdraw into isolation or work may create additional stress or conflict (E. R. Shapiro, 1996). Parents appear to do better when they have both been involved in caring for the child or when they share a consistent philosophy of life or strong religious beliefs (DeFrain, 1991; McCubbin, McCubbin, & Thompson, 1993).

Siblings are also adversely affected by the death of a child (Elizur & Kaffman, 1982; Lehman et al., 1989). Children can experience a range of emotional and behavioral reactions to such a loss, including anxiety, depressive withdrawal, a need to cling to parents, punishment-seeking, accident proneness, declining school performance, or fear of doctors and hospitals. Although these reactions are due in part to their feelings of loss, children are also highly prone to feelings of guilt. Sibling rivalry or feelings of competition for the parents' attention can leave siblings feeling responsible for the death, especially if the deceased child was ill for some time. Such feelings of responsibility can last for as long as ten to twenty years. Children may also experience **anniversary reactions** well into adulthood (Becvar, 2001). This is an emotional reliving of the death each year around the time that the death occurred.

The response by siblings to a death is also dependent on how available the parents remain to their other children. Parents may withdraw emotionally from their surviving children so as to not risk feeling the pain of another loss. In some instances, parents may become overly protective of their surviving children, thereby conveying their own anxiety and insecurity to their children

(Lehman et al., 1989). If the parents have difficulty coming to terms with the loss, they may recruit another sibling into a **replacement role**. This may create stress for the child, who is then affirmed for traits and characteristics that remind the parents of the deceased child. However, these traits may not fit with the child's own identity, leaving the child disconfirmed for acting in accordance with his or her own sense of self (Walsh & McGoldrick, 2004).

Families with young children may encounter another loss as traumatic as the death of a child, namely, the premature death of a parent. Children who lose a parent can experience feelings of depression, anxiety, and even physical illnesses for many years, perhaps well into adult life. Unresolved grieving of a parent can result in fears of separation and feelings of abandonment. This can further affect the individual's capacity to form meaningful intimate relationships at later stages of the life cycle. These reactions can be minimized when parents and other adults include the child in discussions about the deceased and other experiences associated with the loss, rather than trying to protect him or her from the pain. Although children at different ages and levels of cognitive development will cope with death in differing ways, all children need reassurance that other adult figures in their lives will remain available to ensure their safety and well-being.

Finally, the child's ability to cope with the loss of a parent will be affected by the surviving parent's emotional state and method of coping. Children model that which they observe and respond to the emotional expressions (or lack of expression) of significant others. A child's response to the death of a parent, grandparent, or other family members is greatly determined by the response of other adults within the family system. When the parent can openly deal with his or her own feelings of loss, include the child in his or her own grieving process, and remain available to support the child's needs, the child's ability to cope will be fostered (Becvar, 2001; Walsh & McGoldrick, 2004).

Middle Adulthood

During the middle-adult years, it is critical that adult children come to terms with the death of their parents. As a general rule, the reactions of adult children to a parent's death are varied, and appear to be influenced mainly by the quality of the emotional ties that existed between parent and child over time. The closer the tie, the more profound the feelings of loss and grief are likely to be. Compounding the grieving process further are the multiple personal meanings associated with the death of a parent. For instance, a parent's death can bring the adult child to a realization of his or her own mortality. In addition, the loss of a parent terminates one of the last "false assumptions" carried into adulthood from childhood about the nature of life. A parent's death forces children to confront the myth that their parents will always be available to help them. By coming to grips with this myth, individuals are able to grow into an even more independent, complete, and self-directed person (Gould, 1978).

In many respects, the reactions of adult children to the death of elderly parents is tied to the manner in which the separation–individuation drama has been played out during earlier stages in the family life cycle. When the relationships of adult children and aging parents are based on mutuality and intimacy, a situation is created in which the loss of a parent is keenly felt but also accepted more easily. Relationships dominated by antipathy or an ongoing struggle around issues of separateness and connectedness can interfere with the ability of adult children to accept the loss of a parent. Some of these adult children will hold on to their anger and refuse to acknowledge the parent, even in death. Others will experience guilt at not being able to reconcile their differences with the parent. In the broader perspective, the stress and conflict that have dominated the parent–child relationship all along remain a factor that fuels emotional reactivity and interferes with adult children's ability to take personal control over their lives even after the death of the parent (Bowen, 1976; Walsh & McGoldrick, 2004).

Later Life

The death of a spouse constitutes a significant stressor for a surviving spouse. Because of marital customs (men marry women of younger ages) and differences in life expectancy, more women than men experience this particular life crisis. Recent statistics indicate that there are more than 13.7 million widowed persons in the United States, and approximately 80 percent of them are women (American Association of Retired Persons, 2001). In addition, **widowhood** represents a more permanent change in the lifestyle of women when compared to men. The vast majority of men remarry within a two-year period following the death of a spouse (in part, due to the large pool of eligible partners available to them). In contrast, following the death of a spouse, the vast majority of women remain single and live alone (McGoldrick & Walsh, 2005).

Widows are challenged by the multiple losses that accompany the death of a spouse. The loss of a long-term attachment can constitute a significant loss of lifestyle, identity, and support. For most women, the loss of the husband is most keenly felt as a loss of emotional support (Lopata, 1996). Another stress is the loss of income and increased risk of poverty (Hungerford, 2001). In a similar vein, loneliness, depression, and decline in economic well-being are central themes running through the experiences of widowed men (Berardo, 2001; Marshall, 1986).

These reactions of survivors are understandable given the degree to which the loss of a spouse changes both the structure of the family and the strategies and rules employed for the execution of system tasks. Tasks such as managing the household and family finances undergo dramatic restructuring. Shared recreation and leisure activities are disrupted. Learning to live alone requires devising strategies for combating social isolation. Such changes are far-reaching and pervasive (Lopata, 1996).

A considerable amount of time is generally needed to adapt successfully to the changes in lifestyle that widowhood brings (Silverman, 1986). Over time, those who successfully adjust develop strategies for coping with day-to-day problems and establishing ties to others. They find new outlets for their energies and identities (Lopata, 1996). Although widowhood is a stressful event, it is also an event to which most survivors eventually manage to adjust.

Unresolved Grief and Family Strategies

Not all families resolve losses as successfully as others. Families vary in the extent to which they can complete the successive tasks of openly acknowledging the reality of the death, sharing the pain of grief, reorganizing the family system, and reinvesting in other relationships and life pursuits. Some have suggested that even in successful families, the loss is never fully grieved. Memories of the deceased, anniversaries of the death, or other significant family events such as births or marriages can evoke painful feelings of loss and separation (Bagarozzi & Anderson, 1989; E. R. Shapiro, 1996). Each new loss in the family can awaken the emotions and behavioral responses to past losses (Byng-Hall, 1991). When previous losses have been successfully grieved, these reactions are generally more moderate and time-limited. However, when the family has not fully resolved previous losses, the impact of losses can pile up and have significant effects on the family's interactional strategies. In this section, we will discuss the impact of unresolved grief on the family's strategies.

Identity Strategies

As was noted in Chapter 2, information about who we are and how we are expected to behave with others is embedded within the family's primary themes. These themes are passed down from earlier generations as part of the family's legacy. Although a family's themes may be linked to long-standing traditions and ethnic, cultural, or religious values, many are clearly affected by unresolved experiences of loss. Such themes as rejection, abandonment, or deprivation may derive in part from feelings of being left behind following the death of a close family member, and may leave family members feeling overly protective of one another and highly sensitive to future losses. This, in turn, may leave family members reluctant to risk getting close to others who may also abandon, reject, or deprive them.

Themes related to unresolved loss may also lead families to attempt to control the identities of one or more family members. This is the case when a child is expected to take on the identity of a deceased sibling or other family member. In some instances, a child may be conceived with the intention of replacing a family member who has died. Such expectations can undermine the family member's personal control over his or her own identity.

Boundary Strategies

The death of a family member requires the family to open its external boundaries to allow the entrance of others into the system to share in the grieving process. To the extent families are able to do so, they can experience the curative effects of social and emotional support from others, a factor that has been found to foster successful coping with a loss (Eckenrode, 1991). Some families, however, may opt to close their external boundaries, which can intensify the level of stress and tension that must be managed within the system. In some instances, the circumstances surrounding the death may contribute to the closing of the family's boundaries. For example, when the death was caused by random community violence, a flawed public policy, or the actions of corrupt or incompetent public officials, the family's response could be to close ranks. This might also be accompanied by the development of a corresponding theme such as "distrust of outsiders" or "the untrustworthiness of others." Some studies have found that it can be more functional when the family is able to mobilize itself against an external threat than when family members focus the stress internally and blame each other for the death (Patterson & McCubbin, 1983).

Thus, how the family regulates its internal boundaries following a family member's death is a critical factor in the family's successful adaptation. As we have noted, family members may differ in their preferred strategies for coping with a family member's death. Some may require opportunities to express their grief openly, while others may prefer to withdraw to manage their feelings on their own. Although there is no "proper" way for all individuals to grieve, these differences in individual styles can become problematic when members refuse to accept these differences as legitimate or choose to hold others responsible for their own pain and suffering. Externalizing one's pain onto others often takes the form of blaming others, either for the death itself or for failing to ease one's sense of emptiness or sorrow. The critical factor is the extent to which family members are permitted to exercise their own unique styles of grieving and are able to receive the emotional support they require.

Maintenance Strategies

The death of a family member has an immediate impact upon the family's resources of time, energy, and money. If the death was preceded by a lengthy illness, the family's finances, time allocations, and energy are likely to have been depleted dealing with this crisis. Following the death, the family's resources will be devoted to the various tasks associated with grieving. This will include making arrangements for the funeral and burial, setting aside time to talk about and remember the deceased, attending to the emotional needs of various family members, and reorganizing family members' role responsibilities to accommodate the loss. If the deceased was a central adult figure in the household, many of the family strategies for managing tasks such as cooking, cleaning, home repairs, and managing finances will have to be redefined.

However, the demands of grieving may require a postponement of many of these decisions and changes. Thus, the strategies that were once in place are no longer effective, and yet the new strategies that are required to maintain the family system have not yet been defined. The result can be a sense of confusion, disorientation, and disorganization that is common during periods of family crisis. Family members may experience a sense of restlessness and aimless searching for something to do. There may be an accompanying inability to initiate and maintain organized patterns of behavior (Crosby & Jose, 1983; McCubbin & Patterson, 1983).

Another alternative is that family members may instead focus their energies on maintaining the household rather than addressing their grief. They may become so preoccupied with tasks that their grief reactions become delayed for days, weeks, or even years (Littlewood, 1992). This delayed reaction may have the immediate effect of maintaining family morale and helping the family to remain organized and functional. However, over time, the family members' inability to confront their feelings of pain and grief can lead to distorted grief reactions such as the development of symptoms that belonged to the deceased; medical problems (e.g., ulcerative colitis, asthma, rheumatoid arthritis); intense feelings of anger and hostility; agitated depression; alterations in relationships with relatives or friends; self-defeating behaviors; or a loss of social contacts with others (Murray, 1994).

Strategies for Managing the Family's Emotional Climate

One of the critical tasks in adjusting to the death of a family member is developing strategies for nurturing and supporting family members through their grieving process. Families must also be able to maintain a sense of family cohesion and utilize effective strategies for managing conflict and tension. The emotional intensity that accompanies a death can severely test the family's strategies for managing its emotional environment. The essential factors here are whether family members are encouraged and supported in their emotional expressions and the extent to which the family system can remain open to the wide range of emotional expressions, including feelings of anger, resentment, blame, remorse, guilt, emptiness, alienation, rejection, abandonment, embarrassment, helplessness, vulnerability, and hurt.

Families may opt to minimize their pain and sorrow through a variety of strategies that have the effect of narrowing the range of emotions that are permitted expression. One such strategy is maintaining a sense of secrecy about the death. Here facts about the deceased or the circumstances surrounding the death are kept from certain family members. This is especially common when adults in the family attempt to protect children from feeling the pain of their loss. It may also be that some family members are perceived as being too vulnerable to be able to tolerate the whole truth. A more extreme version of this strategy is for the family to develop what has been called a "shroud of silence." Here the family enacts rules that prohibit family members from talking about or remembering the deceased. Another strategy is for one or more family members to distance themselves physically from the family or the grieving process. Examples are when family members state that they are too busy to return home for the funeral, or when a family member decides to take a long trip directly following the death. Another strategy is to distance oneself psychologically from the intense feelings by denying or minimizing one's emotional experiences. Although these strategies may be functional in the short term in that they provide the family with needed time to adjust to the loss, these patterns can become dysfunctional when they are maintained over time, thereby adversely affecting the family's ability to maintain family support, cohesion, and effective conflict management.

Strategies for Managing Family Stress

A final critical task of a family dealing with death is to adapt to the stress engendered by the changes it must now face. As noted in Chapter 2, stress is the degree of pressure exerted on the family to alter the strategies it employs to accomplish its basic tasks. Stress is experienced in response to events that require changes or adaptations on the part of the family. This stress derives from both horizontal and vertical sources that can pile up, thus adding to the overall level of stress that must be managed.

Thus, in assessing the family's capacity to cope with the death of a family member, it is important to take into account these other stressors. For instance, the death of a family member can occur along with other horizontal stressors, such as the birth of a child, the engagement of an adult daughter, a parent's retirement, or the job loss of the family's primary breadwinner. It is also important to consider the vertical, or historical, stressors that have occurred earlier or that have been passed down from generation to generation within the family system. These vertical stressors include the attitudes, expectations, taboos, secrets, and prior unresolved losses that a family has incorporated.

For example, let us consider a family that has dealt with previous losses by closing its external boundaries and coming to view outsiders as dangerous or untrustworthy. Over time, it has developed a theme that equates losses with "being abandoned by significant others when they are most needed." Such a theme can leave family members reluctant to confide or trust in one another for fear of being abandoned by them as well. Their strategy for managing the family's emotional environment is to distance from one another by keeping critical feelings and information secret. As a result, the emotional intensity surrounding deaths and other critical life experiences is never fully expressed. This diminished level of emotional expression is further reinforced by interactional strategies that emphasize avoiding conflict, thus leaving a variety of important issues between family members unresolved. When a death occurs, the family members' response is to enact strategies that deny or minimize its impact and maintain distance and isolation from one another. The capacity of family members to support one another's emotional expressions and reactions to the death is thereby constrained. Thus, the strategies that have been put in place in the family over time become reenacted with each subsequent loss that occurs within the family system.

This example illustrates how the multigenerational patterns of interaction that exist within a particular family contribute to the overall level of stress it experiences as it copes with a death. This historical legacy interacts with the ongoing ordinary and extraordinary demands to influence the level of stress within the family system. Thus, the manner in which previous losses have been resolved becomes an important factor in determining the family's response to the current loss. Previous unresolved losses can pile up and combine with other vertical stresses to magnify the demands upon the family in the present. Legacies, images, themes, myths, and previous strategies of coping with loss comprise a multigenerational process that is enacted with each succeeding loss.

Finally, coping with the loss of a family member is enhanced when the family and its members are able to come to a cognitive understanding of the person's death. Death can dramatically alter the family and individual members' world views. Families must often face daunting questions about the rationality, controllability, and fairness of life, especially when the death was sudden or unexpected (DeFrain, 1991). The family must develop what has been termed a **healing theory** (Figley, 1989). The healing theory helps the family to define the event in such a way so as not to deny the pain of the loss but to make it possible for the family to evolve a new perspective that once again establishes a positive sense of control, fairness, and trust in the future. Some find significance through religious or spiritual beliefs. Others find meaning in other ways, perhaps by attempting to right a perceived wrong by seeking justice or by making positive changes in one's life to honor the memory of the deceased. Whatever the means, finding a sense of meaning and explanation for the death can facilitate the coping process by offering a sense of comfort and cognitive understanding to the event. A sense of meaning can also provide a sense of continuity between the past, present, and future that can positively affect the functioning of future generations of the family system (Bagarozzi & Anderson, 1989; Byng-Hall, 1991; Shapiro, 1996).

As we have seen in this section, the death of a family member can have an immediate impact on all of the basic tasks a family must perform and on the strategies it has evolved over time. Family members can feel alienated and isolated from one another, anxious and perhaps depressed. Roles and responsibilities become confused. The family may split into factions. Coalitions and triangles can disrupt the ability of the family to manage conflict and support its members. The family environment is experienced as chaotic and disorganized. Family members no longer are assured of receiving the needed physical, social, emotional, and/or psychological benefits from the family, and the survival of the family itself may even be in question. However, for most families these immediate reactions are followed by a reorganization of the family system in a way that acknowledges the lost member's place in the family while also allowing the family to move on by developing new strategies, interests, and activities.

Conclusions

At the conclusion of this chapter readers are encouraged to refrain from viewing the family life cycle as a linear process. The family life cycle does not consist simply of a beginning, middle, and end, despite the fact that it is often discussed in this way. The family must address a series of common developmental milestones determined in part by the ages of its members. However, the family can encounter any number of sudden or unexpected life events that have the capacity to alter the family's developmental trajectory, thereby creating stress and disorganization. How the family manages its tasks during these periods is dependent on the number and intensity of other horizontal stressors that pile up simultaneously and on how previous generations of the family managed their tasks as well.

In the case of a family member's death, the horizontal stressors include other normative life-cycle events as well as other non-normative events that occur simultaneously. Horizontal stressors also include the specific context of the death, which takes into account the nature of the death; the role the deceased played in the family; the family's history of previous losses; the family's racial, ethnic, and religious orientations; the family's overall level of openness and adaptability; the overall quality of support within the family system; and the timing of the death. The timing of the death, in turn, is strongly affected by the point in the family life cycle at which it occurs.

As we have seen, a death in the family can severely alter all of the basic tasks families are called on to perform. Strategies for managing individual and family identity, external and internal boundaries, household maintenance, emotional climate, and stressful events are all challenged by the death of a family member.

The family's adaptation to the loss is dependent on how successfully it manages several additional tasks, including how able family members are to acknowledge the reality of the death, share their experiences of pain and grief, reorganize the family system in response to the loss, and move on toward the future by investing in other relationships and new life pursuits.

Key Terms

Anniversary reaction An emotional reliving of a person's death each year around the time that the death occurred.

Emotional shock wave The emotional response to a death felt throughout the family system, producing stress and altering relationships even among family members who are emotionally removed from the deceased.

Healing theory A cognitive understanding of a death that helps the family to accept the pain of the loss and makes it possible for the family to evolve a new perspective that reestablishes a positive sense of control, fairness, and trust in the future.

Replacement role When a child is conceived to take the place of a deceased family member, or when a surviving child is affirmed for traits that remind parents of a deceased child.

Unrecognized or unsanctioned grief Grief that exists even though society does not recognize one's need, right, or capacity to grieve.

Widowhood A role transition brought on by the death of a spouse.

CHAPTER 16

Divorce

Chapter Overview

Divorce has a profound effect on the family system and its members, especially over the short term. The long-term consequences of divorce depend on many factors and may be positive or negative.

In recent years, theorists and researchers have come to view divorce not so much as an atypical or pathological event but rather as an alternate developmental pathway. Today, many families experience divorce, and perhaps single parenthood or remarriage, rather than follow the traditional, intact, two-parent family model.

Like any developmental process, divorce can be viewed as occurring in a series of stages and transitions. Spouses must first cognitively accept that something is wrong in the marriage. Those who divorce must then pass through a period of discussing their dissatisfaction with one another, eventually deciding to separate, and finally reorganizing as a new family unit. Spouses with children must deal with the additional tasks of resolving child custody issues and maintaining a coparenting relationship while severing the marriage relationship.

Healthy adaptation for adults generally includes accepting the reality that the marriage has ended, making peace with the former spouse, accepting one's own role in the marital breakup, developing sources of social support, establishing a sense of competency as a single person, and looking to the future rather than to the past. Children's adaptation is fostered when they, too, can accept the reality that the parents' marriage has ended, have opportunities to express their feelings, and receive reassurance that they are still loved by both parents and that loving one parent will not jeopardize their place in the other parent's affections.

Divorce

Divorce, single parenthood, and remarriage have become significant events in the lives of many contemporary families. Couples of all ages at all stages of the life cycle experience **divorce**, or the legal termination of a marriage. Overall, the national rate of divorce among first marriages has been hovering just under 50 percent (Stevenson & Wolfers, 2007).

Because of these rates of marital disruption, it has been estimated that as many as 40 percent of all children will be faced with their parents' divorce and spend an average of five years in a single-parent home before the custodial parent remarries (Amato, 2000). Seventy-five percent of divorced mothers and eighty percent of divorced fathers remarry (Coleman, Ganong, & Fine, 2000). However, the rates of remarriage among African Americans and Hispanics are lower (Amato, 2000). Given this evidence, it is difficult to view divorce as a static event. Rather, it seems more appropriate to view divorce, single parenthood, and remarriage as a series of developmental transitions, each with the potential to alter the family's structure and patterns of interaction (Carter & McGoldrick, 2005b).

In recent years, researchers have moved away from the view that divorce and its aftermath are atypical or pathological. Instead, research has focused more on the diversity that characterizes family members' responses to divorce. More attention also has been given to the factors that either facilitate or inhibit the family's adaptation. This chapter examines the experience of divorce and its effect on the family system and its members. In Chapter 17, the implications of becoming a single-parent household and the challenges this presents to the family system and its members, including the custodial parent, the children, and the noncustodial parent, will be discussed. The complex process of becoming a remarried family will be the focus of the last chapter.

Although this discussion has been divided into three chapters for organizational purposes, it is important to emphasize that the content of these chapters is highly interrelated. First, as noted above, the experience of divorce often initiates a series of subsequent family developmental transitions. Second, the success or failure of a family to reorganize as a remarried system, as with any developmental process, depends on the manner in which the earlier transitions into divorce and single parenthood were managed. Successful resolution of the stresses and strains of divorce and single parenthood enhances the remarried system's capacity to adapt, while unresolved stresses and conflicts from these earlier periods can interfere with subsequent adaptation.

Divorce as a Family Process

Just as it is possible to view divorce as being one transition in a series of developmental transitions, so too it is possible to view divorce itself as involving a series of stages or transitions. The process of divorce begins long before the actual decision to obtain a legal divorce is made. Couples who divorce first experience a crisis in their relationship characterized by unresolved conflicts and a great deal of frustration, pain, and anger.

Prolonged experiences of marital distress lie at the foundation of the decision to divorce. **Marital distress** is a term that refers to those situations where one or both members of a marriage-like relationship have come to believe that their relationship suffers from serious, long-standing problems that threaten the stability of the relationship (Sabatelli & Chadwick, 2000). While it is common for us to speak of distressed relationships, in this chapter, the term "distress" refers to an individual's experiences of, and beliefs about, his or her lifetime partnership. Extremes of distress are built on a legacy of unhappiness and dissatisfaction resulting from the mismanagement of the ordinary difficulties encountered by all couples. Distress results from (1) a high level of complaints that lead to conflicts; and (2) the inability to manage these conflicts in a way that promotes a sense of cohesion and ongoing intimacy within the relationship.

Divorce generally becomes a viable option after other strategies for resolving marital differences have been tried and found to be unsatisfying or unsuccessful. After all, at some earlier point in the relationship's development, the spouse was viewed as a "good choice" (Kitson & Morgan, 1990), possibly even as the "one and only" choice. Divorce dissolves the family's primary bond and dramatically alters its identity (Ahrons, 2004). Thus, the decision to divorce is generally made over a period of time with a great deal of ambivalence, confusion, and uncertainty.

It is also important to note that many individuals in distressed relationships ultimately will not divorce. This is because, in spite of the unhappiness within the relationship, the costs of, and barriers to, dissolving the relationship can be quite high. That is, because relationships have a history and persist over time, constraints or barriers to the termination of the relationship build and can make it difficult for people to leave a distressed relationship (Levinger, 1999; Sabatelli, 1999). The time invested in the relationship, the social network support for the relationship, financial interdependence, the presence of children, or religious convictions all act as factors that increase the likelihood that a person might remain in a relationship in spite of the erosion of happiness. This is important to keep in mind because we have no way of really knowing how many individuals reside in unhappy marriages and might choose to divorce if it were not so difficult to leave.

Researchers and theorists generally recognize that divorce is just one step in a series of family transitions. Recent studies have emphasized the diversity in patterns of change and adjustment that these families undergo. Characteristics of the individuals involved, family interaction strategies, and extrafamilial factors all serve to undermine or support the adjustment of spouses and children as they cope with separations, loss, and the challenges of changing circumstances (Baum, 2004; Hetherington, 2003a; Kelly, 2003). The process of divorce begins long before the actual filing of legal papers and extends far beyond its impact on the immediate family. Children of divorce may suffer long-term consequences, and subsequent generations of the family system can also be affected (Amato & Cheadle, 2005). These different transitions are described in the following sections.

Predivorce Family Dynamics

A key to understanding the later stages of the divorce process is the spouses' personal characteristics and the predivorce relationship. Longitudinal studies of couples who later divorced have found that partners often had high rates of alcohol and substance abuse, antisocial behavior, depression, economic problems, and stressful life events during the marriage (Hetherington, 2003a). As noted in earlier chapters, an effective spousal relationship involves open and supportive communication between partners. Successful parenting involves regularly discussing matters pertaining to the children, making joint decisions regarding the children, and supporting one another as parents. In contrast, the interactions of couples who are likely to divorce are characterized by high levels of conflict, poor problem solving, and an inability to listen and respond to the other's feelings (Amato & Booth, 1997; Hetherington, 2003b; Kelly, 2003). For instance, Gottman and his colleagues found that married couples with a set of specific interactional characteristics had an almost 100 percent probability of getting divorced within four years. The interactions of these couples were characterized by criticism, defensiveness, contempt, stonewalling, and an inability to repair the relationship by de-escalating conflicts (Gottman, 1999; Gottman & Notarius, 2002). Stonewalling occurred when one partner withdrew from the interaction. In Gottman's research, men were most likely to engage in stonewalling behaviors. Although lesser degrees of criticism, defensiveness, and stonewalling were found to be present in stable marriages as well, contempt was not. The presence of contempt in the marriage was found to be the most severe risk factor among couples who ultimately divorced. Contempt was defined as any statement or behavior that put oneself on a higher plane than one's partner. It was generally accompanied by a mocking or demeaning tone or gesture (Gottman, 1999a).

The parenting practices in families likely to divorce are often inadequate. Parents who will later divorce have been found to have more negativity, irritability, and less warmth and control when compared to parents who remain married (Hetherington, 2003a). Their children exhibit numerous problems before the marital breakup such as conduct disorders, internalizing disorders (anxiety, depression), poor self-esteem, poor social skills, and low achievement (Amato, 2000; Hanson, 1999; Hetherington, 1999). As we will see in later sections, children who live in high-conflict family environments experience many of the same adjustment difficulties as those whose parents actually divorce.

Decision to Divorce

The transition into the divorce process begins with **individual cognition**, which occurs when a spouse first realizes that he or she is feeling dissatisfied or distressed in the marriage (Ahrons, 2005). This first step toward divorce is rarely mutual. Instead, it begins with the spouse who is the most distressed by the marriage being more invested in ending it (Emery & Sbarra, 2002). In about two-thirds to three-fourths of all divorces it is the woman who initiates the process (Ahrons, 2005).

The reasons for contemplating divorce are many. For those who have been married only a few years, the reason may have to do with the partner not fulfilling one's idealized image of "prince (or princess) charming" with whom one will live "happily ever after." Although many individuals are able to balance their expectations for the perfect mate with a more realistic appraisal of the partner as an imperfect human being, those who cannot are likely to become resentful and unhappy about what the other does not provide rather than building on what the partner can actually offer. Other recently married individuals enter marriage feeling empty and hoping their partner will fill the void left from earlier family of origin experiences of physical, emotional, or sexual abuse; parental absenteeism or neglect; substance abuse; poverty; or homelessness. When the partner is unable to fulfill all of their unmet needs, they may re-experience feelings of disappointment and despair that are now attributed to the spouse (Bowen, 1978; Kaslow, 2000). Others may become disaffected when they discover that their partner has been secretive about an addiction, prior involvement in a criminal lifestyle, a history of mental illness in the family, an out-of-wedlock child, or an abortion. Later in the marriage reasons such as sexual incompatibility; an extramarital affair; in-law problems; and disagreements over money, childrearing, lifestyles, values, or religion may be the turning point (Kaslow, 2000).

The first realization that something is wrong in the marriage may begin with a small, nagging feeling of dissatisfaction that grows in strength, retreats, and then flares up again. For others, the initial realization may be experienced indirectly through feelings of depression. The spouse may realize only that he or she is unhappy but be unable initially to attribute this feeling to the marriage. Such denial, or an inability to see the problem situation clearly, is a common characteristic of the individual cognition period. However, the hallmark of this period for the dissatisfied spouse is ambivalence. The experience is an emotional one characterized by obsession, vacillation, and anguish (Ahrons, 2004).

At this point, the prospect of confronting the partner or addressing problems in the marriage is often too threatening to entertain. Instead, during this period the spouse may resort to blaming the other as a way of relieving stress and tension, or the spouse may begin to collect evidence of the partner's annoying behaviors to build a case that can justify the decision to leave (Ahrons, 2005). As this pattern escalates, the spouse may rigidly view the other as the culprit and attribute less and less of the responsibility for the marriage to himself or herself.

This period can also be a highly stressful time, especially for children, who can be drawn into coalitions and triangles and be expected to side with one parent against the other. Such loyalty binds present no-win situations for children. In some instances, one of the children, usually the one most attached or most emotionally tuned into the family system (Bowen, 1978), may develop a problem. He or she may become depressed, begin failing at school, or start to misbehave. Again, the spouses may not connect these changes in the child's behavior with the problems in the marriage.

Some spouses who are used to a high level of conflict in the marriage may decide to remain together at this point rather than risk the changes and uncertainty that would accompany separation or divorce. However, as noted earlier, research has shown that these kinds of stable, highly conflicted marriages can be just as damaging to children's growth and development as the disorganization associated with divorce, especially if the postmarital relationship is less conflicted than the predivorce one (Amato, 2000; Davies & Cummings, 1994; Hanson, 1999).

The kind of resolution chosen by the spouse during this transition will vary according to the couple's earlier coping patterns. Some may decide to delay separation and divorce until a less disruptive time. For some, this might be until the children are grown. Others may decide to "divorce emotionally" (Bowen, 1978). This may entail devoting less time and energy to the marriage, avoiding the partner, and spending more time on outside interests while maintaining the "facade of an intact marriage." Such a strategy may protect the individual from further distress, but this emotional withdrawal will inevitably reverberate through the family system (Ahrons, 2005). Still others may focus all of their attention on a misbehaving child who becomes the family's scapegoat and is blamed for all of the family's problems (Bagarozzi & Anderson, 1989; Vogel & Bell, 1968).

Regardless of the strategy chosen at this time, the outcome is generally one of maintaining the family's homeostasis. Despite the growing tension, family members continue to meet their basic roles and responsibilities, and the family's basic tasks are maintained in the system's customary ways. However, the strategies that are typically chosen by families who proceed further into the divorce process tend to heighten rather than diminish the family's level of stress.

Separation

The degree of crisis that emerges when one parent moves out of the home depends on how well family members have adjusted to the realization that the marriage has come to an end. Couples commonly engage in a long transition of **separation**. There may be one or several separations followed by efforts to reconcile before the final decision to separate is actually made. These efforts are generally tied to lingering feelings of attachment for the spouse, ambivalence about ending the marriage, and feelings of guilt over the spouse's or children's distress.

The separation period is characterized by a high degree of uncertainty and disequilibrium. The most typical pattern, occurring in 90 percent of the families who ultimately divorce, is for the father to move out of the home while the mother and children remain (Ahrons, 2005). Such a change calls into question the family's identity as a cohesive unit, disrupts the family's internal and external boundaries, and alters the manner in which the family manages its daily household tasks. Children may wonder if both of their parents are still part of their family. They may be confused about where the departed parent has gone and upset by their reduced access to him or her. Parental roles and responsibilities change. For example, previous strategies for managing family finances, housecleaning, and child care must be renegotiated to take into account one spouse's move to a separate residence.

This state of **boundary ambiguity**, or confusion about who is in the family and who is not, is highly stressful (Boss, 1980, 1988). If the family reorganizes as a single-parent family and reallocates the separated parents' roles and responsibilities to remaining members, it can stabilize temporarily. However, the family can also look forward to another period of disequilibrium if the absent parent later returns. Furthermore, having achieved a new equilibrium, they may even resist or resent the absent parent's return. On the other hand, if the family maintains the absent parent's psychological presence within the family and chooses not to reallocate his or her role and responsibilities, the family remains disorganized and confused.

Families in the separation transition face other stresses as well. It is at this point that extended family, friends, and the wider community learn about the couple's separation. Significant others can possibly serve as resources and sources of support, but they can also serve as additional sources of stress depending on their reactions to the couple's separation. For instance, responses from one's parents such as, "See, I told you that you were making a big mistake when you married that bum in the first place," may compound feelings of failure and low self-esteem rather than promote coping.

This is also the point at which the couple begins the tasks of the economic and legal divorce (Ahrons, 2005). Economic tasks often involve dividing up finances and assets, possibly selling the family home and negotiating child support arrangements. These activities have the potential to escalate conflict and stress greatly. Power struggles may ensue. Winning the battle for material possessions can come to represent a last-ditch attempt to have one's unfulfilled needs met by the spouse symbolically or to get even with the partner for past wrongs.

Legal Divorce

The separation period also marks the legal system's entrance into the divorce process. Questions regarding spousal support, child custody, child support, and visitation are ultimately decided in the courts. For families with children, a key priority is deciding **child custody** issues.

Child custody decisions define the parameters of each parent's relationship with the children. Custody arrangements define who is responsible for child care, who makes decisions about the children's welfare, where children will live, and how much time each parent will have with the children. In **sole custody** arrangements, one parent assumes complete responsibility for child care with the other parent generally receiving visitation rights, and, in many instances, responsibility for child support. In cases of abuse or neglect, the noncustodial parent may be denied access to his or her children completely. A sole custody arrangement essentially defines the family as a single-parent household. The external and internal boundaries that become established reflect the noncustodial parent's limited access to the family system.

Another possibility is a **split custody** arrangement. In this case, one parent has legal and physical custody of one or more children, and the other parent has legal and physical custody of one or more other children. Research suggests that this type of custody arrangement remains relatively infrequent, occurring in only about 2 percent of child custody cases (Kaplan, Ade-Ridder, & Hennon, 1991). It is more likely to occur when children are older.

In contrast to sole custody or split custody, **joint custody** allows both parents to continue to be parents to all of their children despite the divorce. The family becomes a **binuclear family system** comprised of two active and involved parents and two separate households (Ahrons, 2005). In this instance, both parents remain involved in child-rearing and are responsible for decisions about the children's welfare, ranging from where the children will live to how much allowance they should receive to whether they should go to overnight summer camp. Joint custody requires spouses to negotiate the complex process of creating a rigid boundary between themselves as spouses while maintaining an open and flexible boundary between themselves as parents.

Although no-fault divorce legislation in many states has made the legal process more straightforward, the legal system still requires spouses to become adversaries, each with his or her own attorney. Because the legal context is one of "win or lose," power struggles between spouses can be further exaggerated. Often children become pawns during court motions and hearings and are forced to take sides. The custodial parent, the parent with whom the children reside most regularly, may interfere with visitation or shared parenting arrangements simply by refusing to comply; not having children ready when the noncustodial parent comes to pick them up; or refusing to share information about the children's healthcare, schooling, or out-of-school activities. The custodial parent may also make charges in court or with social service agencies about the noncustodial parent's unfitness as a parent. The noncustodial parent may retaliate by failing to make child-support payments, bringing the children back late from scheduled visits, threatening to take the children away, or undermining the authority of the other parent with the children. Underlying these behaviors are unresolved feelings of attachment, anger, betrayal, and resentment toward the former partner that are now being played out in the legal arena.

In recent years, **divorce mediation** has emerged as an alternative to court litigation. Mediation offers couples the opportunity to minimize conflict over personal, economic, or child-related differences by concretely examining their options in a goal-focused and task-oriented manner. The goal is to make constructive decisions in a more informed manner before appearing in court (Kaslow, 2000). When both spouses share a sense of personal control over the process, conflicts can be minimized and the potential for a win-win outcome is enhanced (Bay & Braver, 1990).

Ultimately, the extent to which power struggles over finances or child custody can be avoided depends on how successfully the family has managed earlier transitions. Spouses who have fully accepted the reality of their marital difficulties and openly communicated their intentions for divorce with other family members are more likely to manage the stresses of the separation transition effectively. Even though lingering feelings of attachment, ambivalence, guilt, anger, or resentment are common at this time, the presence of these feelings often indicates the extent to which unresolved conflicts between spouses remain. The greater the level of unresolved conflict between spouses, the greater the likelihood that subsequent transitions will be stressful.

Family Reorganization

It is during the **family reorganization** transition that the family must clarify its new internal and external boundaries, redefine its identity, stabilize the family's emotional environment, and reestablish strategies for managing the household. In the case of married couples without children, these tasks are undertaken in the context of two separate and independent households. Families with children, however, must face the additional priority of defining a **coparenting relationship**.

In negotiating this task, ex-spouses are required to terminate their spousal role while renegotiating their parental role. Under ideal circumstances, the custodial and noncustodial parents work together to avoid conflict with each other, share resources, and respect their rights and responsibilities, while supporting each other's parenting for the sake of the children. Many therapeutic interventions and social and legal policies such as joint custody are intended to foster these goals (Hetherington & Stanley-Hagen, 1999). However, most do not approach this ideal. Children may witness name-calling, physical or verbal abuse, drunkenness, and other demeaning and frightening behaviors on the part of their parents (Kaslow, 2000). As a general rule, conflict does, in fact, decline in most couples over time. However, research suggests that about one-fourth of all couples continue to have highly conflicted relationships in which children often feel caught in the middle. Another quarter develop cooperative, mutually supportive relationships, but the remaining half develop parallel, disengaged parenting patterns with little communication or cooperation but also little undermining of the other (Baum, 2004; Hetherington & Stanley-Hagen, 1999).

The process of ceasing to be a husband or wife while continuing to be a mother or father forms the nucleus for the reorganization of families with children (Ahrons, 2005). Although divorce brings about structural changes in the family, the ongoing relationship between former spouses remains the key to the family's successful reorganization (Ahrons, 2005; Amato, 2000). Ex-spouses must define new strategies and rules for how their relationship will operate. They must establish patterns that allow them to operate essentially as a team with regard to parenting matters while keeping other aspects of their lives private. They must reach consensus on how to divide their children's time between separate households, how and when to discipline, and what expectations are important to hold for the child.

For example, will picking up the children and returning them to the other parent be smoothly coordinated, or will deadlines be missed and plans disrupted? Will the same bedtimes be implemented in both households? Will parents share the same definitions of misbehavior? Will misbehavior be treated the same by both parents? Will similar expectations for positive behaviors be established, and will the reinforcements or rewards used by both parents be consistent? These and many other decisions must be made jointly by coparents.

It becomes readily apparent that developing an effective coparenting relationship will be extremely difficult so long as unresolved conflicts remain between the former spouses. Children can be drawn into loyalty binds between warring parents and feel compelled to take sides. Children may be used as a source of information about the other parent's lifestyle and activities. For instance, on returning from a visit with the noncustodial parent, the child may be pumped for information about whom the other parent is dating or how much money he or she is spending. If parents continue to act out their anger and lingering attachment with each other in these ways, the children will become upset each time they must go from one parent's home to the other and will find it difficult to maintain a close relationship with both parents.

Research has found that it is not divorce per se that is disruptive to children's adjustment, but rather the extent to which the children are able to maintain a close, independent, personal, and supportive relationship with each parent and how well parents can maintain a cooperative and nonconflicted relationship with one another (Hetherington & Kelly, 2002; Lamb & Kelly, 2001; Warshak, 2003). The importance of the relationship between ex-spouses cannot be overstated. It has been shown that high rates of continued aggression and conflict between divorced parents are associated with the gradual loss of contact between children and their noncustodial parent, generally the father, especially after the noncustodial parent remarries (Amato, 2000; Hetherington, 2003a).

Of course, children's adjustment to divorce is affected by other factors as well. In this regard, the effects of changes in family income, the mother's employment, family relocation, quality of housing, and social support networks will be discussed in Chapter 17 on single parenthood. But even as the effects of these changes are considered, we must keep in mind that many of these stresses are mediated by the quality of relationships established between members of the divorced family system. The resolution of the parents' emotional and legal differences, including child custody issues and the establishment of a collaborative coparenting relationship, will have a direct impact on the family's ability to reorganize successfully following divorce.

Adaptation Following Divorce

Although each family system is different, making it difficult to provide generalizations, most adults and children adapt to divorce in a period of two to three years, if the situation is not compounded by persistent stress or additional adversity (Ahrons, 2005; Carter & McGoldrick, 2005b; Hetherington, 2003b). For adults, adaptation involves two basic individual tasks. First, they must rebuild their personal lives so as to make good use of the new opportunities divorce provides. Second, they must parent their children, making sure that the children's development proceeds with limited interference (Wallerstein & Blakeslee, 1989). Perhaps the most difficult task for children is to come to terms with two profound losses. One is the loss of the intact family, with the symbolic and real protection it provided. The other is the loss of the presence of one parent, usually the father, from their daily lives (Wallerstein & Blakeslee, 1989). There are a number of factors that are helpful to consider when assessing how successfully ex-spouses, children, and the family system as a whole have adapted following divorce.

Ex-Spouses' Adaptation

Coping with the aftermath of divorce involves coming to terms with a host of potential adjustment difficulties. Research has found that adults who divorce are more likely than those who have not divorced to suffer from health problems, depression, higher rates of motor vehicle accidents, elevated drinking and drug use, alcoholism, and suicide (Amato, 2000). They also report more difficulties performing the routine tasks associated with their jobs (Hetherington & Kelly, 2002). There is often a lingering sense of anger toward the former spouse and problems with loneliness (Ahrons, 2005; Hetherington, 2003b). Studies have shown that many of these adjustment difficulties can be attributed to the divorce itself rather than to pre-existing conditions (Greene, Anderson, Hetherington, Forgatch, & DeGarmo, 2003).

However, not all post-divorce changes are negative. Some individuals report improvement in their overall happiness, feelings of autonomy, self-esteem, social involvement, and career development. Those who were the most unhappy during the marriage are more likely than those who felt happy in the marriage to report these kinds of positive changes (Hetherington, 2003b; Hetherington & Kelly, 2002). This suggests that women are more likely to experience these positive benefits from divorce because they were more often the ones who felt distressed in the marriage. Men are more likely to report better health, happiness, and social support when married compared to when they are single and to feel the loss more profoundly following divorce (Baum, 2003; Greene et al., 2003).

Although understanding such trends is important, the key point to remember is that adults follow many different patterns of adjustment over time. In one study, the vast majority (70 percent) experienced distress during the first year following divorce. However, by the sixth year, although problems remained, over three-quarters reported that the divorce had been a good thing, and they were well down the path to building a satisfying new life. Yet another 10 percent continued to feel defeated, in despair, and suffering from a host of emotional problems (Hetherington, 2003b). What is it that determines a given individual's adjustment over time?

For ex-spouses, one of the primary criteria for successful adaptation is acceptance that the marriage has ended. This entails establishing an individual identity that is tied neither to one's former marital status nor to one's ex-spouse. For this to occur, the individual must become convinced that there is no use investing further in a relationship for which there is no return (Sutton & Sprenkle, 1985).

A second consideration is the extent to which the individual has been able to make peace with the ex-spouse. This generally involves a realization that continued "nastiness will only beget nastiness" and that aggressive or hostile action will only hurt oneself. Often with this realization comes the ability to see the relationship from a more balanced perspective. One is able to forgive the ex-spouse for his or her contributions to the marriage's dissolution and to appreciate what is good about the ex-spouse as well as his or her weaknesses and limitations (Sutton & Sprenkle, 1985).

A third factor is whether the individual has established a realistic appraisal of his or her own contribution to the marital breakup. This requires giving up a blaming posture toward the ex-spouse and honestly examining one's own role in the relationship. Such an appraisal includes: (1) examining one's reasons for originally choosing the mate and making the necessary revisions in one's expectations for future mates; (2) accepting one's contributions to the dysfunctional interaction patterns so that they are not repeated in future relationships; and (3) exploring how one's family of origin experiences may have played a role in the marital struggles (Napier, 1988; Sutton & Sprenkle, 1985).

As has been noted throughout this text, the family of origin plays a key role in determining the manner in which interpersonal relationships are organized.

The family of origin is no less instrumental in determining the likelihood of a relationship ending in divorce. Research has shown that individuals raised in divorce-disrupted families are more likely to end their own marriage in divorce compared with those who were raised in intact families (Amato, 2000; Hetherington & Kelly, 2002).

For many, reexamining their own contributions to the marital breakup may require understanding how they were affected by their own parents' marriage. Some may also have to examine how they were affected by their parents' divorce. For instance, individuals who were raised in families in which their own parents divorced may have learned to view divorce as a more viable solution to their own marital problems than someone who was raised in an intact home (happy or unhappy) (Amato & DeBoer, 2001). Having been raised by parents who divorced also may not offer one the opportunity to learn how to enact a more functional or successful marital role. Similarly, someone who experienced divorce in his or her family of origin may bring negative expectations for failure into the marriage that reduce the overall commitment and investments (time, energy, effort) necessary to make the marriage work. Such negative expectations for a failed marriage may then become a self-fulfilling prophecy.

Honestly examining one's contribution to the divorce may also require reassessing how successful one has been at individuating from the family of origin. For instance, was marriage perceived as the only acceptable way to disengage from an overly involved family of origin? Were a clear sense of identity and a capacity for intimacy established before the marriage? If the answer to this latter question is "no," one may have entered the marriage depending on the partner to "complete one's sense of self," only to be disappointed later by the spouse's "inability to measure up to this need" (Napier, 1988). Was a clear boundary defined between the family of origin and the marital relationship? That is, was a clear "couple identity" established during the early transition to marriage? If not, these earlier unresolved tasks may have become chronic strains that played a role in the divorce. Throughout the marriage, was each partner able to recognize and respond to the other spouse's needs for individuality (time apart) and intimacy (emotional support)? If not, this, too, may have played a role in the eventual breakup.

There is one other criterion for assessing one's adaptation following divorce in addition to accepting that the marriage has ended, making peace with the ex-spouse, and establishing a realistic appraisal of one's own contributions to the marital breakup. It is the individual's readiness to move on with life. This includes the extent to which one has been able to (1) establish or reestablish sources of support outside the marriage; (2) develop a sense of mastery, self-esteem, and competency as a single person; and (3) establish future-oriented as opposed to past-oriented goals. Those who are ready to move on toward the future begin to focus their energies on such goals as fulfilling educational or career aspirations, developing new hobbies or leisure activities, or entering into new dating relationships. In contrast, those who are not yet ready to move on may need more time to mourn the loss of the former spouse. These individuals may not have exhausted efforts to rekindle the relationship or come to the realization that the relationship has definitely ended.

Children's Adaptation

A large body of research has documented the many adjustment difficulties children may face following divorce, especially early in the process. Regardless of their circumstances, many children experience problems in the months immediately following divorce. Children are often initially depressed, anxious, angry, demanding, or disobedient; many show a drop in school performance. Difficulties in relationships with parents, siblings, peers, and teachers are common (Kelly, 2003). Beyond the immediate effects, children from divorced families are two to three times more likely to drop out or be expelled from school than children in married families (Kelly, 2003). The strongest impact on adjustment appears to cluster around a set of behaviors often referred to as externalizing disorders. These behaviors include antisocial acts, aggression, noncompliance, a lack of self-regulation, low social responsibility, and lowered achievement motivation. To a lesser degree, children also experience internalizing disorders. These disorders include anxiety, depression, poor self-esteem, and withdrawal from social activities (Hetherington & Kelly, 2002; Kelly, 2003). Even children who experience relatively few problems immediately following divorce may develop problems later in life as they face new transitions and developmental tasks. For instance, whereas some children may continue to have problems from childhood into adolescence, for others, adolescence may trigger problems in those who had previously functioned well (Hetherington & Stanley-Hagen, 1999). Some continue to suffer negative consequences long past the divorce and well into adulthood (Amato, 2000).

As was the case with adults who experienced divorce, we see a variety of differing adjustment outcomes for children exposed to divorce. Not all children from divorced families suffer negative consequences, and for some who do, the negative effects are shortlived. For example, children who move from a highly conflicted, abusive, or neglectful family environment prior to divorce to a more harmonious living arrangement following divorce generally show fewer problems (Amato, 2000; Hetherington & Stanley-Hagen, 1999; Kelly, 2003). Adjustment problems are also fewer for children who were well adjusted prior to the divorce (Hetherington & Stanley-Hagen, 1999). The impact of divorce is also determined in part by the number of other stresses and family transitions the child experiences. These stressors may include living in a single-parent household, moving to a new home or location, or moving with the custodial parent into a remarried or cohabiting living arrangement. Estimates suggest that approximately 20 percent to 25 percent of children in divorced families experience high levels of problem behaviors. This is in contrast to about 10 percent of children in nondivorced homes who experience severe problems (Greene et al., 2003; Hetherington & Kelly, 2002). This means that about 80 percent of children do not show serious problems as a result of divorce. Thus, in spite of the potential pitfalls associated with divorce, most children do show a great deal of resilience and go on to become relatively adjusted adults (Hetherington, 2003a; Moxnes, 2003; Ruschena, Prior, Sanson, & Smart, 2005). Again, the critical question is, what enables children to overcome the various stresses associated with divorce and to achieve a successful quality of life?

For children, successful adaptation to divorce requires that they, too, accept the finality of the parents' breakup. This acceptance is aided by the parents' willingness to discuss with their children, in age-appropriate ways, the reasons for the separation and divorce. It is important that children do not entertain fantasies that their parents may reunite (Sutton & Sprenkle, 1985). Children must be given the opportunity to express their painful emotions to ensure that they feel listened to and cared for. Children may feel guilty or hold themselves responsible for their parents' divorce, and such feelings can only be corrected when they are brought out in the open. It is important, too, that children come to believe that both parents still love them, even if their parents no longer love one another. Furthermore, children must not feel that loving one parent will jeopardize their place in the affections of the other parent (Ahrons, 2005; Greene et al., 2003).

Children who are adapting well to the divorce should be doing satisfactory work in school, be reasonably active in social and recreational activities, and have satisfying peer relationships (Amato, 2000; Sutton & Sprenkle, 1985). If both parents maintain a positive relationship with the child, resolve their parental conflicts after the divorce, and are able to provide sufficient socioeconomic resources for the child, the negative consequences of divorce are not generally found (Ahrons, 2005; Amato, 2000; Green et al., 2003).

The Family System's Adaptation

For the family system as a whole, successful adaptation to divorce requires the reestablishment of effective strategies for meeting the family's basic tasks. In most families with children, the establishment of effective strategies depends on the resolution of child custody and coparenting issues. This will typically be aided by the establishment of a family identity as either a single-parent or binuclear system. A secure family emotional environment will often require a cooperative and nonconflicted relationship between the ex-spouses. In many instances, successful strategies for managing internal boundaries will include each parent's maintenance of a personal relationship with the children and the disengagement of the parental subsystem from the former marital subsystem. Effective strategies for managing the household will generally include mutually agreed on child-care strategies, the equitable distribution of financial resources, and the fair distribution of leisure time between parents through clearly defined visitation schedules. Successful strategies for managing stress require cognitive coping efforts that involve a realistic appraisal of the hardships, unresolved conflicts, and hurt feelings that accompany divorce along with the implementation of appropriate behavioral strategies that support each member's social and emotional development.

However, it is important to emphasize that this general blueprint for successful family adaptation to divorce will not fit all families equally well. Throughout this text, the point has been made that even though all families can be thought of as having to manage the same basic tasks, their strategies for doing so can vary a great deal. African American families offer a good example of how quite different strategies can be equally effective in managing the aftermath of divorce.

For instance, African American women are less likely to remain financially dependent on their former husbands for assistance (Fine, McKenry, & Chung, 1992). They are more likely to maintain strong ties with their extended family and to rely more heavily on the extended family for resources and support than are white women (Taylor, 2000).

As a result, black women's strategies for maintaining a secure emotional environment are likely to depend less on ongoing cooperation between former spouses and more on the emotional environment within the extended family system. Furthermore, black women may be more easily able to adopt a single-parent identity because there is less stigma attached to this identity in the black community (Fine et al., 1992). This may be because there are more successful single-parent models to observe, or because the shortage of available black men relative to women makes single-parent status a more common occurrence among blacks than among whites (Pinderhughes, 2002). Black single parents are, therefore, less likely to establish a binuclear family identity. Their strategies for managing the household often will not emphasize mutually agreed upon child-care strategies between former spouses or the equitable sharing of financial resources or leisure time through clearly defined visitation schedules. These strategies, although different, may be no less effective in adapting to divorce. In fact, some research has found that black adults may adapt more effectively to divorce than their white counterparts (Fine et al., 1992; Gove & Shin, 1989; Menaghan & Lieberman, 1986).

An Intergenerational Systems Perspective on Divorce

As we have seen in this chapter, a variety of contextual factors have been found to affect the ability of parents and children to adjust to divorce. Some of the major factors that can hinder successful adaptation are reduced socioeconomic opportunities and the disruption brought on by multiple transitions such as living in a single-parent family structure, parental remarriage or cohabitation, additional parental divorces, changing schools, or moving to a new home or neighborhood. However, a primary factor in determining the outcome of divorce is the quality of interpersonal relationships. Divorce is the termination of the spousal relationship and the consequent reorganization of many other relationships inside and outside the family. Parent–child, sibling, in-law, grandparent, and friendship relationships are all altered. Stepparent, stepsibling, and new extended family relationships also may be added. Understanding this degree of change in so many relationships in a condensed period of time is a critical factor in understanding the divorce process. The other core element to consider is the presence of conflict in these core relationships prior to, during, and following divorce. More precisely, it is the lack of resolution of conflict that is consistently implicated in the maladjustment of adults and children throughout the divorce process. The ability to resolve conflict, to maintain a cooperative parenting relationship, and the availability of both parents to maintain personal one-to-one relationships with each child have been shown to be the cornerstones of successful adaptation to divorce. These findings are consistent with the intergenerational systems perspective that was described earlier in this text.

As noted in earlier chapters, experiences in the family of origin establish a legacy that affects the development of individual family members and the patterns of adjustment found in subsequent generations of the family. Unresolved conflict, anxiety, effective or ineffective communication, conflict resolution, or parenting strategies are passed from generation to generation and help to determine the system's ability to successfully manage its basic tasks. An important concept in this framework is family differentiation. From this perspective, families with differing levels of differentiation use different interactional strategies to manage highly stressful events such as a divorce. Well-differentiated family systems accept change, tolerate difference, and manage tensions and anxiety by separating their intellectual from their emotional functioning. That is, they manage stressful transitions by maintaining emotional connection with significant others, while responding with thoughtfulness and without defensiveness or the need to counterattack when negotiating differences. Individuals are encouraged to express their individuality, and their personal identities are supported. Personal one-to-one relationships are maintained, and tensions and anxiety are managed within the appropriate dyad. Poorly differentiated family systems operate at the extremes of fusion (overinvolvement) and emotional cutoff (disengagement). Tensions and anxiety are not easily resolved but rather are channeled into high levels of conflict, triangulation, or projection processes that may extend over multiple generations of the family system. The results of these strategies are psychological distress, physical symptoms, or difficulty in establishing intimate and rewarding interpersonal relationships with others.

Research has begun to recognize links between the intergenerational perspective and adaptation during and after the divorce process. For instance, families that function well after parental divorce have been found to have fewer emotional cutoffs than those that function poorly (Johnson & Nelson, 1998). Young adults in well-functioning families following parental divorce have reported less triangulation and greater equality in their relationships with their parents compared to those in poorly functioning families (Johnson & McNeil, 1998). Reports of young adults from divorcing families also indicate that they are more emotionally reactive and less intimate with significant others when compared to young adults in nondivorced families (Johnson, Thorngren, & Smith, 2001). Kitson and Holmes (1992) found that almost 30 percent of the adults in their study reported continued attachment to their former spouse up to four years after the divorce. Such lingering feelings of attachment speak not only to a lack of resolution of the marital breakup but also to the possibility of ongoing fusion and overinvolvement with the former partner. Finally, divorced parents characterized by low differentiation were less successful in establishing an effective coparenting relationship following the divorce (Johnson et al., 2001).

Other studies have produced results consistent with the intergenerational view that the consequences of divorce pass from one generation of the family to another. A number of studies have consistently found that parental divorce significantly increases the risk of marital instability and difficulties in establishing intimate relationships among adult children of divorce (Amato, 2000; Amato & DeBoer, 2001; Bumpass, Martin, & Sweet, 1991; Hetherington, 2003b). In a recent study, Amato and Cheadle (2005) found that divorce between grandparents was associated with a variety of problem outcomes for grandchildren. These outcomes included lower educational attainment, greater marital discord, and poorer relationships with their mothers and fathers. They interpreted these findings as suggesting that parental divorce has consequences not only for the children of these parents but also for subsequent generations not yet born at the time the divorce occurred. Their findings clearly support the intergenerational view that successful or unsuccessful interactional strategies in divorcing families can be passed along over multiple generations of the family system. One limitation of these studies is that they do not indicate whether processes associated with poor differentiation preceded the divorce process or were a result of the divorce. The intergenerational perspective would suggest that these differentiation processes were present prior to divorce and in fact were present in preceding generations of the family system as well, and that they were also accelerated by the stress of the divorce transition.

Conclusions

Divorce dramatically alters the structure of the family system and has the potential to, at least temporarily, disrupt the family's developmental course. Each transitional phase of the divorce process places unique stresses and demands on the family system. Family members must progress from acceptance of the reality of the spouses' breakup to a reorganization of the family as two independent households. In the case of couples with children, this is likely to be a single-parent household, or a binuclear system. Such a reorganization requires a renegotiation of the family's strategies for managing its basic tasks.

Successful adaptation includes family members accepting the divorce as final and gaining an accurate perspective on the factors that led to the divorce. Another factor is the ability of former spouses to develop a nonblaming, cooperative, and nonconflicted relationship. Children must be helped to maintain close, one-to-one relationships with each parent, as these healthy relationships have the potential to facilitate greatly their adaptation following divorce. Successfully managing the divorce transition can greatly aid the family's efforts to cope with the subsequent transition to a single-parent household.

Key Terms

Binuclear family system A system comprised of two active and involved parents and two separate households.

Boundary ambiguity Confusion about who is in the family and who is not.

Child custody The legal parameters of each parent's relationship with the children that are established following divorce.

Coparenting relationship The termination of the spousal role combined with the maintenance of the parental role and the sharing of responsibilities for one's children.

Divorce The legal termination of a marriage.

Divorce mediation A negotiation process designed to minimize divorcing couples' conflicts over personal, economic, or child-related differences by concretely examining their options in a goal-focused and task-oriented manner and making constructive decisions before appearing in court.

Family reorganization The fourth and final transition of the divorce process, during which the family clarifies its new internal and external boundaries, redefines its identity, stabilizes its emotional environment, and reestablishes strategies for managing the newly created household.

Individual cognition The first transition of the divorce process, which begins when a spouse first realizes that he or she is feeling dissatisfied or distressed in the marriage.

Joint custody When both parents continue to be parents to all of their children despite a divorce.

Marital distress When one or both partners in a marriage-like relationship believe that the relationship suffers from serious, long-standing problems that threaten the stability of the relationship.

Separation The third transition of the divorce process, which occurs when one spouse moves out of the home.

Sole custody When one parent assumes complete responsibility for child care with the other parent generally receiving visitation rights and, in many instances, responsibility for child support.

Split custody When one parent has legal and physical custody of one or more children, and the other parent has legal and physical custody of one or more other children.

CHAPTER 17

The Single-Parent Household

Chapter Overview

The single-parent household has become an increasingly common family form. The challenges faced by single-parent families are varied and many. They can include changes in the level of family stress, modifications in one's personal and family identity, and major alterations in how the household is managed. Household management can be severely affected by diminished or altered financial resources, changes in a parent's employment status, and alterations in the family's residence. Additional modifications are likely to occur in the family's boundaries and emotional environment. Parenting strategies may have to be modified, particularly those related to issues of parental custody. Social relationships and sources of support (family, friends) are generally altered, and dating relationships may be initiated. Although these stresses typically affect men and women differently, their effect on the family system can be extensive. The accumulation of demands has the potential to outweigh the system's available coping resources, leaving the family vulnerable to crisis and disorganization. Successful adaptation will depend on the family's capacity to alter its existing strategies and establish new sources of social support.

The Single-Parent Household

Despite the structural diversity found within contemporary families, all families can be thought of as facing the same basic tasks. The single-parent household is no exception. Strategies and rules are required to organize family themes and individual identities, maintain boundaries, manage the household, regulate the emotional climate, and manage family stress. And, as with any family system, adaptations will be required over time. The strategies adopted by single-parent families are influenced by their unique composition, structure, and circumstances.

However, it should also be apparent that the single-parent family system confronts a unique set of challenges and circumstances. The family's ability to adapt in the face of these challenges will depend, in part, on the ordinary and extraordinary stresses and strains it encounters and its available resources. Because of the prevalence of this family form, it is imperative that we develop an understanding of the single-parent family system and the unique challenges it faces.

Diversity within Single-Parent Systems

While all single-parent families are, by definition, headed by a single parent, families differ with respect to the factors that gave rise to their origin (Hill, 1986). Single-parent systems can result from death, divorce, separation, or desertion. Others can occur as a result of out-of-wedlock births. Some single-parent-headed households are the result of single-parent adoptions. In still other instances, single-parent-headed households occur when parents remain separated for extended periods due to out-of-state employment. This diversity is important to note, because different origins produce different challenges that will influence the family's methods of coping and ability to manage system tasks (Hill, 1986). For example, the single-parent system that originates as a result of divorce must deal with the stress and emotional turmoil that spousal separation introduces into the system. Although single-parent systems originating from the death of a spouse face many of the same emotional and systemic issues, social and community support is usually more readily extended to those dealing with a death than with a divorce. Similarly, the social support experienced by a widow with a young child is often considerably different from the support experienced by a teenage mother who gives birth to a child out of wedlock.

Consider, as well, the unique challenges confronted by those single-parent systems in which one partner works away from home or goes on active military duty for extended periods. These systems must develop two sets of strategies for the execution of system tasks—one set that applies when both parents are present and one set that applies when only one parent is present. As a result, these exits and entrances challenge the family to devise different strategies for the division of tasks, equitable allocation of resources, and distribution of power and authority. This further challenges the adaptability and flexibility of the family system. These demands have the potential to strain family relationships and overburden the system's coping resources.

Single-parent families differ not only in terms of their origin but also in terms of their composition. Researchers have tended to use simplistic terms in describing family structures, such as two-parent, one-parent, or stepparent. However, many single-parent mothers and fathers live with other adults, such as a cohabiting partner, grandparents, other relatives, or nonrelatives, which makes these typical designations inaccurate and misleading (Bumpass & Raley, 1995; Eggebeen, Snyder, & Manning, 1996; Manning & Smock, 1997).

In sum, each single-parent system is the result of a unique origin and developmental history. Each must balance its own set of demands and stresses with its available coping resources. These differences must be acknowledged in any effort to understand the unique patterns of interaction found within single-parent systems.

Single-Parent Family Systems: Prevalence and Challenges

A sizable percentage of American families are headed by a single parent. In 1970, 5 percent of all American households were headed by a single parent. Today, 9 percent are headed by a single parent, and this percentage has remained unchanged since 1994 (U.S. Census Bureau, 2007a).

One out of every two children in the United States will live in a single-parent family at some time before he or she reaches age eighteen (U.S. Census Bureau, 2003c). Children in single-parent households are five times more likely to live with their mothers (84 percent) than with their fathers (16 percent) (U.S. Census Bureau, 2007b). The likelihood of a child living in a single-parent household also differs by race. Recent estimates suggest that 22 percent of white children live in single-parent households. However, 34 percent of Hispanic American and 62 percent of African American children live in single-parent households (U.S. Census Bureau, 2005a). The reasons for children living in a single-parent household also differ among racial groups. For instance, most white children are likely to find themselves in a single-parent household as a result of parental divorce (49 percent) or an out-of-wedlock birth (31 percent). In contrast, the majority of African American single mothers were never married (62 percent), and only 20 percent were likely to have been divorced (U.S. Census Bureau, 2004b).

Whether a single-parent household is formed following divorce, separation, widowhood, or an out-of-wedlock birth, it is clear that the single-parent household has become a new family form in contemporary society. Regardless of its origins, the family headed by a single parent must undergo changes in its structure, the role definitions of its members, and the means by which it executes its basic tasks. In the next section, we will examine the unique demands that challenge single-parent families in their efforts to manage their basic tasks. We focus more of our attention on single-parent families formed following divorce because this group has been the most studied by researchers.

Challenges in Meeting Basic Tasks within Single-Parent Systems

Managing Family Stress

One of the most significant challenges to single-parent systems is managing the increased levels of stress within these systems. The ordinary demands of family life must be managed along with the challenges imposed by the demands of single parenthood. The potential for an accumulation of stress is apparent in that the demands on these systems may easily exceed their coping resources. This is particularly true given that coping resources such as finances, time, energy, and social support may be less available to the post-divorce and single-parent system (Anderson, 2003).

A critical challenge facing the single-parent system is the need to balance demands with available coping resources. These demands may be especially great for single-parent systems that must shift from a nuclear family system as a result of divorce or desertion or death of a spouse. At such times, previously available resources for coping may no longer be available. For example, the partner who was once available for assistance and support is no longer present. As a result, demands such as parenting or managing finances and the household will inevitably change. Although not all families are adversely affected by these changes, the situation can easily challenge the resourcefulness and creativity of the system. Under these circumstances, new strategies will be required to meet these system demands. It should be apparent, as well, that new demands place families at potential risk. When stressed beyond manageable levels, coping strategies can become less adaptive, leading to even more stress within the family system. The potential for both individual and family dysfunction is increased as is the likelihood that ineffective strategies will be employed to manage basic tasks and responsibilities.

Developing New Family Themes and Identities

As suggested earlier, themes represent a fundamental view of the "reality of the family." They represent the critical images and identities of the family system that family members hold. Living according to a theme necessitates the development of various patterns of behavior that affect (1) how members interact with the outside world; (2) how they interact with each other; and (3) how they develop personally (Galvin & Brommel, 1991). Themes affect every aspect of the family's functioning. Individual identities, external and internal boundaries, and the establishment of priorities for the allocation of resources are all examples of issues that are influenced by the themes selected. That many forms of single-parent systems in our society are thought of as being non-normative, deviant, or dysfunctional adds to the difficulty that single-parent systems encounter when called on to alter or evolve constructive and positive family themes. For example, often the single-parent system that has come about as a result of divorce is thought of as a "broken family." Politicians routinely talk about the need for strengthening the family and, in the same context, discuss the prevalence of single-parent systems within the United States as an example of the deterioration of the family. The powerful and negative images and identities that are projected onto single-parent systems complicate the process that single-parent systems confront when evolving family themes. The single-parent system must grapple with the difficulties of constructing positive and adaptive themes in what might be fairly characterized as a "hostile societal environment." Adopting the view that the single-parent system represents a broken family makes the task of fostering a positive identity among family members as well as themes that facilitate a positive connection with outside systems more difficult.

Managing Maintenance Tasks in a Changing Family Household

Clearly, some of the most dramatic changes that occur in single-parent families are related to the alterations in their physical environment. Strategies for providing basic necessities such as food, shelter, and education can be adversely affected by a decline in the family's available resources. The resources most likely to be affected by the transition to a single-parent family are finances, employment status, sources of income, and residence.

Financial Stressors. One of the most potentially disabling stressors faced by single parents, especially women, is the absence of financial security that accompanies single parenthood. For example, 28 percent of mother-headed single-parent households with children in the United States live in poverty. The figure for father-headed single-parent households is 11 percent. In addition, poverty is more common among certain subgroups. Single parents who are young (under thiry years of age), Black, or never married have poverty rates between 36 percent to 40 percent (U.S. Census Bureau, 2007b).

Further evidence of the financial stress experienced by single-parent systems comes from the research that has analyzed how divorce affects the financial well-being of women and children. In the aftermath of a divorce, research suggests that the average income of the mother-headed single-parent household drops by 27 percent, in contrast to men, whose incomes increase 10 percent (Peterson, 1996). This is because the husband's salary provided the largest share of the family's income prior to divorce. Many women, especially those with younger children, have left paid employment to raise their children. A two- to four-year hiatus from paid employment can permanently lower the average woman's future earnings by 13 percent. A four-year hiatus has been estimated to lower her future earnings by 19 percent. This decline in earnings is in no way offset by other potential sources of income such as alimony, child support, or government assistance. At least initially, such a dramatic decline in income has a major effect on the family's ability to manage the household and its overall standard of living. Sacrifices must be made, and coping strategies become focused on day-to-day survival patterns rather than on long-term plans for the future, at least until a more realistic appraisal of available resources and current living standards can be made (Anderson, 2003).

This dramatic decline in the overall economic well-being of women-headed households challenges the resourcefulness and creativity of the family system. Economic hardship reverberates throughout the family system and affects other aspects of family life. Furthermore, economic hardship occurs in the context of other financial stresses such as changes in the single mother's work status, sources of family income, and family residence.

Changes in Employment Status. For women whose primary roles prior to divorce involved managing the household and caring for children, the reduction in the standard of living accompanying divorce may force her into the workforce. Some homemakers may be relatively unprepared for such a change. They may have few marketable skills, limited training, and large gaps in their employment record, which can make competing for available jobs difficult. Furthermore, the jobs that are available to them tend to be low paying. For some, the costs of child care may be so high as to offset the economic advantages gained by working. Many will be forced to settle for less-than-adequate child-care arrangements or seek assistance with child care from relatives, friends, or neighbors. The mother's return to work may also leave children feeling that they have been abandoned by both parents (Hetherington & Kelly, 2002).

The economic crunch experienced by single mothers is further complicated by the fact that the wages of women, in general, are lower than the wages of their male counterparts. Women earn 80 percent of what their male counterparts make (U.S. Bureau of Labor Statistics, 2009). Reasons for this include a lack of job skills and experience, irregular work histories, limited child-care options, and sex discrimination in hiring practices. Nevertheless, most single-parent mothers prefer to work rather than turn to other sources of support, like welfare assistance (Mednick, 1987). Data on single-parent mothers indicate that 50 percent work full-time and 29 percent work part-time (U.S. Census Bureau, 2007b). However, the choice to work further complicates the lives of single mothers by requiring them to balance the needs of their children and the demands of their work (Jackson, Brooks-Gunn, Huang, & Glassman, 2000).

Changes in Sources of Income. The decline in family income associated with single parenthood may be augmented by additional sources of support and assistance. Although most single-parent families receive their major source of incomes from wages, they also receive assistance from a variety of other sources. Some may receive government assistance in the form of welfare, foodstamps, or financial aid for job training. Many may receive child-support payments from the children's father. Others receive alimony from their ex-spouses. Although any of these sources of income may mean the difference between sinking into poverty and adequately maintaining the household, each is fraught with potential problems. For instance, reliance on government agencies for subsistence may perpetuate feelings of insecurity, helplessness, and dependency, rather than a sense of competence and self-efficacy. Female single parents on some form of welfare have been found to have poorer social and emotional adjustment than those who are not receiving such assistance (Teachman & Paasch, 1994).

The problems with reliance on ex-spouses for child support are well documented. Ninety percent of single parents who have child support agreements are women. Only 46 percent of these single parents receive full child support, 30 percent receive some but not all payments, and 23 percent receive no child support at all. Also telling is the fact that, on average, receiving full support payments accounts for only 19 percent of the parent's annual income. Receiving partial support payments amount to about 11 percent of the single parent's annual income (U.S. Census Bureau, 2007b). Clearly, the unpredictability and amount of support payments can contribute greatly to an unstable and insecure financial situation.

Alimony is a distinctly different category from child support. It is money that higher-earning spouses provide to their lower-earning counterparts following the end of their marriage. Generally, it is court ordered. Only approximately 15 percent of divorced women receive alimony payments from their ex-spouses. Those who do tend to be older, have been married longer, and have less employment experience (Rowe, 1991). These women are also less likely to be caring for young children. Most alimony awards are "short-term, rehabilitative" awards. They are intended to provide women time to find employment or gain the skills, training, or education necessary to become self-supporting. However, most of these awards are too short-term, and the amounts are too small to cover the time and cost needed to complete training and find employment (Rowe, 1991).

Most states have now implemented no-fault divorce laws that emphasize property settlements instead of alimony. In such cases, assets are equally divided between ex-spouses at the time of divorce. This can be especially unfair to women who typically retain custody of the children and most of the costs. Also, only half of all divorced women actually receive some form of property settlement, and when they do, the average amount is small (Teachman & Paasch, 1994).

Finally, some single-parent women may find themselves on government assistance programs. Recent statistics indicate that 31 percent of custodial single parents receive some kind of government assistance in the form of Medicaid, food stamps, public housing or rent subsidy, or Temporary Assistance for Needy Families (TANF).

The small value of property settlements, the irregularity of child-support payments, the rare granting of alimony, and the minimal assistance offered by entitlement programs do relatively little to alleviate the financial tensions that permeate many single-parent systems. These systems must tolerate a great deal of financial uncertainty and ambiguity. Consequently, considerable physical and emotional energy is devoted to the management of financial tasks, leaving less time and energy for other aspects of family life.

Changes in Residence. Single parents may also find themselves displaced from their homes. Women, in particular, are often forced to sell their homes and find a less expensive place to live in order to manage the downward mobility that comes with single parenthood. Selling the family home involves both an economic and emotional rebalancing of the family system. Economically, selling the family home may be an important step in reorganizing the family's financial resources to meet necessary expenses.

However, selling the family home is also an emotional and symbolic event. Moving to a less expensive residence graphically symbolizes the changes taking place in the family's standard of living. It can also represent conflicting feelings of wanting to be rid of the past while still wishing to feel the security and stability of old and familiar surroundings (Bagarozzi & Anderson, 1989).

Children may also view the sale of the family home as a major loss symbolizing the end of the original family and any lingering fantasies they may have had for it reuniting. Moving also means saying good-bye to old friends, changing schools, and investing energy in making new friends.

Maintenance Tasks in Father-Headed Single-Parent Systems

Most discussions of the issues confronted within single-parent systems focus on women-headed households, primarily because most single-parent systems are headed by women. At this point, less is known about the stressors and strains experienced within male-headed single-parent systems, although as noted earlier, this family structure is becoming increasingly common.

Some initial findings suggest that single-father households are quite diverse in their structure and composition. For instance, 57 percent of these households are formed following divorce or separation. Eighteen percent of single-parent fathers report never having been married (U.S. Census Bureau, 2007b). Many single fathers share the household with a cohabiting partner, parents, or other extended family members (Eggebeen et al., 1996). Roughly one-half of single-parent fathers who live with a cohabiting partner were previously married and then received custody of their children following a divorce. The other half have never been married. Single fathers in a cohabiting relationship tend to be younger, less educated, and have lower incomes than fathers who gained custody of their children following divorce (Eggebeen et al., 1996).

By far, the most extensive attention given to fathers in the single-parent literature has emphasized how divorce affects fathers' financial status and their willingness to support their ex-spouse and children. Financial settlements following divorce and the need to contribute support to two households can tax fathers' financial resources, at least initially. That the father is expected to contribute to a household from which he no longer benefits can also make this as much an emotional as a financial issue for him. When the father did not initiate the separation, he may have even more resistance to providing support.

However, in contrast to single-parent custodial mothers, most custodial and noncustodial fathers generally maintain or improve their standard of living following divorce (Arditti, 1992; Kitson & Morgan, 1990). Most work either full-time (74 percent) or part-time (18 percent) (U.S. Census Bureau, 2007b). Some maintain or improve their standard of living because they refuse to provide child support. For others, it may simply be because they cease to be the primary support for the mother and children. Even when they do provide continuous child support, the amount generally represents a small percentage of fathers' usable income. Some have estimated that fathers are capable of paying more than twice the amounts currently being awarded in child-support settlements (Grall, 2006)).

It appears that the critical factors regarding single fathers' compliance with child support have to do with their overall level of income (the higher the income, the more likely he is to pay), the level of attachment felt toward their children and former spouse, and the extent to which he and his former spouse agree on child-rearing issues (Arditti, 1992). Once again, it is the quality of the emotional relationships between former spouses and the father's level of personal involvement with his children (along with his own financial security) that determine his willingness to share his financial resources. However, it may well be the differences between the financial situations of fathers and mothers that exacerbate conflicts between them. Mothers may come to resent that fathers have more discretionary income, can afford more "extras," and can spend more of their money on themselves, while they must spend their money on their children. Such differences can severely tax efforts to redefine the boundaries between mothers' and fathers' separate households.

Boundary Tasks: Renegotiating Family Members' Roles and Responsibilities

Because many single-parent systems result from divorce and separation, these families must confront several unique parenting issues. Parents and children must adjust to the changes in family relationships that naturally occur. To successfully negotiate this transition, parents and their children must rework family roles and responsibilities within the new single-parent system. These role redefinitions add to the ordinary challenges that parents experience. Chief among these challenges are those related to custody and the clarification of each parent's role with the children.

Resolving Custody Issues. One such challenge faced by parents is resolution of child custody and coparenting issues. This will entail deciding who will assume primary responsibility for the children. In this regard, even though **joint legal custody** (when parents share decision-making and economic support) has become more common, **joint physical custody** (residence) has not (Kitson & Morgan, 1990). Approximately 84 percent of children reside with the custodial mother following divorce (U.S. Census Bureau, 2007b).

Obviously, sharing joint legal custody can be difficult when one parent has sole physical custody of the children. Sharing legal (or physical) custody is sometimes further complicated in that both parents do not always live in the same community (Kelly & Lamb, 2003). The transition to a binuclear family, in which both parents share custody and responsibility for children, is further challenged by the absence of prescribed societal norms, traditions, and rituals for divorced parents. Finally, unresolved personal feelings between former spouses can interfere with their ability to share parenting responsibilities cooperatively.

Reworking Parenting Roles. Even when parents are able to work together to share the tasks of parenthood, divorce precipitates a movement toward greater separateness and autonomy and a corresponding decline in the former couple's level of interdependence. Each parent must establish new personal relationships with their children without the same kind of continuous input, support, or collaboration that was formerly available from the partner. Tasks that were once allocated to the partner must now be assumed by the single parent. For example, father may have to become more involved in chauffeuring children to after-school activities or helping them with their homework when they visit him, even though it was mother who "usually took care of these things in the past." Similarly, mother may now have to establish her own methods of discipline rather than leaving some matters "until father gets home." Therefore, even in the best of circumstances, divorced parents must contend with the task of redefining their parental roles and responsibilities. The family must contend with how some of the tasks that were formerly shared between two parents are now to be managed independently by each parent.

Managing the Family's Emotional Environment

The research literature suggests that the challenges posed by the transition to single parenthood are rarely handled in an optimal manner. The accumulation of stressors brought on by changes in the family's household routines, financial changes, the mother's increased work demands, and unresolved feelings of loss and grief for the ex-spouse tend to increase the risks of psychological or physical dysfunction among parents. This in turn will decrease the effectiveness of their efforts to attend to their children's evolving needs. Specifically, alcoholism, drug abuse, depression, psychosomatic problems, and accidents are all more common among divorced than nondivorced adults (Amato, 2000; Hetherington & Kelly, 2002).

In addition, parents coping with changes following divorce often exhibit marked emotional changes, alternating between periods of euphoria and optimism and periods of anxiety, loneliness, and depression, along with associated changes in self-concept and self-esteem (Hetherington & Kelly, 2002). Many custodial mothers report feeling overwhelmed at this time (Anderson, 2003), and a period of diminished parenting is common among them. Parental attention and discipline are often infrequent or inconsistent (Amato, 2000; Anderson, 2003).

In other words, the greater the accumulation of demands (work, expenses, unresolved issues with ex-spouse, younger versus older children) and the more limited the custodial mother's resources (financial, psychological, extended family, social supports), the greater the potential for ineffective parenting strategies to be established. The critical issue in this regard appears to be the extent to which the single mother is able to assume the role of **sole administrator** for the household. That is, the mother must accept that the single-parent household can no longer operate as it did before, when two parents were present. She must assume complete authority and responsibility, enlisting the help of others when needed without allowing them to take over for her (Anderson, 2003). In structural terms, the parental hierarchy or executive subsystem must be clearly defined with the mother in charge. When others are sought for assistance (e.g., babysitter, grandparent, older child), they are given responsibility but not ultimate authority (Haley, 1987; Minuchin, 1974).

To the extent that the mother feels a gap in her own personal competency, she is likely to enlist her children, her parents, or the children's father into the coparent role, thereby inviting triangles or coalitions that may provide temporary assistance but long-term dysfunction (Anderson, 2003; Byng-Hall, 2002). One such triangle is when the oldest child (often a daughter) is called on to fill the role of **parental child**. Children in single-parent families are often expected to help out more around the home than children from two-parent families, and this can serve as a valuable resource for mothers. There also is evidence to suggest that such increased expectations can contribute to children's heightened senses of independence and competence (Amato, 2000).

However, in other instances this can become problematic. The daughter who becomes a parental child may be given authority over younger children who may not accept her newly elevated status, thereby creating sibling conflicts. The mother may begin to treat the daughter as her confidante, sharing personal information with her about the other children, her dating life, or other aspects of her personal life. Such an arrangement may serve to strengthen the emotional bond between mother and daughter and provide each with a necessary measure of emotional support. However, the demands of this relationship and the parental responsibilities the daughter must fulfill may, over time, interfere with her own growth and development. For instance, responsibilities at home may curtail her own extracurricular activities after school or social interactions with peers, both of which are important to personal adjustment, especially during adolescence (Sabatelli & Anderson, 1991).

The mother may also pull her own mother into the vacuum created by her spouse's absence. She may move in with her parents, or live nearby, so that the grandparents can help care for the children while she works or goes to school. The more overwhelmed the single-parent mother is, the more domineering the grandmother may become. Put another way, the less successful the mother has been at individuating from her own mother, the greater the chances that the grandmother will begin to function as the mother. What may have started as an effort to cope with the pressures of single parenthood may end as an added stress, with increased feelings of failure, incompetence, or low self-esteem for the single mother.

On still other occasions a triangle may develop among the mother, the children, and the children's father. The mother may rely on the father for support payments, child-care responsibilities, or, in some cases, even continued discipline, while also resenting him for his intrusions. The children, too, may learn that they can undermine their mother's decisions by getting their father to agree with them. In each of these cases, the mother's role as sole administrator in her own home is undermined and ineffective, and inconsistent parenting strategies become established.

Managing the Emotional Environment in Father-Headed Single-Parent Households

For fathers, the parenting experience may be quite different than that experienced by mothers. As noted earlier, it has become more common for men to receive sole or joint custody of their children. These fathers experience many of the same parenting stresses that single-parent mothers face. However, they tend to cope with them differently. For instance, they, too, may seek out their own parents to fill in for the missing spouse when it comes to child care. However, men are less likely to view parents or a girlfriend as a competitor for their children's attention and more likely to view them as convenient child-care substitutes (Anderson, 2003).

In most instances, fathers become noncustodial parents, with custody awarded to the mother. As a consequence, men often experience a loss of a sense of home and family. Furthermore, with the loss of legal custody, many men also experience a loss of influence and control over their children (Arditti, 1992; Arendell, 1995). Their contacts with their children may be limited to court-defined visitation schedules. If these schedules are poorly defined (i.e., visits are allowed only at unreasonable times and places) or not closely adhered to by the custodial mother, the father's sense of loss and powerlessness can be even greater.

It may be this sense of loss of contact and control, coupled with feelings of guilt, anxiety, and depression, and loss of self-esteem following the family breakup that leads a father to emotionally withdraw from his children. Numerous studies have documented that fathers tend to decrease the frequency and duration of their visits with their children over time (Amato, 2000; Arditti, 1992; Kelly, 2003). Of course, there are a number of other explanations for this, including unresolved conflicts with the former spouse, inability or unwillingness to continue with child support, the superficiality of the visitation experience, a lack of interest in parenting, relocation to another state, or remarriage and the establishment of a new family.

Take, for example, a situation in which there are unresolved conflicts with the ex-spouse. Struggles may occur over keeping to the agreed upon visitation schedule. Mother may "forget" father was coming or neglect to have the children ready for the visit. Conversely, father may be late returning the children after the visit or deliberately spend the time with them in an activity that was forbidden by mother. In these instances, the children's visits with father simply become another battleground for unresolved feelings between the ex-spouses.

Adaptation to Single Parenthood: Sources of Social Support

Both men's and women's social relationships are disrupted by divorce. The loss of one's supportive social network is a major reason for the stress that accompanies divorce and single parenthood (Anderson, 2003). On the other hand, research also has consistently shown that the availability of social supports in the form of personal friendships, relationships with extended family, and new dating partners is positively related to adaptation to single parenthood (Edin & Lein, 1997; Pledge, 1992). Unfortunately, not all social relationships offer this positive benefit. Some can have the opposite effect and produce greater stress when they are not responsive to single parents' emotional or physical needs, or when they impose even greater demands on the single parent.

The Family of Origin

One's family of origin plays an especially important role in coping with becoming a single parent, especially for women (Kitson & Morgan, 1990). Relationships with one's family of origin often change as a result of becoming a single parent. Most women report increases in the amount of contact they have with family members. About one-fourth of divorced women live with their parents at some point after divorce. However, the kind of contact will depend greatly on the overall quality of the relationship with the family, especially with one's parents. Parents and other family members can be emotionally and instrumentally supportive (running errands, babysitting, sharing information), but they can also be more critical than friends or other acquaintances (Hetherington & Kelly, 2002).

One spouse's parents may have been very fond of the ex-spouse and fail to see the reasons for the marital breakup. They may even hold the single parent responsible for it. Alternatively, parents may not have approved of the marriage and express pleasure that it has ended. This can be perceived as either supportive or unsupportive, depending on the metamessage received. For instance, a message such as, "I told you he was no good from the beginning, but you were too thick-headed to listen," may serve only to heighten feelings of incompetence and failure. On the other hand, a message such as, "We're glad that you had the strength and courage to end a relationship that was causing you so much pain," would probably be received very differently.

One's level of individuation from the family of origin also plays an important role in determining the kinds of relationship changes that may occur. Some single-parent mothers, especially younger ones, move in with their parents following divorce. For those who have managed a "good enough" individuation, such an arrangement can provide the single mother with a host of resources such as financial assistance, help with child care, an easier reentrance into the work force, increased time for leisure activities, and a supportive emotional environment in which to resolve feelings about the divorce.

When individuation has been less successful, this arrangement can result in the single mother becoming overinvolved with her own parents, allowing them to take over her responsibilities and place her in an "incompetent" role. Others who have not yet successfully individuated may choose to separate emotionally from their parents to save themselves from criticism. In so doing, they isolate themselves further and lose a potential source of emotional and practical support (Anderson, 2003; Bowen, 1978). As a result, an important means of releasing emotional tension is lost. This can, in turn, intensify tensions and conflicts within the single-parent household or force the single mother to turn to her children or ex-spouse for emotional support (Bowen, 1978). In so doing, she may compromise her position as sole administrator for the household.

For men, the family of origin often plays a somewhat different role. Men tend to reduce their overall contact with family following divorce rather than increase it. When contacts are maintained, they tend to be more emotionally distant, less personally disclosing, and more instrumentally based than those of women. For instance, fathers may rely on their parents for help with child care, or they may help out around the parental home by doing such things as house repairs, yard work, or errands. These behaviors are in keeping with men's traditional socialization toward being objective (relying on facts, coping by trying to manage the physical environment) and functional (providing for others) (Hetherington & Kelly, 2002).

Friendships

Often a recently divorced single-parent mother does not seek new outside friends because of the financial and parenting stresses she is experiencing. She may feel overwhelmed by her many tasks and responsibilities or still be working through unresolved feelings toward the former spouse. She may still feel a sense of failure about her earlier marriage, which makes the prospect of beginning new relationships or seeking out others for support seem risky (Pledge, 1992). She may also not be able to afford either the cost of recreational activities or the expense of hiring support (child care, domestic work).

The friendships that she does maintain are generally those that have been her own personal friends rather than friends of the former couple. They are generally long-standing rather than recent acquaintances, and they tend to live nearby, generally within the same neighborhood or town. In contrast to family members, friends can be emotionally supportive without tending to be critical. A friend who is critical can much more easily be dismissed than a family member. Friends who are often the most helpful are those who can understand the reasons for the divorce, offer advice, and provide daily help with errands and tasks (Anderson, 2003).

As do most women, men experience a decline in the number of their friends, especially in the initial year following divorce. It has been estimated that both men and women decrease their friendship networks by roughly 40 percent following divorce. Friends who are lost are often those who were closer to the ex-partner or who were friends of the former couple. The divorced man or woman may withdraw from former couple friends because he or she may think that he or she no longer has any overlapping interests with married friends. Couple friends sometimes withdraw from the divorced individuals because they feel caught in the middle and forced to take sides. Others exclude the individuals from couple activities, thinking that they might be uncomfortable participating alone.

However, beyond this similarity, men's experiences with friends are considerably different from women's. Men tend to interact less frequently with their remaining friends following divorce than do women (Anderson, 2003). They are more likely to become involved with social clubs and organizations in contrast to women, who affiliate more with family (Colburn, Lin, & Moore, 1992).

Men also typically experience less support from their friends than do women. This again may be due, in part, to gender differences in socialization. Men generally disclose less personal information to their friends than do women and know considerably less about their friends' attitudes and opinions. Overall, men tend to communicate through more active channels (i.e., doing something together) than verbal ones that require a greater amount of emotional sharing (Meth & Passick, 1990). It may be the difficulty that men have reaching out to potentially supportive people along with losing contact with their children and having to leave the family home that accounts for some research showing that men experience adjustment problems such as loneliness, anxiety, and depression following divorce (Amato, 2000; Emery & Sbarra, 2002; Pledge, 1992).

Therefore, while women tend to increase their involvement with family and friends, men tend to experience a decline overall in these relationships. The relationships that men do maintain with family and friends are focused more on practical matters such as helping with child care and sharing activities rather than providing emotional support. However, the one area from which men do appear to derive emotional support is dating relationships.

Dating Relationships

Men are likely to initiate new dating relationships sooner than women. In addition, whereas women strive for greater independence and autonomy following divorce, men are more likely to redefine their identity in the context of another love relationship (Colburn et al., 1992). Although they may lack the intimate social supports of women, they are more likely to have an established network of acquaintances at work. This offers them a pool of eligible dating partners. They are also generally free of the role overload women may experience and more able to afford the expenses associated with dating. A divorced man may also be viewed as more of a catch by both younger and older women. He may be more established in a career, have more financial resources, and be less likely to be part of a "package deal" that includes the full-time responsibility for children. Therefore, not only are men more likely to seek out new dating partners in an attempt to cope with the changes they are experiencing, but they are more likely to be supported in their efforts by a social context that promotes their efforts.

Differences in men's and women's social networks and socialization may also contribute to the likelihood of men dating sooner. Men, more so than women, may tend to rely on dating partners for their needs for intimacy and support. This may come about because men lack supportive social ties with others and the interpersonal skills necessary to elicit this support. It may be that contact with a regular dating partner provides men with a safer and more secure context within which to express feelings and disclose personal vulnerabilities. Dating relationships also offer men the opportunity to express themselves sexually. This is more in keeping with the prevailing social norms for how men express feelings of closeness and intimacy.

It is important to acknowledge that, despite the obvious differences between men and women, there are no right or wrong ways to establish supportive social relationships during the transition into single parenthood. What is especially important, however, is that social relationships are not static. They change. For instance, when the stress of becoming a single mother is high, the need for stability in one's friendship network may be greater. Close-knit relationships with family and friends can provide stability at a time when many other aspects of the single mother's household are undergoing rapid and dramatic changes. Similarly, a single father may find stability by relying heavily on a new dating partner to alleviate many of the feelings of loss and uncertainty that come from leaving the family home and his children.

However, an emphasis on stability, predictability, and sameness can eventually lead to stagnation rather than growth. As noted earlier, one of the essential tasks of the single parent is to establish a new life, one that offers new opportunities and a greater sense of personal competence, self-esteem, and mastery. Such an adaptation will eventually require relinquishing one's newfound stability and again moving on. Establishing new relationships helps to reorganize one's social network such that it can be more responsive to the individual's changing needs. Social relationships introduce new experiences, options, and information into the system. Such a reorganization is an important indicator of how willing the single parent is to put the past to rest and move on toward the future.

Conclusions

It is apparent that both men and women experience stress during the transition to a single-parent household. Both undergo dramatic changes in their personal and family lives. Both are likely to experience stress due to the unresolved feelings and conflicts that may remain following divorce. They are also equally likely to encounter disruptions in their social support networks at this time.

However, men and women also differ with respect to some of the other stressors they must face. For women, divorce and single parenthood precipitate a dramatic decline in financial well-being and standard of living. This change is further compounded by a host of other potential hardships and stressors, including changes in work status, source of income, and residence. Further compounding the woman's overload is the likelihood that she will assume primary parenting responsibilities.

Most men do not experience the same levels of stress due to finances or parenting responsibilities. Men's financial stress is generally short-term, if it is a factor at all. In addition, with the exception of those fathers who assume sole custody or joint legal and physical custody for their children, most experience fewer parenting demands than their female counterparts. The major source of stress for men appears to be the sense of loss they experience both with regard to their children and with regard to the family home. Finally, men and women differ in the coping strategies they enact to adapt to single parenthood. For men, this often involves rapidly engaging in new dating relationships and initiating a new love relationship. For women, coping often entails reaching out to family and friends for both emotional and practical support. However, regardless of the form coping takes, both men and women rely heavily on supportive relationships with others to manage the stresses and hardships that accompany the transition to single parenthood. It is through these supportive relationships that both men and women attempt to redefine their own personal identities as single persons, gain a sense of mastery over their personal and family environments, and seek out new opportunities and experiences that propel their lives forward toward the future rather than backward toward the past.

Key Terms

Alimony Money that higher-earning spouses provide to their lower-earning counterparts following the end of their marriage.

Joint legal custody When parents legally share responsibility for child care, parental decision-making, and economic support of their children following divorce.

Joint physical custody When parents equally share the responsibility for providing their children with a residence. The term is used to distinguish between this arrangement and joint legal custody, which involves shared parental decision-making and economic support, and a situation in which children generally reside with one parent most of the time.

Parental child A role assumed by a child (often a daughter or older child) requiring him or her to take responsibility for parenting other children (or the parent) in the single-parent family system.

Sole administrator The role assumed by a single parent that involves accepting complete authority and responsibility for the household and all related tasks and enlisting the help of others when needed, without allowing them to take over. That is, the parent accepts that the single-parent household can no longer operate as it did when two parents were present.

CHAPTER 18

Remarriage and Stepparenting

Chapter Overview

Remarried families have a uniquely different structure than that found in traditional nuclear families. For example, the parental subsystem predates the establishment of the new marital subsystem. Also, most children have a biological parent living elsewhere. These and other variations suggest that remarried families will have to develop different strategies for managing basic tasks. Strategies also will vary at different stages of the remarried system's development.

The remarried family can be thought of as passing through four stages over time. First, there is a period of courtship and preparation for remarriage. This gives adults and children an opportunity to accommodate to the changes that are taking place. During the next phase, the early remarriage stage, identity tasks must be addressed. The middle remarriage stage involves the restructuring of the family's boundaries. During the late remarriage stage, attention shifts to strengthening the emotional bonds between family members.

Models of remarried family development offer an ideal set of guidelines against which a given family's adaptation can be compared. Not all families adapt equally well, and some will become bogged down in problematic interactional patterns that can constrain optimal development.

Remarriage and Stepparenting

Consider these facts: Approximately half of all marriages in the United States are estimated to be remarriages for one or both partners (Coleman, Ganong, & Fine, 2000). Almost two-thirds of these individuals have children from a previous relationship, thus forming stepfamilies. It has been estimated that over half of all Americans will be part of a stepfamily at some point in their lives (Visher, Visher, & Pasley, 2003). One-third of all children are expected to live in a remarried family for at least one year before reaching the age of eighteen (Field, 2001).

Remarriages tend to take place quickly after earlier marriages end. Most people who remarry do so within three to four years (U.S. Census Bureau, 2005b). However, 30 percent remarry within one year after their divorce. Men generally remarry at higher rates than do women. However, African American and

Hispanic men remarry at lower rates than white men. For divorced women, the likelihood of remarriage declines as they become older. Remarriage is most likely among women who are under age twenty-five at the time of their divorce (Bramlet & Mosher, 2002). Women who are more educated and employed are also less likely to remarry (Coleman et al., 2000). Finally, remarriages are more likely to end in divorce than first marriages. The divorce rate for remarried couples is about 60 percent (Bramlet & Mosher, 2002). As a result, children in these living situations can be expected to undergo many family transitions.

The remarried family or stepfamily is not a single, clearly defined entity. Rather, stepfamilies vary greatly in their structure and composition. The most common remarried family structure is comprised of a mother, her children from a previous relationship, and a stepfather. This undoubtedly reflects the fact that women are more likely to retain physical custody of children from an earlier marriage than are men (U.S. Census Bureau, 2005). A more complex stepfamily household might include a mother and father who both bring children from a previous relationship plus offspring born to the remarried couple.

However, remarriage rates are now beginning to decline except among older adults. More adults are bringing children into cohabiting relationships (Coleman et al., 2000). In fact, cohabiting couples are more likely (48 percent versus 37 percent) to bring children into their new household than are remarried couples. Some of these cohabiting couples with children will eventually marry. Others will continue to reside together in a cohabiting arrangement (Coleman et al., 2000). Little is known about these permanent cohabiting households with children. Most of what we know comes from research on remarried families.

These data indicate how much stepfamily life has come to characterize our contemporary culture. They also indicate dramatically how the environment in which many young children are being raised has changed from that of earlier generations. When neither spouse brings children from an earlier marriage into a remarriage, the family closely resembles that of a first marriage, and many of the same norms apply. However, numerous theorists, clinicians, and researchers have suggested that the stepfamily with children is profoundly different from the traditional nuclear family (Coleman et al., 2000; McGoldrick & Carter, 2005; Visher et al., 2003). Efforts to understand stepfamilies by applying traditional nuclear family values have been criticized for ignoring the diversity and complexity that characterize these systems. As will be shown throughout this chapter, these differences result in many stresses that are not shared by the traditional nuclear family.

The Unique Characteristics of Stepfamilies

It is important to understand the ways in which stepfamilies differ from the more traditional nuclear family. Along these lines, Visher and Visher (1996) noted that stepfamilies differ structurally from nuclear families in the following ways:

1. *All stepfamily members have experienced important losses.* Losses include parental death or divorce; loss of the single-parent family structure; changes in residence, income, and social and peer networks; changes in relationships with grandparents. Even though nuclear families may experience losses over the course of their development, the nuclear family is not born of numerous and repeated losses, as is the stepfamily.

2. *All members come with histories.* In a first marriage, the couple comes together with differing experiences and expectations based on their family of origin experiences. They gradually work out a shared set of strategies and rules for how their nuclear family will operate. Children are added gradually. In a remarriage, adults and children often come together more suddenly. Every strategy, rule, tradition, and preferred way of doing things must be renegotiated. Even the strategies for negotiating differences must be worked out.

3. *Parent–child bonds predate the new couple relationship.* That biological parent–child bonds predate the marriage relationship means that the couple does not have time to develop an intimate, clearly defined marital subsystem slowly before the arrival of children. Furthermore, in most remarried systems, the parent–child bond not only predates the remarriage but is more central than the marital relationship, at least initially. Failure to recognize this key distinction can lead stepparents to compete with their stepchildren for their new spouse's attention, as if the relationships were on the same level (McGoldrick & Carter, 2005).

4. *A biological parent exists elsewhere.* In stepfamilies, there is another parent elsewhere. Even if the other parent has died, his or her influence will remain. Memories linger and influence present behavior. When the parent lives elsewhere, strategies are required for how children will be shared. As has been noted in Chapters 16 and 17, children can easily become caught in the middle of unresolved conflicts between former spouses. Furthermore, developing a close relationship with a stepparent may be perceived by the other biological parent, the child, or both as a form of disloyalty to the biological parent. As a result, relationships between stepparents and stepchildren may be resisted and become characterized by conflict and stress.

5. *Children often are members of two households.* When children spend time in two separate households, they are generally exposed to two qualitatively different and contrasting family environments. They must learn to operate under two separate systems of rules. If the adults are willing to work cooperatively with regard to the children, children will be able to move in and out of both households easily. If, however, the relationship between the two biological parents continues to be governed by conflict, insecurity, and competitiveness, children will become caught between two warring camps and, once again, struggle with loyalty conflicts.

6. *Stepparents have few legal rights.* State laws give almost no recognition to the role of stepparents living with stepchildren (Mason, Harrison-Jay, Svare, & Wolfinger, 2002). This can lead to confusion and awkward situations when stepparents have no legal or decision-making authority in day care centers, schools, or other important areas of their stepchildren's lives. These restrictions can be especially problematic in long-standing stepfamily households where stepparents and stepchildren have established lasting emotional bonds (Visher et al., 2003). The lack of legal rights for stepparents is part of what Cherlin (1978) referred to as the **incomplete institution**. This refers to a lack of norms and institutional supports for stepfamilies.

These differences are compounded by the boundary ambiguity that exists within stepfamilies. Stepfamilies cannot operate like nuclear families, which have a clearly defined boundary around the immediate family unit. Instead, a more permeable boundary is required to allow interaction between the remarried household (e.g., biological parent, stepparent, siblings, stepsiblings) and the metafamily system. The **metafamily system** includes the other biological parent's household (perhaps another stepparent, siblings, and stepsiblings), biological relatives (e.g., grandparents, aunts, uncles, cousins), and steprelatives (e.g., grandparents, aunts, uncles, cousins) (Sager, Walker, Brown, Crohn, & Rodstein, 1981).

Finally, traditional gender patterns that encourage women to take responsibility for the emotional well-being of family members may add stress to the remarried family system (McGoldrick & Carter, 2005). These traditional assumptions can create antagonism and rivalry between stepchildren (especially stepdaughters) and stepmothers, or between new wives and ex-wives. Successful functioning in remarried families often requires placing more importance on the role of the biological parent in parenting his or her own children rather than on traditional gender role socialization. This means that each spouse, in conjunction with the ex-spouse, must assume primary, coparenting responsibility for raising and disciplining his or her own biological children (McGoldrick & Carter, 2005).

These conclusions are supported by research that has found one of the most frequently reported problems in the remarried family to be in the relationships between stepparents and stepchildren (Bray & Kelly, 1998; Coleman et al., 2000). This is especially true for stepmother–stepdaughter relationships (Coleman & Ganong, 1990). Problems in stepparent–stepchild relationships also have been found to be a critical factor in the level of marital satisfaction reported between remarried husbands and wives (Coleman et al., 2000; Shriner, 2009; Visher et al., 2003). Many of the marital difficulties that remarried couples report are related to tensions between stepparents and stepchildren (Bray & Kelly, 1998; Coleman et al., 2000).

Differences within Remarried Families

The focus on the many differences between remarried and traditional nuclear families often obscures the variations within remarried family systems. It is not surprising, therefore, that the research that has been conducted on remarried families has been criticized for assuming that all remarried families are alike. Inadequate attention has been given to the various family structures these families may assume. Some of these families may be binuclear, with biological parents sharing joint custody arrangements and children spending time in two households. In other families, one of the biological parents may be unavailable and uninvolved in child-rearing. In some families, one spouse brings children from a former marriage, whereas in others, both spouses bring children from a former marriage. In some families, all children were born before the remarriage. In yet others, some children were born before the remarriage and others were born to the remarried couple after the remarriage.

Furthermore, the issues faced by remarried families may be different depending on the stages of development of individual family members. For instance, the younger the children at the time of remarriage, the more likely they are to eventually accept the stepparent as a parent (Coleman et al., 2000; Marsiglio, 2004). Adolescent children may never accept a stepparent as a parent given their longer shared history with their own biological parents and their greater investment in individuating from the family. At a time when the remarried family is moving to establish greater cohesion and intimacy, adolescent children are focusing their attention toward peers and moving out of the family orbit.

Spouses, too, may be at different developmental stages. The tendency of men to remarry women younger than themselves can often produce a situation in which the wife is at the life cycle stage of wanting to bear children while the husband, having already passed this developmental phase, does not wish to raise another family. In general, the greater the discrepancy between the life-cycle experiences of a husband and wife, the greater the difficulty they will have in managing the transition to a new family structure (McGoldrick & Carter, 2005).

A Developmental Model for Remarried Family Systems

As has been noted throughout this text, families continually change as they encounter and adapt to various stressors, transitions, and stages over the life cycle. The family's strategies for coping with each current stage or transition are dependent, to some extent, on the strategies the family has selected for coping with earlier transitions and stages. In this manner, each family develops a distinctive identity, coping style, and structure, within which its patterns of interaction are maintained. However, changes occur that can greatly alter the family's structure and its distinct interactional style. One such change is the merging of two family systems through remarriage. The merging of two families dramatically alters how the family manages its basic tasks. The family's identity, boundaries, household management, emotional climate, and level of stress all must be renegotiated while allowing each separate family system and individual member to maintain some sense of stability and continuity with the past.

In an effort to acknowledge the unique and diverse set of demands that remarried families confront, clinical researchers and theorists have articulated developmental models that take into account the experiences of families at different stages of establishing a remarried family system. These models generally offer an ideal set of guidelines against which a given family's adaptation can be compared. The models are flexible enough to account for the tremendous diversity that characterizes remarried family systems. They also acknowledge the differences between traditional nuclear and remarried families. These models are presented in this chapter because they can help identify how a given family may, or may not, be proceeding successfully along this alternative developmental path.

Courtship and Preparation for Remarriage

The transition to a remarried family system begins before the two adults actually marry. Later adjustment to remarriage and a stepfamily system (for those with children) can be greatly facilitated during the period of **courtship and preparation** for remarriage if several issues are addressed. These issues include the continued resolution of the previous marriage, the gradual modification of the single-parent household structure, and the anticipation of the remarried family structure (Visher et al., 2003).

Resolution of the Previous Marriage. As has been noted in earlier chapters, the resolution of personal feelings about the divorce and the establishment of an effective coparenting relationship with one's former spouse can greatly facilitate adjustment to later family stages and transitions. However, it is not only "unfinished business" from one's first marriage that is brought into a new marriage but the sum total of all unfinished business with each important personal relationship (parents, siblings, former spouse) that makes us emotionally sensitive in the new relationship. When these conflicts are severe, there is a tendency to react in one of two ways. One way is to become self-protective, closed off, and afraid to make ourselves vulnerable to further hurt (i.e., we create barriers to intimacy). The other is to develop unrealistically high expectations and assume that a new partner will make up for, or erase, past hurts. To the extent that either or both remarried partners expect the other to relieve them of their past hurts, the relationship will become over burdened. On the other hand, if each partner can successfully resolve his or her own personal issues with significant persons from the past, the new relationship can start anew on its own terms (Golish, 2003; McGoldrick & Carter, 2005).

Gradual Modification of the Single-Parent Structure. Despite the overload and strain of the single-parent system, the stable patterns of interaction that have evolved within these single-parent systems are not easily altered. Many single parents, for example, develop a greater sense of personal independence as well as close, supportive relationships with their children (Afifi, 2003). Although a new courtship relationship may offer the prospects of adult intimacy, companionship, and security, it also threatens to alter the relationship changes achieved during the earlier single-parent period. Consequently, the courtship period offers time to adjust gradually to the change from a single-parent family structure to a remarried family system. In other words, a gradual period of transition allows the partners and children to maintain a sense of stability and predictability while gradual changes take place. It takes time to alter daily household routines and strategies for financial planning and decision-making. This period also offers an opportunity for prospective stepparents and stepchildren to develop friendships without the pressures that accompany living together on a regular basis. Pleasurable activities that do not place heavy loyalty demands on family members can allow a sense of cohesion and unity to begin to develop (Adler-Baeder & Higgin-Botham, 2004; Bray & Kelly, 1998; Hetherington & Kelly, 2002).

Anticipation of the Remarriage. As the couple becomes more intimate and starts to anticipate remarriage, many new issues may begin to emerge. These issues can include concerns about changes in one's personal identity, the effect of the remarriage on financial and custody arrangements with the former spouse, the response of the former spouse to the remarriage, the role of the new partner with regard to the children, the reactions of the children to the remarriage, and each partner's expectations for the new marriage based on their previous experiences. The more attention the couple is able to devote to negotiating their expectations for such issues as finances, household rules, child-rearing values, custody decisions, or children's visitation schedules, the greater the likelihood that succeeding stages will proceed smoothly (Coleman, Fine, Ganong, Downs, & Pauk, 2001; Visher & Visher, 1996). Failure to address these issues early may indicate that the couple has unclear expectations about the differences between a first family and a remarried family structure or that they are unaware of the complicated emotional issues they will face in a remarried family (Visher et al., 2003).

The Early Remarriage Stage: Defining Critical Identity Tasks

As Papernow (1993) noted, the remarried stepfamily begins with the stepparent as an outsider to a biological subsystem that has a shared history and preferred methods of relating that have been built over many years. This biological subsystem also includes an ex-spouse, dead or alive, with intimate ties to the children. From a structural perspective, such a system would be characterized as pathological due to its weak marital subsystem, an overinvolved parent–child alliance, and a weak external boundary that allows frequent intrusion in the family from an outsider (biological parent). However, such a family structure is the starting point for normal stepfamily development.

In the **early remarriage** stage, the system typically remains divided primarily along biological lines. Research has found that this stage can be turbulent and disorganized and last an average of one to two years for most families (Hetherington & Kelly, 2002). However, some families can remain stuck in this stage for many years (Papernow, 1993). The key task that must be mastered during this period, if the family is to move on to the middle and late stages of development, is establishing an identity as a stepfamily.

Given the lack of clearly defined cultural norms for remarried families, stresses related to defining a clear family identity are almost inevitable (Visher et al., 2003). In fact, our society has not yet even decided what to call these families. Numerous terms have been proposed, including "blended family," "reconstituted family," "restructured family," "stepfamily," and "remarried family." The term **remarried family** has been chosen to acknowledge that one or both spouses have been married previously. A family in which one or both partners bring children into the new household is referred to as a **stepfamily** to emphasize the presence of both biological and nonbiological parents.

Further compounding the task of family definition are the expectations, fantasies, images, and myths that different family members bring to the remarried family. For example, because the nuclear family is still considered the ideal family arrangement, many adults continue to assume that their new family can replicate their previous one, thereby perpetuating the myth of reconstituting the nuclear family (Visher et al., 2003).

Another such myth is the myth of instant love. This myth overlooks that new relationships take time to grow. Children cannot be mandated to love a stepparent. Expecting caring simply because individuals suddenly find themselves living together can easily lead to disappointment, insecurity, and anger. The first step toward developing positive relationships between stepparents and stepchildren is for stepparents to avoid trying to replace the biological parents. When adults relax and let children gauge the pace of the relationship, caring friendships and love are possible, especially when the children are young (Visher et al., 2003).

A third common myth is the myth of the wicked stepmother. Fairy tales such as "Snow White" and "Cinderella" inform children at an early age about the potential dangers of living with a stepparent. Stepmothers, too, have been exposed to this cultural stereotype in their own development and may, as a result, carry this anxiety into their relationships with stepchildren. They may try too hard to be perfect parents. Such unrealistically high expectations can lead to frustration that, in turn, can perpetuate the very myth that they are trying to avoid (Claxton-Oldfield, 2000; Visher et al., 2003).

Family members also differ in the fantasies they bring to the remarried family (Papernow, 1993). One adult may enter the new family with fantasies of "rescuing children from a deprived background" or "healing a broken family." A biological parent may expect the new spouse (stepparent) to "adore my children." The stepparent might expect that the stepchildren "will welcome me with open arms." A struggling single mother may enter remarriage fantasizing that "I have finally found someone with whom to share my load." Her new husband may anticipate that he "can now have the intimate and caring relationship that he has been looking for." On the other hand, children may hold vastly different fantasies: "I really hoped that my parents would get back together," or "If I just ignore this guy, maybe he'll go away" (Papernow, 1993).

Such myths and fantasies are a natural element of the early phase of stepfamily development. However, these myths and fantasies can easily become stressors as they come up against the reality of the situation. The stepparent may find himself or herself on the outside looking in as the new partner's energy remains focused on the children rather than on the couple. The stepparent may reach out to the stepchildren only to find them indifferent or rejecting. The stepchildren's loyalty may remain with their own absent biological parent. They may even view the stepparent as the "cause of their parents not getting back together again." During this phase, the biological parent may interpret the stepparent's failure to engage the children as "a lack of desire to be a part of the family" or as "a refusal to share the burdens of parenthood." The stepparent may perceive the partner as distant or uninvolved in the marriage. Such reactions may invoke fears of having entered into another bad marriage and of having failed again (Papernow, 1993).

It is also important to point out that the confusion experienced within the remarried family reverberates throughout the entire extended family system (Papernow, 1993). For instance, what is the relationship between the grandparents and their now ex-daughter-in-law going to be like? Will these grandparents be welcome in the new remarried family and continue to have a relationship with their grandchildren? In general, research has indicated that paternal grandparents are more likely than maternal grandparents to lose frequent or regular contact with their grandchildren following divorce and remarriage (Dunn, 2002). Finally, how are the stepchildren to be received by the stepparent's parents?

Families that successfully progress through this early stage will gradually clarify their confusion and begin to develop common expectations and a shared sense of family identity. This process also will involve clarifying each member's personal feelings and coming to some understanding of the primary strategies and rules by which the family has been operating. It is often stepparents who first become aware of the need for change in the family. This may be because their more peripheral position in the family allows them to see the situation from a more detached perspective. On the other hand, this may be due to the discomfort that comes from entering the family as an outsider. Since many of the new stepfamily's strategies and rules are determined by those inherited from the biological family, stepparents may come to experience the boundary between themselves and the rest of the family as a "biological force field" (Papernow, 1993).

However, the biological parent, too, must begin to clarify the stresses he or she is experiencing as a result of holding the central role in the family. This role includes nurturing and controlling children, maintaining a close and supportive relationship with the new spouse, and negotiating with the ex-spouse around financial and parenting issues. Biological parents naturally want to protect their children from further pain or too much change. On the other hand, they must also begin to alter their previous strategies for managing the household, caring for children, and fostering the family's emotional climate to make room for the new spouse. The biological parent's position in the middle will be even more stressful if unresolved issues with the former spouse remain.

Although awareness of the major issues confronting the family may be heightened, the family's structure is not dramatically altered at this time. The biological parent–child subsystem remains the center of family activity. However, a supportive spouse appears to offer the best chance of moving smoothly through the early stage. Such a spouse appears to be able to empathize with the partner without imposing heavy expectations that the situation change (Papernow, 1993; Visher et al., 2003).

The Middle Remarriage Stage: Restructuring Family Boundaries

Movement from the early stage to the **middle remarriage** stage is often related to an infusion of support from someone or something outside the couple's relationship (Papernow, 1993). This support might come from another stepparent who understands the situation, a self-help book for remarried families, a therapist, a support group, or a move out of the biological family's home to avoid the feeling of "living in someone else's house" (McGoldrick & Carter, 2005).

With this added thrust, the stepparent may begin to demand changes in the family's structure. The stepparent may want to spend more time as a couple, set a clearer limit on the amount of contact between the partner and his or her ex-spouse, or have a greater say in the disciplining of children. Alternatively, if the stepparent (especially a stepmother) has been expected to assume the traditional role of caretaker for the spouse's children, she or he may now demand that she or he be relieved of this excessive burden.

These bids to alter the family's structure may provoke a renewed period of stress and potential conflict as many highly charged differences are openly expressed for the first time. Although the fights that emerge at this time may seem trivial, they may actually reflect major struggles over whether the system is going to remain differentiated along biological lines or undergo change (Papernow, 1993). For example, a stepmother's temper outburst when ten-year-old Johnny leaves his dirty clothes all over the house may actually be about whether she has a right to discipline her husband's children and have a say in how the house is to be maintained. Similarly, an argument over how the stepfather sets the dinner table may actually be about whether sixteen-year-old Donna is losing the role of parental child that she assumed while living with her mother and siblings in a single-parent household. Each of these interactions can be viewed as an effort to loosen the boundaries around the biological subsystem (Afifi, 2003; Coleman et al., 2001; Golish, 2003).

As couples and children work together to resolve their differences, the structure of the family will gradually undergo change. This will require involving all family members in the process and ensuring that each individual member's needs, expectations, and feelings are attended to. It is through mutual participation, open communication, shared empathy, and respect for individual differences that family cohesion and unity are developed (Golish, 2003; Visher et al., 2003). The most successful strategies that emerge from this process are generally those that leave some of the old ways of doing things intact while also creating new rituals, rules, and boundaries (Papernow, 1993). Thus, sixteen-year-old Donna may have to give up her responsibilities for caring for younger children in the family, although she and her mother may find other ways to maintain a special mother–daughter bond. The family may have to create new holiday rituals that respect the history and legacies of both families.

Clarifying the family's boundaries also entails defining the relationship that will exist between the custodial household and the other biological parent's household. This includes establishing a routine and mutually acceptable schedule of visitation, child support, and parental decision-making (Visher et al., 2003). For example, both biological parents may have to agree that children will be required to finish their homework before being allowed to play. However, it also is important to the adjustment of all family members, but especially for children who have loyalties to two families, that differences between the two households be openly accepted without connotations of right or wrong (Papernow, 1993). For instance, it may be permissible to eat dinner while watching television in one home but not in the other.

As was true in the early stage of the remarried family's development, changes in the family's boundaries during the middle stage also reverberate throughout the extended family system. For example, should the family change its rituals around Christmas or Hanukkah, these changes might alter how four sets of grandparents, aunts, and uncles (biological mother's, biological father's, stepparent's, and stepparent's ex-spouse's) celebrate their holiday rituals. Fulfilling obligations to each family's traditions and legacies while also redefining the present family structure can become exceedingly complex.

Nonetheless, by the time most families complete this stage, they have begun to function as a cohesive unit with more clearly defined boundaries and a shared sense of belonging. It appears that most families complete this stage after about three to five years (Hetherington & Kelly, 2002).

The Late Remarriage Stage: Strengthening Emotional Bonds

The **late remarriage** stage is marked by a greater sense of shared intimacy and authenticity in family relationships (Papernow, 1993). With the restructuring of the family's boundaries comes greater flexibility in roles and interactional patterns among family members. The family at this stage is characterized by a higher level of differentiation with dyadic personal relationships taking precedence over disruptive triangles and coalitions.

It becomes possible for stepparents and stepchildren to have more personal one-to-one relationships without interference from the biological parent. Although issues of inclusion and exclusion may periodically reappear because biological ties often remain more intense than steprelationships (Coleman & Ganong, 1990), these issues by now have been essentially resolved. In some families, this may mean that members have agreed to accept a more distant relationship between a stepparent and a stepchild. In other families, these issues may be resolved by the stepparent assuming a role of "primary parent" to the stepchild equal in authority to the biological parent. Whichever is the case, the role of stepparent has now been clearly defined.

The clearly defined stepparent role is defined by the following characteristics: (1) the role does not usurp or compete with the biological parent of the same sex; (2) the role includes an intergenerational boundary between stepparent and stepchild; (3) the role is sanctioned by the rest of the stepfamily, especially the spouse; and (4) the role incorporates the special qualities this stepparent brings to the family (Papernow, 1993). Whereas the stepparent's differentness may have been a source of conflict in the past, these qualities may now be appreciated for the diversity they bring to the family. For example, a stepmother's interest in clothing styles and fashion that may have been criticized as extravagant or weird during earlier stages may now be considered a resource by an adolescent stepdaughter who is more conscious of her appearance with her peers.

With the establishment of personal stepparent–stepchild relationships and the clarification of boundaries with extended family and the other parental households with which children are shared, the couple's relationship may now assume a more central position in the family system. The couple may now be able to turn their attention to "getting to know each other all over again" and experience their relationship in more personally supportive and intimate ways (Golish, 2003; Papernow, 1993).

As in any family, new stresses will continue to emerge for families at this stage of remarriage development. Decisions about childbearing; changes in children's visitation and financial arrangements; renegotiations of coparenting decisions with biological parents; or routine stressors brought on by changes in employment, residence, or income can stress the family and precipitate changes in family interactions. When the stress becomes great, families may find themselves reexperiencing the entire remarriage developmental cycle. Periods of confusion or conflict, accompanied by alterations in the family's structure and perhaps polarization along biological lines, may all occur. However, these changes now occur within the context of a solid couple and stepfamily structure with a history of successful coping and problem resolution.

Problematic Family System Dynamics in Remarried Stepfamilies

Not all families will proceed through the various stages of remarried family development noted above. Some families will become stuck in an earlier stage indefinitely or for an extended period (Braithwaite, Olson, Golish, Soukup, & Turman, 2001). Others will end their remarriage through divorce. As was noted earlier, divorce rates among the remarried tend to be even higher than for those in first marriages. Thus, it is clear that remarriage is fraught with potential complications that can interfere with successful adjustment.

Relatively little research has examined the system dynamics that foster or interfere with stepfamilies' adjustment and adaptation. The research that has been undertaken generally suggests that stepfamilies are less cohesive and slightly less effective than nuclear families at problem solving and communicating. However, the differences between the two groups of families on these factors are generally small (Coleman et al., 2000; Hetherington & Kelly, 2002). This combined with the fact that members of stepfamilies and nuclear families generally report similar levels of well-being and marital satisfaction has led researchers to conclude that patterns of effective functioning in stepfamilies are different from those in nuclear families (Coleman et al., 2000).

One important factor in the patterns of interaction found in stepfamilies appears to be the extent to which triangles and coalitions form between family members. Although research has found that even well-functioning stepfamilies are more likely to have coalitions than well-functioning nuclear families, these coalitions are far more extensive and intense in dysfunctional stepfamilies (Afifi, 2003). Given the complexity of the stepfamily system, there are a great many forms that these triangles and coalitions can take. Descriptions of some of the most common ones follow.

Triangles Involving an Ex-Spouse

When the former married couple has not succeeded in reaching an emotional divorce, these unresolved conflicts may produce stress for the remarriage. Remarried spouses may disagree over how to deal with the former spouse over child custody, child support, or other issues. In addition, the ex-spouse may frequently intrude into the new marriage by remaining dependent on the former spouse for emotional, practical, or financial support. The effect of this triangle is to interfere with the establishment of the remarried couple's identity and the creation of a clear boundary around the new marital relationship.

Another triangle that can occur when spouses have not resolved their earlier divorce involves one or more children. Here conflicts develop between the remarried couple and an ex-spouse over the care of a child. In this situation, the tension in the triangle is most often felt by the child, who begins to misbehave, develop problems at school, or asks to have custody shifted to the other biological parent. The remarried couple tends to unite in blaming the other parent or the child for the problem, while the noncustodial parent blames the remarried couple.

Successful resolution of both of these triangles will require the two former spouses to resolve their feelings toward one another regarding their separation and divorce. In the case of triangles involving a child, the management of the child should be placed in the hands of the biological parents. The new spouse can then assume a neutral position rather than siding against the child. The new remarried couple can then work toward individuating from one another in their own relationship so that differences and disagreements can be aired and the biological parent can have a personal relationship with the child without interference from the new spouse (Afifi, 2003; McGoldrick & Carter, 2005; Visher et al., 2003).

Triangles within the Remarried System

Sometimes the new wife is expected to assume the traditional role of primary caretaker for her new husband's children. The children will generally resent the stepmother's involvement, especially when they still have regular contact with their own biological mother. The resolution of this situation will generally require that the father assume the primary responsibility for enforcing discipline and providing support to the children. The stepmother then can have time to develop a trusting relationship with the children (Carter & McGoldrick, 2005b).

Another possible triangle puts the new husband in a stressful position in relation to his new wife and her children. The second husband may be seen as both rescuer and intruder (McGoldrick & Carter, 2005). He is expected to share the single mother's financial and parental burdens, but he may also be viewed as disrupting the close bonds that have become established between his new wife and her children during the single-parenthood period (Papernow, 1993; Visher et al., 2003).

The stepfather's expressions of authority are then resented by the stepchildren, who go to their biological parent for support.

Here again, resolution will require that parental responsibility be assumed by the biological mother, with her new husband assuming a role that is supportive of his wife's efforts. Relationships between stepparents and stepchildren require time to develop. Unresolved issues with former spouses also must be addressed such that children are not caught in the middle, thereby reactivating stress in the remarried marital subsystem.

A third possible triangle involves the remarried couple, his children, and her children. In this triangle, the couple may report that they are happily married and that their only problem is that their two sets of children are constantly fighting. In this instance, the children may be fighting out the unexpressed differences or disagreements between the remarried spouses (McGoldrick & Carter, 2005). These disagreements may involve unexpressed feelings about ex-spouses, about how to manage their own and each other's children, or about any of the myriad of tasks associated with establishing a new household. It is not uncommon for remarried partners to be cautious with one another, fearing that disagreements or conflicts may result in another failed marriage and loss (Papernow, 1993). However, the resolution of this triangle requires that spouses begin to communicate openly about their differences and implement problem-solving strategies that are mutually acceptable to both (Adler-Baeder & Higginbotham, 2004; Visher et al., 2003).

A fourth possible triangle involves one parent, instead of the couple, caught between two sibling subsystems. This triangle may appear on the surface to represent simple household conflict, with the parent caught between two "opposing camps" of children. However, the source of this conflict can be quite complex. It can represent a series of interlocking triangles including the children, the remarried couple, and the couple's ex-spouses (McGoldrick & Carter, 2005). Although it is quite common during the early stages of remarriage, when this arrangement continues over time, it can come to represent the system's failure to alter its structure toward a more cohesive, integrated, and flexible family unit.

Instead, the family remains divided primarily along biological lines. The children act out the unresolved issues of each spouse with their former spouses or the children's own conflicted loyalties to their noncustodial parent and the new remarried system. Resolution of this impasse will require active efforts by both parents to establish clearly defined relationships with their own and each other's children. Open communication and sharing of parental responsibilities with the children's other biological parent are also essential.

Triangles Involving the Extended Family

Triangles with parents or in-laws are especially likely when the latter disapprove of the remarriage or when they have had an active role in raising their grandchildren (McGoldrick & Carter, 2005). For instance, the grandparents may remain loyal to the ex-spouse (their grandchildren's biological parent), thereby causing the new spouse to feel excluded. When the grandparents have been active in parenting their grandchildren, they may resent forfeiting this role to the new stepparent, thereby creating a triangle among the children, the grandparents, and the stepparent. This may force the children to take sides, leaving the stepparent again feeling excluded or forcing the grandparents to withdraw. The resolution of this triangle generally requires that each spouse take responsibility for clarifying the boundary between his or her parents and the remarried system. The other spouse must generally agree to stay out of it and to stop arguing or criticizing the in-laws.

Conclusions

Adults marry, divorce, become single parents, and remarry with great frequency in contemporary society. These events alter the family's developmental course in dramatic fashion. The structure of the family undergoes many changes in a typically short period. Members are added or lost to the system. Relationships undergo a series of changes as previous roles (e.g., marital partner) are redefined and new roles are created (e.g., ex-spouse, coparent, stepparent). The family is called on to alter continually its strategies and rules as it seeks to fulfill its basic tasks.

It is also important to emphasize that the changes in structure that accompany divorce, singlehood, and remarriage occur in conjunction with other typical and expected developmental changes in the family and its members. In the course of this text, patterns of change or stages through which families must pass have been discussed as basic or universal. For instance, one underlying assumption has been that individuals are continually individuating by negotiating and renegotiating their levels of individuality and intimacy with significant others over the entire life course. Another has been that the family system must continually alter its strategies and rules in response to individuals' changes so that an environment conducive to each member's growth and development is maintained. Still another has been that it is possible to anticipate the kinds of stresses that families will often face at each developmental stage and that certain coping strategies (e.g., effective communication, conflict-resolution skills) can ease the transition from one developmental stage to another.

However, it has been also repeatedly emphasized that expected developmental stages interact with each family's unique set of coping strategies, internal and external stressors (e.g., disability of a family member, unemployment, natural disasters), family background, and intergenerational legacy to produce untold complexity and diversity. No two families are alike. Families vary greatly in how they manage the stresses and strains of divorce, remarriage, or any of the other developmental stages examined in this text. Each family must ultimately be understood by examining its own unique context. In the final analysis, the theories and models presented here provide raw, primitive snapshots of the family's inner world. None of them, however, comes close to approximating the actual experience of being a member of a family.

Key Terms

Courtship and preparation An initial stage in the process of remarriage that provides time to resolve issues related to the earlier divorce of one or both partners and a gradual introduction of the new stepparent into the present single-parent system.

Early remarriage The second stage of the process of remarriage beginning immediately after the remarriage, during which the system typically remains divided primarily along biological lines.

Incomplete institution A lack of norms and institutional supports for stepfamilies.

Late remarriage The fourth and final stage of the remarriage process, marked by a greater sense of shared intimacy and authenticity in family relationships. Restructuring is now complete, and the family is characterized by flexibility in roles and interactional patterns. Personal one-to-one relationships take precedence over disruptive triangles and coalitions.

Metafamily system A remarried family system that includes the households of both biological parents (perhaps other stepparents, siblings, and stepsiblings), biological relatives (perhaps grandparents, aunts, uncles, and cousins), and steprelatives (perhaps grandparents, aunts, uncles, and cousins).

Middle remarriage The third stage of the remarriage process during which the structure of the family will gradually undergo change.

Remarried family A family in which one or both spouses have been married previously.

Stepfamily A family in which one or both partners bring children into the household, resulting in the presence of both biological and nonbiological parents.

References

Adler-Baeder, F., & Higginbotham, B. (2004). Implications of remarriage and stepfamily formation for marriage education. *Family Relations, 53,* 448–458.

Administration for Children and Families (2006). Child maltreatment: 2004. U.S. Department of Health and Human Services. www.acf.hhs.gov/programs/cb/pubs/cm04/index.htm

Afifi, T. (2003). Feeling caught in stepfamilies: Managing boundary turbulence through appropriate communication privacy rules. *Journal of Social and Personal Relationships, 20,* 729–755.

Ahrons, C. R. (2004). *We're still family: What grown children have to say about their parents' divorce.* New York: HarperCollins.

Ahrons, C. R. (2005). Divorce: An unscheduled family transition. In B. Carter & M. McGoldrick (Eds.), *The expanded family life cycle: Individual, family, and social perspectives* (3rd ed., pp. 381–398). Boston: Allyn & Bacon.

Aldous, J. (1978). *Family careers: Developmental change in families.* New York: John Wiley & Sons.

Aldous, J., & Klein, D. M. (1991). Sentiment and services: Models of intergenerational relationships in mid-life. *Journal of Marriage and Family, 53,* 595–608.

Allegretto, S. A. (2005). *Basic family budgets: Working families' income often fails to meet living expenses around the U.S.* Washington, DC: Economic Policy Institute.

Allen, K., Blieszner, R., & Roberto, K. A. (2000). Families in the middle and later years: A review and critique of research in the 1990s. *Journal of Marriage and Family, 62,* 911–926.

Allen, K. R., Fine, M. A., & Demo, D. H. (2000). An overview of family diversity: Controversies, questions, and values. In D. H. Demo, K. R. Allen, & M. A. Fine (Eds.), *Handbook of family diversity* (pp. 1–14). New York: Oxford University Press.

Alline, K., & Johnson, L. (2002). Sexuality. In R. Ham, P. Sloane, & G. Warshaw (Eds.), *Primary care in geriatrics* (4th ed., pp. 427–436). New York: Mosby.

Allison, M. D., & Sabatelli, R. M. (1988). Differentiation and individuation as mediators of identity and intimacy in adolescence. *Journal of Adolescent Research, 3,* 1–16.

Almeida, D. M., Maggs, J. L., & Galambos, N. L. (1993). Wives' employment hours and spousal participation in family work. *Journal of Family Psychology, 7,* 233–244.

Amato, P. R. (2000). The consequences of divorce for adults and children. *Journal of Marriage and Family, 62*(4), 1269–1287.

Amato, P. R., & Booth, A. (1997). *A generation at risk: Growing up in an era of family upheaval.* Cambridge, MA: Harvard University Press.

Amato, P. R., & Cheadle, J. (2005). The long reach of divorce: Divorce and child well-being across three generations. *Journal of Marriage and Family, 67,* 191–206.

Amato, P. R., & DeBoer, D. D. (2001). The transmission of marital instability across generations: Relationship skills or commitment to marriage. *Journal of Marriage and Family, 63,* 1038–1051.

American Association of Retired Persons (2001). Coping with grief and loss: Statistics about widowhood. www.aarp.org/griefandloss/stats.html

American Medical Association (1990). *America's adolescents: How healthy are they?* Chicago: Author.

American Psychiatric Association (2000). *Diagnostic and statistical manual of mental disorders* (4th ed., Text Revision). Washington, DC: Author.

American Psychiatric Association Work Group on Eating Disorders (2000). Practice guidelines for the treatment of patients with eating disorders (revision). *American Journal of Psychiatry, 57*(1 Suppl.), 1–39.

Ammerman, R. T. (1990). Etiological models of child maltreatment: A behavioral perspective. *Behavior Modification, 14,* 230–254.

Anderson, C. (2003). The diversity, strengths, and challenges of single-parent households. In F. Walsh (Ed.), *Normal family processes: Growing diversity and complexity* (pp. 121–152). New York: Guilford.

Anderson, S. A. (1988). Parental stress and coping during the leaving home transition. *Family Relations, 37,* 160–165.

Anderson, S. A. (1990). Changes in parental adjustment and communication during the leaving home transition. *Journal of Social and Personal Relationships, 7,* 47–68.

Anderson, S. A., & Cramer-Benjamin, D. (1999). The impact of couple violence on parenting and children: An overview and clinical implications. *American Journal of Family Therapy, 27,* 1–19.

Anderson, S. A., & Fleming, W. M. (1986). Late adolescents' home-leaving strategies: Predicting ego identity and college adjustment. *Adolescence, 21,* 453–459.

Anderson, S. A., & Gavazzi, S. M. (1990). A test of the Olson Circumplex model: Examining its curvilinear assumption and the presence of extreme types. *Family Process, 29,* 309–324.

Anderson, S. A., & Sabatelli, R. M. (1990). Differentiating differentiation and individuation: Conceptual and operational challenges. *American Journal of Family Therapy, 18,* 32–50.

Anderson, S. A., & Sabatelli, R. M. (1992). Differentiation in the family system scale: DIFS. *American Journal of Family Therapy, 20,* 77–89.

Andrews, B., & Brewin, C. R. (1990). Attributions of blame for marital violence: A study of antecedents and consequences. *Journal of Marriage and Family, 52,* 757–767.

Appel, W. (1983). *Cults in America.* New York: Holt, Rinehart and Winston.

Aquilino, W. S. (1990). Likelihood of parent–adult child co-residence. *Journal of Marriage and Family, 52,* 405–419.

Aquilino, W. S., & Supple, K. (1991). Parent–child relationship and parent's satisfaction with living arrangements when children live at home. *Journal of Marriage and Family, 53,* 178–198.

Arditti, J. A. (1992). Factors related to custody, visitation, and child support for divorced fathers: An exploratory analysis. *Journal of Divorce and Remarriage, 17*(3–4), 23–42.

Arendell, T. (1995). *Fathers and divorce.* Thousand Oaks, CA: Sage.

Arendell, T. (2000). Conceiving and investigating motherhood: The decade's scholarship. *Journal of Marriage and Family, 62*(4), 1192–1207.

Arnett, J. J. (2000). Emerging adulthood: A theory of development from the late teens through the twenties. *American Psychologist, 55,* 469–480.

Arnett, J. J. (2006). Understanding the new way of coming of age. In. J. J. Arnett & J. L. Tanner (Eds.), *Emerging adults in America: Coming of age in the 21st century* (pp. 3–19). Washington, DC: American Psychological Association.

Avis, J. M. (1992). Where are all the family therapists? Abuse and violence within families and family therapy's response. *Journal of Marital and Family Therapy, 18,* 225–232.

Ayoub, C. C., & Willett, J. B. (1992). Families at risk of child maltreatment: Entry-level characteristics and growth in family functioning during treatment. *Child Abuse and Neglect, 16,* 495–511.

Babcock, J. C., Walz, J., Jacobson, N. S., & Gottman, J. M. (1993). Power and violence: The relation between communication patterns, power discrepancies, and domestic violence. *Journal of Consulting and Clinical Psychology, 61,* 40–50.

Bagarozzi, D. A., & Anderson, S. A. (1989). *Personal, marital, and family myths: Theoretical formulations and clinical strategies.* New York: W. W. Norton.

Bagarozzi, D. A., Bagarozzi, J. I., Anderson, S. A., & Pollane, L. (1984). Premarital education and training sequence (PETS): A three year follow-up of an experimental study. *Journal of Counseling and Development, 63,* 91–100.

Barber, B. K. (1996). Parental psychological control: Revisiting a neglected construct. *Child Development, 67*(6), 3296–3319.

Barber, B. K. (2002). *Intrusive parenting: How psychological control affects children and adolescents.* Washington, DC: American Psychological Association Press.

Barnes, G. M., & Farrell, M. P. (1992). Parental support and control as predictors of adolescent drinking, delinquency, and related problem behaviors. *Journal of Marriage and Family, 54,* 763–776.

Barnett, O. W., Miller-Perrin, C. L., & Perrin, R. D. (1997). *Family violence across the lifespan.* Thousand Oaks, CA: Sage.

Barnett, R. C., Marshall, N. L., & Pleck, J. H. (1992). Men's multiple roles and their relationship to men's psychological distress. *Journal of Marriage and Family, 54,* 358–367.

Barnett, R. C., & Shen, Y. C. (1997). Gender, high- and low-schedule-control housework tasks, and psychological distress: A study of dual-earner couples. *Journal of Family Issues, 18,* 403–428.

Bartle, S. E., & Anderson, S. A. (1991). Similarity between parents' and adolescents' levels of individuation. *Adolescence, 26,* 913–924.

Bartle-Haring, S., & Sabatelli, R. M. (1998, November). Can we "see" family process and would it matter if we could? Paper presented at the National Council on Family Relations Theory Construction and Research Methodology Workshop, Milwaukee, WI.

Baruch, G. K., Biener, L., & Barnett, R. C. (1987). Women and gender research on work and family stress. *American Psychologist, 42,* 130–136.

Barusch, A. S. (1995). Programming for family care of elderly dependents: Mandates, incentives, and service rationing. *Social Work, 40,* 315–322.

Bates, J. E., & Pettit, G. S. (2007). Temperament, parenting and socialization. In J. E. Grusec & P. D. Hastings (Eds.), *Handbook of socialization* (pp. 153–177). New York: Guilford Press.

Baum, N. (2003). The male way of mourning divorce: When, what, and how. *Clinical Social Work Journal, 31,* 37–50.

Baum, N. (2004). Typology of post-divorce parental relationships and behaviors. *Journal of Divorce and Remarriage, 41,* 53–79.

Baumrind, D. (1991a). The influence of parenting style on adolescent competence and substance use. *Journal of Early Adolescence, 11*(1), 56–95.

Baumrind, D. (1991b). Parenting styles and adolescent development. In J. Brooks-Gunn, R. Lerner, &

A. C. Petersen (Eds.), *The encyclopedia of adolescence* (pp. 746–758). New York: Garland.

Baxter, L. A., & Bullis, C. (1986). Turning points in developing romantic relationships. *Human Communication Research, 2,* 469–493.

Baxter, L. A., & Wilmot, W. W. (1984). Secret tests: Social strategies for acquiring information about the state of the relationship. *Communication Research, 11,* 171–201.

Bay, R. C., & Braver, S. L. (1990). Perceived control of the divorce settlement process and interparental conflict. *Family Relations, 39,* 382–387.

Beach, S. R., Schulz, R., Yell, J. L., & Jackson, S. (2000). Negative and positive health effects of caring for a disabled spouse: Longitudinal findings from the caregiver health effects study. *Psychology and Aging, 15,* 259–271.

Beavers, W. R., & Hampson, R. B. (2003). Measuring family competence: The Beavers Systems model. In F. Walsh (Ed.), *Normal family process* (3rd ed., pp. 549–580). New York: Guilford Press.

Becker, A. E., Grinspoon, S. K., Klibanski, A., & Herzog, D. B. (1999). Eating disorders. *New England Journal of Medicine, 340*(14), 1092–1098.

Becvar, D. S. (2001). *In the presence of grief: Helping family members resolve death, dying, and bereavement issues.* New York: Guilford.

Becvar, D. S., & Becvar, R. J. (2000). *Family therapy: A systemic integration* (4th ed.). Boston: Allyn & Bacon.

Bedford, V. H., & Blieszner, R. (1997). Personal relationships in later life families. In S. Duck (Ed.), *Handbook of personal relationships* (2nd ed., pp. 523–539). New York: Wiley.

Belitz, J., & Schacht, A. (1992). Satanism as a response to abuse: The dynamics and treatment of satanic involvement in male youths. *Adolescence, 27,* 855–872.

Belsky, J. (1984). The determinants of parenting: A process model. *Child Development, 55,* 83–96.

Belsky, J., & Kelly, J. (1994). *The transition to parenthood.* New York: Dell.

Belsky, J., & Rovine, M. (1990). Patterns of marital change across the transition to parenthood. *Journal of Marriage and Family, 52,* 5–19.

Belsky, J., Steinberg, L., & Draper, P. (1991). Childhood experience, interpersonal development, and reproductive strategy: An evolutionary theory of socialization. *Child Development, 62,* 647–670.

Belsky, J., Youngblade, L., Rovine, M., & Volling, B. (1991). Patterns of marital change and parent–child interaction. *Journal of Marriage and Family, 53,* 487–498.

Bem, S. (1993). *Lenses of gender.* New Haven, CT: Yale University Press.

Berardo, D. H. (2001). Social and psychological issues of aging and health. In J. C. Delafuente & R. B. Stewart (Eds.), *Therapeutics in the elderly* (3rd ed.) Cincinnati, OH: Harvey Whitney Books.

Berger, P., & Kellner, H. (1985). Marriage and the construction of reality: An exercise in the microsociology of knowledge. In G. Handel (Ed.), *The psychosocial interior of the family* (3rd ed., pp. 3–20). New York: Aldine.

Bernard, J. (1974). *The future of motherhood.* New York: Dial Press.

Bernardo, D. H., Shehan, C. L., & Leslie, G. R. (1987). A residue of tradition: Jobs, careers, and spouses' time in housework. *Journal of Marriage and Family, 49,* 381–390.

Berscheid, E. (1985). Interpersonal attraction. In G. Lindzey & E. Aronson (Eds.), *Handbook of social psychology* (3rd ed., pp. 413–484). New York: Random House.

Berscheid, E., & Reis, H. T. (1998). Attraction and close relationships. In D. T. Gilbert, S. T. Fiske, & G. Lindzey (Eds.),*The handbook of social psychology* (4th ed., pp. 193–281). New York: McGraw-Hill.

Berscheid, E., & Walster, E. (1974). A little bit about love. In T. L. Huston (Ed.), *Foundations of interpersonal attraction* (pp. 356–382). New York: Academic Press.

Best, K. R., Cox, M. J., & Payne, C. (2002). Structural and supportive changes in couples' family and friendship networks across the transition to parenthood. *Journal of Marriage and Family, 64,* 517–531.

Bianci, S. (2000). Maternal employment and time with children: Dynamic change or surprising continuity? *Demography, 37,* 401–414.

Billingsley, A. (1974). *Black families and the struggle for survival: Teaching our children to walk tall.* New York: Friendship Press.

Blacker, L. (1999). The launching phase of the family life cycle. In B. Carter & M. McGoldrick (Eds.), *The expanded family life cycle: Individual, family, and social perspectives* (3rd ed., pp. 287–306). Boston: Allyn & Bacon.

Blain, J. (1994). Discourses on agency and domestic labor: Family discourse and gendered practice in dual-earner families. *Journal of Family Issues, 15,* 515–549.

Blair, S. L., & Lichter, D. T. (1991). Measuring the division of household labor: Gender segregation of housework among American couples. *Journal of Family Issues, 12,* 91–113.

Blau, P. M. (1964). *Exchange and power in social life.* New York: Wiley.

Blumstein, P., & Schwartz, P. W. (1983). *American couples.* New York: William Morrow & Co.

Bogenschneider, K., Wu, M., Raffaelli, M., & Tsay, J. C. (1998). Parent influences on adolescent peer orientation and substance use: The interface of parenting practices and values. *Child Development, 69,* 1672–1688.

Bolton, C. D. (1961). Mate selection as the development of a relationship. *Marriage and Family Living, 23,* 234–240.

Bomar, J. A., & Sabatelli, R. M. (1996). Family system dynamics, gender, and psychosocial maturity in late adolescence. *Journal of Adolescent Research, 11*, 421–439.

Boss, P. (1988). *Family stress management.* Newbury Park, CA: Sage.

Boss, P. A. (1980). Normative family stress: Family boundary change across the life-span. *Family Relations, 29*, 445–450.

Boszormenyi-Nagy, I., & Krasner, B. (1986). *Between give and take: A clinical guide to contextual therapy.* New York: Brunner/Mazel.

Boszormenyi-Nagy, I., & Spark, G. (1973). *Invisible loyalties.* New York: Harper & Row.

Boszormenyi-Nagy, I., & Ulrich, D. (1981). Contextual family therapy. In A. S. Gurman & D. P. Kniskern (Eds.), *Handbook of family therapy.* New York: Brunner/Mazel.

Bowen, M. (1966). The use of family theory in clinical practice. *Comprehensive Psychiatry, 7*, 345–374.

Bowen, M. (1976). Family reaction to death. In P. Guerin (Ed.), *Family therapy: Theory and practice* (pp. 335–349). New York: Gardner Press.

Bowen, M. (1978). *Family therapy in clinical practice.* New York: Jason Aronson.

Bowlby, J. (1979). *The making and breaking of affectional bonds.* London: Taristock.

Bowlby, J. (1988). *A secure base: Parent–child attachment and healthy human development.* London: Basic Books.

Boyd-Franklin, N. (2003). Race, class, and poverty. In F. Walsh (Ed.), *Normal family processes: Growing diversity and complexity* (3rd ed., pp. 260–279). New York: Guilford.

Bradbury, T. N., Rogge, R., & Lawrence, E. (2001). Reconsidering the role of conflict in marriage. In A. Booth, A. C. Crouter, & M. Clements (Eds.), *Couples in conflict* (pp. 59–81). Mahway, NJ: Lawrence Erlbaum.

Bradley, R. H., & Corwyn, R. F. (2002). Socioeconomic status and child development. *Annual Review of Psychology, 53*, 371–399.

Braithwaite, D. O., Olson, L. N., Golish, T. D., Soukup, C., & Turman, P. (2001). Becoming a family: Developmental processes represented in blended family discourse. *Journal of Applied Communication Research, 29*, 221–247.

Bramlett, M. D., & Mosher, W. D. (2001). *First marriage dissolution, divorce and remarriage in the United States. Advanced data from vital and health statistics* (No. 323). Hyattsville, MD: National Center for Health Statistics.

Bramlett, M. D., & Mosher, W. D. (2002). *Cohabitation, marriage, divorce, and remarriage in the United States* (Vital Health Statistics Series 23, Number 22). Hyattsville, MD: National Center for Health Statistics.

Bray, J. H., Adams, G., Getz, G., & Baer, P. (2000). Adolescent individuation and alcohol use in multiethnic youth. *Journal of Studies on Alcohol, 61*(4), 588–597.

Bray, J. H., Adams, G., Getz, G., & Baer, P. (2001). Developmental, family, and ethnic influences on adolescent alcohol usage: A growth curve approach. *Journal of Family Psychology, 15*(2), 301–314.

Bray, J. H., Adams, G. J., Getz, G. J., & Stovall, T. (2001). The interactive effects of individuation, family factors, and stress on adolescent alcohol use. *American Journal of Orthopsychiatry, 71*, 436–449.

Bray, J. H., & Kelly, J. (1998). *Stepfamilies: Love, marriage, and parenting in the first decade.* New York: Broadway.

Bray, J. H., Williamson, D. S., & Malone, P. (1984). Personal authority in the family system: Development of a questionnaire to measure personal authority in intergenerational family processes. *Journal of Marital and Family Therapy, 10*, 167–178.

Brehm, S. S., Miller, R. S., Perlman, D., & Cambell, S. M. (2002). *Intimate relationships* (3rd ed.). New York: McGraw Hill.

Briggs, C. L. (1986). *Learning how to ask: A sociolinguistic appraisal of the role of the interview in social science research.* Cambridge: Cambridge University Press.

Broderick, C. B. (1993). *Understanding family process.* Newbury Park, CA: Sage.

Brown, F. H. (1989). The impact of death and serious illness on the family life cycle. In B. Carter & M. McGoldrick (Eds.), *The changing family life cycle* (pp. 457–482). Boston: Allyn & Bacon.

Buckley, W. (1967). *Sociology and modern systems theory.* Englewood Cliffs, NJ: Prentice Hall.

Buehler, C., Anthony, C., Krishnakumar, A., Stone, G., Gerard, J., & Pemberton, S. (1997). Interparental conflict and youth problem behaviors: A meta-analysis. *Journal of Child and Family Studies, 6*, 233–247.

Bumpass, L. L., & Lu, H. (2000). Trends in cohabitation and implications for children's family contexts. *Population Studies, 54*, 29–41.

Bumpass, L. L., Martin, T. C., & Sweet, J. A. (1991). The impact of family background and early marital factors on marital disruption. *Journal of Family Issues, 12*, 22–42.

Bumpass, L. L., & Raley, R. K. (1995). Redefining single-parent families: Cohabitation and changing family reality. *Demography, 32*, 97–109.

Burman, B., John, R., & Margolin, G. (1992). Observed patterns of conflict in violent, nonviolent, and nondistressed couples. *Behavioral Assessment, 14*, 15–37.

Burns, T. (1973). A structural theory of social exchange. *Acta Sociologica, 16*, 188–208.

Burr, W., Leigh, G. K., Day, R. D., & Constantine, J. (1979). Symbolic interaction and the family.

In W. R. Burr, R. Hill, F. I. Nye, & I. L. Reiss (Eds.), *Contemporary theories about the family, Volume II.* New York: Free Press.

Burr, W. R., Day, R. D., & Bahr, K. S. (1993). *Family science.* Pacific Grove, CA: Brooks/Cole.

Byng-Hall, J. (1980). Symptom bearer as marital distance regulator: Clinical implications. *Family Process, 19,* 355–367.

Byng-Hall, J. (1982). Family legends: Their significance for the family therapist. In A. Bentovim, G. Barnes, & A. Cooklin (Eds.), *Family therapy: Complementary frameworks of theory and practice* (Vol. 1, pp. 213–228). New York: Grune & Stratton.

Byng-Hall, J. (1991). Family scripts and loss. In F. Walsh & M. McGoldrick (Eds.), *Living beyond loss: Death in the family* (pp. 130–143). New York: Norton.

Byng-Hall, J. (2002). Relieving parentified children's burdens in families with insecure attachment patterns. *Family Process, 41,* 375–388.

Calhoun, L. G., & Allen, B. G. (1991). Social reactions to the survivor of a suicide in the family: A review of the literature. *Omega, 23,* 95–108.

Cannuscio, C. C., Jones, C., Kawachi, I., Colditz, G. A., Berkman, L., & Rimm, E. (2002). Reverberation of family illness: A longitudinal assessment of informal caregiver and mental health status in the nurses' health study. *American Journal of Public Health, 92,* 305–311.

Carpenter, C., & Gates, G. J. (2008). Gay and lesbian partnership: Evidence from California. *Demography, 45,* 573–590.

Carter, B., & McGoldrick, M. (2005a). The expanded family life cycle: Individual, family, and social perspectives. In B. Carter & M. McGoldrick (Eds.), *The expanded family life cycle* (pp. 1–24). Boston: Allyn & Bacon.

Carter, B., & McGoldrick, M. (2005b). The divorce cycle: A major variation in the American family life cycle. In B. Carter & M. McGoldrick (Eds.), *The expanded family life cycle: Individual, family, and social perspectives* (3rd ed., pp. 373–380). Boston: Allyn & Bacon.

Cassidy, J., Parke, R., Butkovsky, L., & Braungart, J. (1992). Family-peer connections: The roles of emotional expressiveness within the family and children's understanding of emotions. *Child Development, 63,* 603–618.

Catalano, S. (2006). Intimate partner violence in the United States. Bureau of Justice Statistics. http://www.ujp/usdoj.gov/bjs/pub/pdf/ipvus.pdf

Chan, S. (1992). Families with Asian roots. In E. W. Lynch & M. J. Hanson (Eds.), *Developing cross-cultural competence: A guide for working with young children and families* (pp. 181–257). Baltimore, MD: Paul H. Brooks.

Charles, R. (2001). Is there any empirical support for Bowen's concepts of differentiation of self, triangulation, and fusion?*American Journal of Family Therapy, 29,* 279–292.

Cherlin, A., & Furstenberg, F. (1986). *The new American grandparent: A place in the family.* New York: Basic Books.

Cherlin, A. J. (1978). Remarriage as an incomplete institution. *American Journal of Sociology, 84,* 634–650.

Cherlin, A. J. (1992). *Marriage, divorce, remarriage.* Cambridge, MA: Harvard University Press.

Child Trends (2006). *Facts at a glance.* Washington, DC: Author.

Christensen, A., & Jacobson, N. (2000). *Reconcilable differences.* New York: Guilford.

Chu, J. A., & Dill, D. L. (1990). Dissociative symptoms in relation to childhood physical and sexual abuse. *American Journal of Psychiatry, 147,* 887–892.

Cicchetti, D., & Toth, S. L. (2005). Child maltreatment. *Annual Review in Clinical Psychology, 1,* 409–438.

Cicchetti, D., & Valentino, K. (2006). An ecological transaction perspective on child maltreatment: Failure on the average expectable environment and its influence upon child development. *Developmental Psychopathology, 3,* 129–201.

Claxton-Oldfield, S. (2000). Deconstructing the myth of the wicked stepparent. *Marriage and Family Review, 30,* 51–58.

Cohler, B., & Geyer, S. (1982). Psychological autonomy and interdependence within the family. In F. Walsh (Ed.), *Normal family processes* (pp. 196–228). New York: Guilford Press.

Coie, J. D. (1996). Prevention of violence and antisocial behavior. In R. D. Peters & R. J. McMahon (Eds.), *Preventing childhood disorders, substance abuse, and delinquency* (pp. 1–18). Thousand Oaks, CA: Sage.

Colburn, K., Lin, P., & Moore, M. C. (1992). Gender and the divorce experience. *Journal of Divorce and Remarriage, 17*(3–4), 87–108.

Coleman, M., Fine, M. A., Ganong, L. H., Downs, K., & Pauk, N. (2001). When you're not the Brady Bunch: Identifying perceived conflicts and resolution strategies in stepfamilies. *Personal Relationships, 8,* 55–73.

Coleman, M., & Ganong, L. H. (1990). Remarriage and stepfamily research in the 1980s: Increased interest in an old family form. *Journal of Marriage and Family, 52,* 925–940.

Coleman, M., Ganong, L., & Fine, M. (2000). Reinvestigating remarriage: Another decade of progress. *Journal of Marriage and Family, 62*(4), 1288–1307.

Collins, N. L., & Read, S. J. (1990). Adult attachment, working models, and relationship quality in dating couples. *Journal of Personality and Social Psychology, 58,* 644–663.

Collins, W. A., Laursen, B., Mortensen, N., Luebker, C., & Ferreira, M. (1997). Conflict processes and transitions in parent and peer relationships: Implications for autonomy and regulation. *Journal of Adolescent Research, 12,* 178–198.

Coltrane, S. (2000). Research on household labor: Modeling and measuring the social embeddedness of routine family work. *Journal of Marriage and Family, 62,* 1208–1233.

Conger, R. D., Conger, K. J., Elder, G. H., Lorenz, F. O., Simons, R. L., & Whitbeck, L. B. (1992). A family process model of economic hardship and adjustment of early adolescent boys. *Child Development, 63,* 526–554.

Cornell, S., & Hartmann, D. (1998). *Ethnicity and race: Making identities in a changing world.* Thousand Oaks, CA: Pine Forge Press.

Cowan, C. P., & Cowan, P. A. (2000). *When partners become parents: The big life change for couples.* Mahwah, NJ: Erlbaum.

Cox, M. J., Paley, B., & Harter, K. (2001). Interparental conflict and parent–child relationships. In J. H. Grych & F. D. Fincham (Eds.), *Interparental conflict and child development.* Cambridge, UK: Cambridge University Press.

Crespi, T. D., & Sabatelli, R. M. (1993). Adolescent runaways and family strife: A conflict-induced differentiation framework. *Adolescence, 28,* 867–878.

Crosby, J. F., & Jose, N. L. (1983). Death: Family adjustment to loss. In C. R. Figley & H. I. McCubbin (Eds.), *Stress and the family: Vol. 2. Coping with catastrophe* (pp. 76–89). New York: Brunner/Mazel.

Cuber, J. F., & Harroff, P. B. (1972). Five kinds of relationships. In I. L. Reiss (Ed.), *Readings on the family system.* New York: Holt, Rinehart and Winston.

Cummings, E. M., & Davies, P. (1994). *Children and marital conflict: The impact of family dispute and resolution.* New York: Guilford.

Cummings, E. M., Davies, P. T., & Campbell, S. B. (2000). Children and the marital subsystem. In E. M. Cummings, P. T. Davies, & S. B. Campbell (Eds.), *Developmental psychopathology and family process: Theory, research, and clinical implications.* New York: Guilford Press.

Curran, M., Hazen, N., Jacobvitz, D., & Feldman, A. (2005). Representations of early family relationships predict marital maintenance during the transition to parenthood. *Journal of Family Psychology, 19,* 189–197.

Darling, N., & Steinberg, L. (1993). Parenting style as context: An integrative model. *Psychological Bulletin, 113*(3), 487–496.

Darling-Fisher, C., & Tiedje, L. B. (1990). The impact of maternal employment characteristics on fathers' participation in child care. *Family Relations, 39,* 20–26.

Davies, P. T., & Cummings, E. M. (1994). Marital conflict and child adjustment: An emotional security hypothesis. *Psychological Bulletin, 116,* 387–411.

DeFrain, J. (1991). Learning about grief from normal families: SIDS, stillbirth, and miscarriage. *Journal of Marital and Family Therapy, 17,* 215–232.

Demaris, A., & Longmore, M. A. (1996). Ideology, power, and equity: Testing competing explanations for the perception of fairness in household labor. *Social Forces, 74,* 1043–1071.

Demo, D. (1992). Parent–child relations: Assessing recent changes. *Journal of Marriage and Family, 54,* 104–117.

Demo, D. H., & Acock, A. C. (1993). Family diversity and the division of domestic labor: How much have things really changed? *Family Relations, 42,* 323–331.

Demo, D. H., & Cox, M. J. (2000). Families with young children: A review of research in the 1990's. *Journal of Marriage and Family, 62*(4), 876–895.

Devries, H. M., Kerrick, S., & Oetinger, S. (2007). Satisfaction and regrets of mid-life parents: A qualitative analyses. *Journal of Adult Development, 14,* 6–15.

Dibble, U., & Straus, M. A. (1980). Some social structure determinants of inconsistency between attitudes and behavior: The case of family violence. *Journal of Marriage and Family, 42,* 71–80.

Dindia, K., & Canary, D. (2006). *Sex differences and similarities in communication.* Mahway, NJ: Lawrence Erlbaum.

Dodge, K. A., Pettit, G. S., McClaskey, C. L., & Brown, M. M. (1986). *Social competence in children. Monographs of the Society for Research in Child Development, 51* (2, serial no. 213).

Doumas, D., Margolin, G., & John, R. (1994). The intergenerational transmission of aggression across three generations. *Journal of Family Violence, 9,* 157–175.

Dow, B., & Wood, J. T. (2006). *Handbook of gender and communication.* Thousand Oaks, CA: Sage.

Driver, J., Tabares, A., Shapiro, A., Nahm, E. Y., & Gottman, J. M. (2003). Interactional patterns in marital success of failure: Gottman laboratory studies. In F. Walsh (Ed.), *Normal family processes* (3rd ed., pp. 493–513). New York: Guilford.

Dung, T. N. (1984, March–April). Understanding Asian families: A Vietnamese perspective. *Children Today,* 10–12.

Dunn, J. (2002). The adjustment of children in stepfamilies: Lessons from community studies. *Child and Adolescent Mental Health, 7,* 154–161.

Dutton, D. G. (1988). *The domestic assault of women: Psychological and criminal justice perspectives.* Boston: Allyn & Bacon.

Dutton, D. G. (1995). *The batterer: A psychological profile.* New York: Basic Books.

Dutton, D. G., & Hemphill, K. J. (1992). Patterns of socially desirable responding among perpetrators and victims of wife assault. *Violence and Victims, 7,* 29–39.

Duxbury, L., Higgins, C., & Lee, C. (1994). Work-family conflict: A comparison by gender, family type, and perceived control. *Journal of Family Issues, 15,* 449–466.

Dwyer, J. (1985). Nutritional aspects of anorexia nervosa and bulimia. In S. W. Emmett (Ed.), *Theory and treatment of anorexia nervosa and bulimia* (pp. 20–50). New York: Brunner/Mazel.

Eckenrode, J. (1991). *The social context of coping.* New York: Plenum.

Edelson, J. L., Miller, D. M., Stone, G. W., & Chapman, D. G. (1985). Group treatment for men who batter. *Social Work Research and Abstracts, 21,* 18–21.

Edin, K., & Lein, L. (1997). *Making ends meet: How single mothers survive welfare and low-wage work.* New York: Russell Sage Foundation.

Egeland, B., Yates, T., Appleyard, K., & van Dulmen, M. (2002). The long-term consequences of maltreatment in the early years: A developmental pathway model to antisocial behavior. *Children's Services: Social Policy, Research, and Practice, 5,* 249–260.

Eggebeen, D. J., Snyder, A. R., & Manning, W. D. (1996). Children in single-father families in demographic perspective. *Journal of Family Issues, 17,* 441–465.

Elder, G. H. (1979). Historical change in life patterns and personality. In P. B. Baltes & O. G. Brim (Eds.), *Lifespan development and behavior* (pp. 117–159). New York: Academic Press.

Elizur, E., & Kaffman, M. (1982). Factors influencing the severity of childhood bereavement reactions. *American Journal of Orthopsychiatry, 52,* 668–676.

Elkin, M. (1984). *Families under the influence.* New York: W. W. Norton.

Ellyson, S. L., Dovidio, J. F., & Brown, C. E. (1992). The look of power: Gender differences in visual dominance behavior. In C. L. Ridgeway (Ed.), *Gender, interaction, and inequality* (pp. 50–80). New York: Springer-Verlag.

Emerson, R. (1962). Power dependence relations. *American Sociological Review, 27,* 31–40.

Emerson, R. (1976). Social exchange theory. In A. Inkeles, J. Coleman, & N. Smelser (Eds.), *Annual Review of Sociology* (Vol. 2, pp. 335–362). Palo Alto, CA: Annual Reviews.

Emery, R. E., & Sbarra, D. A. (2002). Addressing separation and divorce during and after couple therapy. In A. S. Gurman & N. S. Jacobson (Eds.), *Clinical handbook of couple therapy* (3rd ed.). New York: Guilford.

Emmett, S. W. (1985). *Theory and treatment of anorexia nervosa and bulimia.* New York: Brunner/Mazel.

Epstein, N. B., Ryan, C. E., Bishop, D. S., Miller, I. E., & Keitner, G. I. (2003). The McMaster model: A view of healthy family functioning. In F. Walsh (Ed.), *Normal family processes* (3rd ed., pp. 581–607). New York: Guilford.

Erickson, B. (2005). Scandinavian families: Plain and simple. In M. McGoldrick, J. Giordano, & N. Garcia-Preto (Eds.), *Ethnicity and family therapy* (3rd ed., pp. 641–653). New York: Guilford Press.

Erikson, E. (1968). *Identity: Youth and crisis.* New York: Norton.

Falicov, C. J. (1995). Training to think culturally: A multidimensional comparative framework. *Family Process, 34,* 373–388.

Falicov, C. J. (2003). Immigrant family processes. In F. Walsh (Ed.), *Normal family processes: Growing diversity and complexity* (3rd ed., pp. 280–300). New York: Guilford.

Farley, J. (1979). Family separation-individuation tolerance: A developmental conceptualization of the nuclear family. *Journal of Marital and Family Therapy, 5,* 61–67.

Farnsworth, E. B., & Allen, K. R. (1996). Mothers' bereavement: Experiences of marginalization, stories of change. *Family Relations, 45,* 360–367.

Farrington, D. P. (2005). Childhood origins of antisocial behavior. *Clinical Psychology and Psychotherapy, 12,* 177–190.

Feeney, J., Alexander, R., Noller, P., & Hohaus, L. (2003). Attachment insecurity, depression, and the transition to parenthood. *Personal Relationships, 10,* 475–493.

Feeney, J. A. (1999). Adult romantic attachment and couple relationships. In J. Cassidy & P. R. Shaver (Eds.), *Handbook of attachment: Theory, research, and clinical applications* (pp. 355–377). New York: Guilford.

Feeney, J. A., & Noller, P. (1990). Attachment style as a predictor of adult romantic relationships. *Journal of Personality and Social Psychology, 58,* 281–291.

Feeney, J., & Noller, P. (1996). *Adult attachment* (pp. 111–116). Thousand Oaks, CA: Sage.

Feinberg, M. E. (2002). Coparenting and the transition to parenthood: A framework for prevention. *Clinical Child and Family Psychology Review, 5,* 173–195.

Ferreira, A. J. (1966). Family myths. *Psychiatric Research Reports of the American Psychiatric Association, 20,* 85–90.

Field, J. (2001). *Living arrangements of children: Fall 1996.* Current Population Reports, P70-74. Washington, DC: U.S. Census Bureau.

Figley, C. R. (1989). *Helping traumatized families.* San Francisco: Jossey-Bass.

Fincham, F. D. (1994). Understanding the association between marital conflict and child maladjustment: An overview. *Journal of Family Psychology, 8,* 123–127.

Fincham, F. D. (2000). The kiss of the porcupines: From attributing responsibility to forgiving. *Personal Relationships, 7,* 1–23.

Fincham, F. D. (2009). Conflict in marriage. In Harry T. Reis & Susan K. Sprecher (Eds.), *Encyclopedia of Human Relationships.* Thousand Oaks, CA: Sage.

Fincham, F. D., & Beach, S. R. (1999). Marital conflict: Implications for working with couples. *Annual Review of Psychology, 50,* 47–77.

Fincham, F. D., & Beach, S. R. H. (2002). Forgiveness in marriage: Implications for psychological aggression and constructive communication. *Personal Relationships, 9,* 239–251.

Fine, M., McKenry, P., & Chung, H. (1992). Postdivorce adjustment of black and white single parents. *Journal of Divorce and Remarriage, 17*, 121–134.

Fine, M., & Norris, J. E. (1989). Intergenerational relations and family therapy research: What we can learn from other disciplines. *Family Process, 28*, 301–315.

Fingerman, K. L. (2001). *Aging mothers and their adult daughters: A study of mixed emotions*. New York: Springer.

Fish, M., Belsky, J., & Youngblade, L. (1991). Developmental antecedents and measurement of intergenerational boundary violation in a nonclinic sample. *Journal of Family Psychology, 43*, 278–297.

Fisher, L., Nakell, L. C., Terry, H. E., & Ransom, D. C. (1992). The California family health project III: Family emotion management and adult health. *Family Process, 31*, 269–287.

Fisher, L., Ransom, D. C., Terry, H. E., & Burge, S. (1992). Family structure/organization and adult health. *Family Process, 31*, 399–417.

Fitzpatrick, J. P. (1988). The Puerto Rican family. In C. H. Mindel & R. W. Habenstein (Eds.), *Ethnic families in America: Patterns and variations* (pp. 89–214). New York: Elsevier.

Fitzpatrick, M. A., Mulac, A., & Dindia, K. (1995). Gender preferential language use in spouse and stranger interaction. *Journal of Language and Social Psychology, 14*, 18–39.

Florsheim, P. et al. (2003). The transition to parenthood among African American and Latino couples: Relational predictors of risk for parental dysfunction. *Journal of Family Psychology, 17*, 65–79.

Framo, J. (1970). Symptoms from a family transactional viewpoint. In N. W. Ackerman, J. Lieb, & J. K. Pearce (Eds.), *Family therapy in transition* (pp. 125–171). Boston: Little, Brown.

Framo, J. (1976). Family of origin as a therapeutic resource for adults in marital and family therapy: You can and should go home again. *Family Process, 15*, 193–210.

Framo, J. (1981). The integration of marital therapy with sessions with the family of origin. In A. S. Gurman & D. P. Kniskern (Eds.), *Handbook of family therapy* (Vol. 1, pp. 133–158). New York: Brunner/Mazel.

Francoeur, R. T., & Noonan, R. J. (2004). *International encyclopedia of sexuality*. New York: Continuum International.

Frank, S., & Jackson, S. (1996). Family experiences as moderators of the relationship between eating symptoms and personality disturbance. *Journal of Youth and Adolescence, 25*(1), 55–72.

Friedman, E. H. (1991). Bowen theory and therapy. In A. S. Gurman & D. P. Kniskern (Eds.), *Handbook of family therapy* (Vol. 2, pp. 134–170). New York: Brunner/Mazel.

Friesen, B. J. (1996). Family support in child and adult mental health. In G. H. Singer, L. E. Powers, & A. L. Olson (Eds.), *Redefining family support: Innovations in public-private partnerships*. Baltimore, MD: Paul Brookes.

Fullinwider-Bush, N., & Jacobvitz, D. B. (1993). The transition to young adulthood: Generational boundary dissolution and female identity development. *Family Process, 32*, 87–103.

Furstenberg, F. F. (2000). The sociology of adolescence and youth in the 1990s: A critical commentary. *Journal of Marriage and Family, 62*(4), 896–910.

Gable, S., Belsky, J., & Crnic, K. (1992). Marriage, parenting and child development: Progress and prospects. *Journal of Family Psychology, 5*, 276–294.

Gagnon, J. (1977). *Human sexuality*. Glenview, IL: Scott Foresman.

Gallagher, M. (1996). *The abolition of marriage: How we destroy lasting love*. Washington, DC: Regnery Publishing, Inc.

Galvin, K. M., & Brommel, B. J. (1991). *Family communication: Cohesion and change*. New York: HarperCollins.

Garbarino, J., & Kostelny, K. (1992). Child maltreatment as a community problem. *Child Abuse and Neglect, 16*, 455–464.

Garcia-Coll, C. T. (1990). Developmental outcome of minority infants: A process-oriented look into our beginnings. *Child Development, 61*, 270–289.

Garcia-Coll, C., & Pachter, L. M. (2002). Ethnic and minority parenting. In M. H. Bornstein (Ed.), *Handbook of parenting, volume 4: Social conditions and applied parenting* (2nd ed., pp. 1–20). Mahwah, NJ: Lawrence Erlbaum Associates.

Garcia-Preto, N. (2005). Latino families: An overview. In M. McGoldrick, J. Giordano, & N. Garcia-Preto (Eds.), *Ethnicity and family therapy* (3rd ed., pp. 153–165). New York: Guilford Press.

Gates, R. et al. (2000). Diversity of new American families: Guidelines for therapists. In W. Nichols, M. Pace-Nichols, & D. Becvar (Eds.), *Handbook of family development and intervention*. New York: John Wiley.

Gavazzi, S. M., & Blumenkrantz, D. G. (1991). Teenage runaways: Treatment in the context of the family and beyond. *Journal of Family Psychotherapy, 2*, 15–29.

Gecas, V., & Seff, M. A. (1990). Families and adolescents: A review of the 1980s. *Journal of Marriage and Family, 52*, 941–958.

Gelles, R. J. (1998). The youngest victims: Violence toward children. In R. K. Bergen (Ed.), *Issues in intimate violence* (pp. 5–24). Thousand Oaks, CA: Sage.

Gelles, R. J., & Straus, M. A. (1988). *Intimate violence*. New York: Simon & Schuster.

Gilbert, L. A. (1988). *Sharing it all: The rewards and struggles of two-career families*. New York: Plenum Press.

Giordano, J., McGoldrick, M., & Klages, J. G. (2005). Italian families. In M. McGoldrick, J. Giordano, & N. Garcia-Preto (Eds.), *Ethnicity and family therapy* (3rd ed., pp. 616–628). New York: Guilford Press.

Glade, A. C., Bean, R. A., & Vira, R. (2005). A prime time for marital/relational intervention: A review of the transition to parenthood literature with treatment recommendations. *American Journal of Family Therapy, 33,* 319–336.

Glick, P. C. (1977). Updating the life cycle of the family. *Journal of Marriage and Family, 48,* 107–112.

Gold, J., & Wilson, J. S. (2002). Legitimizing the child-free family: The role of the family counselor. *The Family Journal, 10,* 70–74.

Goldenberg, I., & Goldenberg, H. (2000). *Family therapy: An overview* (5th ed.). Belmont, CA: Brooks/Cole.

Goldner, V. (1988). Generation and gender: Normative and covert hierarchies. *Family Process, 27,* 17–31.

Goldscheider, F. (1997). Recent changes in U.S. young adult living arrangements in comparative perspective. *Journal of Family Issues, 18,* 708–724.

Golish, T. D. (2003). Stepfamily communication strengths: Understanding the ties that bind. *Human Communication Research, 29,* 41–80.

Gorchoff, S. M., Oliver, J. P., Helson, R. (2008). Is empty-nest best? Changes in marital satisfaction in middle age. *Psychological Science, 13,* 5–22.

Gottman, J. M. (1994). *Why marriages succeed or fail.* New York: Simon & Schuster.

Gottman, J. M. (1999). *The marriage clinic.* New York: Norton.

Gottman, J. M., Coan, J., Carrère, S., & Swanson, C. (1998). Predicting marital happiness and stability from newlywed interactions. *Journal of Marriage and Family, 60,* 5–22.

Gottman, J. M., Katz, L. F., & Hooven, C. (1997). *Meta-emotion: How families communicate emotionally.* Mahwah, NJ: Lawrence Erlbaum Associates.

Gottman, J. M., & Levenson, R. W. (1992). Marital processes predictive of later dissolution: Behavior, physiology, and health. *Journal of Personality and Social Psychology, 63,* 221–233.

Gottman, J. M., & Levenson, R. W. (1999a). How stable is marital interaction over time? *Family Process, 38,* 159–166.

Gottman, J. M., & Levenson, R. W. (1999b). What predicts change in marital interaction over time: A study of alternative models. *Family Process, 38,* 143–158.

Gottman, J., Levenson, R. W., Seanson, C., Swanson, K., Tyson, R., & Yoshimoto, D. (2003). Observing gay, lesbian, and heterosexual couples' relationships: Mathematical modeling of conflict interaction. *Journal of Homosexuality, 45,* 65–82.

Gottman, J. M., & Notarius, C. I. (2002). Marriage research in the 20th century and a research agenda for the 21st century. *Family Process, 41,* 159–197.

Gottman, J. M., & Silver, N. (1999). *The seven principles for making marriage work.* New York: Crown Publishers.

Gould, R. L. (1978). *Transformations: Growth and change in adult life.* New York: Simon & Schuster.

Gove, W. R., & Shin, H. (1989). The psychological well-being of divorced and widowed men and women: An empirical analysis. *Journal of Family Issues, 10,* 122–144.

Grall, T. S. (2006). *Custodial mothers and fathers and their child support: 2003.* Current Population Reports, P60-230. www.census.gov/prod/2006pubs/p60-230.pdf

Greenberg, M. S. (1980). A theory of indebtedness. In K. J. Gergen, M. S. Greenberg, & R. H. Willis (Eds.), *Social exchange: Advances in theory and research* (pp. 3–26). New York: Plenum Press.

Greene, S. M., Anderson, E., Hetherington, E. M., Forgatch, M. S., & DeGarmo, D. S. (2003). Risk and resilience in divorce. In F. Walsh (Ed.), *Normal family processes* (3rd ed., pp. 96–120). New York: Guilford.

Greenstein, T. N. (1996). Husbands' participation in domestic labor: Interactive effects of wives' and husbands' gender ideologies. *Journal of Marriage and Family, 58,* 585–595.

Grossman, F., Pollack, W., Golding, E., & Fedele, N. (1987). Affiliation and autonomy in the transition to parenthood. *Family Relations, 36,* 263–269.

Grotevant, H., & Cooper, C. (1986). Individuation in family relationships. *Human Development, 29,* 82–100.

Grusec, J. E., & Davidov, M. (2007). Socialization in the family: The role of parents. In J. E. Grusec & P. D. Hastings (Eds.), *Handbook of socialization* (pp. 284–308). New York: Guilford Press.

Guerrero, L. K. (1997). Nonverbal interactions with same-sex friends, opposite-sex friends, and romantic partners: Consistency or change? *Journal of Social and Personal Relationships, 14,* 31–58.

Guisinger, S., & Blatt, S. (1994). Individuality and relatedness: Evolution of a fundamental dialectic. *American Psychologist, 49,* 104–111.

Guttman, H. A. (1991). Parental death as a precipitant of marital conflict in middle age. *Journal of Marital and Family Therapy, 17,* 81–87.

Haapasalo, J., & Pokela, E. (1999). Child-rearing and child abuse antecedents of criminality. *Aggression and Violent Behavior, 1,* 107–127.

Haas, D. F., & Deseran, F. A. (1981). Trust and symbolic exchange. *Social Psychology Quarterly, 44,* 3–13.

Haas, S. M., & Stafford, L. (2005). Maintenance behaviors in same-sex and marital relationships: A matched sample comparison. *The Journal of Family Communication, 5,* 43–60.

Haley, J. (1980). *Leaving home.* New York: McGraw-Hill.

Haley, J. (1987). *Problem-solving therapy* (2nd ed.). San Francisco: Jossey-Bass.

Hall, J. A. (1984). *Nonverbal sex differences. Accuracy of communication and expressive style.* Baltimore, MD: The Johns Hopkins University Press.

Hammer, H., Finkelhor, D., & Sedlak, A. J. (2002). Runaway/thrownaway children: National estimates and characteristics (National Incidence Studies of Missing, Abducted, Runaway, and Thrownaway Children Bulletin, NCJ 196469). Washington, DC: US Department of Justice, Office of Juvenile Justice and Delinquency Prevention.

Handelsman, M. M., Gottlieb, M. C., & Knapp, S. (2005). Training ethical psychologists: An acculturation model. *Professional Psychology: Research and Practice, 36,* 59–65.

Hanson, T. L. (1999). Does parental conflict explain why divorce is negatively associated with child welfare? *Social Forces, 77,* 1283–1316.

Hareven, T. K. (2000). *Families, history and social change: Life-course and cross-cultural perspectives.* Boulder, CO: Westview Press.

Harkness, S., & Super, C. M. (2002). Culture and parenting. In M. H. Bornstein (Ed.), *Handbook of parenting, volume 2: Biology and ecology of parenting* (2nd ed., pp. 253–280). Mahwah, NJ: Lawrence Erlbaum Associates.

Harvey, J., Wenzel, A., & Sprecher, S. (2004). *Handbook of sexuality in close relationships.* Mahway, NJ: Lawrence Erlbaum.

Harwood, R. L. (1992). The influence of culturally derived values on Anglo and Puerto Rican mothers' perceptions of attachment behaviors. *Child Development, 63,* 822–839.

Hawkins, A. J., Roberts, T. A., Christiansen, S. L., & Marshall, C. M. (1994). An evaluation of a program to help dual-earner couples share the second shift. *Family Relations, 43,* 213–220.

Hawkins, D. J., Herrenkohl, T., Farrington, D. P., Brewer, D., Catalano, R. F., & Harachi, T. W. (1998). A review of predictors of youth violence. In R. Loeber & D. P. Farrington (Eds.), *Serious and violent offenders: Risk factors and successful interventions.* Thousand Oaks, CA: Sage.

Hawkins, J. D., Catalano, R. F., & Miller, J. Y. (1992). Risk and protective factors for alcohol and other drug problems in adolescence and early adulthood: Implications for substance abuse prevention. *Psychological Bulletin, 112,* 64–105.

Hazan, C., & Shaver, P. (1987). Romantic love conceptualized as an attachment process. *Journal of Personality and Social Psychology, 52,* 511–524.

Hazan, C., & Shaver, P. R. (1994). Attachment as an organizational framework for research on close relationships. *Psychological Inquiry, 5,* 1–22.

Hazan, C., & Zeifman, D. (1999). Pair bonds as attachments: Evaluating the evidence. In J. Cassidy & P. R. Shaver (Eds.), *Handbook of attachment: Theory, research, and clinical applications* (pp. 336–354). New York: Guilford.

Heiss, J. (1981). Social roles. In M. Rosenberg & R. H. Turner (Eds.), *Social psychology: Sociological perspectives* (pp. 94–129). New York: Basic Books.

Helms-Erikson, H. (2001). Marital quality ten years after the transition to parenthood: Implications of the timing of parenthood and the division of labor. *Journal of Marriage and Family, 63,* 1099–1110.

Helsen, M., Vollebergh, W., & Meeus, W. (2000). Social support from parents and friends and emotional problems in adolescence. *Journal of Youth and Adolescence, 29,* 319–335.

Hendrick, S., & Hendrick, C. (1992). *Liking, loving, and relating.* Pacific Grove, CA: Brooks/Cole.

Henricson, C., & Roker, D. (2000). Support for the parents of adolescents: A review. *Journal of Adolescence, 23,* 763–783.

Herman, M. R., Dornbusch, S. M., Herron, M. C., & Gerting, J. R. (1997). The influence of family regulation, connection, and psychological autonomy on six measures of adolescent functioning. *Journal of Adolescent Research, 12,* 34–57.

Hess, R. D., & Handel, G. (1985). The family as a psychosocial organization. In G. Handel (Ed.), *The psychosocial interior of the family* (3rd ed., pp. 33–46). New York: Aldine.

Hetherington, E. M. (1989). Coping with family transitions: Winners, losers, and survivors. *Child Development, 60,* 1–14.

Hetherington, E. M. (1999). Should we stay together for the sake of the children? In E. M. Hetherington (Ed.), *Coping with divorce, single parenting, and remarriage: A risk and resiliency perspective* (pp. 93–116). Hillside, NJ: Erlbaum.

Hetherington, E. M. (2003a). Social support and the adjustment of children in divorced and remarried families. *Childhood, 10,* 217–236.

Hetherington, E. M. (2003b). Intimate pathways: Changing patterns in close personal relationships across time. *Family Relations, 52,* 318–331.

Hetherington, E. M., & Kelly, J. (2002). *For better or worse: Divorce reconsidered.* New York: Norton.

Hetherington, E. M., & Stanley-Hagen, M. (1999). The adjustment of children with divorced parents: A risk and resiliency perspective. *Journal of Child Psychology and Psychiatry, 40,* 129–140.

Hill, R. (1986). Life cycle stages for types of single parent families: Of family development theory. *Family Relations, 35,* 19–29.

Hines, P., & Boyd-Franklin, N. (2005). African American families. In M. McGoldrick, J. Giordano, &

N. Garcia-Preto (Eds.), *Ethnicity and family therapy* (3rd ed., pp. 88–100). New York: Guilford.

Hines, P., Preto, N., McGoldrick, M., Almeida, R., & Weltman, S. (2005). Culture and the family life cycle. In E. A. Carter, M. McGoldrick, & B. Carter (Eds.), *The expanded family life cycle: Individual, family, and social perspectives* (3rd ed., pp. 69–87). Boston: Allyn & Bacon.

Ho, D. Y. F. (1981). Traditional patterns of socialization in Chinese society. *Acta Psychologia Taiwanica, 23,* 81–95.

Hochschild, A. (1997). *The time bind: When work becomes home and home becomes work.* New York: Metropolitan Books.

Hochschild, A., & Machung, A. (1989). *The second shift: Working parents and the revolution at home.* New York: Viking.

Hoff, E., Laursen, B., & Tardif, T. (2002). Socioeconomic status and parenting. In M. H. Bornstein (Ed.), *Handbook of parenting, volume 2: Biology and ecology of parenting* (2nd ed., pp. 231–252). Mahwah, NJ: Lawrence Erlbaum Associates.

Hoffman, K., Demo, D., & Edwards, J. (1994). Physical wife abuse in a non-Western society: An integrated theoretical approach. *Journal of Marriage and Family, 56,* 131–146.

Holmes, S. E., & Sabatelli, R. M. (1997). The quality of the mother-daughter relationship and caregiving dynamics. Unpublished manuscript, University of Connecticut, Storrs.

Holzworth-Munroe, A., & Stuart, G. L. (1994). Typologies of male batterers: Three subtypes and the differences among them.*Psychological Bulletin, 116,* 476–497.

Holzworth-Munroe, A., Stuart, G. L., & Hutchinson, G. (1997). Violent versus nonviolent husbands: Differences in attachment patterns, dependency, and jealousy. *Journal of Family Psychology, 11,* 314–331.

Homans, G. C. (1961). *Social behavior: Its elementary forms.* New York: Harcourt, Brace, & World.

Horesh, N. et al. (1996). Abnormal psychosocial situations and eating disorders in adolescence. *Journal of the American Academy of Child and Adolescent Psychiatry, 35,* 921–927.

Hotaling, G. T., & Sugarman, D. B. (1990). A risk marker analysis of assaulted wives. *Journal of Family Violence, 5*(1), 1–13.

Hudson, J. I., Hiripi, E., Pope, H. G., & Kessler, R. C. (2007). The prevalence and correlates of eating disorders in the national comorbidity survey replication. *Biological Psychiatry, 61,* 348–358.

Hughes, D., Galinsky, E., & Morris, A. (1992). The effects of job characteristics on marital quality: Specifying linking mechanisms. *Journal of Marriage and Family, 54,* 31–42.

Humphrey, L. L. (1986). Family relations in bulimic, anorexic, and nondistressed families. *International Journal of Eating Disorders, 5,* 223–232.

Hungerford, T. L. (2001). The economic consequences of widowhood on elderly women in the United States and Germany. *Gerontologist, 41,* 103–110.

Huston, T. L. (1983). Power. In H. H. Kelley, E. Berscheid, A. Christensen, J. H. Harvey, T. Huston, G. Levinger, E. McClintock, L. A. Peplau, & D. R. Peterson (Eds.), *Close relations* (pp. 169–221). New York: W. H. Freeman.

Huston, T. L., & Levinger, G. (1978). Interpersonal attraction and relationships. In M. R. Osenzweig & L. W. Porter (Eds.), *Annual Review of Psychology* (Vol. 29, pp. 264–292). Palo Alto, CA: Annual Reviews.

Huston, T. L., Surra, C. A., Fitzgerald, N. M., & Cate, R. M. (1981). Mate selection as an interpersonal process. In S. Duck & R. Gilmour (Eds.), *Personal relationships: Vol. 2. Developing personal relationships* (pp. 53–88). London: Academic Press.

Igoin-Apfelbaum, L. (1985). Characteristics of family background in bulimia. *Psychotherapy and Psychosomatics, 43,* 161–167.

Isser, N. (1988). The Linneweil affair: A study in adolescent vulnerability. *Adolescence, 19,* 629–642.

Jackson, A. P., Brooks-Gunn, J., Huang, C. C., & Glassman, M. (2000). Single mothers in low-wage jobs: Financial strain, parenting, and preschoolers' outcomes. *Child Development, 71,* 1409–1423.

Jacob, T. (1987). *Family interaction and psychopathology: Theories, methods, and findings.* New York: Plenum Press.

Jacobson, N. S., & Margolin, G. (1979). *Marital therapy: Strategies based on social learning and behavior exchange principles.* New York: Brunner/Mazel.

Jencius, M., & Duba, J. (2002). Creating a multicultural family practice. *The Family Journal, 10,* 410–414.

Jessor, R. (1993). Successful adolescent development among youth in high-risk settings. *American Psychologist, 48,* 117–126.

Johnson, C. (1994). Gender, legitimate authority, and conversation. *American Sociological Review, 59,* 122–135.

Johnson, E. M., & Huston, T. L. (1998). The perils of love, or why wives adapt to husbands during the transition to parenthood. *Journal of Marriage and Family, 60,* 195–204.

Johnson, L., O'Mally, P., & Bachman, J. (2001). Drug use among American High School Seniors, College Students, and Young Adults, 1975–2000. National Institute on Drug Abuse (NIH Publication No. 01-4923). Rockville, MD.

Johnson, P., & McNeil, K. (1998). Predictors of developmental task attainment for young adults from divorced families. *Contemporary Family Therapy, 20,* 237–250.

Johnson, P., & Nelson, M. D. (1998). Parental divorce, family functioning, and college student development: An intergenerational perspective. *Journal of College Student Development, 39,* 355–363.

Johnson, P., Thorngren, J. M., & Smith, A. J. (2001). Parental divorce and family functioning: Effects of differentiation levels of young adults. *The Family Journal, 9,* 265–272.

Jorgenson, S. R., Thornburg, H. D., & Williams, J. K. (1980). The experience of running away: Perceptions of adolescents seeking help in a shelter care facility. *High School Journal, 64,* 87–96.

Josselson, R. L. (1980). Ego development in adolescence. In J. Adelson (Ed.), *Handbook of adolescent psychology* (pp. 188–210). New York: Wiley.

Julian, T. W., McKenry, P. C., & McKelvey, M. W. (1994). Cultural variations in parenting: Perceptions of Caucasian, African-American, Hispanic, and Asian-American parents. *Family Relations, 43,* 30–37.

Kalmuss, D., Davidson, A., & Cushman, L. (1992). Parenting, expectations, experiences, and adjustments to parenthood: A test of the violated expectations framework. *Journal of Marriage and Family, 54,* 516–526.

Kaminer, Y. (1991). Adolescent substance abuse. In R. Frances & S. Miller (Eds.), *Clinical textbook of addictive disorders* (pp. 320–346). New York: Guilford.

Kandel, D. B. (1990). Parenting styles, drug use, and children's adjustment in families of young adults. *Journal of Marriage and Family, 52,* 183–196.

Kantor, D. (1980). Critical identity image: A concept linking individual, couple, and family development. In J. K. Pearce & L. J. Friedman (Eds.), *Family therapy: Combining psychodynamic and family systems approaches* (pp. 137–167). New York: Grune & Stratton.

Kantor, D., & Lehr, W. (1975). *Inside the family.* New York: Jossey-Bass.

Kaplan, L., Ade-Ridder, L., & Hennon, C. B. (1991). Issues of split custody: Siblings separated by divorce. *Journal of Divorce and Remarriage, 16,* 253–274.

Karpel, M. (1976). Individuation: From fusion to dialogue. *Family Process, 15,* 65–82.

Kaslow, F. W. (2000). Families experiencing divorce. In W. C. Nichols, M. A. Pace-Nichols, D. Becvar, & A. J. Napier (Eds.), *Handbook of family development and intervention* (pp. 341–368). New York: John Wiley & Sons.

Kaslow, F. W., & Schwartz, L. (1983). Vulnerability and invulnerability to the cults. In D. Bagarozzi, A. P. Jurich, & R. Jackson (Eds.), *New perspectives in marriage and family therapy* (pp. 165–190). New York: Human Sciences Press.

Kaufman, G. K., & Straus, M. A. (1990). Response of victims and the police to assaults on wives. In M. A. Straus & R. J. Gelles (Eds.), *Physical violence in American families: Risk factors and adaptations to violence in 8,145 families.* New Brunswick, NJ: Transaction Books.

Kaufman, J., & Zigler, E. (1993). The intergenerational transmission of abuse is overstated. In R. J. Gelles & D. Loseke (Eds.), *Current controversies on family violence* (pp. 209–221). Newbury Park, CA: Sage.

Kelley, H. H. et al. (1983). Analyzing close relationships. In H. H. Kelley, E. Berscheid, A. Christensen, J. H. Harvey, T. Huston, G. Levinger, E. McClintock, L. A. Peplau, & D. R. Peterson (Eds.), *Close relations* (pp. 20–67). New York: W. H. Freeman.

Kelly, J. B. (2003). Changing perspectives on children's adjustment following divorce: A view from the United States. *Childhood, 10,* 237–254.

Kelly, J. B., & Lamb, M. E. (2003). Developmental issues in relocation cases involving young children: When, where, and how? *Journal of Family Psychology, 17,* 193–205.

Kelley, M. L., Power, T. G., & Wimbush, D. D. (1992). Determinants of disciplinary practices in low-income black mothers. *Child Development, 63,* 573–582.

Kerr, M. E., & Bowen, M. (1988). *Family evaluation: An approach based on Bowen theory.* New York: W. W. Norton.

Kilpatrick, D. G., Aciero, R., Saunders, B., Resnick, H. S., Best, C. L., & Schnurr, P. P. (2000). Risk factors for adolescent substance abuse and dependence: Data from a national sample. *Journal of Consulting and Clinical Psychology, 68,* 19–30.

Kitson, G. C., & Holmes, W. M. (1992). *Portrait of divorce: Adjustment to marital breakdown.* New York: Guilford.

Klein, D. (1983). Family problem solving and family stress. *Marriage and Family Review, 6,* 85–111.

Klein, G. H., Pleasant, N. D., Whitton, S. W., & Markman, H. J. (2006). Understanding couple conflict. In A. L. Vangelisti & D. Perlman (Eds.), *The Cambridge handbook of personal relationships.* (pp. 445–462). Cambridge, UK: Cambridge University Press.

Kluwer, E. S., & Johnson, M. D. (2007). Conflict frequency and relationship quality across the transition to parenthood. *Journal of Marriage and family, 69,* 1089–1106.

Knapp, M. L., & Hall, J. A. (2002). *Nonverbal communication in human interaction* (5th ed.). Belmont, CA: Wadsworth.

Knapp, M. L., & Vangelisti, A. L. (2005). *Interpersonal communication and human relationships* (5th ed.). Boston: Allyn & Bacon.

Kobak, R. R., & Hazan, C. (1991). Attachment in marriage: Effects of security and accuracy of working models. *Journal Personality and Social Psychology, 60,* 861–869.

Kramer, J. R. (1985). *Family interfaces: Transgenerational patterns.* New York: Brunner/Mazel.

Krause, N., & Rook, K. S. (2003). Negative interaction in late life: Issues in the stability and generalizability of conflict across relationships. *Journals of Gerontology: Psychological Sciences, 58B,* P88–P99.

Kroneman, L., Loeber, R., & Hipwell, A. E. (2004). Is neighborhood context differently related to externalizing problems and delinquency for girls compared with boys? *Clinical Child and Family Psychology Review, 7*(2), 109–122.

Kupers, T. A. (1993). *Revisioning men's lives: Gender, intimacy & power.* New York: Guilford Press.

Kurdek, L. (2004). Are gay and lesbian cohabiting couples really different from heterosexual married couples? *Journal of Marriage and Family, 66,* 880–900.

Kurdek, L., & Schmitt, J. P. (1986a). Interaction of sex role self-concept with relationship quality and relationship beliefs in married, heterosexual cohabitating, gay, and lesbian couples. *Journal of Personality and Social Psychology, 51,* 365–370.

Kurdek, L., & Schmitt, J. P. (1986b). Relationship quality of partners in heterosexual married, heterosexual cohabitating, gay and lesbian couples. *Journal of Personality and Social Psychology, 51,* 711–720.

Laing, R. D. (1971). *The politics of the family.* New York: Random House.

Laird, J. (2003). Lesbian and gay families. In F. Walsh (Ed.), *Normal family processes: Growing diversity and complexity* (3rd ed., pp. 176–209). New York: Guilford Press.

Lamb, M. E., & Kelly, J. B. (2001). Using the empirical literature to guide the development of parenting plans for young children: A rejoinder to Solomon and Biringen. *Family Court Review, 39,* 365–371.

Lamb, M. W. (2004). *The role of the father in child development* (4th ed.). Hoboken, NJ: Wiley.

Lamborn, S. D., Mounts, N. S., Steinberg, L., & Dornbusch, S. M. (1991). Patterns of competence and adjustment among adolescents from authoritative, authoritarian, indulgent, and neglectful families. *Child Development, 62,* 1049–1065.

Langan, P. A., & Innes, C. A. (1986). *Preventing domestic violence against women* (Bureau of Justice Statistics Special Report). Washington, DC: Department of Justice. (NCJ No. 102037)

LaRossa, R., & LaRossa, M. (1981). *Transition to parenthood: How infants change families.* Beverly Hills, CA: Sage.

LaRossa, R., & Reitzes, D. (1992). Symbolic interactionism and family studies. In P. Boss, W. Doherty, R. LaRossa, W. Schumm, & S. Steinmetz (Eds.), *Sourcebook of family theories and methods: A contextual approach* (pp. 135–166). New York: Plenum.

Lee, E. (1996). Asian American families. In M. McGoldrick, J. Giordano, & J. K. Pearce (Eds.), *Ethnicity and family therapy* (pp. 227–248). New York: Guilford.

Lehman, D. R., Lang, E., Wortman, C., & Sorenson, S. (1989). Long-term effects of sudden bereavement: Marital and parent–child relationships and children's reactions. *Journal of Family Psychology, 2,* 344–367.

Leigh, G. K., Homan, T. B., & Burr, W. R. (1987). Some confusions and exclusions of the SVR theory of dyadic pairings: A response to Murstein. *Journal of Marriage and Family, 49,* 933–937.

Leik, R., & Leik, S. (1977). Transition to interpersonal commitment. In R. Hamblin & J. Kunkel (Eds.), *Behavioral theory in sociology* (pp. 299–321). New Brunswick, NJ: Transaction.

Lennon, M. C., & Rosenfield, S. (1994). Relative fairness and the division of housework: The importance of options. *American Journal of Sociology, 100,* 506–531.

Lerner, R. M., Rothbaum, F., Boulos, S., & Castellino, D. R. (2002). Developmental systems perspective on parenting. In M. H. Bornstein (Ed.), *Handbook of parenting, volume 2: Biology and ecology of parenting* (2nd ed., pp. 315–344). Mahwah, NJ: Lawrence Erlbaum Associates.

Levenson, R. W., & Gottman, J. M. (1983). Marital interaction: Physiological linkage and affective exchange. *Journal of Personality and Social Psychology, 45,* 587–597.

Levine, B. L. (1985). Adolescent substance abuse: Toward an integration of family systems and individual adaptation. *American Journal of Family Therapy, 13,* 3–16.

Levinger, G. (1982). A social exchange view on the dissolution of pair relationships. In F. I. Nye (Ed.), *Family relationships: Rewards and costs* (pp. 97–122). Beverly Hills, CA: Sage.

Levinger, G. (1999). Duty to whom? Reconsidering attractions and barriers as determinants of commitment in a relationship. In J. Adams & W. H. Jones (Eds.), *Handbook of interpersonal commitment and relationship stability* (pp. 37–52). New York: Plenum Press.

Levinson, D. J. (1986). A conception of adult development. *American Psychologist, 41,* 3–13.

Lewinsohn, P. M., Striegel-Moore, R. H., & Seeley, J. P. (2000). The epidemiology and natural course of eating disorders in young women from adolescence to young adulthood. *Journal of the American Academy of Child and Adolescent Psychiatry, 39,* 1284–1292.

Lewis, R. A. (1972). A developmental framework for the analysis of premarital dyadic formation. *Family Process, 11,* 17–48.

Lewis, R. A., & Spanier, G. B. (1979). Theorizing about the quality and stability of marriage. In W. R. Burr, R. Hill, F. I. Nye, & I. L. Reiss (Eds.), *Contemporary theories about the family* (Vol. 1, pp. 268–294). New York: Free Press.

Littlewood, J. (1992). *Aspects of grief: Bereavement in adult life.* London: Tavistock/Routledge.

Lopata, H. (1996). *Current widowhood: Myths and realities.* Thousand Oaks, CA: Sage.

Lum, K., & Char, W. F. (1985). Chinese adaptation in Hawaii: Some examples. In W. Tseng & D. Y. H. Wu (Eds.), *Chinese culture and mental health* (pp. 215–226). Orlando: Academic Press.

Maccoby, E., & Martin, J. (1983). Socialization in the context of the family: Parent–child interaction. In E. M. Hetherington (Ed.) & P. H. Mussen (Series Ed.),

Handbook of child psychology: Vol. 4. Socialization, personality and social development (pp. 1–102). New York: Wiley.

MacDermid, S., Huston, T., & McHale, S. (1990). Changes in marriage associated with the transition to marriage. *Journal of Marriage and Family, 52,* 475–486.

MacDonald, K. (1992). Warmth as a developmental construct: An evolutionary analysis. *Child Development, 63,* 753–773.

Mace, D. R. (1983). *Prevention in family services: Approaches to family wellness.* Beverly Hills, CA: Sage.

Mahler, M., Pine, F., & Bergman, A. (1975). *The psychological birth of the human infant.* New York: Basic Books.

Manning, W. D., & Smock, P. J. (1997). Children's living arrangements in unmarried-mother families. *Journal of Family Issues, 18,* 526–544.

Marcia, J. E. (1966). Development and validation of ego identity status. *Journal of Personality and Social Psychology, 34,* 551–558.

Marcia, J. E. (1976). Identity six years after: A follow-up study. *Journal of Youth and Adolescence, 5,* 145–160.

Marcia, J. E. (1980). Identity in adolescence. In J. Adelson (Ed.), *Handbook of adolescent psychology* (pp. 159–187). New York: Wiley.

Marciano, T. (1982). Families and cults. *Marriage and Family Review, 4,* 101–118.

Marks, N. F. (1996). Caregiving across the lifespan: National prevalence and predictors. *Family Relations, 45,* 27–36.

Marks, N. F. (1998). Does it hurt to care: Caregiving, work-family conflict, and mid-life well-being. *Journal of Marriage and Family, 60,* 951–966.

Marshall, V. W. (1986). A sociological perspective on aging and dying. In V. Marshall (Ed.), *Later life: The social psychology of aging* (pp. 125–146). Beverly Hills, CA: Sage.

Marsiglio, W. (2004). When stepfathers claim stepchildren: A conceptual analysis. *Journal of Marriage and Family, 66,* 22–39.

Marsiglio, W., Amato, P., Day, R. D., & Lamb, M. E. (2000). Scholarship on fatherhood in the 1990s and beyond. *Journal of Marriage and Family, 62,* 1173–1191.

Mason, M. A., Harrison-Jay, S., Svare, G. M., & Wolfinger, N. H. (2002). Stepparents: De facto parents or legal strangers? *Journal of Family Issues, 23,* 507–522.

Mason, M. J. (2004). Preadolescent psychiatric and substance use disorders and the ecology of risk and protection. *Journal of Child and Adolescent Substance Abuse, 13*(4), 61–81.

Maynard, R. A. (1997). *Kids having kids.* Washington, DC: Urban Institute.

McAdoo, H. P. (1991). Family values and outcomes for children. *Journal of Negro Education, 60,* 361–365.

McCubbin, H. I., Joy, C. B., Cauble, A. E., Comeau, J. K., & Needle, R. H. (1980). Family stress and coping: A decade review. *Journal of Marriage and Family, 42,* 125–142.

McCubbin, H. I., McCubbin, M. A., & Thompson, A. I. (1993). Resiliency in families: The role of family schema and appraisal in family adaptation to crises. In T. H. Brubaker (Ed.), *Family relations: Challenges for the future* (pp. 153–180). Newbury Park, CA: Sage.

McCubbin, H. I., McCubbin, M. A., Thompson, A. I., Han, S. V., & Allen, C. T. (1997). Families under stress: what makes them resilient? *Journal of Family and Consumer Sciences, 89,* 2–11.

McCubbin, H. I., & Patterson, J. (1983). The family stress process: The Double ABCX model of adjustment and adaptation. *Marriage and Family Review, 6,* 7–37.

McCullough, P., & Rutenberg, S. (1989). Launching children and moving on. In B. Carter & M. McGoldrick (Eds.), *The changing family life cycle: A framework for family therapy* (2nd ed., pp. 286–310). Boston: Allyn & Bacon.

McDonald, G. W. (1981). Structural exchange and marital interaction. *Journal of Marriage and Family, 43,* 825–839.

McGoldrick, M. (2003). Culture: A challenge to concepts of normality. In F. Walsh (Ed.), *Normal family processes* (3rd ed., pp. 235–259). New York: Guilford Press.

McGoldrick, M. (2005a). Irish families. In M. McGoldrick, J. Giordano, & N. Garcia-Preto (Eds.), *Ethnicity and family therapy* (3rd ed., pp. 595–615). New York: Guilford Press.

McGoldrick, M. (2005b). Becoming a couple. In B. Carter & M. McGoldrick (Eds.), *The expanded family life cycle: Individual, family, and social perspectives* (3rd ed., pp. 231–248). Boston: Allyn & Bacon.

McGoldrick, M., & Carter, B. (2005). Remarried families. In B. Carter & M. McGoldrick (Eds.), *The expanded family life cycle: Individual, family, and social perspectives* (3rd ed., pp. 417–435). Boston: Allyn & Bacon.

McGoldrick, M., Gerson, R., & Petry, S. (2008). *Genograms in family assessment* (3rd ed.). New York: W. W. Norton.

McGoldrick, M., & Walsh, F. (2005). Death and the family life cycle. In B. Carter & M. McGoldrick (Eds.), *The expanded family life cycle: Individual, family, and social perspectives* (3rd ed., pp. 185–201). Boston: Allyn & Bacon.

McLoyd, V., Cauce, A., Tacheuchi, D., & Wilson, L. (2000). Marital processes and parental socialization in families of color: A decade review of research. *Journal of Marriage and Family, 62,* 1–27.

McLoyd, V. C. (1990). The declining fortunes of black children: Psychological distress, parenting, and socioemotional development in the context of economic hardship. *Child Development, 61,* 311–346.

Mederer, H., & Hill, R. (1983). Critical transitions over the family life span: Theory and research. *Marriage and Family Review, 6,* 39–60.

Mednick, M. T. (1987). Single mothers: A review and critique of current research. In A. S. Skolnick & J. H. Skolnick (Eds.), *Family in transition* (6th ed., pp. 441–456). Boston: Scott Foresman.

Menaghan, E. (1983). Individual coping efforts and family studies: Conceptual and methodological issues. *Marriage and Family Review, 6,* 113–135.

Menaghan, E. G., & Lieberman, M. A. (1986). Changes in depression following divorce: A panel study. *Journal of Marriage and Family, 48,* 319–328.

Menaghan, E. G., & Parcels, T. L. (1990). Parental employment and family life: Research in the 1980s. *Journal of Marriage and Family, 52,* 1079–1098.

Meth, R., & Passick, R. (1990). *Men in therapy.* New York: Guilford Press.

Meyer, D., & Russell, R. (1998). Caretaking, separation from parents, and the development of eating disorders. *Journal of Counseling and Development, 76*(2), 166–173.

Mezey, M. et al. (2001). *Sexual health. The encyclopedia of eldercare.* New York: Springer.

Milkie, M., & Peltola, P. (1999). Playing all roles: Gender and the work-family balancing act. *Journal of Marriage and Family, 61,* 476–490.

Miller, B., & Myers-Walls, J. (1983). Parenthood: Stresses and coping strategies. In H. McCubbin & C. Figley (Eds.), *Stress and the family: Coping with normative transitions* (pp. 54–73). New York: Brunner/Mazel.

Milner, J. S., & Chilamkurti, C. (1991). Physical child abuse perpetrator characteristics: A review of the literature. *Journal of Interpersonal Violence, 6,* 345–366.

Minuchin, S. (1974). *Families and family therapy.* Cambridge: Harvard University Press.

Minuchin, S. (1986). *Structural family therapy.* Presentation at the Master Therapists Series, University of Connecticut Medical School, Farmington.

Minuchin, S., Montalvo, B., Guerney, B. G., Rosman, B. L., & Schumer, F. (1967). *Families of the slums.* New York: Basic Books.

Minuchin, S., Rosman, B., & Baker, L. (1978). *Psychosomatic families: Anorexia nervosa in context.* Cambridge: Harvard University Press.

Mirkin, M., Raskin, P., & Antognini, F. (1984). Parenting, protecting, preserving: Mission of the adolescent female runaway. *Family Process, 23*(1), 63–74.

Mitchell, B. A., & Gee, E. M. (1996). "Boomerang kids" and midlife parental marital satisfaction. *Family Relations, 45,* 442–448.

Mitchell, V., & Helson, R. (1990). Women's prime of life: Is it the 50's? *Psychology of Women Quarterly, 14,* 451–470.

Moen, P., Kim, J. E., & Hofmeister, H. (2001). Couples' work/retirement transitions, gender, and marital quality. *Social Psychology Quarterly, 64,* 55–71.

Montgomery, B. M. (1981). The form and function of quality communication in marriage. *Family Relations, 30,* 21–30.

Moskowitz, D. S. (1993). Dominance and friendliness: On the interaction of gender and situation. *Journal of Personality, 61,* 387–409.

Moxnes, K. (2003). Risk factors in divorce: Perceptions by the children involved. *Childhood, 10,* 131–146.

Murray, C. I. (1994). Death, dying, and bereavement. In P. McKenry & S. Price (Eds.), *Families and change: Coping with stressful events* (pp. 173–194). Thousand Oaks, CA: Sage.

Myers, S. M., & Booth, A. (1996). Men's retirement and marital quality. *Journal of Family Issues, 17,* 336–358.

Nace, E. P., & Isbell, P. G. (1991). Alcohol. In R. J. Frances & S. I. Miller (Eds.), *Clinical textbook of addictive disorders* (pp. 43–68). New York: Guilford Press.

Napier, A. Y. (1988). *The fragile bond: In search of an equal, intimate, and enduring marriage.* New York: Harper & Row.

National Alliance for Caregiving & AARP (2005). Family caregiving in the U.S.: Findings from a national survey. Washington, DC: Author.

National Institute of Mental Health (NIMH) (2007). *Eating disorders* (Publication No. 07-4901). Bethesda, MD: Author.

Newman, D. (2007). *Identities and inequalities.* New York: McGraw-Hill.

O'Leary, K. D., Malone, J., & Tyree, A. (1994). Physical aggression in early marriage: Prerelationship and relationship effects. *Journal of Consulting and Clinical Psychology, 62,* 594–602.

Ogbu, J. U. (1981). Origins of human competence: A cultural-ecological perspective. *Child Development, 52,* 413–429.

Ogbu, J. U. (1987). Variability in minority school performance: A problem in search of an explanation. *Anthropology and Education Quarterly, 18,* 312–334.

Olson, D. H., & Gorall, D. M. (2003). Circumplex model of marital and family systems. In F. Walsh (Ed.), *Normal family processes* (3rd ed., pp. 514–548). New York: Guilford.

Olson, D. H., Russell, C. S., & Sprenkle, D. H. (1989). *Circumplex model: Systematic assessment and treatment of families.* New York: Haworth Press.

Omni, M., & Winant, H. (1994). *Racial formation in the US: From the 1960s to the 1990s* (2nd ed.). New York: Routledge.

Ordman, A. M., & Kirschenbaum, D. S. (1986). Bulimia: Assessment of eating, psychological adjustment, and familial characteristics. *International Journal of Eating Disorders, 5,* 865–878.

Osofsky, J. (1997). *Children in a violent society.* New York: Guilford.

Paley, B., Cox, M. J., Kanoy, K., Harter, K., Burchinal, M., & Margand, N. (2005). Adult attachment and marital interaction as predictors of whole family interactions during the transition to parenthood. *Journal of Family Psychology, 19,* 420–429.

Palkovitz, R. (2002). *Involved fathering and men's adult development: Provisional balances.* Mahwah, NJ: Lawrence Erhbaum.

Papernow, P. L. (1993). *Becoming a stepfamily: Patterns of development in remarried families.* San Francisco: Jossey-Bass.

Papero, D. V. (1991). The Bowen theory. In A. M. Horne & J. L. Passmore (Eds.), *Family counseling and therapy* (pp. 47–75). Itasca, IL: F. E. Peacock.

Pare, D. (1996). Culture and meaning: Expanding the metaphorical repertoire of family therapy. *Family Process, 35,* 21–42.

Parke, R. D. (1996). *Fatherhood.* Cambridge, MA: Harvard University Press.

Parke, R. D. (2004). Fathers, families, and the future: A plethora of plausible predictions. *Merrill-Palmer Quarterly, 50,* 456–470.

Parke, R. D., & Buriel, R. (2002). Socialization concerns in African-American, American Indian, Asian American and Latino families. In N. V. Benokraitis (Eds.), *Contemporary ethnic families in the United States: Characteristics, variations and dynamics.* Upper Saddle River, NJ: Prentice Hall.

Pasch, L. A., & Bradbury, T. N. (1998). Social support, conflict, and the development of marital dysfunction. *Journal of Consulting and Clinical Psychology, 66,* 219–230.

Patterson, J. M., & McCubbin, H. I. (1983). Chronic illness: Family stress and coping. In C. R. Figley & H. I. McCubbin (Eds.), *Stress and the family: Vol. 2. Coping with catastrophe.* New York: Brunner/Mazel.

Pearlin, L., & Schooler, C. (1978). The structure of coping. *Journal of Health and Social Behavior, 19,* 2–21.

Pearson, J. C. (1985). *Gender and communication.* Dubuque, IA: Wm. C. Brown.

Peplau, L. A., & Fingerhut, A. W. (2007). The close relationships of lesbians and gay men. *Annual Review of Psychology, 58,* 10.1–10.20.

Perry-Jenkins, M., Repetti, R. L., & Crouter, A. C. (2000). Work and family in the 1990s. *Journal of Marriage and Family, 62*(4), 981–998.

Peters, M. F. (1985). Racial socialization of young black children. In H. P. McAdoo & J. McAdoo (Eds.), *Black children: Social, educational, and parental environments* (pp. 159–173). Beverly Hills, CA: Sage.

Peterson, R. R. (1996). A re-evaluation of the economic consequences of divorce. *American Sociological Review, 61,* 528–536.

Piazza, E., Piazza, N., & Rollins, N. (1980). Anorexia nervosa: Controversial aspects of therapy. *Comprehensive Psychiatry, 17,* 3–36.

Pike, K. M. (1995). Bulimic symptomology in high school girls: Toward a model of cumulative risk. *Psychology of Women Quarterly, 19,* 373–396.

Pillari, V. (1991). *Scapegoating in families: Intergenerational patterns of physical and emotional abuse.* New York: Brunner/Mazel.

Pillemer, K., & Suitor, J. J. (1998). Violence and violent feelings: What causes them among family caregivers? In R. K. Bergen (Ed.), *Issues in intimate violence* (pp. 255–266). Thousand Oaks, CA: Sage.

Pinderhughes, E. (1982). Afro-American families and the victim system. In M. McGoldrick, J. Pearce, & J. Giodano (Eds.), *Ethnicity and family therapy* (pp. 108–122). New York: Guilford Press.

Pinderhughes, E. B. (2002). African American marriage in the 20th century. *Family Process, 41,* 269–282.

Pine, V. et al. (1990). *Unrecognized and unsanctioned grief: The nature and counseling of unacknowledged loss.* Springfield, IL: Charles C. Thomas.

Pinsoff, W. M. (2002). The death of "till death do us part": The transformation of pair-bonding in the 20th century. *Family Process, 41,* 135–157.

Piper, A. (1992). Passing for white, passing for black. *Transition, 58,* 4–32.

Pleck, J. H. (1997). Paternal involvement: Levels, sources, and consequences. In M. E. Lamb (Ed.), *The role of the father in child development* (3rd ed., pp. 66–103). New York: John Wiley & Sons.

Pledge, D. S. (1992). Marital separation/divorce: A review of individual responses to a major life stressor. *Journal of Divorce and Remarriage, 17*(3–4), 151–181.

Popenoe, D. (1996). *Life without Father: Compelling new evidence that fatherhood and marriage are indispensable for the good of children and society.* New York: The Free Press.

Preto, N. G. (2005). Transformation of the family system during adolescence. In B. Carter & M. McGoldrick (Eds.), *The expanded family life cycle: Individual, family, and social perspectives* (3rd ed., pp. 274–286). Boston: Allyn & Bacon.

Proulx, C. M., & Helms, H. M. (2008). Mothers' and fathers' perceptions of change and continuity in their relationships with young adult sons and daughters. *Journal of Family Issues, 29,* 234–261.

Qualls, S. H., & Roberto, K. A. (2006). Diversity and caregiving support interventions: Lessons from elder care research. In B. Hayslip & J. Hicks Patrick (Eds.), *Custodial grandparents: Individual, cultural, and ethnic diversity* (pp. 37–54). New York: Springer.

Rando, T. A. (1986). *Parental loss of a child.* Champaign, IL: Research Press.

Rank, M. R. (2001). The effect of poverty on America's families: Assessing our research knowledge. *Journal of Family Issues, 22,* 882–903.

Rapoport, R. (1963). Normal crises, family structure and mental health. *Family Process, 2,* 68–80.

Riggs, D. S., Murphy, C. M., & O'Leary, K. D. (1989). Intentional falsification in reports of interpartner aggression. *Journal of Interpersonal Violence, 4,* 220–232.

Robbins, T., & Anthony, D. (1982). Cults, culture and community. *Marriage and Family Review, 4,* 57–80.

Roberto, K. A. (2006). Family gerontology. *Family Relations, 55,* 100–145.

Roberto, K. A., & Jarrott, S. E. (2008). Caregiving in late life: A life-span human development perspective. *Family Relations, 57,* 100–111.

Roberto, L. G. (1987). Bulimia: Transgenerational family therapy. In J. E. Harkaway (Ed.), *Eating disorders* (pp. 1–11). Rockville, MD: Aspen.

Roberto, L. G. (1992). *Transgenerational family therapies.* New York: Guilford Press.

Robinson, J., & Godbey, G. (1997). *Time for life.* University Park, PA: Pennsylvania State University Press.

Robinson, J. P., & Godbey, G. (1999). *Time for life. The surprising ways Americans use their time* (2nd ed.). State College: Pennsylvania State University Press.

Rohner, R. P. (1984). Toward a conception of culture for cross-cultural psychology. *Journal of Cross-Cultural Psychology, 15,* 111–138.

Rohner, R. P. (1986). *The warmth dimension: Foundations of parental acceptance-rejection theory.* Beverly Hills, CA: Sage.

Roland, A. (1988). *In search of self in India and Japan: Towards a cross-cultural psychology.* Princeton: Princeton University Press.

Rolland, J. S. (1994). *Families, illness and disability: An integrated treatment model.* New York: Basic Books.

Root, M. P., Fallon, P., & Friedrich, W. N. (1986). *Bulimia: A systems approach to treatment.* New York: W. W. Norton.

Rosen, E. J., & Weltman, S. F. (2005). Jewish families: An overview. In M. McGoldrick, J. Giordano, & N. Garcia-Preto (Eds.), *Ethnicity and family therapy* (pp. 667–679). New York: Guilford Press.

Rosenkoetter, M. M., & Garris, J. M. (2001). Retirement planning, use of time, and psychosocial adjustment. *Issues in Mental Health Nursing, 22,* 703–722.

Rossi, A. (1968). Transition to parenthood. *Journal of Marriage and Family, 30,* 26–39.

Rowe, B. R. (1991). The economics of divorce: Findings from seven states. *Journal of Divorce and Remarriage, 16,* 5–17.

Ruschena, E., Prior, M., Sanson, A., & Smart, D. (2005). A longitudinal study of adolescent adjustment following family transitions. *Journal of Child Psychology and Psychiatry, 46,* 353–363.

Sabatelli, R. M. (1984). The marital comparison level index: A measure for assessing outcomes relative to expectations. *Journal of Marriage and Family, 46,* 651–662.

Sabatelli, R. M. (1988). Exploring relationship satisfaction: A social exchange perspective on the interdependence between theory, research, and practice. *Family Relations, 37,* 217–222.

Sabatelli, R. M. (1999). Marital commitment and family life transitions. In J. Adams & W. H. Jones (Eds.), *Handbook of Interpersonal Commitment and Relationship Stability* (pp. 181–192). New York: Plenum Press.

Sabatelli, R. M., & Anderson, A. S. (1991). Family system dynamics, peer relationships, and adolescents' psychological adjustment. *Family Relations, 40,* 363–369.

Sabatelli, R. M., & Chadwick, J. J. (2000). Marital distress: From complaints to contempt. In P. C. McKenry & S. J. Price (Eds.), *Family and Change: Coping with Stressful Events and Transitions* (pp. 22–44). Thousand Oaks, CA: Sage Publications.

Sabatelli, R. M., & Pearce, J. K. (1986). Exploring marital expectations. *Journal of Social and Personal Relationships, 3,* 307–321.

Sabatelli, R. M., & Ripoll, K. (2003). An ecological/exchange perspective on recent marital trends. In M. Coleman & L. Ganong (Eds.), *Handbook of Contemporary Families: Considering the Past and Contemplating the Future.* Thousand Oaks, CA: Sage Publications.

Sabatelli, R. M., & Shehan, C. L. (1992). Exchange and resource theories. In P. Boss, W. Doherty, R. LaRossa, W. Schumm, & S. Steinmetz (Eds.), *Sourcebook of family theories and methods: A contextual approach* (pp. 385–417). New York: Plenum.

Sager, C. J., Walker, E., Brown, H. S., Crohn, H. M., & Rodstein, E. (1981). Improving functioning of the remarried family system. *Journal of Marital and Family Therapy, 7,* 3–13.

Sanchez, L., & Thomson, E. (1997). Becoming mothers and fathers: Parenthood, gender, and the division of labor. *Gender and Society, 11,* 747–772.

Sanders, G. S., & Suls, J. (1982). Social comparison, competition, and marriage. *Journal of Marriage and Family, 44,* 721–730.

Satir, V. (1972). *Peoplemaking.* Palo Alto, CA: Science and Behavior Books.

Scanzoni, J. (1979a). Social exchange and behavioral interdependence. In R. Burgess & T. Huston (Eds.), *Social exchange in developing relationships* (pp. 61–98). New York: Academic Press.

Scanzoni, J. (1979b). Social processes and power in families. In W. Burr, R. Hill, F. I. Nye, & I. Reiss (Eds.), *Contemporary theories about the family* (pp. 295–316). New York: Free Press.

Scanzoni, J., & Polonko, K. (1980). A conceptual approach to explicit marital negotiation. *Journal of Marriage and Family, 42,* 31–44.

Schnaiberg, A., & Goldenberg, S. (1989). From empty nest to crowded nest: The dynamics of incompletely launched young adults. *Social Problems, 36,* 251–269.

Schwartz, D. M., Thompson, M. G., & Johnson, C. L. (1985). Anorexia nervosa and bulimia: The sociocultural context. In S. W. Emmett (Ed.), *Theory and treatment of anorexia nervosa and bulimia* (pp. 95–112). New York: Brunner/Mazel.

Schwartz, L., & Kaslow, F. (1982). The cult phenomena: Historical, sociological, and family factors contributing to their development and appeal. *Marriage and Family Review, 4,* 15–25.

Seltzer, J. A. (2000). Families formed outside of marriage. *Journal of Marriage and Family, 62*(4), 1247–1268.

Serbin, L., & Karp, J. (2003). Intergenerational studies of parenting and the transfer of risks from parent to child. *Current Directions in Psychological Science, 12,* 138–142.

Shapiro, E. R. (1994). *Grief as a family process: A developmental approach to clinical practice.* New York: Guilford Press.

Shapiro, E. R. (1996). Family bereavement and cultural diversity: A social developmental perspective. *Family Process, 35,* 313–332.

Shapiro, P. G. (1996). *My turn: Women's search for self after children leave.* Princeton, NJ: Peterson's.

Sharpley, C. F., & Yardley, P. G. (1999). What makes me happy now that I'm older: A retrospective report of attitudes and strategies used to adjust to retirement as reported by older persons. *Journal of Applied Health Behavior, 1,* 31–35.

Shearer, S. L., Peters, C. P., Quayman, M. S., & Ogden, D. L. (1990). Frequency and correlates of childhood sexual and physical abuse histories in adult female borderline patients. *American Journal of Psychiatry, 147,* 214–216.

Shisslak, C. M., Crago, M., McKnight, K. M., Estes, L. S., Gray, N., & Parnaby, O. G. (1998). Potential risk factors associated with weight control behaviors in elementary and middle school girls—a defined population study. *Journal of Psychosomatic Research, 44*(3), 301–313.

Shriner, M. (2009). Marital quality in remarriage: A review of methods and results. *Journal of Divorce & Remarriage, 50,* 81–99.

Sieburg, E. (1985). *Family communication: An integrated systems approach.* New York: Gardner Press.

Silber, S. (1990). Conflict negotiation in child abusing and nonabusing families. *Journal of Family Psychology, 3,* 368–384.

Silverstein, M., Giarrusso, R., & Bengston, V. L. (2005). *Intergenerational relations across time and place.* New York: Springer

Silverman, P. R. (1986). *Widow to widow.* New York: Springer.

Simons, R., Whitbeck, L., Conger, R., & Melby, J. (1990). Husband and wife differences in determinants of parenting. *Journal of Marriage and Family, 52,* 375–392.

Simpson, J. A. (1990). Influence of attachment styles on romantic relationships. *Journal of Personality and Social Psychology, 39,* 971–980.

Singley, S. G., & Hynes, K. (2005). Transition to parenthood: Work-family policies, gender, and couple context. *Gender & Society, 19,* 376–397.

Smith, C. A., & Stern, S. B. (1997). Delinquency and antisocial behavior: A review of family processes and intervention research. *Social Service Review, 71,* 382–420.

Smith, K., Downs, B., & O'Connell, M. (2001). *Maternity leave and employment patterns: 1961–1995.* Current Population Reports, P70-79. Washington, DC: U.S. Census Bureau.

Smolak, L., & Levine, M. P. (1993). Separation-individuation difficulties and the distinction between bulimia nervosa and anorexia nervosa in college women. *International Journal of Eating Disorders, 14,* 33–41.

Snyder, H. N. (August, 2005). Juvenile arrests 2003. *Juvenile Justice Bulletin,* Washington, DC: U.S. Department of Justice, Office of Juvenile Justice and delinquency Prevention.

Spitze, G. (1988). Women's employment and family relations: A review. *Journal of Marriage and Family, 50,* 595–618.

Spotts, J. V., & Shontz, F. C. (1985). A theory of adolescent substance abuse. *Advances in Alcohol and Substance Abuse, 4,* 117–138.

Sprey, J. (1978). Conflict theory and the family. In W. R. Burr, R. Hill, F. I. Nye, & I. L. Reiss (Eds.), *Contemporary theories about the family* (Vol. 2, pp. 130–159). New York: Free Press.

Stacey, J. (1996). *In the name of the family: Rethinking family values in the postmodern age.* Boston: Beacon.

Stanton, M. D. (1977). The addict as savior: Heroin, death, and the family. *Family Process, 16,* 191–197.

Stanton, M. D., & Todd, T. C. (1982). *The family therapy of drug abuse and addiction.* New York: Guilford Press.

Steck, G. M., Anderson, S. A., & Boylin, W. M. (1992). Satanism among adolescents: Some empirical and clinical considerations. *Adolescence, 27,* 901–914.

Steffensmeier, R. (1982). A role model of the transition to parenthood. *Journal of Marriage and Family, 44,* 319–334.

Steinberg, L. (2005). *Adolescence* (7th ed.). New York: McGraw-Hill.

Steinglass, P. (1987). A systems view of family interaction and psychopathology. In T. Jacob (Ed.), *Family interaction and psychopathology* (pp. 25–65). New York: Plenum.

Stephen, T. (1984). A symbolic exchange framework for the development of intimate relationships. *Human Relations, 37,* 393–408.

Stephen, T. (1987). Taking communication seriously? A reply to Murstein. *Journal of Marriage and Family, 49,* 937–938.

Sternberg, R. J. (1988). *The triangle of love.* New York: Basic Books.

Stevenson, B., & Wolfers, J. (2007). Marriage and divorce: Changes and their driving forces. Working Paper 12944. National Bureau of Economic Research. http://bpp.wharton.upenn.edu/jowlfers/Papers/MarriageandDivorce (JEP).pdf

Stevenson, H. W., & Lee, S. (1990). Contexts of achievement: A study of American, Chinese, and Japanese children. *Monographs of the Society for Research in Child Development, 55* (1–2, Serial No. 221).

Stierlin, H. (1981). *Separating parents and adolescents.* New York: Jason Aronson.

Stierlin, H. (1994). Centripetal and centrifugal forces in the adolescent separation drama. In G. Handel & G. Whitchurch (Eds.), *The psychosocial interior of the family* (4th ed., pp. 465–491). New York: Aldine de Gruyer.

Stierlin, H., Levi, L., & Savard, R. (1971). Parental perceptions of separating children. *Family Process, 10,* 411–427.

Stierlin, H., & Weber, G. (1989). *Unlocking the family door: A systemic approach to the understanding and treatment of anorexia nervosa.* New York: Brunner/Mazel.

Stinson, K. M., Lasker, J. N., Lohmann, J., & Toedter, L. J. (1992). Parents' grief following pregnancy loss: A comparison of mothers and fathers. *Family Relations, 41,* 218–223.

Storaasli, R., & Markman, H. (1990). Relationship problems in the early stages of marriage: A longitudinal investigation. *Journal of Family Psychology, 4,* 80–98.

Straus, M. A. (1974). Sexual inequality, cultural norms, and wife beating. *Journal of Marriage and Family, 36,* 13–30.

Straus, M. A. (1977). A sociological perspective on the prevention and treatment of wifebeating. In M. Roy (Ed.), *Battered women* (pp. 194–238). New York: Van Nostrand.

Straus, M. A. (1979). Measuring intrafamily conflict and violence: The conflict tactics scales. *Journal of Marriage and Family, 41,* 75–88.

Straus, M. A., & Gelles, R. J. (1986). Societal change and change in family violence from 1975 to 1985 as revealed by two national surveys. *Journal of Marriage and Family, 48,* 465–479.

Straus, M., & Sweet, S. (1992). Verbal/symbolic aggression in couples: Incidence rates and relationships to personal characteristics. *Journal of Marriage and Family, 54,* 346–357.

Strober, M., Freeman, R., Lampert, C., Diamond, J., & Kaye, W. (2000). Controlled family study of anorexia nervosa and bulimia nervosa: Evidence of shared liability and transmission of partial syndromes. *American Journal of Psychiatry, 157*(3), 393–401.

Strober, M., & Humphrey, L. L. (1987). Family contributions to the etiology and course of anorexia nervosa and bulimia nervosa. *Journal of Consulting and Clinical Psychology, 55,* 654–659.

Substance Abuse and Mental Health Services Administration (SAMHSA) (2003). Results from the 2002 National Survey on Drug Use and Health: National Findings (Office of Applied Studies, NHSDA Series H-22, DHHS Publication No. SMA 03-3836). Rockville, MD.

Sugg, N. K., & Inui, T. (1992). Primary care physicians' response to domestic violence: Opening Pandora's box. *Journal of the American Medical Association, 267,* 3157–3160.

Suitor, J. J., & Pillemer, K. (1987). The presence of adult children: A source of stress for elderly couples' marriages? *Journal of Marriage and Family, 49,* 717–725.

Surra, C. A., & Huston, T. L. (1987). Mate selection as a social transition. In D. Perlman & S. Duck (Eds.), *Intimate relationships: Development, dynamics, and deterioration* (pp. 88–120). Newbury Park, CA: Sage.

Sutton, P. M., & Sprenkle, D. H. (1985). Criteria for a constructive divorce: Theory and research to guide the practitioner. *Journal of Psychotherapy and the Family, 1*(3), 39–51.

Suzuki, B. H. (1980). The Asian-American family. In M. D. Fantini & R. Cardenas (Eds.), *Parenting in a multicultural society* (pp. 74–102). New York: Longman.

Swett, C., Surrey, J., & Cohen, C. (1990). Sexual and physical abuse histories and psychiatric symptoms among male outpatients. *American Journal of Psychiatry, 147,* 632–636.

Szinovacz, M. (1998). Grandparents today: A demographic profile. *The Gerontologist, 38,* 37–52.

Szinovacz, M. (2000). Changes in housework after retirement: A panel analysis. *Journal of Marriage and Family, 62,* 78–92.

Szinovacz, M., & Davey, A. (2008). *Caregiving contexts: Cultural, familial, and social implications.* New York: Springer.

Szinovacz, M., & DeViney, S. (2000). Marital characteristics and retirement decisions. *Research on Aging, 22,* 470–489.

Szinovacz, M., & Schaffer, A. M. (2000). Effects of retirement on marital conflict management. *Journal of Family Issues, 21,* 367–389.

Szinovacz, M., & Washo, C. (1992). Gender differences in exposure to life events and adaptation to retirement. *Journal of Gerontology: Social Sciences, S47,* S191–S196.

Tannen, D. (1986). *That's not what I meant: How conversational style makes or breaks your relationships with others.* New York: William Morrow.

Tannen, D. (1990). *You just don't understand: Women and men in conversation.* New York: Ballantine Books.

Tannen, D. (2001). *I only say this because I love you.* New York: Ballantine Book.

Taylor, R. L. (2000). Diversity within African American families. In D. H. Demo, K. R. Allen, & M. A. Fine (Eds.), *Handbook of family diversity* (pp. 232–251). New York: Oxford University Press.

Teachman, J. D., & Paasch, K. M. (1994). Financial impact of divorce on children and their families. *The Future of Children, 4*(1), 63–83.

Teachman, J. D., Tedrow, L. M., & Crowder, K. D. (2000). The changing demography of America's families. *Journal of Marriage and Family, 62,* 1234–1246.

Thibaut, J. W., & Kelley, H. H. (1959). *The social psychology of groups.* New York: Wiley.

Thomas, D. D. (1993). Minorities in North America: African-American families. In J. L. Paul & R. J. Simeonsson (Eds.), *Children with special needs: Family, culture and society* (pp. 114–125). New York: Harcourt Brace Jovanovich.

Thompson, L., & Walker, A. J. (1989). Gender in families: Women and men in marriage, work, and parenthood. *Journal of Marriage and Family, 51,* 845–871.

Tjaden, P., & Thonnes, N. (2000). Extent, nature and consequences of intimate partner violence. National Institute of Justice Report #NCJ 1811867. http://www.ncjrs.org/pdffiles1/nij/181867

Todd, T. C., & Selekman, M. (1989). Principles of family therapy for adolescent substance abuse. *Journal of Psychotherapy and the Family, 6*(3–4), 49–70.

Turner, R. H. (1970). *Family interaction.* New York: Wiley.

Umberson, D. (1995). Marriage as support or strain? Marital quality following the death of a parent. *Journal of Marriage and Family, 57,* 709–723.

U.S. Bureau of Justice Statistics (2006). *Criminal victimization in the United States, 2004.* Statistical tables. NCJ213257. http://www.ojp.usdoj.gov/bjs/pub/pdf/vsus0402.pdf

U.S. Bureau of Labor Statistics. (2009). *Employed persons by full-and-part-time status and sex, 1970–2007 annual averages.* Table 20. www.bls.gov/cps/wlf-table20-2007.pdf.

U.S. Census Bureau (2001a). *Money income in the United States: 2000.* Current Population Reports, P60-213. Washington, DC: U.S. Printing Office.

U.S. Census Bureau (2003a). *Fertility of American women: June 2002.* Current Population Reports, P20-548. Washington, DC.

U.S. Census Bureau (2003b). *Children's living arrangements and characteristics: March 2002.* Current Population Reports. http://www.census.gov/prod/2003pubs/p20-547.pdf

U.S. Census Bureau (2004). *America's families and living arrangements: 2003.* Current Population Reports, P20-553. Washington, DC.

U.S. Census Bureau (2005a). *Living arrangements of children: 2001.* Current Population Reports, P70-104. Washington, DC.

U.S. Census Bureau (2005b). *Number, timing, and duration of marriage and divorces: 2001.* http://www.census.gov/prod/2005pubs/p70-97.pdf

U.S. Census Bureau (2006). *America's families and living arrangements: 2006.* http://www.census.gove/population/www/socdemo/hh-fam/cps2006.html

U.S. Census Bureau (2007a). *Families and living arrangements: 2006.* http://www.census.gov/Press-Release/www/release/archives/families_households/009842.html

U.S. Census Bureau (2007b). *Custodial mothers and fathers and their child support: 2005.* http://www.censue.gov/prod/2007pubs/p60-234.pdf

U.S. Census Bureau (2007c). *Statistical abstract of the United States.* http://www.census.gov/compendia/statab/2007edition.html

U.S. Census Bureau (2008). *Statistical abstract of the United States.* http://www.census.gov/compendia/statab/2008edition.html

U.S. Department of Health and Human Services (USDHHS) (2000). *Eating disorders.* Washington, DC: Office on Women's Health.

Vakalahi, H. F. (2002). Family-based predictors of adolescent substance use. *Journal of Child and Adolescent Substance Abuse, 11*(3), 1–15.

van der Hart, O. (1988). *Coping with loss: The therapeutic use of leave-taking rituals.* New York: Irvington.

Van Egeren, L. A. (2004). The development of the coparenting relationship over the transition to parenthood. *Infant Mental Health Journal, 25,* 453–477.

van Schoor, E. P., & Beach, R. (1993). Pseudoindependence in adolescent drug abuse: A family systems perspective. *Family Therapy, 20,* 191–202.

Vega, W. A. (1990). Hispanic families in the 1980s: A decade of research. *Journal of Marriage and Family, 52,* 1015–1024.

Vinick, B. H., & Ekerdt, D. J. (1991). Retirement: What happens to husband–wife relationships? *Journal of Geriatric Psychiatry, 24,* 16–23.

Visher, E. B., & Visher, J. S. (1996). *Therapy with stepfamilies.* New York: Brunner/Mazel.

Visher, E. B., Visher, J. S., & Pasley, K. (2003). Remarriage families and stepparenting. In F. Walsh (Ed.), *Normal family processes* (3rd ed., pp. 153–175). New York: Guilford.

Vogel, E. F., & Bell, N. W. (1968). The emotionally disturbed child as the family scapegoat. In N. W. Bell & E. F. Vogel (Eds.), *A modern introduction to the family* (pp. 412–427). New York: The Free Press.

Von Bertalanffy, L. (1975). *Perspectives on general systems theory: Scientific-philosophical studies.* New York: George Braziller.

Voydanoff, P., & Donnelly, B. W. (1999). Risk and protective factors for psychological adjustment and grades among adolescents. *Journal of Family Issues, 20,* 328–349.

Walker, L. E. (1979). *The battered woman.* New York: Harper & Row.

Walker, L. E. (1984). *The battered woman syndrome.* New York: Springer.

Wallerstein, J. S., & Blakeslee, S. (1989). *Second chances: Men, women, and children a decade after divorce.* New York: Ticknor & Fields.

Walker, A., Manoogian-O'Dell, M., McGraw, L., & White, D. (2001). *Families in later life: Connections and transitions.* Thousand Oaks, CA: Pine Forge Press.

Walsh, F. (1998). *Strengthening family resilience.* New York: Guilford.

Walsh, F. (2003). Changing families in a changing world: Reconstructing family normality. In F. Walsh (Ed.), *Normal family processes* (3rd ed., pp. 3–26). New York: Guilford.

Walsh, F., & McGoldrick, M. (2004). *Living beyond loss: Death in the family* (2nd ed.). New York: Norton.

Walsh, F., & Pryce, J. (2003). The spiritual dimensions of family life. In F. Walsh (Ed.), *Normal family processes* (3rd ed., pp. 337–372). New York: Guilford.

Walster, E., Walster, G. W., & Berscheid, E. (1978). *Equity: Theory and research.* Boston: Allyn & Bacon.

Walter, M., Carter, B., Papp, P., & Silverstein, O. (1988). *The invisible web: Gender patterns in family relationships.* New York: Guilford.

Walters, S. D. (2001). *All the rage: The story of gay visibility in America.* Chicago: University of Chicago Press.

Wamboldt, F. S., & Wolin, S. J. (1989). Reality and myth in family life: Change across generations. In S. A. Anderson & D. A. Bagarozzi (Eds.), *Family myths: Psychotherapy implications* (pp. 141–166). New York: Haworth Press.

Ward, R., Logan, J., & Spitze, G. (1992). Influence of parent and child needs on coresidence in middle and later life. *Journal of Marriage and Family, 54,* 209–221.

Warshak, R. A. (2003). Payoffs and pitfalls of listening to children. *Family Relations, 52,* 373–384.

Watzlawick, P., Beavin, J. H., & Jackson, D. D. (1967). *The pragmatics of human communication.* New York: Norton.

Watzlawick, P., Weakland, J., & Fisch, R. (1974). *Change: Principles of problem formation and problem resolution.* New York: W. W. Norton.

Weiss, B., Dodge, K. A., Bates, J. E., & Pettit, G. S. (1992). Some consequences of early harsh discipline: Child aggression and maladaptive social information processing style. *Child Development, 63,* 1321–1335.

Whipple, E. E., & Webster-Stratton, C. (1991). The role of parental stress in physically abusive families. *Child Abuse and Neglect, 15,* 279–293.

Whitchurch, G. G., & Constantine, L. L. (1993). Systems theory. In P. G. Boss, W. J. Doherty, R. LaRossa, W. R. Schumm, & S. K. Steinmetz (Eds.), *Sourcebook of family theories and methods: A contextual approach* (pp. 325–355). New York: Plenum.

White, L., & Edwards, J. N. (1993). Emptying the nest and parental well-being. *American Sociological Review, 55,* 235–242.

White, L., & Rogers, S. J. (2000). Economic circumstances and family outcomes: A review of the 1990s. *Journal of Marriage and Family, 62,* 1035–1051.

Wiehe, V. R. (1998). *Understanding family violence.* Thousand Oaks, CA: Sage.

Wilder, C., & Collins, S. (1994). Patterns of interactional paradoxes. In W. R. Cupach & B. H. Spitzberg (Eds.), *The dark side of interpersonal communication.* New York: Lawrence Erlbaum.

Wiley, N. F. (1985). Marriage and the construction of reality: Then and now. In G. Handel (Ed.), *The psychosocial interior of the family* (3rd ed., pp. 21–32). New York: Aldine.

Williamson, D. S. (1981). Personal authority via termination of the intergenerational hierarchical boundary: A new stage in the family life cycle. *Journal of Marital and Family Therapy, 7,* 441–452.

Williamson, D. S. (1982). Personal authority in family experience via termination of the intergenerational hierarchical boundary: Part III—Personal authority defined and the power of play in the change process. *Journal of Marital and Family Therapy, 8,* 309–323.

Willis, W. (1992). Families with African-American roots. In E. W. Lynch & M. J. Hanson (Eds.), *Developing cross-cultural competence: A guide for working with young children and their families* (pp. 121–150). Baltimore, MD: Paul H. Brookes.

Wills, T. A., Resko, J. A., Ainette, M. G., & Mendozza, D. (2004). Role of parent support and peer support in adolescent substance use: A test of mediated effects. *Psychology and Addictive Behaviors, 18,* 122–134.

Wilmot, W. W. (1975). *Dyadic communication: A transactional perspective.* Reading, MA: Addison-Wesley.

Wilson, W. J. (1996). *When work disappears: The world of the new urban poor.* New York: Alfred A. Knopf.

Winch, R. F. (1958). *Mate selection: A study of complementary needs.* New York: Harper & Brothers.

Wolf-Smith, J. H., & LaRossa, R. (1992). After he hits her. *Family Relations, 41,* 324–329.

Wood, J. T. (2009). *Gendered lives: Communication, gender, and culture* (8th ed.). Belmont, CA: Wadsworth Cengage.

Wright, S., & Piper, E. (1986). Families and cults: Familial factors related to youth leaving or remaining in deviant religious groups. *Journal of Marriage and Family, 48,* 15–25.

Wynne, L. C. (1988). The epigenesis of relational systems: A model for understanding family development. *Family Process, 23,* 297–318.

Youniss, J., & Smollar, J. (1985). *Adolescent relations with mothers, fathers, and friends.* Chicago, IL: University of Chicago Press.

Zimmerman, L., Mitchell, B., Wister, A., & Gutman, G. (2000). Unanticipated consequences: A comparison of expected and actual retirement timing among older women. *Journal of Women and Aging, 12,* 109–128.

Zuniga, M. E. (1988). Chicano self-concept: A proactive stance. In C. Jacobs & D. Bowles (Eds.), *Ethnicity and race: Critical concepts in social work* (pp. 71–85). Silver Spring, MD: National Association of Social Workers.

Zuniga, M. E. (1992). Families with Latino roots. In E. W. Lynch & M. J. Hanson (Eds.), *Developing cross-cultural competence: A guide for working with young children and their families* (pp. 151–179). Baltimore, MD: Paul H. Brookes.

Name Index

Subject Index